Software Testing

Martin Pol, Ruud Teunissen and Erik van Veenendaal

Software Testing
A Guide to the TMap® Approach

Addison-Wesley

An imprint of **PEARSON EDUCATION**

Boston · San Francisco · New York · Toronto · Montreal · London · Munich ·
Paris · Madrid · Cape Town · Sydney · Tokyo · Singapore · Mexico City

PEARSON EDUCATION LIMITED

Head Office
Edinburgh Gate
Harlow CM20 2JE
Tel: +44 (0)1279 623623
Fax: +44 (0)1279 431059

London Office
128 Long Acre
London WC2E 9AN
Tel: +44 (0)20 7447 2000
Fax: +44 (0)20 7240 5771

Website: www.aw.com/cseng

First Published in Great Britain in 2002

ISBN 0 201 74571 2

British Library Cataloguing in Publication Data
A catalogue record for this book is available from the British Library.

Library of Congress Cataloging in Publication Data
Applied for.

10 9 8 7 6 5 4 3 2 1

Typeset by Pantek Arts Ltd, Maidstone, Kent.
Printed and bound in Great Britain by Biddles Ltd, Guildford and King's Lynn.

The Publishers' policy is to use paper manufactured from sustainable forests.

Contents

Foreword

There is a real hunger in the software testing world for a more structured approach for testing. Testing professionals find satisfaction in knowing that they have done a good job. But how can you do a good job if you don't know what to do? This book will tell you how to do a more professsional job of testing. Is a structured approach the right way to go in today's speed-driven culture of ever-increasing time pressure? In my experience, the greatest benefits of speed come in partnership with a structured approach. Speed without structure gives chaos (automated chaos if you then introduce tools!). A structured approach gives control and manageability at any speed.

TMap (Test Management approach) provides a structured approach for the ful spectrum of software testing concerns, from the highest-level management issues for large organizations, to the details of using TMap techniques. TMap is a well-established and proven methodology. It has been developed in the Netherlands and Belgium, where it has been very successful. The full detail of TMap has not been available in English before and will now prove equally valuable to English-speaking readers. This book provides the foundation for good practices that can be and have been adapted to many different situations. Reading this useful and practical advice will help you accelerate towards better testing.

There are a number of things I particularly like about the TMap approach. It describes many techniques for use at the higher levels of testing. This is particularly useful, as most other testing books describe techniques mainly at lower levels rather than at system and acceptance testing. The test process lifecycle emphasizes testing activities as early as possible, and also includes a specific phase (completion) to achieve closure of a testing project. TMap covers organization and infrastructure issues, which can prove critical to a testing effort. I liked the useful checklists scattered throughout the book; they are clearly based on solid experience. I was particularly interested in the test specification techniques section of the book and found it fascinating reading. I recognized some familiar favorites, some original ways of applying them, some I have known under other names, and some I haven't seen before.

TMap lays a sound foundation for good-quality software testing. Such a foundation is the only way to safely achieve responsiveness needed for the challenges of today – and tomorrow. This book will speed you to a structured but adaptable approach for better testing.

Dorothy Graham, Grove Consultants, Macclesfield, UK, August 2001
www.grove.co.uk

Preface

TMap: the book

The TMap **T**est **M**anagement **ap**proach is based on years of practical software testing experiences and developed by the R&D department of IQUIP Informatica B.V. It enjoyed an overwhelming interest from its first publication in Dutch in 1995. Many companies and government departments arranged their organization and performed their test processes as much as possible according to TMap. Within a few years, it became the standard for software testing within the Dutch-speaking countries. The generic approach of the model offers ample space to tune the TMap standard to specific applications and organizational needs. TMap withstands the frequent innovations in IT since one of its main advantages is the possibility to create extensions for progressing IT developments, such as object orientation (OO), enterprise resource planning (ERP), component-based development (CBD), test automation, the Internet, etc.

In 1998, the English summary 'Structured testing: an introduction to TMap' was published. It caught the attention of several international organizations, and the demand for the complete English version became enormous, especially through the well-attended TMap-courses. These courses are successfully organized in the Benelux and other parts of the world (UK, USA, Scandinavia, etc.).

Through these courses and, in particular, the continuously increasing international use of the TMap approach, the number of TMap experts is constantly growing, thereby creating an unprecedented flow of information on the application of TMap within different organizations and projects. As authors, we felt obliged to gather all experiences and new developments and share them with the TMap user community: publications in the press and on the Internet; papers, tutorials and track presentations at international test conferences; publication of the German version and TMap-related books regarding test process improvement (TPI); test automation; and finally the reviewed Dutch edition of the standard in 1999. But the demand of the English-speaking community kept on growing.

The authors are proud to present this book: the first complete English version of testing according to TMap. We wish you success in applying TMap, and are keen to share your experiences and critics. Let us continue to improve the testing profession and, by doing so, help the IT industry to introduce even better products to society.

TMap: the approach

This book describes TMap as the approach for the structured (white-box and black-box) testing of information systems. It answers the what, when, how, by what, and by whom questions regarding testing.

In order to make the design and execution of test processes more structured, TMap is based on four cornerstones related to those questions. The 'what/when' questions are answered by the *lifecycle model*, a description of the test cycle related to the development cycle. The 'how' question is answered in the description of the *techniques* for planning, preparation and execution of several tests. The 'by what' question is considered in the description of the *infrastructure*. And the description of the *organization* aspects answers the 'by whom' question.

Structure of the book

TMap is a generic approach to structured testing. The theory is described in a universal way because the one and only test approach does not exist. Testing occurs in several variations that demand their own application of the standard. In this book, ample attention is given to the way in which the right components of TMap in any kind of test process could be selected. This book is divided into six parts. Part I describes the phenomenon of testing and TMap in general. Parts II to V describe the respective cornerstones of TMap: lifecycle, techniques, organization and infrastructure. Part VI consists of several important applications of TMap towards modern developments in IT.

Part I describes the importance and the context of software testing in general and the relation with quality assurance in particular. The need for testing and the possibilities of a structured application are described in detail. Part I is concluded with an overview of the test management approach.

Part II contains a detailed description of the lifecycle for test processes. Test activities are described systematically for master test planning, and the low-level and high-level tests. The lifecycle is the central cornerstone of TMap. It describes the relation between the activities in a test process and all the components of the remaining cornerstones: techniques, organization and infrastructure.

Part III describes the available testing techniques in detail. As well as extensive test-specification techniques, the TMap set contains, among others, techniques for test strategy, test effort estimation, and an extensive set of checklists for static testing.

Part IV contains a detailed description of the organizational aspects of testing. It describes the different test functions, including required knowledge and skills, the organization within the test team – tasks and responsibilities – and the incorporation of the test team in the line or project organization. It also pays attention to the recruitment, selection and training of test personnel. Due to the need for 'hard figures' about the test process the implementation of metrics is discussed. Part IV is concluded by a chapter on test process improvement: a practical step-by-step guide to structured testing.

Part V describes the infrastructure needed for testing. Guidelines are included for the test environment, test tools and the office environment.

Part VI contains a number of specific applications of TMap. Among others, extensions are created for object orientation (OO), enterprise resource planning (ERP), component-based development (CBD), test automation, and the Internet.

The appendices contain an elaborated example of a test plan, and a description of relations between TMap quality characteristics and ISO9216 quality characteristics definitions.

Target audience

The primary audience of this book is the group of people involved directly in the test process. A test team may use this book as a guide to perform test activities. For those who operate at more of a distance from the basic test process, such as clients, end users, and IT auditors, this book offers a good insight into the phenomenon of testing. For this purpose, in Part I some chapters have been added in which the background and the set-up of testing are discussed. This book does not have to be read from beginning to end. Depending on the involvement in testing, readers will look at some parts thoroughly, briefly or not at all. All readers are advised to look in the first place at Chapter 5 or preferably Part I in its entirety. After that, the interest and use will differ according to the target group.

- Test managers, test coordinators and the like are advised to study the entire book, especially Parts II and IV, and Chapters 10, 11 and 12. Depending on the assignment of supporting test tasks, it is also advisable to read Part V.
- For those people in charge of the primary test activities (testers, developers, users and system managers), you are recommended to study thoroughly Part II and (parts of) Parts III and V.
- IT auditors and employees charged with quality care should look at Parts II and III.
- Clients for development and test processes and line management will, after reading Part I, probably make a selection according to their own interests, for instance organizational aspects (Part IV) or the master test plan (Chapter 7).
- For students (information engineering/business economy) and teachers, the study of the total theoretical framework is important.
- For employees of the personnel and organization departments, Part IV and especially Chapters 19 and 20 offer good references.

Acknowledgments

In respect to the great number of contributors, it is unfeasible to mention everyone by name. Yet we do want to mention the most important supporters here, and to thank them for their cooperation.

Many people enthusiastically devoted a lot of effort, often in the evenings and at weekends, and shared their knowledge and experiences of testing with us. Without their contribution, the now-achieved quality could not have been realized. Special thanks goes to our IQUIP colleagues, who besides their contribution to the content, also coordinated the publishing activities with unceasing energy: Rob Baarda and Klaas Brongers. We would especially like to mention Tim Koomen. His enormous knowledge of the test profession, combined with an unbridled devotion and the ability to write his ideas down, were crucial for the realization of this edition of TMap. Many employees of IQUIP and the Belgian sister company Gitek n.v. have added indispensable practical experience and the wishes of everyday users of TMap. TMap may consider itself lucky to have the invaluable support and expert contribution of internationally renowned test experts Dorothy Graham, Hans Schaefer and Ross Collard: thanks a lot for your indispensable comments and contribution to reach the quality needed for this edition. Finally, thanks to those many, many others not mentioned by name. The results belong to you all!

Martin Pol
Ruud Teunissen
Erik van Veenendaal

Recommendations

In the information era, IT determines the success of organizations. Structured testing is of crucial importance to determine the right quality level and possible risks while realizing IT solutions. IQUIP contributes in a trend-setting way by making available the test approach TMap, which has been developed by the R&D department of Software Control and appeared to be a long-lasting standard.

J.P.E. van Waayenburg
General Director
IQUIP Informatica B.V.

'Cap Gemini Ernst & Young as a worldwide services organization is constantly working to improve its capabilities. One of these capabilities is system testing, as delivered very successfully by IQUIP through TMap. TMap has set the standard for structured testing in the Benelux as well as in many other European countries, and has the potential to become a worldwide standard; a new milestone in sophisticated structured testing has been established. My congratulations to Martin Pol and his co-authors for their work and their success.'

P. Hessler
Member of the Executive Board
Cap Gemini Ernst & Young S.A.

'The term "Information Age" forces businesses to acknowledge that information can be their best competitive advantage. Reliability of systems that deliver that knowledge will define business success or failure. The Information Age will thus be the Age of Testing. Manoeuvrability, dynamic infrastructure, process control and reuse of IT are the testing challenges business must meet to succeed.'

Emily Nagle Green
Managing Director
Forrester Research B.V.

General principles   PART 1

Introduction 1

According to a dictionary, testing means 'to ascertain (the worth, capability or endurance) (of a person or thing) by subjection to certain examinations'. Information engineering has gradually developed a general idea of testing, but a clear-cut and universally applied definition still does not exist. The many kinds of tests with different aims, the vague demarcations, and the frequently informal application of the phenomenon make it difficult to formulate an unambiguous definition.

1.1 What is testing?

Testing always means comparing. It requires an item that is to be tested and terms of reference with which the item must comply. Testing satisfies the need for information about the difference between the item and the requirements. The International Standardization Organization (ISO) describes testing in the following terms: '*Technical operation that consists of the determination of one or more characteristics of a given product, process or service according to a specified procedure*' (ISO/IEC, 1991).

Testing provides an insight into the difference between the actual status and the required status of an item. Since quality can be defined as 'meeting the requirements', testing therefore results in recommendations on quality. It consequently provides an insight into the risks that will be incurred if lower quality is accepted. This is also the principal objective of testing. Testing is one of the detective measures of a quality system. It is related to reviewing, simulating, inspecting, auditing, examining, desk-checking, walk-throughs, etc. The various detective measures are divided into two groups: evaluation and testing.[1]

Evaluation means reviewing or inspecting intermediate products and development processes, and performing all activities aimed at finding out whether the development process is satisfactory. *Testing* means inspecting the final

---

[1] In the theory, the terms 'verification' and 'validation' are also used. Verification means evaluating (part of) the system to determine whether the products of a development phase meet the requirements set for that phase. Validation means determining whether the system development products meet the user needs and requirements (IEEE, 1994).

products in order to determine whether they meet the requirements, answering the question of whether the right products have been constructed.

It is obvious that this distinction cannot be absolute. Evaluating the testability of specifications, for instance, is an important activity during the preparation of testing. Evaluation activities also include reviewing the test process.

Within the framework of this book, the scope of evaluation is narrowed down to evaluation of intermediate products.

In simple terms, it can be said that the main objective of testing is to detect defects: tests are conducted in an attempt to show a lack of quality as revealed by defects. Formally, it means establishing the difference between the product and the requirements. It would be more agreeable to think in terms of acquiring confidence in a product, including items such as the relevant documentation and user procedures. Hence a manageable definition of testing is as follows: *'A process of planning, preparing, executing and analyzing, aimed at establishing the characteristics of an information system, and demonstrating the difference between the actual status and the required status.'*

1.2 Why use testing?

In many organizations, information technology (IT) supports the business processes to an important extent. It is expected that this importance will increase. Trends such as globalization, individualization and shorter lifecycles of products place great demands on the flexibility of organizations. In order to compete as an organization in the present market, a constantly decreasing time to market for new products is essential. An important part of those new products is often the supporting information systems. The pressure from the organization to bring new or modified systems into production in the shortest possible time is increasing. In addition, more information systems are introduced for communication with the client, and the integration of several information systems is gaining importance. The success of the business process is becoming more dependent on qualitatively well-functioning information systems.

Many organizations are finding themselves with projects that have got out of hand in terms of time and budget, and software defects that occur during the operation of developed information systems. It appears that customers accept applications – or are obliged to accept them – without having any real understanding of their quality. In most instances, good management information is lacking. The application's release is a gamble, either intentionally or unintentionally, and often leads to taking major financial risks, potentially resulting in high repair costs, damage to the image, and loss of competitive advantage because of the late availability of the new product.

Before an information system goes into production, the organization should consider whether the green light really can be given. Have all parts and characteristics of the information system been checked sufficiently? As well as the functionality, have the suitability, performance and, for instance, security been checked? Or like ISO formulates, has it been determined whether the product has the properties and characteristics to satisfy the stated needs or, even more difficult, the *implied needs*? What is an 'implied need' for one is an 'eye-opener' for another.

Have all defects been corrected without any new ones being introduced during the re-work process? Can the management rely on this system? Does the system genuinely provide a reliable solution of the information problem for which it was designed? What are the risks, and what measurements are eventually taken to reduce those risks? Answers to these crucial questions must not be postponed until the operational phase. Therefore, a well-structured and reliable test process is required. This calls for a structured test approach, organization and infrastructure.

A structured test approach offers the following advantages:
- Testing gives insight into and advice about the risks regarding the quality of the tested system.
- Defects are found at an early stage.
- Defects can be prevented.
- Testing is performed in as short a time as possible on the critical path of the total development cycle, so the development time will be shorter.
- The deliverables of the test process (such as test cases) can be reused.
- The test process is transparent and manageable.

1.3 Where does testing fit in?

In many organizations, testing is underdeveloped and frequently still at an experimental stage. There is often a tendency to delay the introduction of a robust quality system, of which testing is a major component. The required organizational basis for providing quality development and testing is often lacking. Even though the quality is taken seriously, structured testing is frequently not introduced until the very end of the process.

There is a definite view that the implementation of quality management, quality systems and quality assurance can reduce the number of defects to (almost) zero. This situation can, of course, never be achieved in the relatively young IT industry – wherever there is work, errors are made and the resulting defects must be tracked down in good time.

Testing is one of the efforts required for this purpose. The ultimate objective is prevention – not the relatively expensive detection of defects in the final product. For the time being, however, the emphasis must be on the reduction of the time lapse between the moment of introduction of a defect and the moment of its detection. This requires an effective combination of preventive and detective measures.

Detection, with testing as a part of this, may serve as a major lever for raising the standards for quality systems. The testing safety net inspires developers with awe and forces them to avoid errors. This phenomenon is sometimes called the 'quality push' or 'reverse quality assurance'. In more mature industries, such as the aviation and hardware industries, testing has developed into a full and substantial part of the quality system. That is what lies ahead of us.

Framework and importance

2

You want to start testing. In fact, you do not want to test but you want to control the risks associated with the introduction of a new or changed information system. This book is therefore more about risk control than testing itself. Testing is merely a means to an end; a rough remedy maybe, but one that is currently indispensable.

2.1 The aim of testing

The development and maintenance of information systems requires that special attention is paid to their quality, i.e. to satisfying the expectations of the users. This has proved to be a delicate matter in the software industry – there are not many branches of industry that battle to the same extent with the image of providing poor quality. Quality in this context has a bearing on reliability, completion on time and within budget, and achieving the object of the exercise, providing a solution to a specific problem.

Increasingly, many measures are taken to achieve quality. According to some people, preventive measures should suffice as errors are then avoided. This idea, however, will remain utopian for some time. The development process is still essentially a craft that is difficult to complete without making errors. The causes of defects are therefore varied and unpredictable, and, for the time being, it is still necessary to devote a great deal of energy to tracking down these defects.

On the basis of this, the obvious conclusion would be that exposing a lack of quality with a view to remedying the situation was the principal objective of testing: testing is aimed at removing defects. Although it cannot be denied that testing will improve quality, it is not the appropriate means of achieving quality.

Testing is solely an aid to the observation of symptoms. Consequently, there is a considerable risk that testing will lead merely to fighting symptoms, and only the detected defects will be corrected.

Testing should lead to diagnoses, to seeking the *underlying* causes of a problem. A diagnosis is not founded on an isolated defect but is based on the recognition of a pattern of defects. The improvement process may subsequently be started on the basis of the diagnosis, and that, in the case of information systems, is more than just solving an isolated problem. *The structural improvement of quality must be brought about from the top down.* Quality must be *built in*, not *tested in*!

One of the fundamentals of quality is that prevention is better – and above all cheaper – than detection and correction. Prevention should be an important focus within the development process. Improving quality solely by means of testing is extremely expensive. On the basis of this principle, testing should stop in the case of a poor system and redesign should start. It is rare for organizations to be bold enough to accept that something is definitely wrong with the system, and that it is essential to redesign it if the defects are to be genuinely corrected. Only afterwards, when it is too late, do people realize that they might have avoided all the misery if they had taken action in good time.

As mentioned above, the observed symptoms enable an organization to make a diagnosis and to solve the problems. It is, however, at least equally important that the observed symptoms also provide an opportunity for making a statement about the risks that will be taken if a particular version of a system is put into operation. On the basis of observations made during testing, it is possible to make a prediction about the system's behavior in production by means of extrapolation. Such an assessment is of major importance to anyone responsible for releasing or accepting the system. Reaching the conclusion on the basis of a solid risk report that implementation or release of a system is not advisable may prevent many problems.

Postponement of a system's implementation is painful and often very costly. The implementation of a poor system, however, is much more costly and much more painful. Desperate diseases require desperate remedies. The costs of poor quality are high because they are multiplied by the number of the system's users. A defect costing ten times five minutes daily may cost a company more than ten percent of the productivity of its users. This represents more than the profit margins of many companies.

Testing is therefore an activity that must be taken seriously, but the necessary serious approach is frequently lacking. Testing is not merely a phase that comes after system development. As an activity, it is comparable with system development, and therefore it deserves an equal amount of attention.

2.2 What testing is not

Testing is not just the measuring but is also the planning and preparation. Testing may be compared with an iceberg, with only its tip visible above the surface of the ocean. The greater part of the iceberg is below the surface and is not immediately recognizable. The actual execution of the tests is regarded as testing, although on average it represents a mere 40 percent of the test activities. The other activities – planning and control, preparation, specification and completion – make up 60 percent of the test effort (Figure 2.1).

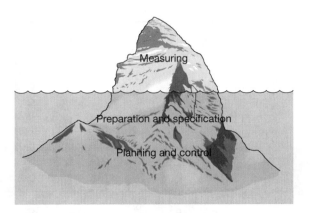

Figure 2.1
The 'iceberg'

This percentage is not usually recognized as such by the organization, but it accounts for the major part of the gain in time that may be achieved during testing. There is a tendency that through technical developments such as test automation, the percentage of time used for executing is decreasing compared to planning and control, preparation, specification and completion.

Testing is not the same as release or acceptance. Testing gives advice on quality; decisions on the release are the responsibility of others, often the customer who commissioned the test. Nor is testing the correction of defects, since it is only during unit testing that it is possible to test as well as to correct. In the case of all other tests, it is essential to adhere to the principle that the person who has built it does not test it, and the person who has tested it does not correct it.

Testing is not a post-development phase. It comprises a series of activities that must be carried out from an early stage in the development. At the same time as the functional specifications, a test plan must be prepared in which the tests to be carried out by various people are planned and harmonized. Preparations for testing begin immediately after the functional specifications have been agreed.

Testing differs from implementing an information system. In principle, testing and implementing are opposite activities. Test results frequently frustrate implementation plans. It is important, however, to provide a well-structured organization for these often closely related activities.

The purpose of testing is not primarily to check the completeness and the correctness of the system's functionality. Although one should obviously not be blinkered when testing, checking whether the right solution was specified is something of a different order.

Testing is not cheap. Depending on the type of system, the costs will vary from 20 percent to 50 percent of the development costs after the functional specification phase. A good test executed in good time will, however, have a positive effect on the development process, and may result in a qualitatively

Figure 2.2
Correction costs
increase exponentially
(Boehm, 1981)

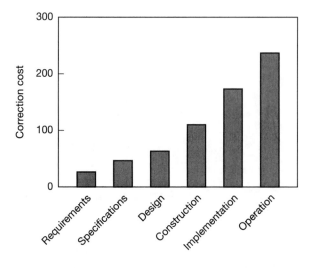

improved information system in which fewer faults occur during operation. Boehm demonstrated as far back as 1981 that the greater the time lapse between the moment of introduction of an defect and the moment of detection, the more effort, time and money its correction costs (Figure 2.2)

Testing is not training for use and operation control. Because a test process is, as a rule, highly suitable for such a purpose, this phenomenon tends to be included too readily as a secondary assignment, although it is to be preferred to separate testing and training. A combination of the two is possible provided that particular conditions are met. There should be proper agreements to prevent both testing and training from being of inferior quality. Money and time must be made available for training, and sound agreements on priorities will be required since the need to make choices may occur at some time.

Although the situation has begun to change, testing is still unpopular. This arises on the one hand from the natural human urge to make things, build, generate and innovate, and on the other hand from a lack of familiarity. People are often unaware of how challenging, creative and innovative testing is. *Unknown, unloved!*

2.3 Quality management and testing

Quality is a problem in the software industry, and testing does not provide the ultimate solution. Testing is one of the instruments that contribute to efforts to improve the quality of information systems. It should be embedded in a system of measures to achieve quality: it should be embedded in the organization's *quality management system*. Several concepts have been formulated during the development of theories on quality management. ISO has played a major part in arriving at standard definitions, and its definition of quality is: '*the totality of characteristics of a product or service that bear on its ability to satisfy stated or implied needs*' (ISO8402,

1994). This definition clearly indicates the intangible nature of quality. What is implied or obvious to one person is not so to another. 'Implied' is essentially a subjective concept. Important aspects of quality management therefore include minimizing implied needs by converting them into stated requirements, and demonstrating to what extent the stated requirements are being met. Measures should be taken to state those requirements, making the development process more manageable. The ISO definition of quality assurance is: '*the totality of planned and systematic activities implemented within the quality system, and demonstrated as needed, to provide adequate confidence that an entity will fulfill requirements for quality*' (ISO, 1994). These measures should ensure that:

- there are measurement points and quantities that provide an indication of the quality of the process (standardization);
- it is clear to individual employees what requirements their work ought to meet, and that they can check them against the above standards;
- it is possible for an independent party to check the products/services against the above standards;
- in the event of proven defects in products or services, it is possible for management to trace the causes and decide how they might be avoided in future.

These measures can be divided into preventive, detective and corrective measures:

- The objective of *preventive measures* is to prevent poor quality. We may think in terms of documentation standards, methods, techniques, etc.
- The objective of *detective measures* is to detect poor quality, e.g. by organizing reviews, walk-throughs and, of course, testing.
- The objective of *corrective measures* is to eliminate poor quality, e.g. by correcting defects exposed by testing.

Cohesion between the various measures is essential. Testing is not an activity in itself but just a small cog in the machinery of quality management. It is merely one of the forms of quality detection that may be employed. Quality detection in turn is merely one of the activities necessary to assure quality. Finally, quality assurance is one of the dimensions of quality management.

2.4 The quality of information systems

Any attempt to convert implied needs into stated requirements soon comes up against the problem that there is no obvious way of rendering the quality of information systems discussable. What is lacking is a 'language' in which it is possible to talk about quality.

What we need is a number of (independent and measurable) properties that cover the whole quality concept of the information system. For each property, a metric should be described. Then agreements could be made about the extent to which that aspect should be present in the product: standardization.

McCall *et al*, (1977) proposed the idea to break down the concept of quality into a number of properties – the so-called quality characteristics. Others followed this idea by connecting these characteristics to several metrics and creating a model of software product quality. In these varying models, some elementary characteristics keep on reappearing, although their places in the model may differ.

An important result in this field was the definition by ISO and the International Electrotechnical Commission (IEC) of an international standard for quality characteristics (ISO9126-1, 2001). These standard quality characteristics form the next step on the way to consensus in the information industry, and are directed at a general notion of software quality. The ISO9126 standard defines six quality characteristics, subdivided into a number of subcharacteristics:

- *Functionality*, which consists of five subcharacteristics: suitability, accuracy, interoperability, security and functionality compliance.
- *Reliability*, which consists of four subcharacteristics: maturity, fault tolerance, recoverability and reliability compliance.
- *Usability*, which consists of five subcharacteristics: understandability, learnability, operability, attractiveness and usability compliance.
- *Efficiency*, which consists of three subcharacteristics: time behavior, resource utilization and efficiency compliance.
- *Maintainability*, which consists of five subcharacteristics: analyzability, changeability, stability, testability and maintainability compliance.
- *Portability*, which consists of five subcharacteristics: adaptability, installability, co-existence, replaceability and portability compliance.

The exact definitions of the various quality characteristics are given in Appendix B. From these quality characteristics, an optimal set is composed within TMap that are specifically fit for testing. This set of quality characteristics is described in Chapter 11. Basically, the TMap approach can be applied in relation to any other quality model. In such a case, a 'translation' of those quality characteristics into TMap quality characteristics should take place.

An approach to testing should include tools needed for establishing whether the quality characteristics meet the requirements. TMap includes such tools in the form of techniques for the development of test strategy, estimation and planning, test strategy and test execution (see Part III).

The context of testing

3

There are many types of testing. As testing is still a relatively new discipline, clear objectives and boundaries have not yet been established adequately in most cases; where they have been established, traditional concepts rather than a new kind of testing are used. Because several disciplines, often with different interests, are involved in the same development process, it is important to identify the various test levels and types. This chapter describes several ways, levels and types of testing, and indicates to what extent they are considered in this book.

3.1 Dynamic explicit testing

In the execution of dedicated test cases by running programs, the actual result is compared with the expected result to determine whether the system behaves as required. This so-called *dynamic explicit testing* is the most common way of testing, and for a long time was considered the only one. Myers (1979) formulated the following definition: *'Testing is the process of executing a program or system with the intention of finding errors.'*

3.2 Dynamic implicit testing

During the course of explicit testing, data about the test process may be collected simultaneously with the execution of the test cases. Information about the good and bad characteristics of the system may be derived from these data. An assessment of the system's reliability may be based on its behavior during the test period: noting the frequency of failures and specifically looking for trends in their incidence will allow the tester to estimate the failures that are likely to occur during operation. This is called *implicit testing*. Implicit testing may be both planned and unplanned. An example of the latter might be to infer that there is something wrong with the user-friendliness of the system following a remark by a tester that he or she is 'being driven mad from the flashing of a field on the screen'.

3.3 Static testing

Not everything can be tested dynamically. An information system is more than just a piece of software: it is the combination of structures and resources that are used to provide an organization with information. In addition to the application software, it therefore includes:

- the technical infrastructure, i.e. the hardware, system software, etc. required for running the software;
- the organization of both the users and the systems operations; this includes the interaction between the manual and automated parts of the system, security procedures, etc.;
- the documentation belonging to the system, e.g. user manuals, and a description of administrative procedures;
- implementation and conversion schemes for introducing a new system, including appropriate training programs.

In the case of several of these aspects, it is impossible to check by dynamic testing whether the specified requirements are met. Other kinds of testing are therefore required, such as checking and examining products without executing programs. Possible examples include spell-checking documents, checking the code against standards, evaluating security procedures, training schemes, and user manuals. This is called *static testing*.

Particular measures are carried out during a development process to achieve a specific quality level. The use of a tool to check whether all program variables have been initialized is a measure to increase the reliability of the system. Estimating the quality of an information system by judging these measures may also be regarded as static testing. Activities of this kind are on the borderline between evaluation and testing. It is necessary to determine for each organization or development process where the responsibility for these activities lies.

3.3.1 Terminology
In the literature on quality and testing, no agreement exists yet regarding the terminology that should be used. Although several standards exist (IEEE, 1990; ISO, 1994; BS, 1998), often these are not followed. TMap employs the most common terms.

3.4 Test levels and techniques

To gain insight into the actual status and the required status of the IT system, it is important to realize that there is not a single specific document that contains the required status. There are, for instance, user and technical requirements on which a functional design is specified, followed by a technical design and the actual coding of the software. To get an insight into the quality of the system, it is not sufficient to test only whether the software works according to the functional or technical design, because this design can be flawed. It is also not sufficient to test only whether the software works according to user requirements, because these are at such an abstract level that the derived test cases do not cover enough of the software code or even the total system functionality.

The answer to these problems is that several kinds of tests need to be used. Tests are required to validate whether the programs work according to the technical design, whether the application works according to the functional design, and whether the system fulfils the users' needs and wishes.

To organize these tests in an efficient way, different test levels are used, where each test level addresses a certain group of requirements or functional or technical specifications. *A test level is a group of test activities that are organized and directed collectively.* Examples of test levels are the unit test, integration test, system test and acceptance test.

Based on the assigned requirements and the risks involved if the requirements are not met, each test level defines a test strategy to find the most important defects as early as possible and in the most efficient way.

An important aspect in the definition of the strategy is the choice of which test-specification techniques to use. These techniques are a structured approach to derive test cases from the test basis (e.g. requirements, functional or technical specifications), and are aimed at detecting certain kinds of defects. Use of well-chosen techniques results in far more effective detection of defects than random identification of test cases.

To measure how thoroughly tested a product is, we use the term 'coverage', i.e. the ratio between that which can be tested (possible number of test objectives) and that which is actually tested. Coverage is often used in relation to program code ('with the available test cases, $x\%$ of all statements or conditions is covered'), but it can also be used in relation to the functional specifications or requirements (paths, conditions or interfaces).

3.4.1 White-box and black-box

The test-specification techniques can be split into two groups: white-box and black-box. White-box testing techniques are based on the program code, the program descriptions or the technical design. Knowledge about the internal structure of the system plays an important role. Other terms used for this kind of techniques are glass-box or structural testing. Black-box testing techniques are based on the functional specifications and the quality requirements. In black-box techniques, the system is viewed as it would be in actual use. In theory, knowledge about the structure of the system is not used; judgement is made merely from a functional point of view of the system. Does the 'black-box' deliver output B on input A, in time frame C, in environment D, etc. (Figure 3.1)? Functional or behavioral testing are synonyms for this kind of testing.

Figure 3.1
Black-box testing

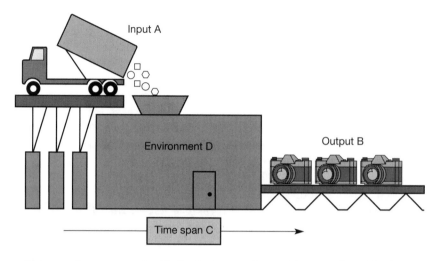

Figure 3.1
Black-box testing

This may be compared with testing a car. A test drive, maybe with the specifications to hand, will help the driver to assess whether the car comes up to his or her expectations: can it really do 100 miles per hour, and does it really go from 0 to 60 miles per hour in 10 seconds? Is the power steering working properly, and is there a vanity up mirror on the sun visor? That is black-box testing. It is then possible to open up the hood and check whether the cylinder capacity agrees with the specifications, whether the camshaft is on top, and whether the windshield wiper motor is adequately protected from moisture. That is white-box testing.

In practice, the use of black-box techniques is often aided by some knowledge of the design methods employed and the risks inherent in them. This is referred to as *gray-box* testing.

The test levels can be grouped into two categories in the context of this book: low- and high-level.

Low-level tests

These test levels involve testing the separate components of a system, e.g. programs, individually or in a combination (Kit, 1995). Developers almost exclusively execute these tests. From the beginning of the first building blocks of the system, unit, program and module tests are executed, although it depends on the infrastructure and programming language as to what extent separate tests are performed. It needs to be checked whether the most elementary parts or collections of parts are coded in accordance with the technical specifications. This book uses the term 'unit test' with regards to this subject. *A unit test is a test executed by the developer in a laboratory environment, and should demonstrate that the program meets the requirements set in the design specifications.*

After it has been determined that the most elementary parts of the system are of a sufficient quality, larger parts of the system are tested as a whole during the integration tests. The emphasis is on data throughput and the interface between the programs on a level of system parts. The integration test represents an assembly test. Depending on the development strategy, the system will be delivered step by step and integration tested with an increasing number of parts. *An integration test is executed by a developer in a laboratory environment, and should demonstrate that a logical set of programs meets the requirements set in the design specifications.*

As the low-level tests require good knowledge of the internal structure of the software, mainly white-box testing techniques are applicable.

High-level tests

These tests involve testing complete products (Kit, 1995). High-level tests offer the developer insight into the quality of the system. In addition, the tests inform the customer, user and manager about the extent to which the requirements are met, and the system can (again) be taken in production. After the low-level tests have been executed and any defects corrected, the developer executes a *system test* to determine whether the system meets the functional and technical requirements. In practice, this means that parts of the system are tested 'tile-wise' until the whole system can be tested integrally. The system test requires a controllable environment with regard to the program versions and test data. *A system test is executed by the development organization in a (properly controlled) laboratory environment, and should demonstrate that the developed system or subsystems meet the requirements set in the functional and quality specifications.*

After the development organization has performed the system test, and has corrected all or most defects, the system will be offered to the customer for acceptance. Then the specified acceptance tests can be performed. The *acceptance test* should answer questions such as: Can the system (again) be taken in production? Which risks am I taking when I do this? Has the supplier met their obligations? The execution of the acceptance test requires an environment that is, for most aspects, representative of the production environment ('as-if production'). *An acceptance test is executed by the user(s) and manager(s) in an environment simulating the operational environment to the greatest possible extent, and should demonstrate whether the developed system meets the functional and quality requirements.*

Within the acceptance test, two test levels can be recognized, which, as a result of their special characters, are usually prepared and executed separately. The functional acceptance test focuses mainly on the functionality, while the production acceptance test validates whether the system meets the requirements for operation. The functional acceptance test is performed by the users and the application managers. In terms of planning, it usually links tightly to the system test and will, in many cases, be organized 'tile-wise' at the start. In most cases, the system managers will perform the production acceptance test shortly before production begins.

The high-level tests in particular can be regarded as individual processes (and can therefore be organized as such). These are processes parallel to the development process that start during the functional design phase. Good management of these processes, and tuning in with the rest of the project by means of reporting and communication, is vital. Experience has shown that the awareness of the importance of a good test process is larger with the high-level tests than with low-level tests.

As their focus is often the externally visible properties of an object, high-level tests commonly use black-box techniques. However, the line between low-level/white-box and high-level/black-box tests is not as black and white as it seems. High-level tests increasingly appear to require knowledge of the internal operation and structure of the system. On the other hand, typical low-level tests, such as unit tests, increasingly use functional specifications as a test basis.

3.5 The development and test process

The waterfall model, the much-used lifecycle model, is still employed for developing information systems. This method proceeds as follows:

1   The process first defines the opportunities presented by IT throughout the business for solving problems or optimizing business processes, then allocates priorities (information strategy, information planning).
2   A general study is then made of the requirements that the functionality should meet (definition study, requirements analysis).
3   Next it is decided what functionality should be created in order to solve the problem (functional design).
4   The next concern is how that should be resolved (technical design).
5   The system is built and subsequently tested, introduced and used.

The terminology used above is derived from one of a number of lifecycle models. They all have a similar kind of approach. In general, this also applies to the more modern development approaches, for example rapid application development (RAD) and evolutionary development. For further information on testing in these variations, see Chapter 29.

The V-model (Figure 3.2) is a popular graphical representation used to relate test levels to the lifecycle model for system development. The phases in which the system is developed or maintained – from wish, idea, need, law, strategy, amendment, requirement, to solution – are shown on the left. The appropriate tests appear on the right. The dotted line indicates the division of responsibilities between consumer, user and systems manager (above the line), and software developer, supplier and programmer. In practice, software developers will obviously be involved in the requirements analysis and in preparing the specifications; they will also give support during the acceptance test. The

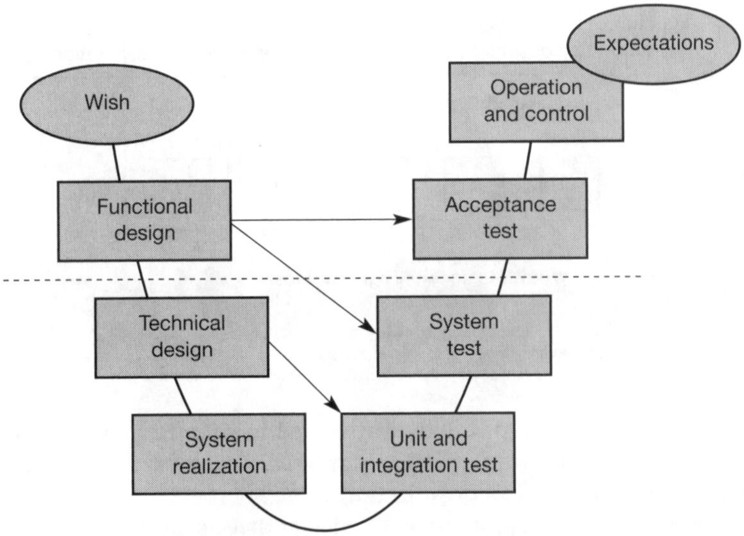

Figure 3.2
The V-model

expertise of users and systems managers will also be called upon during development activities.

How these responsibilities are handled is very important, particularly when it comes to testing, e.g. who will act as the customer for the test, or who will require advice on quality? One or more test levels are shown on the right opposite each development phase. The figure suggests that the test levels may be regarded as phases in the development process, but this is not correct. Only the measuring phases of the various tests appear in the V-model. They represent a mere 40 percent of the total effort of that test level, as shown in the iceberg in Figure 2.1. The arrows indicate the path of the initial documentation (the test basis) to the execution of the test, the 60 percent that makes up the planning and preparation activities. These early test activities on the left-hand side of the V-model should force testers to think through the specifications, design and code, and thus lead to the detection of defects and potential problems at a stage where they cost less to resolve.

It is true that the execution phases of the various test levels are located on the critical path of the development process, and constitute an intersection between the test and development processes. It is obviously important to finalize the planning and preparation activities before the actual execution of the tests.

3.6 Boundaries between test levels

Traditionally, specific criteria have been used for setting boundaries between various test levels: only one discipline (software developers, users or system managers) is responsible for each test level. Likewise, only one test environment

Figure 3.3
Traditional test levels.

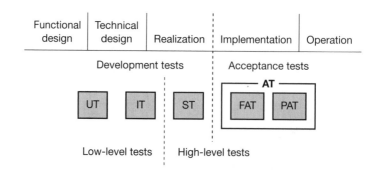

AT, acceptance test; FAT, functional acceptance test; IT, integrated test;
PAT, production acceptance test; ST, system test; UT, unit test.

(laboratory or production lookalike) is involved in each test level (Figure 3.3). Furthermore, the various tests are usually strictly consecutive. This procedure is customary in 90 percent of all organizations.

As a result of this set-up, however, particular defects are not detected until a late stage, and sometimes not until it is too late. A further consequence may be the execution of superfluous test activities, particularly between the system test and the functional acceptance test. The traditional procedure frequently does not lead to the required objective: the introduction of a well-tested system on time. In most cases, the testers get into trouble because of classic problems such as lack of time, incomplete delivery, lack of tools and management instruments, incompatible interests and, strangely enough, complaints by the customer ('all that testing is taking so long'). Developers are rarely in a position to execute a complete system test based on the specifications. It is extremely rare for a system to be handed over complete, let alone provided with all the documentation that the acceptance test asks for, such as the user manual or help texts.

In the case of high-level tests (system and acceptance tests), the need has therefore gradually arisen to deal pragmatically with the matter of test level boundaries, mainly concerning the amount of coverage to be achieved and the test environment to be employed. Because of this integration, however, the boundaries between responsibilities have become less clear cut. It is therefore essential for sound agreements on the responsibilities of the various disciplines to be made well in advance. Then cooperation can lead to a win–win situation resulting in a reduction in the time required for the process, earlier detection of defects, and better quality.

In view of this situation, many organizations are now adopting a so-called 'integrated test', in which the system test and the functional acceptance test are combined either completely or in part (Figure 3.4). This integrated test is described in detail in Chapter 29.

This kind of cooperation involves users and managers at an early stage, and gives them knowledge of the system and the (test) environment, as well as test know-how and influence on planning. It provides developers with an under-

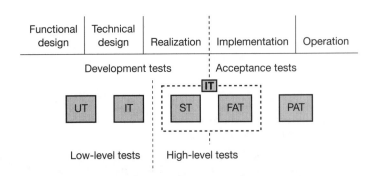

Figure 3.4
Integrated testing

FAT, functional acceptance test; IT, integrated test;
PAT, production acceptance test; ST, system test; UT, unit test.

standing of the organizational needs, and encourages earlier defect detection. Because of their early participation, an integrated test will also increase the degree of acceptance by the end users. This is, of course, a significant advantage.

Abandonment of the principle that people should execute their own complete tests in their 'own' environment will enable them to use different environments for each type of test. System tests will usually be executed in a laboratory environment, but an environment that is the same size as the production environment might, for example, be used for some specific tests. The functional acceptance test is traditionally executed exclusively in a production lookalike environment, although this is not always necessary.

Testing in a production lookalike environment is far more laborious because of the (justifiably) strict procedures. Many kinds of test tools, monitors and simulators that would be banned in a production (lookalike) situation are available in a laboratory situation. In a laboratory, several systems may be started up simultaneously. It is sometimes possible to let each tester have their own system, which means gaining time. If something can be done in the laboratory environment, there is no good reason why it should not be done there.

3.7 Test types

Because the boundaries between the various test levels are becoming less clear cut, some other means of achieving more detailed arrangements about the boundaries should be sought. Decisions should be made on *what* should be tested in each test level. An obvious solution would be to base such decisions on quality characteristics, as introduced in Chapter 2 and elaborated on in Chapter 11. The trouble with quality characteristics, however, is that they are difficult to manage; they still need to be specified in some way that would enable them to be used in practice. Test types are introduced to this end. *A test type is a group of activities aimed at checking the information system on a number of interrelated quality characteristics.*

Table 3.1

Test types

Test type	Description	Quality characteristics, including
Functionality	Testing functionality (includes dealing with input errors)	Functionality
Interfaces	Testing links with other systems	Connectivity
Load and stress	Allowing large quantities and numbers to be processed	Continuity, performance
Manual support	Testing the relationship between the software and the manual procedures of the system	Suitability
Production	Test production procedures	Operability, continuity
Recovery	Testing recovery and restart facilities	Recoverability
Regression	Testing whether all components still function correctly after the system has been changed	All
Security	Testing security	Security
Standards	Testing standards	Security, user-friendliness
Use of resources	Measuring the required amount of resources (disk, data communication, memory)	Efficiency

   Table 3.1 relates the most common test types (Perry (1995) speaks about 'techniques') to quality characteristics. This list is not exhaustive. In the development of a test strategy, decisions are taken on how, and therefore in what form, tests will be executed. New test types are devised if required. Arrangements about who is to execute which tests may then be made based on these test types.

3.7.1 Regression tests

A frequently used test type is the regression test. The building phase of an information system takes on average about 20 percent of the lifecycle of the system. In the remainder of the time, the system is in the production and maintenance phase. In this phase, changes to the existing system are applied regularly, mostly due to defects having been solved or proposals for changes. These adaptations should be tested to ensure that they do not unwittingly introduce defects into the unchanged parts of the system, a phenomenon called regression, and the reason why unchanged parts of the system still have to be tested. The regression test is aimed mainly at the integration between functions where the risk of regression is greatest.

Because regression is the sole quality risk, testing of unchanged parts of the system may take place with relatively less effort compared with a new or changed part of the system. The total effort for the regression test is, however, often much greater than the test effort needed for the detailed testing of the changes. The reason for this is that in maintenance, usually just a limited number of functions change.

Because the regression test is meant to test whether the system as a whole still functions, the test will be executed frequently (at least once for every release). New releases of a system usually concern minor changes; the system functionality as a whole remains largely the same. As a consequence, regression test cases are very reusable, and in general require only minor adaptations for each new system release. This is quite different to a test to validate a specific change: that test is usually executed only for the release concerned. The combination of frequent use and high stability means that good reusability is important. It is therefore important to create and maintain a well-structured and documented set of tests. This set of tests is usually composed during the development of the system, using existing test cases, in particular those that check integration. Suitable test specification techniques are the data combination test, the data cycle test and the process cycle test (described in Chapter 15). The regression test is maintained by adapting and enlarging the set of tests based on changes in the system, both functional adaptations and defects that have been solved. Thus, the regression test always remains up to date and is a primary candidate for automation.

Structured testing   **4**

Testing is usually regarded as a necessary evil that costs money and, above all, a lot of time. Many organizations are still seeking a solution after countless attempts at structuring the test process. Most attempts at raising the standard of testing fail as a result of many causes, usually predictable ones. In addition to the functional and technical complexity of information systems, and continually changing development methods, techniques and tools, these causes can usually be traced back to the organization of testing: to the organization of the test structuring process on the one hand, and to the organization and control of the test process itself on the other.

4.1 Unstructured testing: findings

In an attempt to alert readers to the traditional pitfalls that accompany the structuring of testing, this section discusses the most frequent findings of various studies dealing with the subject.

4.1.1 Time pressure
An unstructured test process is nearly always defeated by test enemy number one: time pressure. Major causes include:

- lack of test planning and proper estimation method;
- starting too late in preparing the test;
- insufficient and poor-quality test staff;
- the development process over-running its schedule when the delivery date has already been fixed;
- poor testing in a preceding test level;
- lack of satisfactory arrangements for deadlines and delivery procedures, and for correcting applications.

4.1.2 Waiting attitude
Strangely enough, starting too late on preparations is one of the causes. This is more or less at odds with time pressure. A characteristic wait-and-see attitude is often observed among (acceptance) testers. Preparations are delayed until the very last moment. A major reason for this is that users and testers are so

preoccupied with day-to-day problems, such as keeping the current system going, that it is simply impossible to set aside time for test preparations. The effort required for testing is inadequately foreseen and accepted. This is in addition to the often 'strategic' delivery dates that allow the developers to finish their work just before they go on holiday. Thorough preparation is essential, and it is impossible to make up for the lack of it while tests are in progress.

4.1.3 No lifecycle model for test activities

A mandatory approach whereby test activities are at least divided into specified phases and described as such is often lacking. When should a test process begin? What activities should be carried out, and by whom? All sorts of ad hoc methods and lifecycle models are created because of a lack of test instructions, and the wheel is reinvented in every organization and for every test process – an extremely expensive hobby.

4.1.4 Ignoring test techniques and tools

Test techniques and tools are often ignored even though they are available. Testers may have attended courses on test techniques and have some promising tools at their disposal, but for various reasons, including lack of time, they often fall back on an unstructured test approach. High-level testers make use of white-box test cases. Test cases are sometimes simply borrowed from the programmer or, even worse, users take a programming course and derive their test cases from, for example, the Working Storage Section of COBOL programs. This may be fun, but it is a waste of effort since low-level tests have already been carried out.

Acquiring test tools on the assumption that they will solve the test problems is a common pitfall. Record and playback tools that allow tests to be recorded and played back make a genuine contribution to the efficiency of (maintenance) testing. Structuring aspects, however, are often overlooked. It has been established time and time again that the available test tools do not lead to the desired result because nearly all of them require experience in the application of a structured approach to testing.

4.1.5 Unclear specifications

In contracts for the development or servicing of information systems, testing is often considered to be a minor detail, and in most cases formal grounds for delivery or non-acceptance are not included. Specifications often turn out to be neither established nor managed, and untraceable changes are commonplace. The connection between the 'order' (the specification) and the 'product' (the test object) is then lost. Testing subsequently becomes very difficult, since specifications form the basis for test activities.

4.1.6 Lack of management and control

A test process is quite frequently wrecked because of the absence of the required management and control functions, such as configuration and change control.

There is often a reasonable test plan that proves highly satisfactory in its preliminary phases. During the test execution phase, however, when time pressure causes many ad hoc management problems, the plan collapses. The test plan lacks flexibility, and there is not enough anticipatory capability.

4.1.7 Low quality of low-level tests

The quality of low-level tests often leaves much to be desired. System and acceptance testers are then faced with elementary program defects at too late a stage and in the wrong environment. Correction thus becomes a rather expensive activity (Boehm, 1981).

4.1.8 Conflicting interests

Testing takes place within a spectrum of (seemingly) conflicting interests. Developers, system managers, testers, users, application managers and, above all, customers have their own ideas about the best way of arriving at the most suitable solution or creating the optimal product.

Developers want as much time as possible to optimize the product. As long as this is compatible with the plans, there is nothing against it, and it is very much to the advantage of the testers. After all, the fewer defects there are, the more manageable the test process will be. Unfortunately, however, the development process tends to run short of time. Whatever time is available is then spent largely on development activities, while low-level tests and system tests go by the board.

The *system managers* will require an understanding of many aspects before the system goes into production. It is necessary to answer the question of whether the new or amended system can be operated to the customer's satisfaction within the framework of technical infrastructure, procedures and competitive systems without making excessive demands on (standard) facilities. Yet coming up with an answer to this question requires (test) time and a great deal of consultation. Having learned from bitter experience, system managers are often fated to take a hard line. In many instances, this attitude has deteriorated unwittingly into an insurance premium for operational continuity. Opportunities for conflict abound, and polarization replaces cooperation.

Testers, *users* and *managers* want to execute tests as planned. For the purpose, the test object should therefore be available fully in good time, including components such as the operational instructions, user manuals and descriptions of administrative procedures. The system manager should also organize the required test infrastructure on time, and (trained) staff should be available. Organizing all this requires much patience and, above all, tact.

The *customer* simply wants the best solution to the problem at the lowest possible cost and with the least effort. He or she also wants their wishes to be carried out instantly, even though they have a habit of expressing them in vague terms and far too late. All that fuss about lifecycle models, development and testing methods, design tools and architectures is unlikely to impress the customer very much. He or she merely wants his or her solution – and on time!

4.1.9 Poor coordination of test activities

Projects and organizations often lack rules about the test methods and techniques to be adopted. They muddle along, even when it comes to using the test infrastructure, test databases and test tools. When these facilities are used, many of the test processes compete with one another. As a rule, the required coordination is lacking, even in matters such as training, recommendations, and the collection and exchange of experiences and metrics. This causes proliferation and insularity. Individuals and individual projects make good progress, and there may even be good test gurus who come to the fore. This is excellent, but after an inevitable promotion, or by the end of the process, all good things are binned and the process begins all over again.

4.2 Structured testing: recommendations

The principal findings of the various studies may serve as bases for structuring the test process within a project or the test process in an organization. This obviously depends on the extent to which the organization's test processes already have some structure. The findings may simply be converted into concrete recommendations. They have made a significant contribution to the development of TMap and will be referred to again in the next chapter. A more reflective approach may suffice here.

4.2.1 Reducing time pressure
This is effected by:

- flexible planning in good time;
- progress monitoring;
- starting on time;
- sufficient and suitable staffing;
- sound arrangements.

Efforts to reduce the pressure will be boosted by the timely creation of a master test plan, which specifies who will execute which tests, and when they will do so. Test strategy development and test point analysis (TPA®) techniques will provide the support required for this purpose. The use of good-quality tools for planning and progress monitoring is obviously recommended. Monitoring the progress of the test process is of great importance. Testing is a final process, and it depends on all parties involved in the system's development. It is essential to make early arrangements with the various parties on matters such as delivery, quality standards, retests, support, etc. All problems concerning the quality of the development process and the test object, together with the related planning, have a direct effect on test planning.

Because a test process is aimed primarily at detecting defects, it may, in principle, have a negative effect on its own planning. Test planning should therefore be flexible and revised periodically. This requires further planning, and capacity should be set aside for it.

After the test plan has been completed and accepted by the customer, test preparation should begin as soon as possible. This might include setting up management procedures, arranging for the required functional, methodological and technical support, and accommodating and recruiting sufficient and suitable test staff. As soon as the specifying documentation for the test (the test basis) has become available, depending on the quality of it the specification of test cases may begin.

4.2.2 Project approach, free from line concerns

Test activities should be tackled in a project on the basis of a test plan. 'Line' noise, caused by departmental meetings, subsidiary activities and nonspecific training, should be reduced to a minimum. It is advisable to separate test activities strictly from everyday operational concerns. Possible measures include choosing a different location and recruiting only full-timers. These are not easy measures, since operation always has priority, and the test process must be included in the regular organization on completion. This is a challenge for test management.

4.2.3 A lifecycle model for test activities in parallel with development activities

Test activities should begin at some stage during the process of system development, and should be conducted in association with other activities. This requires careful phasing. A lifecycle model should specify the activities for each test level in phases up to the questions what? and when? For each activity, the objective, procedure, techniques, products to be delivered, etc. should be identified.

4.2.4 Setting standards and monitoring their application

The standards to be adopted for testing (lifecycle model, documentation, techniques, tools, etc.) should be set in good time, unambiguously and centrally. Ideally, this should be done at a corporate level for the whole organization. As the need arises, it will be necessary to settle matters for individual departments or projects. Setting standards involves establishing, implementing and maintaining them. Periodic monitoring of their application and usefulness must also be arranged, if possible as a separate task.

4.2.5 Structured and appropriate use of test tools

In theory, most test activities can be automated, i.e. there are test tools available for them. When the required structure has been incorporated in the test process (organization, infrastructure and setting standards), test tools may be employed as appropriate. Initially, one should consider supporting tools for estimating, planning, progress monitoring, test data management, coverage analysis and reporting. At a later stage, so-called primary test tools should be considered, e.g. test design and test execution.

The stability of the test process is a prerequisite for tools of this kind. If changes to the specifications and consequently to the test object continue to come through in large numbers, the use of such tools is usually not advisable and would merely lead to extra expense. As yet, primary test tools are suitable only for maintenance testing. Simple tools, such as spreadsheets and word processors, may also provide excellent support for the test process.

4.2.6 Organizing management and control

Everything, including the environment, is in motion during the test process. The availability of appropriate management and control tools is essential if sound recommendations on quality are to be made at the end of the test process. We cover here the management and control of the test process itself, its environment and test attributes such as the test object, specifications and the testware. Management and control instruments for this purpose include:

- organizing and planning test activities;
- progress and budget monitoring;
- periodic risk analysis of the test process;
- procedures and tools for configuration management and change control, which will provide structural insight into the relationship between (frozen) specifications, the test object, testware and the test infrastructure;
- procedures for analyzing and making decisions on defects, and tracing possible solutions and retests;
- collecting metrics on the test process and the quality of the test object;
- progress and quality (risk) reports;
- external quality assurance (audits on the test process by third parties).

4.2.7 Reduction of conflicting interests, and team building

Early preparation of a master test plan that includes as many arrangements as possible between the parties involved will prevent conflicts subsequently having an adverse effect on progress and the atmosphere at work. Such arrangements will help to clarify everyone's contribution, and start people in the same or desired direction later on. Although it is necessary to guard against excess, setting up a sound communication structure is very important in this context. Experience has shown that identifying points of cooperation is an excellent way of converting conflicting interests into shared ones. Efforts should be made to allow test activities by the various disciplines to take place on the basis of maximum cooperation whilst preserving individual responsibilities. If everyone's interests are considered, mutual assistance will follow automatically. However, this requires professionalism and tact.

4.2.8 Organizing test coordination and/or a test help-desk function

Testers are just like everyone else. They need methods, techniques, tools, training and support. They like to benefit from the experience of others, and they have an interest in the metrics of test processes. They sometimes need advice on specific aspects and, if possible, ready-made test facilities equipped by experts. They also want to be able to gear their planning towards competitive test processes and, if possible, make use of the same (generic) test data. Such facilities should preferably be provided at an organization level, or alternatively for each department or project. There should be a door marked 'Test' and a facilities discipline that coordinates test activities and operates as a help-desk when required. In a broad outline, the following facilities would be required:

- standards on test methods, techniques and tools;
- maintaining these standards;
- monitoring their application and usability;
- overall test planning in the event of concurrent test activities;
- collecting test metrics, and making them available;
- training and coaching test staff;
- assembling and servicing the test infrastructure;
- making test tools available, and servicing them;
- technical management of test data;
- advice on testing in the broadest sense of the word.

4.3 The four cornerstones of a structured approach to testing

The various recommendations for structuring the test process may be seen as a tetrahedron, with four cornerstones supporting a structured approach to testing (Figure 4.1). The four cornerstones consist of a lifecycle of test activities associated with the development *lifecycle*, sound *organizational embedding*, the right *infrastructure* and usable *techniques* for performing the activities.

Figure 4.1
The four cornerstones supporting a structured approach to testing

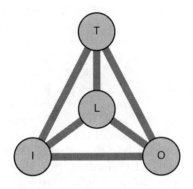

L, lifecycle; I, infrastructure; O, organization; T, techniques.

4.3.1 Lifecycle

Like a system development process, a test process consists of a number of activities. There are lifecycle models for system development that make it possible for the various activities, their sequence and interdependence to be mapped out. In a lifecycle model, the entire process is divided into a number of phases, which in turn are subdivided into activities. The objective, procedure, deliverables, techniques, etc. of each activity are described in detail. The use of a lifecycle model makes it possible to retain an overview during the system development process. There are also lifecycle models for the test process, which are essential for retaining an overview during testing. The lifecycle model is like a thread running through the test process. By describing what, when, how, where, with what, by whom and so on needs to be done in the course of the test process, demands on and relations with the other three cornerstones (techniques, infrastructure and organization) are automatically established. A good test lifecycle model is therefore the first cornerstone supporting a structured test process.

4.3.2 Techniques

There are many techniques for supporting the testing process – for supporting the planning process, for study and review of the test basis, and for reporting. Test-specification techniques constitute the most important group, and vary from very informal to very formal (mathematical). A test-specification technique may be used to measure particular quality characteristics of an information system. However, there is not a single test-specification technique that can measure all quality characteristics. It is therefore necessary to use a combination of techniques for this purpose. A 'toolbox', well stocked with test techniques, is the second cornerstone supporting a structured test process.

4.3.3 Infrastructure

A test environment is needed if tests are to be executed. Such an environment must be stable, controllable and representative. It must also be separated from other environments (e.g. the development environment). It is only under such conditions that reproducible tests can be carried out. If this is to be done efficiently, particular aids – test tools – will be required. The office environment of the test team is also important. A good infrastructure is therefore the third cornerstone supporting a structured approach to testing.

4.3.4 Organization

A test process is performed by people, therefore it requires organization – on the one hand, an organization within the test team whereby everyone must be given tasks and responsibilities, and on the other hand, incorporation of the test team in the project organization. It is essential to specify for each test who is to prepare and execute it, who is in charge, who is to check the quality, and to whom the results are to be communicated. It is only under these conditions that the test process can proceed in an orderly fashion. A good test organization is therefore the fourth cornerstone supporting a structured approach to testing.

4.4 TMap

TMap enlarges upon the four cornerstones of lifecycle, techniques, infrastructure and organization. TMap was created and applied most frequently as an approach to high-level testing (system and acceptance tests). Since then, it has proved convenient for other test levels and types. TMap represents an extensive collection of standards, instruments, tools and procedures that may be selected for a specific test using the test strategy development technique (see Chapter 11).

The theoretical treatment of TMap is grouped in this book by cornerstone:

- Lifecycle: Part II
- Techniques: Part III
- Organization: Part IV
- Infrastructure: Part V

For a quick introduction, read the next chapter.

TMap in a nutshell

5

This chapter gives the reader a quick global understanding of the aspects of TMap. Depending on your involvement in testing, you may then work through the remainder of the book selectively.

TMap (test management approach) starts with the notion that testing is a process. A process is performed by executing activities. TMap defines all possible activities, and groups those in phases into a lifecycle model. This model and the activities are described as the L-cornerstone of TMap in Part II.

To execute the activities in a controlled way, many useful techniques are introduced. Together they form the T-cornerstone described in Part III.

To have the activities executed in time with the desired quality, TMap states that infrastructure and an organization with professionals and procedures must be in place. The organization (O-)cornerstone is described later in this chapter and in full in Part IV. The infrastructure (I-)cornerstone is described briefly in this chapter, and in full in Part V.

The lifecycle model describes how and when the details of the T-, I- and O-cornerstones have to be used and to what extent, depending on the customer specific situation. In this way TMap is like an organ that can be played softly for delicate music or in full to support great symphonies.

5.1 Testing as a process

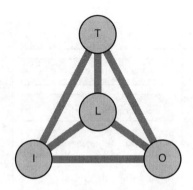

The principal activities – planning, preparation and execution – are included in all test levels. A significant part of the effort should be devoted to planning and preparation. An appropriate rule of thumb for allocating time is to allow 20 per cent for planning, 40 per cent for preparation, and 40 per cent for executing tests.

During the creation or adaptation of the functional specifications, a master test plan is produced that determines who will be responsible for a specific test level or test type, and when that responsibility will begin. Ideally, this master test plan should work for all test levels and types, starting with the unit tests and ending with the acceptance tests. Sometimes it is limited to high-level tests (system and acceptance tests) or, for example, the developer's tests (low-level and system tests). Because a master test plan touches upon more than one discipline, the various tasks, responsibilities, milestones and deliverables must be specified accurately.

In large projects, the order to produce and coordinate the execution of this kind of master test plan is often issued to a (high-level) test team, which may or may not be independent. On the basis of the agreed master test plan, more detailed subtest plans are prepared – usually one for low-level tests, one for the system test, and one for the acceptance tests. Apart from these levels, it is possible to enter evaluations such as inspecting and reviewing as a part of the master test plan (Figure 5.1). The preparation and execution of subtest plans is the responsibility of the disciplines designated for the purpose.

After the test plans have been agreed, test cases and infrastructure are developed in line with the system development process. The actual tests will be executed as soon as the test object has been supplied.

A test process therefore includes a second design process, the test design, in addition to system design. This may appear to be expensive, but sound planning and agreements, risk assessment, careful test strategy development and above all starting on time will reduce costs considerably. Experience has shown that designing test cases and reviewing specifications required for this purpose reveal so many ambiguities and inconsistencies that the costs are recovered before the first test is executed. The cost of correcting defects, after all, has shown to increase exponentially for each development phase (Boehm, 1981).

Figure 5.1
Test plan hierarchy

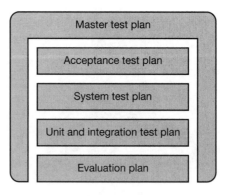

5.2 Lifecycle

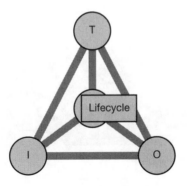

Test activities are incorporated in a lifecycle model, which can be used by analogy with the lifecycle models for system development. In the TMap lifecycle model, the principal test activities are grouped into five phases (Figure 5.2). In addition to the phases of planning and control, preparation, specification and execution, a completion phase has been designed to round off the test process satisfactorily and to hand over the testware to the organization for the first or subsequent maintenance releases.

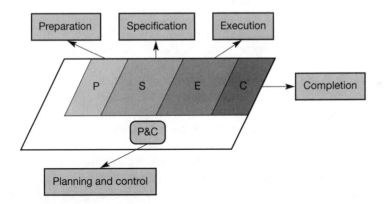

Figure 5.2
TMap lifecycle model

It should be noted that the line between phases is not vertical. The reason for this is that phases may overlap. For instance, testing of part of the system has already started, while the test cases are still being specified for other parts of the system.

The TMap lifecycle model is a generic model – it may be applied to any test level. In every phase, several activities are distinguished. It usually includes too many activities for low-level testing. Only in extreme circumstances will all registers be used. It is up to the person responsible for the tests to make an appropriate selection from the TMap arsenal. Within the hierarchy of test plans, several TMap models will be used for various types of tests in a system development process (Figure 5.3)

Figure 5.3
TMap per test level

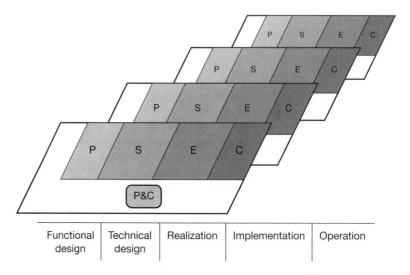

| Functional design | Technical design | Realization | Implementation | Operation |

A global description of the generic TMap lifecycle model follows. It includes definitions of the terminology (the term 'specifications' refers to the program descriptions as well as to the 'functional design').

5.2.1 The planning and control phase

The planning and control phase begins during the functional specification phase of the project. The activities included in this phase lay the foundations for a manageable and high-quality test process. Hard though it is, at this early system development stage, everything that makes the test process so difficult to direct and control must be anticipated. To appreciate this, just consider the reliability of the milestone planning of the development, the quality of the test object, and the number of amendments and retests, the organization of the management tasks, and the availability of personnel, tools, money and time. The planning phase, which is the most important test phase, is nearly always underestimated.

After confirmation of the test assignment, a global record is made of the available system and project documentation, the quality requirements set for the system, and the organization of the system development process. It is impossible to test the entire system, as test techniques providing 100 per cent coverage of everything exist only in theory. Moreover, no single company would be willing to designate the time and the resources for this purpose. So the test strategy is then developed by way of risk assessment – depending on the risks, which parts of the information system will get the highest attention and which parts somewhat less, and so on. Such matters are, of course, agreed with stakeholders such as the customer – testers should not make these decisions by themselves. The object is to provide *the best possible degree of coverage in the right place*. In addition, the testers initiate the set-up of the test organization and the test infrastructure. These activities are carried out at the beginning of the test process and are described in a test plan. This test plan has to be approved by the customer, and will be the baseline for the execution of all further test activities: a consolidated test plan.

The other activities belonging to this phase continue throughout the test process and are aimed at managing the use of time and resources during testing. Detailed plans for each test phase are prepared throughout the test process.

Reports on the progress of the process and the quality of the test object are prepared as agreed in the test plan (Figure 5.4). Frequency and format should be stipulated here. Recommendations on quality and therefore risks are the most important deliverables of a test process. Testers begin to form an impression of the test object's quality at the time of the first test activities. It is important to note indications of quality during every phase of the test process.

The customer is given information periodically on the condition of the system as well as in response to an ad hoc request – and definitely not only on completion of the job. The test must produce properly structured management information. It is not enough to say at the end of the test process, 'No, you can't go into operation yet, I haven't finished testing.' No customer is likely to tolerate that kind of claim. They want to know what risks are being taken, if possible backed up by statistical information, and therefore what measures should be implemented. It may be decided, for example, to continue testing, to go into partial operation, or to keep the old system operating in parallel (shadow production).

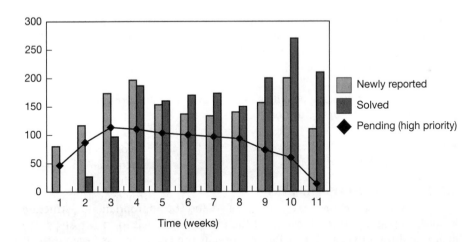

Figure 5.4
Statistical information about defects

For the purpose of preparing a test plan, TMap defines the following activities as part of the planning and control phase:

- formulating the assignment
- global review and study
- establishing the test basis

- determining the test strategy
- setting up the organization
- specifying test deliverables
- specifying the infrastructure
- organizing management and control
- setting up schedules
- consolidating the test plan.

The following activities can be identified within the framework of the coordination, monitoring and control of the test process:
- maintaining the test plan
- controlling the test
- reporting
- establishing detailed schedules.

5.2.2 The preparation phase

The preparation phase begins with the testability review of the specifications and other documentation forming the test basis. If the documentation is insufficiently or not available, this activity is aimed more at composing the test basis by performing interviews with users and developers and by collecting prototypes and requirements. The testability review provides an insight into testability by evaluating aspects such as clarity, uniformity in notation, separability and recognizability. The quality of the test basis may improve as a result. After the review, the system is divided into independently deliverable and testable system components with the cooperation of the developers. Based on the test strategy, test techniques are subsequently allocated to these test units, and the continuation of the test activities is planned.

TMap defines the following activities as part of the preparation phase:
- testability review of the test basis
- defining test units
- allocating test techniques
- specifying the infrastructure.

5.2.3 The specification phase

During this phase, the test cases are specified and the appropriate infrastructure is put into place. The specification of the test cases is effected in two steps: the logical and the physical test design. As soon as the test basis has become available, it is used for the specification of logical test cases (test specifications). Later, as more information becomes available on the technical implementation, the logical test cases are translated into physical test cases and test scripts. A test case consists of the description of the starting situation, the actions to be performed, and the prediction of the expected result. During this process, the initial contents of the various test databases are also specified. The test infrastructure (hardware and software environment, and so on) is set up parallel to the test design.

TMap defines the following activities as part of the specification phase (Figure 5.5):

- preparing test specifications
- defining initial test databases
- producing test scripts
- producing a test scenario
- specifying the review of the test object and infrastructure
- setting up the infrastructure.

5.2.4 The execution phase

The execution phase begins with the first delivery of testable components. Arrangements for this and for the infrastructure to be employed have been made during the previous phases. The supplied (parts of) applications are first checked for completeness and installed in the test environment. Then it is assessed whether the applications and technical infrastructure function properly in relation to each other (review). In order to start the real testing, the initial test databases should be set up, an important, painstaking task that is carried out mostly using genuine system functions. This is already part of the actual testing.

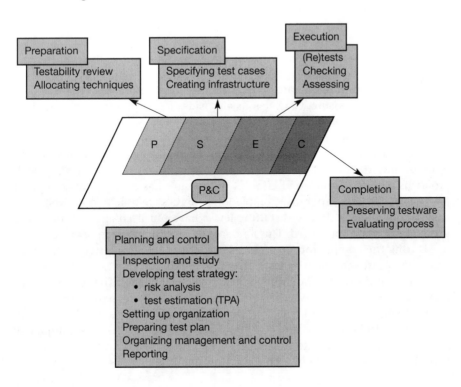

Figure 5.5
Activities in the TMap lifecycle

When (parts of) the applications and infrastructure as well as parts of the initial test databases are ready, pretests (also known as smoke tests) are executed for the purpose of checking the principal tasks of the object to be tested. Pretests provide an answer to the question: is the quality of the test object such that it is of sufficient quality to start testing? If the outcome of the pretests is satisfactory, executing the designed test scripts may begin.

The difference between a test's actual result and the predicted one may point to a programming error, a defect or ambiguity in the specifications, a defect in the test infrastructure, or an invalid test case. This is sorted out during the compare and analyze activities. After any defects have been corrected, the tests may be executed again, and so on.

Rapid, reliable reporting of risks is prepared for throughout the execution phase. Management may expect fast, reliable reports on the risks that should be taken into account. Management wants to know how much of what was agreed has been tested, how much still needs to be done, how many defects there are, what the trends are, which risks are still open, and whether they can stop testing.

TMap defines the following activities for the execution phase:

- review of test object/infrastructure
- setting up initial test databases
- executing (re)tests
- comparing and analyzing the test results
- maintaining the testware.

5.2.5 The completion phase

The completion phase consists of conserving testware and evaluating the test object and the test process.

The reason for this separate phase is that the final tests are usually executed under great time pressure. Concessions are made to control procedures, such as maintaining test documentation.

Another tiresome phenomenon that tends to interfere with clear-up operations is the fact that problems that cannot wait for a solution are almost bound to occur after the delivery of the test object ('post-natal stress'). Tackling such problems requires a concerted effort. The test staff has a part to play in all of this, e.g. in the necessary tests. Completion activities are usually not given sufficient priority, and if time and staffing levels have not been allowed for it, the testware will not be preserved. This amounts to sheer destruction of capital.

During the completion phase, a selection is made of the frequently large amounts of testware, such as test cases, test results and, for example, descriptions of the infrastructure and the tools that were employed. The objective is to preserve those parts of the testware that are likely to be reused, so that in the event of amendments and corresponding maintenance tests, the testware will merely need to be adapted and it will not be necessary to design a completely new set of tests. During the test process, an attempt will have been made to keep the test cases consistent with the specifications and the developed system.

The test process is also evaluated in this phase in the hope that a better process will be implemented next time. The metrics and evaluations collected during the previous phases are combined with the results of a final evaluation. The subject is not only the test process but also, for example, the quality of the product. It is also advisable to prepare an account on the costs and benefits of the test process. This is a difficult activity, but it is also fascinating and above all instructive. The quantities of statistics that often become available are indispensable for planning and optimizing future testing and development processes, and for organizing quality systems. Following the evaluation, preservation and presentation of the evaluation report, the testing process stops and the customer may discharge the test team from their assignment.

TMap defines the following activities for the completion phase:

- evaluating the test object
- evaluating the test process
- preparing an evaluation report
- preserving testware
- discharging the test team.

5.3 Techniques

TMap is supported by a large number of techniques offering testers elaborated,

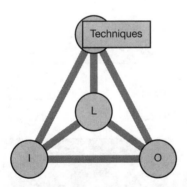

well-proven and universal working methods, as well as enabling the management (and auditors) to track the content of the test process (Figure 5.6). *A test technique is a system of actions aimed at providing a universally applicable method of creating a test product.*

In the description of the activities in the lifecycle model, some of the possible techniques that can be used are hinted at. The characteristics of the various (groups of) test techniques are described briefly below.

5.3.1 Strategy development

Deciding on a test strategy is a means of communicating with the customer on matters such as the organization of testing and the strategic choices that go with it. A customer commissioning the tests will expect the released system to include specific qualities, which may vary considerably from case to case. It is important to be able to communicate with the customer on these matters, and to incorporate their wishes in the chosen testing approach.

A test strategy is based on risk assessment because it is important to deploy test effort (i.e. test coverage) in an optimal way. The strategy development technique makes an analysis of how much should be invested in a test in order to find an optimal balance between the required insight in quality and the amount of time and money needed for it.

5.3.2 Test point analysis

Once the test approach has been more or less determined, the test effort should be estimated. How much time will be needed for having subsystem x tested by means of technique y by staff member z? Answering this kind of question requires metrics, but since testing is a relatively new discipline, few statistics and metrics are available. The test effort is often measured in terms of development effort, for instance as a percentage.

The size of a system's functionality can be determined by means of function point analysis (FPA). Test point analysis (TPA) was developed by analogy with FPA for budgeting test processes; the technique has been applied in practice in a

Figure 5.6
Techniques in the TMap
lifecycle

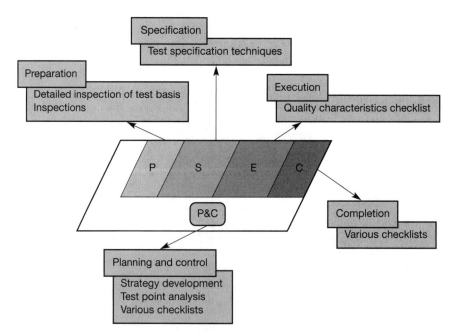

large number of projects. TPA is suitable for estimating the effort for high-level tests such as the system and acceptance tests. It converts function points into test points, on the basis of which the number of test hours is calculated. The TPA technique analyzes the impact of specific factors that affect tests, such as quality requirements, the system's size and complexity, but also the quality of the test basis and the extent to which test tools are used.

5.3.3 Testability review of the test basis

The test basis consists of the documentation used to prepare the tests. It is obvious that the review (study and assessment) of that test basis is a major condition for making good progress during the actual preparations for the tests. The review checks whether the documentation is sufficiently complete, accurate and consistent to serve as a reference for the tests.

5.3.4 Test-specification techniques

Test cases should be based on reference information. An elementary test case consists of a description of the starting situation, the actions to be performed, and a prediction of the expected result (Figure 5.7). A test case can aim to test one or more quality characteristics of one or more functions of the software to be tested. *A test-specification technique is a standardized way of deriving test cases from reference information.*

The individual test cases are subsequently grouped into test scripts that prescribe which starting situation and which sequence of actions and checks are applicable during the execution of the test. The collection of test scripts is subsequently incorporated into a full test scenario, which establishes the relationship with the required test infrastructure.

Several test-specification techniques are available for testing the various functional and quality characteristics. However, the application of a technique depends largely on the way in which the reference information is structured.

During the preparation phase, test-specification techniques are selected and adapted on the basis of the quality characteristics specified in the strategy, and on the basis of the structure of the reference information.

5.3.5 Checklists

TMap offers a great number of checklists. During the planning and control and preparation phases, there are useful checklists for global study, defining preconditions, identifying risks relating to the test project and specifying test facilities. Also included are checklists for testing several quality characteristics.

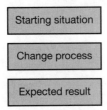

Figure 5.7
Elementary test case

5.4 Infrastructure

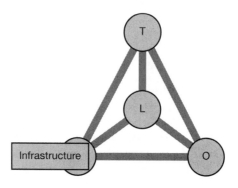

The infrastructure for testing includes all facilities and resources required for structured testing. It is possible to distinguish between facilities needed for executing the test (test environment), facilities needed for supporting test execution (test tools) and, often underestimated, the office environment.

The 'choice' of infrastructure for the test is usually not a choice at all but a fait accompli. There *is* a test environment, there *are* test tools, and there *are* workstations for test purposes. The choice usually consists of requests for a few changes to the existing infrastructure and the arrangement of test databases. The arrangement of the test infrastructure also depends largely on the type of IT platform and the organization. TMap is therefore obliged to keep within general terms in this context and merely offers some suggestions.

5.4.1 Test environment

Traditionally, there are three types of environment available for testing purposes: the laboratory environment for low-level tests, the rather more controllable environment for system tests, and the simulated production environment for acceptance tests (Figure 5.8)

Figure 5.8
Traditional test
environments

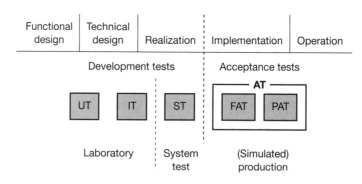

AT, acceptance test; FAT, functional acceptance test; IT, integration test;
PAT, production acceptance test; ST, system test; UT, unit test.

For considerations of efficiency, however, it is becoming more and more common to abandon the fixed link between the person involved in the test and his or her 'own' environment. It is more efficient to let the environment required for testing purposes depend on the test type concerned.

The demands on the infrastructure made by low-level tests, for example, are quite different from those made by the production acceptance test, but sometimes a production acceptance test need not necessarily be executed in a 'simulated production' environment. Which quality characteristics are to be tested? Are formal rules of simulated production required? Is the possibility of quickly adapting the test object most important for the continuity of the test process?

These kinds of questions should be answered at an early stage in the test process, partly because it takes considerable time to implement environment. System managers, who usually make this kind of facility available to testers, should be fully notified of the 'order' at an early date. To avoid disappointment it is advisable – or even essential – to call in one of the system managers to assist in formulating an 'order' of this kind.

5.4.2 Test tools

The development of test tools has matured over recent years. Their scope, diversity and application have increased enormously. Test tools may be classified according to the activities (and therefore the TMap phases) they support (Figure 5.9).

Here we give, grouped by TMap phase, an enumeration of test tools related to the TMap phase:

- *Planning and control phase*:
    - Defect administration – tool for supporting the administration and control of the defects found.

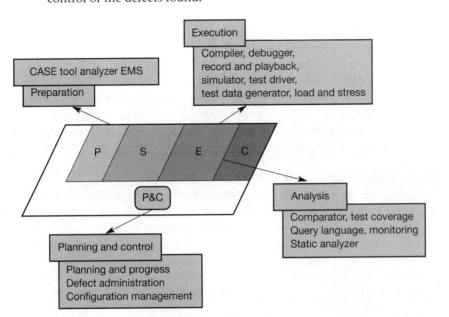

Figure 5.9
Test tools and TMap

- Configuration management – tool for supporting product control.
- Planning and progress control – tool for supporting the planning progress and/or the monitoring and controlling of the project progress.
- Test management – tool with an integrated set of functionalities concerning planning, progress control, defect management and configuration management.

- *Preparation phase:*
    - CASE tool analyzer – tool by which the test basis is checked on completeness and correctness (if the test basis is documented in a CASE tool).
    - Electronic Meeting System (EMS) – tool for supporting the communication and inspection process.
- *Specification phase:*
    - Test design – tool for supporting the specification of test cases by means of test specification techniques.
- *Execution phase:*
    - Test data generator – tool for supporting the building of physical test sets.
    - Debugger – aid for tracing specific defects that are hard to find.
    - Record and playback – the possibility to play back test scripts automatically after they have been recorded or constructed for that purpose.
    - Load and stress – tool for load and stress tests, by which large numbers of users may be simulated.
    - Simulator – tool by which the 'realistic' environment may be imitated in order to test, for example, the performance.
    - Stubs and drivers – a replacement of a calling or called program that has not been delivered yet.
    - Static analyzer – tool by which the program code is checked and analyzed.
    - Comparator – tool to compare automatically the test results with the results of a previous test session.
    - Test coverage tool – tool that measures the degree to which the test object has been covered by test cases.
    - Query language – tool for requesting information about the content of databases.
    - Monitoring tool – tool that measures the use of resources (memory, central processing unit (CPU), etc.).

5.4.3 Office environment

From planning to completion, the test process requires a suitable environment for people to work in. It seems simple enough, but in reality testers all too often find that their desks and workstations are not ready on time or that they are obliged to share them with colleagues. The work environment for tests should be equipped fully by the beginning of the specification phase, not merely by the time the tests are to be executed.

Since testing often requires a lot of consultation, the availability of a dedicated meeting area is essential, not just a luxury. Testing often takes place out of office hours, and catering facilities are therefore essential, as is adequate access to the offices, e.g. transport facilities at night. Experience has shown that excessive physical distance between system management, development organization and testers is likely to cause problems.

5.5 Organization

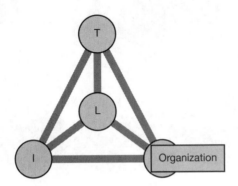

Test processes with an organization of insufficient quality will be a failure. The involvement of many different disciplines (Figure 5.10), conflicting interests, unpredictability, complicated management tasks, lack of experience (and metrics), and time constraints make the set-up and management of the test organization a difficult task. Test organization is the representation of *effective relations* between test functions, test facilities and test activities in order to allow a high standard of quality recommendations to be given in good time

The organization of structured testing requires attention to the following areas:

- the operational test process
- the structural test organization
- test management and control
- staff and training
- structuring the test process.

5.5.1 The operational test process

At departmental or project level, where the real testing takes place, it is important to choose a flexible but stable form of organization. This requires experience, tact, patience and a feeling of timing by the (test) management. The set-up of the functions and the means of control demand a permanent tuning with the process and the quality of system development of which the test process is a part. Classical problem areas in test processes include introducing staff or installing tools too early or too late.

Figure 5.10
The variety of disciplines
involved in testing

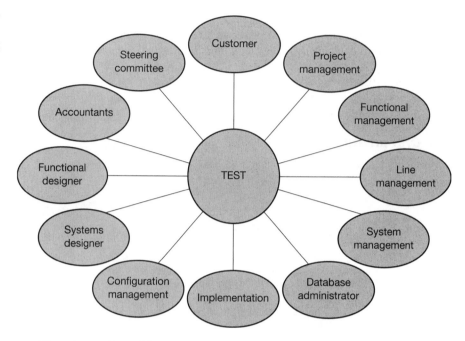

Figure 5.10
The variety of disciplines
involved in testing

There is a variety of functions in an operational test organization. Depending on the test level and the size of the test object, for instance, these functions are carried out by one or more people. Sometimes, the test team consists of just one part-timer, whereas for larger projects a (high-level) test team may consist of 20–30 employees. The main test functions are testing, test management and control. TMap advises high-level tests to be executed as a project (test team). It is important to assemble in an operational test organization the right mixture of expertise:

- the subject matter
- the developed system
- the infrastructure (test environment, developing platform, test tools)
- testing
- test management.

5.5.2 The structural test organization

Just like any other process within information services, testing asks for regulations and assessments on their application. These regulations indicate on what preconditions, and according to what rules and standards, people, resources and methods should be deployed in order to achieve the strategic goals.

Test functions exist to make the regulations and to check the assessment of these regulations. In large organizations, where IT represents almost all the primary process, e.g. in banks, insurance companies and some government institutions, these functions are incorporated into the structural test organization. In other organizations, the functions are performed within the test project.

There are no rules for the set-up and control of the structural test organization. Rather, it is dependent on a great number of factors, such as the maturity of automation and the size of the organization. Of course, the demands that the organization is making on the IT are of great importance: is a little mistake permitted, or does the smallest incident lead to front-page news in a national newspaper? How important is time to market? Is insufficient quality fatal to the public or just to some careers?

Often, the regulatary and assessment functions are part of the department of quality management and/or methodology and techniques. In other cases, a special test office or a test service department is operational. Sometimes, something is arranged simply at department or project level. In short, *there is no universal kind of test organization.*

5.5.3 Test management and control

One of the real problems of testing is that everything, even the environment, is in motion. All that movement needs to be managed and controlled in order to provide a satisfactory indication of the quality of the test object at the end of it.

There are three forms of management and control in a test process:

- management and control of the test process;
- management and control of the test infrastructure;
- management and control of test deliverables.

Depending on the form of organization chosen, management and control are exercised as a whole or as a part within operational level (department or project) or within the structural organization. Some control tasks, such as the control of the test object and the test basis, should be based outside the test organization. Management and control tasks are basically allocated to anyone involved in a test process. Controlling the test processes and deliverables is so important that it is an attitude, an automatic action, a way of handling things, besides a set of firm procedures.

5.5.4 Staff and training

Staff

Over recent decades, testing has developed into a profession. Its evaluation, alongside comparable functions in the field of information services, has evolved from a part-time occupation to a separate discipline. The ever-increasing demand for high-quality tests and associated developments in the area of testing require specialized knowledge, skills and training. This does not imply that testing is now the exclusive preserve of specialists. Users, systems managers and developers may – or must – execute tests in addition to their primary tasks. A test organization is made up of a large number of different areas of expertise. It is essential that specialists make adequate contributions in both test management and test techniques.

Providing staff for testing requires adequate attention from (test) management. Aspects such as working with part-timers who take on testing as a sideline should not be underestimated, nor should the unpredictability of staffing requirements – since plans have a tendency to over-run their original schedules – or even the varying composition required for each TMap phase.

In order to have the necessary test staff available at the right time, it is essential to have a sound understanding of the test functions and tasks, and of the knowledge and skills needed for them. Such an understanding is necessary for communicating with personnel officers and trainers, and for any selection procedure for prospective testers.

Training

Job requirements for testers cover a wide range of knowledge and skills. A training program for test staff should obviously include specific components such as test management and test techniques, but it should also provide for a general build-up of knowledge about quality management and system development. Social skills should not be overlooked either.

There is a large variety of training courses for testing on offer. A mixture of theory and practice is undoubtedly required for testing, just as it is for many other training schemes. Optimum results are obtained by a short theoretical introduction followed by adequate on-the-job training. An interesting development is that the British Computer Society's Information Systems Examinations Board (ISEB) certifies people for up to three levels of qualification in software testing.

5.5.5 Structuring the test process

The change process towards a structured test organization has its own approach and dynamics. It is an understatement to say that test structuring processes often fail. Unfortunately, they fail most of the time. The blame usually lies with the underestimation of the organizational and financial implications. A lack of attention after the first successful implementation of structured testing is also often to blame.

Test structuring is usually caused by an expensive failure or disaster, at which point the management will decide that something should be done at last. Someone is charged with structuring, and a project or system is selected as a pilot by which structuring should prove itself.

As we have said, it often goes wrong. A structuring process requires a strategy and know-how regarding both changing an organization and testing. After the assessment of the actual test practice, and the possibilities for the structuring process, there should be a step-by-step transformation from the present situation to the situation you are aiming for. Time and tact play an important role.

Lifecycle PART 2

Introduction to the lifecycle

6

6.1 The cornerstones

As mentioned before, the four cornerstones of a structured test approach consist of a lifecycle of test activities, a good organizational embedding, the right infrastructure and usable techniques. This lifecycle is related to the development lifecycle. In this part of the book, the lifecycle of test activities is outlined in more detail.

The lifecycle may be seen as the central cornerstone. While elaborating the lifecycle for both high-level and low-level tests, for each phase in the lifecycle the relation is shown with techniques, infrastructure and organization (Figure 6.1)

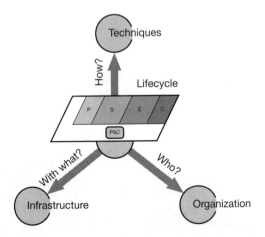

Figure 6.1
The lifecycle as the
central cornerstone

6.2 Test levels

The test process begins with setting up a master test plan in which agreements are made concerning several evaluation activities and test levels. The strategy is described in terms of aspects to be tested grouped by evaluation activities and test level. In addition, procedures are described that are valid for the entire test process. At the same time, a global plan is set up.

During the various phases of the system-development process, evaluation activities are carried out on intermediate products of these phases, e.g. the functional specifications. Consequently, the activities belonging to the system tests and the acceptance tests are started. Both aim to test the system, but from different perspectives.

During the technical design, the first activities of the integration test begin. In this test, the loose parts of the system are joined step by step, and the functioning of the 'growing' system is tested after each step, guided by the technical specifications. Simultaneously with the programming phase, the unit tests are started. In this case, the functioning of the programs is tested against the technical specifications and the program design.

For the test levels mentioned above, a lifecycle model of the activities has been described. The lifecycle model aims to structure the test approach and make the process controllable. In doing so, it will be obvious who should do what and when, and the various activities may be planned and controlled in their interdependencies.

The set-up of the master test plan is explained in detail in Chapter 7. The system test and acceptance test, are high-level tests, and are carried out in a similar way. The lifecycle model for high-level tests is elaborated on in Chapter 8. The unit test and integration test are both low-level tests, and are carried out in a similar way. The lifecycle model for low-level tests is discussed further in Chapter 9.

6.3 Describing the lifecycle

The description of the lifecycle of high-level tests is as follows. For each *phase*, it is indicated *what* the phase is about, under which *preconditions* the phase is carried out, and which *activities* are part of the phase. A short description of the *procedure* is included. For each activity, you will find the *aim*, the *procedure* used and the *deliverables*. As far as applicable, a connection is made between the test techniques and the infrastructural and organizational aspects as described in this book.

For the low-level tests, a description of the phases is presented, with the activities to be carried out grouped by phase. The description concentrates on the differences from the high-level test lifecycle. However, to make the chapter on the low-level testing lifecycle applicable without reading the previous high-level chapter, all necessary details are included. Readers who work through the descriptions sequentially will find that the lifecycles have common characteristics.

Master test planning **7**

By gearing the various test levels to one another, an optimalization of the total test process takes place. This chapter describes how the gearing is shaped by the set-up of a master test plan.

7.1 Introduction

At the start of a system-development lifecycle several parties, including the customer, the end users and the managers, offer up their demands, wishes and restrictions. A project manager will be appointed who defines and arranges the system-development process based on these demands, wishes and restrictions. The project manager is responsible for the execution of all necessary activities within this process, including the test activities. The organization of the requisite test activities usually implies the division of the test process over the separate test levels. Certain tasks and responsibilities are assigned to each test level, and each level looks at whether parts of the information system meet particular demands and functional and/or technical specifications.

For each test level, a test strategy and plan are drawn up, based on the demands and specifications to be tested and the risks for the organization if the demands are not met. The purpose of this is to find the major defects as early and as cheaply as possible, and to make the critical path of the system development as short as possible. Sometimes, the strategy is determined implicitly ('each programmer should test his/her own program as seems to him/her the best, provided that the available time is not exceeded'), and sometimes it is determined explicitly, according to the techniques described in Chapter 11.

When a proper strategy has been determined for each level, the real possibility exists that some tests will be performed twice or that 'holes' exist within the test. Quite often, for instance, in the system test and the acceptance test the same test specification techniques are applied for the same functional specifications. Another risk is that test levels do not fit in the planning, and the total test process stays much longer on the critical path of the system-development lifecycle.

It is obvious that the different test levels should be geared to one another. This prevents redundancy and omissions between the various tests, and increases considerably the quality of the test (strategy). It enables testers to perform the tests at the right moment, i.e. when (with identical depth of testing) the costs of testing, repairing and retesting are minimized and the total test process is on the critical path of the system development for as short a time as possible.

Organizing tests in such a way is a complex affair for which the project manager usually does not have sufficient time. The solution is to appoint a test manager who is responsible for all test activities. The test manager tunes the various test levels and optimizes the total test process, drawing up a master test plan. The master test plan forms the basis for the detailed test plans of the various test levels. Figure 7.1 shows the place of testing, the test manager and the master test plan within the system development.

Figure 7.1
Master test plan within
system development

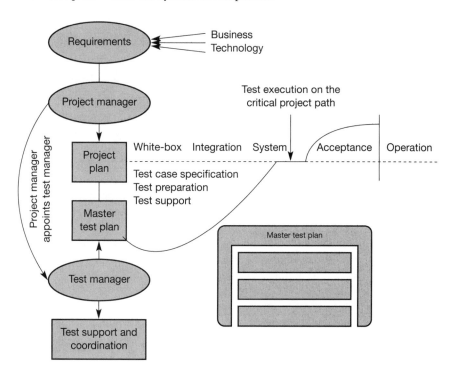

7.2 Scope

An important issue is the scope of the master test plan. This may vary from the high-level tests (system and acceptance test) to all test levels and evaluation activities (Figure 7.2). An important factor for coordinating the tests in a master test plan is the extent of understanding of what each test and evaluation is testing or not testing, and with which depth testing is performed. How, for instance, can you coordinate with the unit test when you know that a programmer tests but you do not know how? If the insight into a particular test level cannot be given or is refused, it is quite difficult to involve this test level in the master test plan. In practice, a master test plan mainly coordinates the high-level tests because these tests are already sufficiently transparent or one is prepared to make them sufficiently transparent. Less commonly, the low-level tests and the evaluations are incorporated in the plan.

It is important to involve the low-level tests and evaluations in the master test plan because this offers all kinds of possibilities to optimize the total test process. Both low-level testing and evaluation take place in an earlier stage of the system-development lifecycle than high-level testing. As such, they are likely to detect defects sooner and closer to the source, leading to lower repair costs and the option of an opinion on the quality of the system at a earlier stage. It is preferable that evaluation is part of the plan. In this chapter, we talk only about 'testing', but we also mean evaluation.

It is possible that the person responsible for a particular test level is not always interested in tuning by a master test plan if that means that some tasks have to be given up or extra ones assigned. Tuning is then felt to be (deserved or undeserved) the unwanted influence of other parties. It is, however, still useful to involve this test level in the master test plan because the plan shows explic-itly a double test on the same characteristic or a missing test on some characteristic. If, for instance, a third party develops the system, there some-times are not enough opportunities to tune the test levels in advance. The master test plan is then limited to the tuning of the test levels that fall under the organization's own responsibility, such as the functional acceptance test and the production acceptance test. However, the master test plan may describe demands made on the the third party's way of testing. The master test plan serves then as a means of communication to the third party.

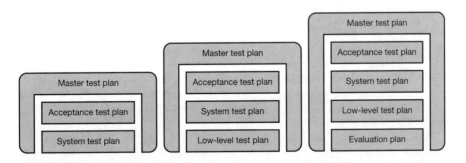

Figure 7.2
Possible scope of the master test plan

7.3 Preconditions

The following preconditions should be met before the set-up of a master test plan:

- There is insight in:
  - the aim and the significance of testing at organizational level;
  - the global system demands;
  - the organization of the system-development process;

–   the global (delivery) planning of the system-development process;
–   the development environment;
–   the future production environment;
–   the procedure regarding the set-up of the test basis (system-development methodology).
●   There is readiness and contractual possibilities to make general agreements on testing.

7.4 Procedure

The process starts with the formulation of the assignment in order to state the scope of the master test plan and the test levels. Then an orientation is made to gain knowledge of the system-development process and the project. Thus, the position of testing within the total range of quality management measures is determined, and a description is given of which quality characteristics of the system will be tested and to what depth. Then the selected quality characteristics will be spread over the recognized test levels, and a global estimation is made. At the same time, there is an assessment of the requisite test organization and infra-structure beyond the various test levels. The arrangement at project level of some test functions and of agreements concerning infrastructure may lead to cost reduction. Finally, a global plan is drawn up for the entire test process. Based on the activities outlined, the master test plan is drawn up and consolidated.

Although these activities have been described in sequence, it is possible that some activities have to be carried out repeatedly and in another sequence – if, for instance, the customer does not accept the planning, more staff may be needed or the strategy may have to be adapted.

7.5 Activities

The set-up of the master test plan involves:
1   Formulating the assignment;
2   Global review and study;
3   Determining test strategy;
4   Defining the organization;
5   Specifying the infrastructure;
6   Setting up schedules;
7   Consolidating the master test plan.

Figure 7.3 shows the sequence and dependencies between the different activities.

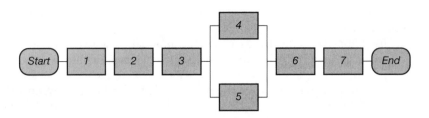

Figure 7.3
Activities of drawing up a
master test plan

7.5.1 Formulating the assignment

Aim

The aim of this activity is threefold. In the first place, it states who the customer is and who is responsible for setting up the master test plan. Then it determines the scope and the aim of the entire test process. Finally, it determines which test levels will be involved in the master test plan.

Procedure

There are no subactivities defined for the activity. The following matters will be stated:

- *Customer.* The originator of the assignment to execute tests and to draw up the master test plan. This is usually the general (project) manager for the system development process, coming from or appointed by the user organization.
- *Responsible.* The person responsible for setting up the master test plan.
- *Test levels.* The test levels involved in the master test plan. Consider here evaluation, unit test, integration test, system test, functional acceptance test and the production acceptance test.
- *Scope.* The restrictions and limitations of the entire test process. For instance:
  - unique identification of the information system to be tested;
  - interfaces with neighboring systems;
  - conversion;
  - administrative organization.

It is at least as important to state what does *not* belong to the scope of the test assignment.

- *Aim.* What the test process intends to achieve. For instance:
  - the risks and quality characteristics to be covered by the tests, and to give advice for a go/no go to implement the system based on risks and quality, e.g. regarding functionality, maintainability after implementation of the system, suitability to the administrative organization and the performance;
  - the deliverables of the various test levels.

- *Preconditions.* The preconditions describe the conditions imposed on the test process 'externally', e.g.
  - fixed final date – the date by which the information system must be tested is usually already fixed by the time the test assignment is commissioned;
  - planning – the planning for delivery of the test basis, the test object and the infrastructure is usually fixed when the test assignment is commissioned;
  - available resources – the customer often sets limits on the people, means, budget and time.
- *Assumptions.* Assumptions describe the conditions imposed by the test process on third parties, e.g.
  - requested support – the test process requires various types of support concerning, for instance, the test basis, the test object and/or the infrastructure;
  - changes in the test basis – the test process must be informed about changes in test basis. In most cases, a tester can participate in the existing project change control procedures.

During the further planning process, the preconditions and assumptions are elaborated on in detail.

Products
The formulating of the assignment, set down in the master test plan.

Techniques
Not applicable.

7.5.2 Global review and study
Aim
The aim of this activity is to get an insight into the (project) organization, the objective of the system-development process, the information system to be developed, and the requirements the system should meet.

Procedure
The procedure involves the following activities:
- the study of the available documentation
- interviews.

The study of the available documentation
The documentation, made available by the customer, is studied. Consider here:
- system documentation, such as the results of information analysis or a definition study;
- project documentation, such as the scheme of action for the system development process, the organization scheme and responsibilities, the quality plan, and a (global) function point analysis;

- a description of the system development method, including standards;
- contracts with suppliers.

If the system-development process relates to maintenance, then an investigation is made into the presence and applicability of existing testware.

Interviews
Various people involved in the system development process are interviewed. Consider here:

- the representatives of the customer to get insight in the company objectives, the organizational culture as well as in the system objectives, and the importance of the system to the organization;
- specialists from the user organization to gain insight into the functionality of the system;
- system management to get insight into the (future) production environment of the system;
- the suppliers of the test basis, the test object and the infrastructure in order to ensure a tuning between the various parties involved at an early stage.

It is also advisable to consult people who are involved indirectly, such as accountants, the implementation manager, and the future maintenance organization.

Products
A file of collected materials and interview reports.

Techniques
Checklist 'global investigation of the information system' (see Chapter 17).

7.5.3 Determination of test strategy
Aim
During this activity, it is determined which quality characteristics of the information system should be tested and at which test level those tests should take place. This strategy determination is based on the risks to the organization if the system is of insufficient quality.

Procedure
The determination of the test strategy involves the following activities:
- getting insight into existing quality management procedures
- determining strategy
- drawing up a (global) estimation of the test levels.

Getting insight into existing quality management procedures
Testing is a part of the total quality management within the system development process. In order to determine which characteristics should be tested, the way of dealing with quality management is described. Especially important is the presence of the quality system used by the project, and the stated quality plan. In order to use the total effort for quality management as efficiently as possible, the quality management activities, which are already determined, are assessed.

Determining strategy
The steps to obtain a test strategy are described here only briefly (a detailed description is given in Chapter 11).
- *Determination of quality characteristics.* In consultation with the customer and any other involved parties, the risks are assessed and the quality characteristics on which the testing should aim are determined. These characteristics will be reported to the customer during the test process.
- *Determination of the relative importance of the quality characteristics.* Based on the results of the previous step, the relative importance of the various quality characteristics is determined.
- *Allocating quality characteristics to test levels.* In order to utilize the test effort as efficiently as possible, an indication is made of which test level(s) cover the selected quality characteristics. In this way, tuning is achieved between the various test levels, which are executed within the frame of the master test plan. Of course, the various responsibilities and competencies should be taken into account.

Drawing up a (global) estimation of the test levels
On the basis of the size of the system (possibly expressed in function points) and the chosen strategy, a global estimation is drawn up for the various test levels. For the high-level tests, a global test point analysis may be applied here. During the planning and control phase of the various test levels, the final estimate is determined.

Products
The test strategy including a global estimate set down in a master test plan.

Techniques
Development of a test strategy (see Chapter 11), and test point analysis and estimation (see Chapter 12).

7.5.4 Defining the organization
Aim
This activity defines the functions, tasks, competences and responsibilities that are applicable for the entire test process across the test levels.

Procedure
There is a detailed description of conceivable forms of organization at testing and all aspects that play a role there in Part IV. The set-up of the organization involves the following activities:
- determination of the requisite functions
- establishing training
- assigning tasks, competences and responsibilities.

Determination of the requisite functions
In order to obtain a good tuning between the test levels, positions at the umbrella level over the test levels must be determined. Consider here especially:
- (general) test management and coordination;
- control (at umbrella level) e.g. central control of infrastructure and defect administration.

Some test functions may be involved in the test process from the line organization, namely:
- test regulation
- control
- coordination and advice
- monitoring.

The determination of the test functions within the various test levels is made during the planning and control phase of each test level.

Establishing training
If the staff who will be involved at the test levels are not familiar enough with the test approach, techniques and tools to be applied, they should be trained (see Chapter 20). The plan should therefore reserve sufficient time for training.

Assigning tasks, competences and responsibilities
Specific tasks, competences and responsibilities are assigned to specific test functions. This applies especially for the tasks related to the tuning between the various test levels and the decisions to be taken. For instance:
- drawing up regulations for the products to be delivered by the various test levels;
- monitoring the appliance of the regulations (internal review);
- coordinating the various test activities that are similar for the various test levels, such as the set-up and control of the technical infrastructure;
- drawing up guidelines for communication, and reporting between the test levels to one another and the test process and the various suppliers;
- setting up the methodology, technical and subject matter support;
- preserving consistency of the various test plans.

Products
A description of the test organization set down in the master test plan.

Techniques
Not applicable.

7.5.5 Specifying the infrastructure
Aim
The aim of this activity is to specify at an early stage the infrastructure needed for the test process, especially for the parts that should be arranged for several test levels or have a relatively long delivery time.

Procedure
The procedure involves the following activities:
- defining the test environment
- defining test tools
- determining the planning of the infrastructure.

Defining the test environment
The test environment is defined in general terms. This consists of the facilities needed to execute the test, and is dependent on the system development environment and the future production environment (see Chapter 26). It is important to state a number of specific demands for the test process. Consider here, for instance, the availability to the test team of multiple logical environments, a system date to be manipulated, and the representativeness (to what degree the test environment is equal to the future production environment). In practice, the environment is often a fixed situation, which should be taken into account when setting up the test process.

It is inevitable that differences will occur between the test environment and the future production environment. The risks introduced by these differences will be indicated, and possible measures based on such risks will be described.

Defining test tools
The requisite test tools are defined in rough lines. Test tools may offer support to test activities concerning planning and control, constructing initial data sets, test execution and assessment (see Chapter 27).

Determining the planning of the infrastructure
Responsibility for the further elaboration, selection and acquisition of all necessary parts of the infrastructure will be determined, and the agreements will be recorded. In addition, the availability of the various facilities will be outlined.

Products
The description of the necessary infrastructure, including planning, set down in the master test plan.

Techniques
Checklist 'test facilities' (see Chapter 17).

Although the activity 'set-up of control' has not been distinguished as a separate activity during the drawing up of the master test plan, it is useful to organize some aspects of control centrally beyond test levels. This applies in particular to the control of infrastructure (see Chapter 22).

7.5.6 Setting up schedules
Aim
The aim of this activity is to design a global plan for the entire test process.

Procedure
Based on the planning of the system-development process, a global plan for the entire test process is drawn up. For each test level, the starting and final dates as well as the deliverables, are stated. In the planning and control phase of the various test levels, the planning is elaborated in detail. The global planning should contain at least:
- activities to be carried out (phases per test level);
- relations with and dependencies on other activities (within or outside the test process, and between the various test levels);
- time to be spent for each test level;
- required and available lead time;
- deliverables.

The interdependencies between the various test levels are especially important. After all, the execution phases of several test levels are executed mostly sequentially: unit test, integration test, system test, and finally acceptance test.
   The planning is shown by a bar chart, depending on the technique employed by the organization. The financial consequences of the choices will be translated in a financial plan. The following division may be applied:
- *Personnel.* The costs of the chosen form of organization should be determined, with respect to personnel hired externally and internally. Possible training costs should be included.
- *Infrastructure.* An estimate is made of the costs that the chosen infrastructure may add to the test process.

Products
A global plan for the entire test process, set down in the master test plan.

Techniques
Not applicable.

7.5.7 Consolidating the master test plan

Aim

The aim of this activity is to document the results of all activities executed so far, and to acquire the customer's approval of the chosen approach.

Procedure

The procedure involves the following activities:

- recording threats, risks and measurements
- drawing up the master test plan
- approval and settlement of the master test plan.

Recording threats, risks and measurements

It is essential to state explicitly the conceivable threats and risks for the test process. Among others, they may refer to:

- *Feasibility.* To what extent the formulated test planning and the planning of various suppliers is feasible and realistic.
- *Testability.* To what extent the expected quality of the specifications is sufficient for the test process to be performed.
- *Stability.* To what extent the specifications will be exposed to alternations during the test process.
- *Experience.* To what extent the experience of the personnel involved is sufficient for the test process to be executed.

The master test plan states which measurements have been adopted to tackle the spotted risks. Consider here preventive measurements to avoid the risks, but possibly also detective measurements to spot problems in due time.

Drawing up the master test plan

The results of the activities carried out so far are set down in the master test plan, which contains at least the following chapters:

- the formulation of the assignment
- test strategy
- threats, risks and measurements
- organization
- infrastructure
- global planning.

Approval and settlement of the master test plan

The master test plan will be presented for approval to the customer. It is advisable to have the plan formally ratified with a signature from the customer. In addition, a presentation to the steering committee and various involved parties, for instance, may help to gain approval and, at least as important, support within the organization.

Products
The master test plan.

Techniques
Checklist 'test project risks' (see Chapter 17).

Lifecycle of high-level tests 8

8.1 Introduction

Both the system test and the acceptance test are high-level tests. They can be regarded – and hence organized – as virtually independent processes, each with its own lifecycle model. These processes run parallel to the developing process and should be started when the functional specifications are being drawn up.

The supplier carries out the *system test* to determine whether the system meets the functional and technical requirements. In practice, parts of the system are usually tested in overlapping sections until the entire system can be tested integrally. After the supplier has carried out the system test and corrected any defects, they will perform a retest before handing over the system to the customer for acceptance.

The *acceptance test* should provide answers to questions such as can the system be put it into operation (again) and can it be managed? What risks do I run in doing so? Has the supplier met their obligations? The execution of an acceptance test requires an environment that is, in most aspects, representative of the production stage (simulated production).

8.2 Planning and control phase

Aim

A test plan is used to describe how, by whom, with what and when the test activities will be carried out. After this, the activities are aimed at coordinating, monitoring and controlling the test process, and at providing insight into the quality of the test object. The customer is informed in periodic and ad hoc reports.

Preconditions

The following conditions must have been met before the planning and control phase can start:
- The organization of the system development process must have been set up.
- In those cases in which a master test plan has been set up for the test process as a whole, this plan should be approved.

- Insight into the (delivery) planning of the system development process.
- Insight into the development environment.
- Insight into the future production environment in order to define the test environment.
- Insight into the procedure of creating the design documentation (system development method).

Procedure

The planning and control phase begins during the functional specification or design phase. During this phase, a test plan lays the foundations for the test process. After determining the test assignment, an overall inventory is made of the available system and project documentation, the demands made on the system in terms of functionality and quality, the organization of the system-development process, the available knowledge and experience in the field of testing, and, with respect to the acceptance test, the user organization. Then a test strategy is determined that specifies which characteristics of the system will be assessed with the high-level test, which characteristics are given priority, which parts of the system will receive the most attention, and which parts will receive the least attention. The object is to provide the best possible degree of coverage in the right place.

In addition, an initiative is taken to structure the organization, the test products (to be delivered), the infrastructure and control; an overall plan is also set up. On the basis of the previous activities, the test plan is compiled and written.

Although these activities have been described in succession, it is possible that some activities must be completed several times and in a different order. For example, if the customer does not accept the schedule that is submitted, it may be necessary to deploy more employees.

The activities of this phase, after establishing the test plan, are carried out throughout the test process and are aimed at coordinating, monitoring and controlling the test process, and at providing insight into the quality of the test object. Detailed plans for each test phase are prepared and maintained during the test process.

The progress of the process and the quality of the test object are reported in the specified format and with the frequency agreed upon in the test plan, or ad hoc at the customer's request.

Activities

The planning and control phase consists of the following activities:
1   Formulating the assignment.
2   Global review and study.
3   Establishing the test basis.
4   Determining the test strategy.
5   Setting up the organization.
6   Specifying test deliverables.
7   Specifying the infrastructure.

8   Organizing management and control.
9   Setting up schedules.
10   Consolidating the test plan.

The following activities can be identified within the framework of the coordination, monitoring and control of the test process:
11   Maintaining the test plan.
12   Controlling the test.
13   Reporting.
14   Establishing detailed schedules.

Figure 8.1 indicates the sequence and interdependencies between the various activities:

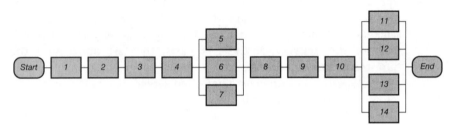

Figure 8.1
Planning and control phase

8.2.1 Formulating the assignment

Aim
The aim of this activity is threefold. In the first instance, the customer and the supplier are identified. Then the scope and the aim of the test process are determined. Lastly, an inventory is made of the assumptions and preconditions of the test process.

Procedure
No subactivities have been defined for this activity. The following issues are determined:
- *Customer.* The provider of the test assignment and therefore also the person to whom reports are addressed.
- *Supplier.* The person who is responsible for carrying out the test assignment, known from now on as the 'test manager'.
- *Scope.* The limits and demarcation of the assignment, e.g.
    - unique identification of the information system to be tested;
    - interfaces with adjoining systems;
    - conversion;
    - the administrative organization.

It is also important to specify what does *not* belong to the scope of the test assignment.

- *Aim.* The expected output of the test process, e.g.
  - the products to be supplied;
  - the quality characteristics to be tested and sound advice concerning this, e.g. regarding:
    - functionality
    - maintainability after production has started
    - ability to fit in the administrative organization
    - performance aspects.
- *Preconditions.* These describe the 'external' conditions imposed upon the test process, e.g.
  - frozen deadline – in many cases when the test assignment is given, the deadline for production has already been set;
  - schedules – in many cases when the test assignment is given, the schedules for the delivery of the test basis, the test object and the infrastructure are already set;
  - available resources – the customer often sets limits regarding human resources, means, budget and time.
- *Assumptions.* These describe the conditions imposed upon others from the test process, e.g.
  - support regarding the test basis – from the test process, there is a need for support in the case of questions and/or uncertainties regarding the test basis;
  - support regarding the test object – if a defect occurs while the test is being carried out, agreements must have been made as to the way in which the supplier of the test object can provide support. In many cases, the supplier will be asked to start repairs as soon as the defects occur and the continuation of the test process has been compromised. There must be a limit to the number of versions of the test object installed in the test environment;
  - support regarding the infrastructure – in most cases, it is necessary to have specialized knowledge regarding the infrastructure in order to set up, in particular, the technical infrastructure, which should resemble the future production environment as closely as possible;
  - changes in the test basis – the test process must be informed of the changes that have been introduced. In most cases, this means simply linking up with the existing procedures within the system development process.

During the scheduling process, the preconditions and the assumptions are specified in greater detail.

Products

The assignment as specified in the test plan.

Techniques

Checklist 'preconditions and assumptions' (see Chapter 17).

8.2.2 Global review and study

Aim

The aim of this activity is to gain insight into the available system and project documentation, the demands made on the system in terms of functionality and quality, the organization of the system-development process, the available knowledge and experience in the field of testing, and, with respect to the acceptance test, the user organization.

Procedure

The procedure consists of the following:

- studying the available documentation
- conducting interviews.

Studying the available documentation

The available documentation is studied. If the test process concerns a maintenance test, there will also be an investigation into the presence and usefulness of existing testware.

Conducting interviews

The various people involved in the system development process are interviewed. These include the following:

- the (representatives of the) customer, to gain insight into both the business objectives and the 'culture', and the objectives and the strategic importance of the system;
- the subject experts from the user organization, to gain insight into the functionality of the system;
- the system manager, to gain insight into the (future) production environment of the information system;
- the suppliers of the test basis, test object and the infrastructure, to establish at an early stage a degree of agreement between the various parties involved;
- testers from the project or the line department, to gain insight into the available knowledge and experience in the field of testing.

It is also advisable, where possible, to consult those involved indirectly. These include the implementation manager, the future maintenance organization, etc.

Products
A file of collected material and interview reports.

Techniques
Checklist 'global investigation of the information system' (see Chapter 17).

8.2.3 Establishing the test basis
Aim
The aim of this activity is the unequivocal definition of the test basis and the basic documentation.

Procedure
The procedure consists of the following:
- selecting relevant documentation
- identifying documentation.

Selecting relevant documentation
To be able to perform a test properly and to complete the test assignment successfully, it is necessary to know the requirements with respect to the functionality and quality of the system. All documentation that describes these requirements is included in the test basis.

Other types of documentation are also used, in particular for the planning process. These include:
- a function point analysis, if this forms a basis for the budget and the planning of the test process;
- the schedules of the suppliers of the test basis, the test object and the infrastructure;
- the documentation that has been made available and studied.

Identifying documentation
Identify, as far as possible, the relevant documentation. This includes delivery dates, versions, status, etc.

Products
The test basis and other necessary documentation, recorded in the test plan.

Techniques
Not applicable.

8.2.4 Determining the test strategy
Aim
The aim of this activity is to determine what to test, how, and with what coverage. In fact, optimization takes place with the aim of distributing correctly the

available resources over the test activities. Starting from the strategy, a reliable estimate of the required number of hours for the test process is made.

Procedure
The assignment is converted into a concrete approach of the test process. The procedure consists of the following:
- strategy development
- drawing up a budget.

Strategy development
The steps to be taken to arrive at a test strategy are outlined below (see Chapter 11).

1   *Risk assessment.* In consultation with the users and the developers, the risks of defects occurring during production are assessed.
2   *Identifying quality characteristics.* In consultation with the customer and any others who are involved, it is decided which quality characteristics the test should address. During the test process, reports must be submitted to the customer regarding the quality characteristics that have been selected.
3   *Determining the relative importance of quality characteristics.* On the basis of the results from the previous step, an indication is drawn up of the importance of the selected quality characteristics in relation to each other.
4   *Subdividing into subsystems.* During this step, the information system is subdivided into subsystems, with the aim of determining the importance of the various subsystems. Not all subsystems need to be tested with the same coverage.
5   *Determining the relative importance of the system components.* On the basis of the results from the previous step, the relative importance of the various subsystems is defined.
6   *Detailing the test importance of each subsystem and each quality characteristic.* In this step, the importance of the combination of quality characteristic and subsystem is identified.
7   *Determining the test techniques to be used.* The last step in the test strategy consists of selecting the techniques that will be used to test the selected quality characteristics and the identified subsystems. The test techniques include both the test-specification techniques and the checklists.

Drawing up a budget
On the basis of the strategy, and taking into account the available resources, a reliable budget is drawn up for the test process. An instrument that can be used here and that links up with the technique of strategy development is the test point analysis (see Chapter 12). If the test point analysis cannot be carried out, e.g. because of the absence of a function point analysis, then testers should use any available figures or rules of thumb.

High-level testing covers approximately 30–40 per cent of the total efforts required to draw up the functional design up to and including implementation in production. About 10–15 per cent of the total effort is needed for carrying out a system test, and 20–25 per cent is needed to perform the acceptance test.

A test process has many uncertainties, and it may be useful to anticipate this by incorporating an item 'Unforeseen' in the budget. This item generally amounts to between 10–15 per cent of the entire budget.

Products

The strategy, including the accompanying budget, specified in the test plan. Test point analysis specified in the test plan.

Techniques

Strategy development (see Chapter 11) and test point analysis (see Chapter 12).

8.2.5 Setting up the organization

Aim

The aim of this activity is to determine how the organization of the test process will be set up: positions, tasks, authorities, responsibilities, consultation structures, and reporting lines. The need for any training will also be considered.

Procedure

A detailed description of the organization of the test process and all aspects that play a role is included in Part IV.

The procedure consists of the following:

- determining the required positions
- assigning tasks, authorities and responsibilities
- describing the organization
- allocating staff
- establishing training courses
- establishing consultation structures
- establishing reporting lines.

Determining the required positions
It is decided which of the possible test roles should be carried out in order to execute the test process properly (see Chapter 19). The test roles below are relevant for setting up the test process:

- testers
- team leaders
- test management
- methodological support
- technical support
- subject matter support
- intermediaries
- control.

Assigning tasks, authorities and responsibilities
The specific tasks, authorities and responsibilities within the test process are described and assigned to the test roles (see Chapter 21). The tasks are related to the activities that are described in this lifecycle model. The authorities and the responsibilities concern the decisions that are to be taken within the test process, e.g.

- maintaining the test plan;
- setting up and adjusting the detailed schedules;
- approving test specifications, test scripts, test scenarios, etc.;
- starting and/or stopping test activities (on the basis of insufficient quality of the test basis, the test object or the infrastructure);
- deploying/hiring (extra) testers;
- classifying defects;
- arranging for any external tests to be carried out;
- starting with a new version of the test basis and/or test object.

Describing the organization
The relationships between the various test functions, the internal relationships within the test team, and the relationships with the other parties involved in the system development process are described in Figure 8.2 (see also Chapter 21).

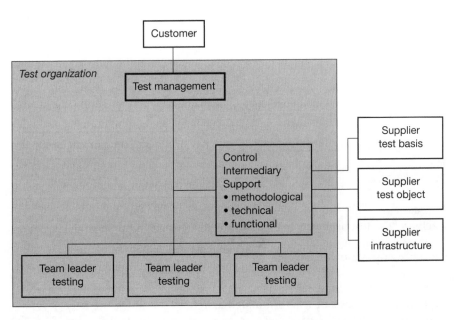

Figure 8.2
Organization of the test process

Allocating staff
When it has been decided which test roles should be carried out within the test process, the necessary staff are recruited, taking into consideration the skills of

the available staff and the knowledge and skills required for each test role (see Chapter 19). It is possible for one person to occupy several positions, but care should be taken when multiple responsibilities are brought together.

Establishing training courses
Using strategy development, it has been determined how tests should be conducted. If the recruited personnel are not familiar enough with (the advantages of) the test approach and the test techniques and tools to be used, then training activities should be arranged. It is also advisable to organize a presentation to inform those involved indirectly in the test process, such as project or line managers, of the importance of (structured) testing. Time for training must be built in to the test process schedule (see Chapter 20).

Establishing consultation structures
The consultation structures that are important for proper functioning of the test organization are described. This includes the internal consultations – the team/work meetings and the test team/department meetings – as well as the external meetings – the project or management meetings, the analysis forum/defect management and the decision forum/change management (see Chapters 21 and 22).

Establishing reporting lines
The various reporting lines, types of report and the reporting frequency (TMap standard: weekly) are described. This includes both internal and external reports on progress and quality.

Products
Test organization, specified in the test plan.

Techniques
Not applicable.

8.2.6 Specifying test deliverables
Aim
The aim of this activity is the unequivocal definition of the test deliverables.

Procedure
Specifying the test deliverables includes the following subactivities:
● establishing the test deliverables
● setting up standards.

Establishing the test deliverables
Working on the basis of the formulated assignment and the strategy development, an inventory is made of the test deliverables to be supplied. The following test deliverables are distinguished within TMap:

- *Testware.* Defined as all test documentation that is produced during the test process and that can be used for maintenance purposes, and therefore that must be transferable and maintainable. In regression tests, for example, use is often made of existing testware. Testware includes:
  - test plans
  - logical test specifications
  - physical test specifications
  - test scenarios
  - test input files and test output
  - test specification and test output dossier.
- *Other test documentation.* During the test process, various documents are received or compiled, including:
  - project plans
  - meeting reports (listing decisions and activities)
  - correspondence
  - memos
  - standards and guidelines
  - reports on progress and quality.

A brief description indicates the contents and the aim of the various deliverables or documents.

Setting up standards
Standards and agreements on the naming of the test deliverables are determined. It is advisable to comply with the general standards applicable within the system-development process for documentation and the use of word processors, etc. When possible, templates are created for the various documents, and made available to the test team.

Products
A description of the test deliverables to be supplied, including the standards, recorded in the test plan. Templates for the various documents.

Techniques
Not applicable.

8.2.7 Specifying the infrastructure

Aim
The aim of this activity is to determine at an early stage the required infrastructure for the test process. The infrastructure includes the test environment, test tools and the office environment.

Procedure
The procedure consists of the following subactivities:
- specifying the test environment;
- specifying the test tools;
- specifying the office environment;
- establishing the infrastructure schedule.

Specifying the test environment
The required test environment is outlined. The test environment contains the facilities that are necessary to perform the test, and is dependent on the system-development environment and the future production environment (see Chapter 26). It is important to specify a number of specific requirements for the test process. One requirement could be, for example, that several logical test environments are available for the test team so tests can run parallel to each other without interference. Other possible requirements could be a system date that can be manipulated, or an environment that is as representative as possible (to what extent does the test environment correspond with the future production environment?).

There will always be differences between the test environment and the future production environment. The risks that are introduced because of this are identified, and possible measures that can be taken are described.

Specifying the test tools
The required test tools are outlined. Test tools can offer support to the test activities with respect to planning and control, constructing initial test databases, carrying out tests and analyzing the results (see Chapter 27).

Specifying the office environment
The required office environment is outlined. This concerns the office environment in the widest sense, because the testers must also be able to carry out their work under proper circumstances (see Chapter 28).

Establishing the infrastructure schedule
For all the required components of the infrastructure, it is determined who is responsible for their detailing, selection and acquisition. Agreements reached must be recorded. A schedule is also set up, specifying the times when items are made available to the test team.

Products
The description of the required infrastructure, including schedules, recorded in the test plan.

Techniques
Not applicable.

It is possible that the required infrastructure is not feasible: the proposed solution may be too expensive, or may not be technically possible, or may not be ready on time. In such cases, an inventory is made of the consequences for the test process. This might lead to an adjustment of the test assignment and the test strategy, in which a number of tests no longer appear to be possible. Obviously, the customer will be informed accordingly, and an inventory is made of the alternatives and possible measures that can be taken.

8.2.8 Organizing management and control

Aim
The aim of this activity is to describe how the management and control of the test process, the infrastructure and the test deliverables will be arranged.

Procedure
The procedure consists of the following subactivities:
- specifying the test process control
- specifying the infrastructure control
- specifying the test deliverables control
- specifying defect procedure.

A detailed specification of test control and all aspects that play a role in it is given in Chapter 22.

Specifying the test process control
The aim of test process control is to control the test process and the quality of the test object. Test process control therefore distinguishes the following control objects or aspects:
- progress
- quality
- statistics
- reports.

The following main tasks must be defined:
- registration, administration, storage and interpretation:
  - progress, spending and time
  - quality indicators
  - test statistics;
- reports.

Specifying the infrastructure control
The test infrastructure is divided into three groups of facilities:
- test environment
- test tools
- office environment.

The technical control tasks to be carried out are part of the technical support role. If necessary, support is provided by the supplier or the system manager when these tasks are carried out.

Specifying the test deliverables control
It is of great importance to carefully distinguish and control the various test deliverables. External and internal deliverables are distinguished. Within the framework of this activity, a test deliverables control procedure should be set up. An example of this procedure is included in Chapter 22.

Specifying defect procedure
Two types of defects are found during testing: internal defects (a test error), and external defects (error made outside the test). An defect procedure must be set up that is capable of handling and controlling all defects. Particular attention should be paid to authorities and responsibilities within the procedure. An example of an defect procedure is included in Chapter 22.

Products
A description of the various control processes, recorded in the test plan.

Techniques
Not applicable.

8.2.9 Setting up schedules
Aim
The aim of this activity is to set up an overall schedule for the entire test process and a detailed schedule for the preparation phase.

Procedure
The procedure consists of the following subactivities:
- setting up an overall schedule
- setting up a financial schedule
- setting up a detailed schedule for the preparation phase.

Setting up an overall schedule
Working on the basis of the established (hours) budget, the available means and resources, and the delivery schedules of the various suppliers, an overall sched-

ule is set up for the rest of the test process. Both the recruited personnel and the products to be delivered are assigned to the activities that are to be carried out within the test process.

To divide up the (hours) budget over the various phases within TMap, the rule of thumb displayed in Figure 8.3 can be used.

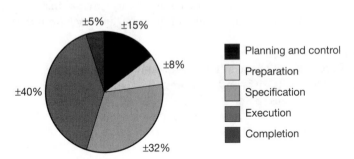

Figure 8.3
Approximate division
across the phases

The schedule is displayed in, for example, a network schedule or a bar diagram, depending on the procedure used within the organization.

Setting up a financial schedule
The financial consequences of the choices made in the activities that have been carried out so far are mapped out. The following division has proved realistic:
- *Personnel.* The cost of the chosen organization and the recruited personnel must be determined. These include not only the deployment of hired personnel (external capacity), but also the cost of internal personnel.
- *Infrastructure.* An estimate is made of the costs relating to the chosen infrastructure for the test process.

Setting up a detailed schedule for the preparation phase
A detailed schedule is set up for the preparation phase. This detailed schedule should include at least the following aspects:
- activities to be carried out (per subsystem);
- links with and dependencies on other activities (inside or outside the test process);
- time to be spent per activity;
- available overall project time;
- products to be delivered;
- employee(s) involved.

Products
The schedule for the test process as a whole, specified in the test plan. Detailed schedule for the preparation phase.

Techniques
Not applicable.

8.2.10 Consolidating the test plan
Aim
The aim of this activity is to record the results of the activities that have been carried out so far, and to acquire approval for the chosen approach from the customer.

Procedure
The procedure consists of the following subactivities:
- identifying threats, risks and measures
- establishing the test plan
- establishing the change procedure for the test plan
- consolidating the test plan.

Identifying threats, risks and measures
It is necessary to identify possible threats for the test process in the test plan. These may relate to the following:
- *Feasibility.* To what degree are the proposed test plans and schedules of the various suppliers feasible and realistic?
- *Testability.* To what degree is the expected quality of the test basis sufficient for the completion of the test process?
- *Stability.* To what degree will the test basis be subject to changes during the test process?
- *Experience.* To what degree is the test team's experience or knowledge level adequate for carrying out the test process properly?

The test plan lists the measures that have been taken for each risk. These include preventive measures taken to avoid risks, and any detective measures to identify risks sooner.

Establishing the test plan
The results of the activities carried out so far are recorded in the test plan. The test plan contains the following chapters:
- formulating the assignment
- test basis
- strategy
- organization
- test deliverables
- infrastructure
- control

- scheduling
- threats, risks and measures.

Appendices include:
- change procedure for the test plan;
- justification of the (hours) budget, possibly based on the test point analysis that was carried out.

A management summary that outlines the strategy, schedules, budget, threats, risks and measures is optional. It is useful if the test plan has become large, or if the test plan's target group consists not only of the customer, but also a steering committee or general management.

Establishing the change procedure for the test plan
A change procedure is set up with regard to the approved test plan. This procedure details both the criteria and the required authority for the changing of the test plan.

Consolidating the test plan
The test plan is submitted to the customer for approval. It is advisable to record the approval formally by means of the signatures of both the test management and the customer. In addition, a presentation for the steering committee and the various other parties involved may be helpful to obtain approval and, equally important, the support within the organization.

Products
The test plan, including the appendices.

Techniques
Checklist 'test project risks' (see Chapter 17).

8.2.11 Maintaining the test plan
Aim
The aim of this activity is to keep the test plan and the overall schedule up to date.

Procedure
Maintenance of the test plan is carried out at a time when changes are introduced that lead to adjustment of the test plan in accordance with the established criteria. Maintenance of the overall schedule is carried out at a time when a delay or an acceleration takes place that has consequences for the overall schedule. The procedure consists of the following subactivities:
- readjusting the test plan and/or test strategy
- maintaining the schedule.

Readjusting the test plan and/or test strategy

Changes to the test plan affect almost all activities carried out in the test process. In theory, the activities 'formulating the assignment' up to 'consolidating the test plan' are carried out again. The test strategy in particular is often subject to change. A good reason to change the strategy is if certain tests find many more or fewer defects than was expected. It is then decided to specify extra tests and carry them out, or to carry out planned tests only in part, or even to cancel them altogether. A lesser reason to change the strategy is to try to compensate extra costs or time in the rest of the development process by testing less.

The changes are recorded in a new version of the test plan or in a supplement, which must also be submitted to the customer for approval. It is the responsibility of the test manager to communicate clearly the consequences of the changes to the customer.

Maintaining the schedule

The most common and expected changes are those regarding the schedule. Reasons for maintaining the schedule may be:

- delayed/faster delivery of the test basis;
- delayed/faster delivery of the test object;
- delayed/faster availability of the infrastructure;
- disappointing/better than anticipated quality of the test basis;
- disappointing/better than anticipated quality of the test object;
- insufficient availability of the test personnel;
- insufficient contribution of knowledge and skills in the test team;
- lower/higher productivity of the test team;
- too many staffing changes;
- too many functional changes in the test basis and the test object.

If the consequences of rescheduling lead to a delay in the delivery date, all parties involved are informed; if necessary, their approval should be obtained. It may be that the changes made make it necessary to adjust the test assignment and/or test strategy.

Products

Changed test plan. Adjusted test schedule.

Techniques

These depend on the activities from the planning and control phase that need to be carried out (again).

8.2.12 Controlling the test
Aim
The aim of this activity is to control the test process, infrastructure and test deliverables in order to be able to constantly provide insight into the progress of the test process and the quality of the test object.

Procedure
Proper control is a precondition for a good test process. It forms the basis of progress monitoring and the reports on the quality of the test object. In accordance with the procedures established in the test plan, three different forms of control are carried out: control of the test process, control of the infrastructure, and control of the test deliverables.

Products
A controlled test process.

Techniques
Not applicable.

8.2.13 Reporting
Aim
The aim of this activity is to draw up reports to provide insight into both the progress of the test process and the quality of the test object.

Procedure
Periodically, and ad hoc upon request, reports are provided on the progress of the test process and the quality of the test object. The test plan lists the form and the frequency of reports in the chapter 'Control'. The procedure consists of the following subactivities:

- drafting progress and quality reports
- drafting ad hoc reports.

Drafting progress and quality reports
Reports are in accordance with the reporting structure described in the test plan. The progress and quality reports contain data of the most recent reporting period and the accumulated data of the entire test process. The report may contain the following elements:
- How much of what was indicated in the test plan has been tested?
- What still needs to be tested?
- Can any trends be recognized with respect to the quality of the test object and the defects found? A well-known trend is symbolized in the Demonic Quadrangle, with time, money, functionality and quality as angles (see also section 22.2.4).

Drafting ad hoc reports

In addition to periodic and structural reports, it is possible for the customer or others involved to request ad hoc reports. The recording of progress and quality should be set up in such a way that reports can be drawn up quickly (usually within one working day).

Products

Progress and quality reports: Ad-hoc reports.

Techniques

Not applicable.

8.2.14 Establishing detailed schedules

Aim

The aim of this activity is to set up and maintain the detailed schedules for the phases of preparation, specification, execution and completion.

Procedure

The detailed schedule should include at least the following aspects for each phase:

* activities to be carried out (per test unit);
* links with and dependencies on other activities (inside or outside the test process);
* time to be spent per activity;
* necessary and available overall project time;
* products to be delivered;
* employee(s) involved.

Products

Detailed schedules for each phase.

Techniques

Test point analysis (see Chapter 12).

8.3 Preparation phase

Aim

The most important aim of the preparation phase is to determine whether the test basis has sufficient quality for the successful specification and execution of the test cases (testability).

Preconditions

The test basis should be available and frozen before the preparation phase can be started.

Procedure

After the frozen test basis has been made available to the test team, a start is made on the testability review of the test basis. This provides insight into testability by investigating aspects such as uniformity of formats, consistency and completeness. Once the review has been completed, the information system is divided into testable units (test units) and test techniques are assigned to the individual units. All of this is done with the previously defined test strategy as a reference. Lastly, the definition of the infrastructure, as recorded in the test plan, may be changed into a detailed specification.

Activities

The following activities are distinguished in the preparation phase:
1   Testability review of the test basis.
2   Defining test units.
3   Assigning test-specification techniques.
4   Specifying the infrastructure.

Figure 8.4 shows the sequence and dependencies of the various activities.

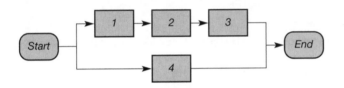

Figure 8.4
Preparation phase

8.3.1 Testability review of the test basis

Aim

The aim of the testability review is to establish the testability of the test basis. Testability here means completeness, consistency, accessibility and the convertibility into test cases.

Procedure

The procedure consists of the following:
●   carrying out the testability review
●   drawing up a report of the testability review.

Carrying out the testability review

The testability review is described only briefly here. An extensive description is given in Chapter 13.
●   *Selecting relevant documentation.* It is determined whether the definition of the test basis that is recorded in the test plan is still correct. If any changes have been introduced in the meantime, the test plan must be adapted. Ultimately, the test team should have the correct version of the test basis.

- *Drafting checklists.* Using the established test strategy of the test plan, checklists are set up for the various subsystems. These checklists function as guides for the assessment of the test basis.
- *Assessing documentation.* The test basis is assessed using the drafted checklists in order to gain insight into the applicability of the established test strategy and the related test techniques. If it is found that the test basis is inadequate, it is important to report this via the customer to the supplier of the test basis so that they can remove any obscurities as quickly as possible. The registration and notification of such defects is done by means of the procedures established in the chapter 'Control' of the test plan.

Drawing up a report of testability review

On the basis of the results of the assessment of the test basis, a report of the testability review is drawn up. This includes a record of the conclusions regarding the testability.

Products

Test basis defects. Report of testability review.

Techniques

Testability review of test basis (see Chapter 13). Inspections (see Chapter 14).

8.3.2 Defining test units

Aim

To make testing manageable and controllable, the subsystems to be tested should be divided into test units. It must be possible to test these units independently of each other.

Procedure

The procedure regarding the definition of test units contains the following:
- determining test units;
- drawing up a test unit matrix.

Determining test units

During this activity, it is assessed which actions within each subsystem have a logical coherence and/or are highly dependent on each other. For example, a modify function can be tested in combination with a create function. After all, to be able to change the data, they will first have to be entered. There are certain limitations to this joining. If the inter-related actions are very large, then combining them may make test units too large. This would make the process of specifying the test cases a difficult one, in which the overview would be lost.

Drawing up a test unit matrix

For each subsystem it is indicated which test units it contains. This subdivision is preferably recorded in a test unit matrix (Table 8.1).

Information system	Test units
Subsystem 1	1
	2
	3
	etc.
Subsystem 2	1
	2

Table 8.1
Test unit matrix

Products

Test unit matrix.

Techniques

Not applicable.

8.3.3 Allocating test techniques

Aim

On the basis of the established test strategy and the subdivision into test units, the test strategy is detailed, resulting in the allocation of test techniques to the units.

Procedure

On the basis of the test unit properties and the characteristics of the selected test techniques in the test strategy, the test strategy is defined. A matrix is set up (Table 8.2) that records the test techniques to be applied to each unit. It is possible to apply several techniques to each test unit, taking into consideration the features of the techniques. The test units matrix set up during the previous activity can be extended with a test techniques column.

Information system	Test units	Test techniques
Subsystem 1	1	Data combination test
	2	Syntactic test
	3	Elementary comparison test
	etc.	Elementary comparison test
Subsystem 2	1	Process cycle test
	2	Process cycle test
		Syntactic test

Table 8.2
Techniques to be applied to each unit

Products
Test unit matrix, including test techniques.

Techniques
Not applicable.

8.3.4 Specifying the infrastructure
Aim
The definition of the infrastructure is specified further, where necessary, describing in detail the required infrastructure.

Procedure
Using the definition of the infrastructure as recorded in the test plan, an investigation is conduced into whether further specification and detailing are necessary. This concerns in particular the test environment and the test tools. On the basis of discussions with the people in the organization and/or the various suppliers, it is decided whether the definition needs to be adjusted or detailed. The agreements made with the various suppliers are recorded, and a detailed schedule is set up for the deliveries of the infrastructure.

Products
Detailed specification of the infrastructure.

Techniques
Not applicable.

8.4 Specification phase

Introduction
During the specification phase, the test cases are prepared and the infrastructure is set up.

Preconditions
The following conditions should be met before the specification phase can be started:
● the test basis should be available and frozen;
● the test basis defects from the testability review of the test basis must have been processed;
● a description of the physical data tables should be available for the definition of the initial test databases;
● the delivery schedule of the test object and the infrastructure should be available for the creation of the test scenario.

Procedure

During the specification phase, the test cases are specified and the appropriate infrastructure is put into place. The creation of test cases is done per test, on the basis of the assigned test specification techniques. When the test basis defects from the testability review have been dealt with, the test cases are derived from the test basis and recorded in test specifications. During this process, the contents of the various initial data sets are also defined. Lastly, the defined test cases in the test specification are placed in an executable sequence in the test scripts. The infrastructure, as described in the detailed specification, is created parallel to the creation of the test cases.

Activities

The following activities are distinguished in the specification phase:
1   Preparing test specifications.
2   Defining initial test databases.
3   Drafting test scripts.
4   Producing a test scenario.
5   Specifying the review of the test object and infrastructure.
6   Setting up the infrastructure.

Figure 8.5 indicates the sequence and dependencies of the various activities.

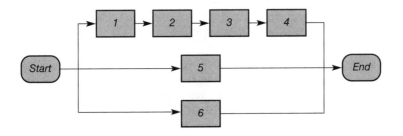

Figure 8.5
Specification phase

8.4.1 Preparing test specifications

Aim

The aim of this activity is to set up the test specifications or test cases for each test unit.

Procedure

To derive test cases from the test basis, use is made of test-specification techniques that allow the test cases to be derived in an unequivocal and reproducible way. A test case consists of a description of the starting situation, the action to be taken and a forecast of the result. Production files (or parts of them) may be used for the physical implementation of the test cases. This can save time.

During the test case specification, agreements must be made so that the tests do not interfere with each other during execution, which may be the case if different test cases use the same data (competition). If one test case is testing 'delete order lines' and another 'change order lines', then there is a strong chance that the forecasted results will not be achieved. A solution may be to agree on certain series of numbers for the order lines, one per test of each function. The test specifications are set up according to the recorded standards in the test plan. After completion, the test specifications are transferred to control.

It is possible that during this activity, shortcomings and/or obscurities will be detected in the test basis. It is, of course, important to report these immediately (via the customer) to the supplier of the test basis so that steps can be taken as quickly as possible to clarify and possibly improve the obscurities and/or omissions. The registration and notification of these defects is done by means of the determined procedures of the test plan in the chapter 'Control'.

Products
Test basis defects. Test specifications.

Techniques
Test-specification techniques (see Chapter 15).

8.4.2 Defining initial test databases
Aim
The aim of this activity is to collect the initial data described in the test specifications and to define them centrally.

Procedure
The test specifications detail the necessary initial data sets for each test unit. To prevent redundancy and to limit the number of required physical files, the data are collected, particularly the table data, and added to a single central description of the initial data set, which is set up according to the standards recorded in the test plan and on completion is transferred to control.

It is possible that during this activity, shortcomings and/or obscurities will be detected in the test basis. It is important to report these via the customer to the supplier of the test basis so that they can remove any obscurities as quickly as possible. The registration and notification of these defects is done by means of the determined procedures of the test plan in Chapter 22.

Products
Test basis defects. Description of the initial data set.

Techniques
Test-specification techniques (see Chapter 15).

8.4.3 Drafting test scripts
Aim
The aim of this activity is to convert the test cases described in the test specifications into executable, concrete test actions. This includes establishing the sequence of the actions and the conditions for their execution in test scripts.

Procedure
To be able to confront the information system with the test cases described in the test specifications in a logical and easy-to-execute sequence, test scripts are set up. During the creation of the test scripts, the test cases are converted into executable and verifiable test actions that are placed in an executable sequence. This takes into account the fact that a test action may fail. It is not advisable to set up the test script in such a way that when a test action does indeed fail, this prevents a large part of the script from being executed. One should therefore try to have as few interdependencies between the actions to be carried out as possible. In a number of cases, this will result in the existence of several scripts per test specification.

The test script also describes which initial data are required in order to carry out the test actions described. These are included as conditions (preconditions) for the execution of the test script. In addition, it is possible to include the loading and/or saving of certain data sets as a separate action in the test script.

During this activity, shortcomings and/or obscurities may be detected in the test basis. The registration and notification of these defects are again done by means of the procedures established in the test plan.

Products
Test basis defects. Test scripts.

Techniques
Test-specification techniques (see Chapter 15).

8.4.4 Producing a test scenario
Aim
The aim of this activity is to record in a test scenario the sequence in which the test scripts will be executed.

Procedure
The test scenario constitutes the basis for a structured approach of the execution phase. The order in which the test scripts are to be executed is recorded. This takes into account the fact that the execution of a test script may fail. It is not advisable to set up the test scenario in such a way that when the script does indeed fail, this prevents a large part of the scenario from being executed. One should try to have as few interdependencies between the test scripts to be executed as possible. This can be achieved, for example, by ensuring that the initial

test databases are reloaded before the next test script is executed. In addition, it is possible to save the files after execution of a script. Any defects can then easily be analyzed and reproduced.

To detect the most important defects, the test scripts that relate to the most crucial parts of the system, as recorded in the test strategy, are executed during the initial phase of the test execution, if possible.

The most important condition that the test scenario must meet is flexibility. It must be set up in such a way that when disrupting defects occur in certain parts of the system, a change can be introduced quickly, enabling the execution of the test to continue.

There may be situations in which setting up a test scenario can be a complex activity e.g.

- a test script spans several days, which means that particular attention must be paid to synchronization of the various test scripts;
- reports that derive their data from the initial data set as a whole must be tested. Creating a scenario on the basis of the initial data set and the accompanying test script is a complex process. Care should be taken in particular to ensure that other test scripts do not interfere with this test. If possible, such a test should be executed under isolated conditions.

This activity is strongly related to the activity 'maintaining the test plan' (see section 8.2.11).

Products
Test scenario.

Techniques
Not applicable.

8.4.5 Specifying the review of the test object and infrastructure
Aim
The aim of this activity is to record the way in which the review of the test object and the infrastructure is to be carried out.

Procedure
This activity includes the following:

- setting up a test object checklist
- setting up an infrastructure checklist
- setting up a pre-test test script.

Setting up a test object checklist

Within the framework of the review of the test object, it is recorded which products will be delivered as test object or part of the test object. This should correspond with the contracts signed with the various suppliers. This will result in a short checklist that can be used to establish that the delivery is complete. The following documents may be included in the test object checklist:

- the operating manual
- the user manual
- the installation manual
- a version overview of the software supplied.

Setting up an infrastructure checklist

A checklist is set up with respect to the infrastructure, based on its specification. This is used to determine whether all specified components are present. Its operation is determined by means of the pretest.

Setting up a pretest test script

In the pretest scripts, it is recorded how to determine whether the delivered test object or its components function in such a way that the structural test execution can start. This is often done by making a selection from the test cases for the 'real' test, with or without a checklist of the functions to be accessed. This results in a test script, which is used to access a representative section of the functions.

Products

Infrastructure review checklist. Test object review checklist. Pretest test script.

Techniques

Not applicable.

8.4.6 Setting up the infrastructure

Aim

The aim here is to set up the infrastructure in accordance with the drafted specifications.

Procedure

The infrastructure is set up parallel to the other activities of the specification phase. Execution of this activity usually consists of the following elements:

- checking whether all agreements are still valid;
- solving bottlenecks and problems, and recording any measures taken in new agreements;
- installation check;
- trial run;

- (as far as possible) executing the drafted checklists for the review of the infrastructure;
- testing recovery and back-up procedures, and any roll-back facilities.

Since the test team is not responsible directly for the supply of the required products, this process is often difficult to manage. It therefore requires careful coordination.

Products
Operational infrastructure.

Techniques
Not applicable.

8.5 Execution phase

Introduction
The aim of the execution phase is to perform the specified tests in order to gain insight into the quality of the test object.

Preconditions
The test object and the related infrastructure must have been set up or supplied before the execution phase can be started.

Procedure
The actual execution of the test starts at the moment when the first testable test units are supplied. The supplied test units are first checked for completeness and are installed in the test environment in order to assess whether they work properly. The first test to be carried out is the pretest (also known as the smoke test). This is a general test that investigates whether the information system to be tested, in combination with the test infrastructure, is of sufficient quality to be tested extensively. If the quality of the entire set-up is sufficient, then the initial data sets are filled with their initial values. Subsequently, the test scripts from the test scenario are carried out.

During the activity 'comparing and analyzing the test results', the causes of any differences between the forecast results and the achieved test results are investigated. The cause may be a program defect, but other causes are also possible, e.g. obscurities in the test basis, defects in the test environment, or defects in the test cases. After correction of a defect, the tests concerned are carried out and assessed again until all tests have been carried out and there are no longer any known defects present.

Activities

The following activities are distinguished in the execution phase:

1   Reviewing the test object/infrastructure.
2   Setting up initial test databases.
3   Executing (re)tests.
4   Comparing and analyzing the test results.
5   Maintaining the test scenario.

Figure 8.6 indicates the sequence and dependencies of the various activities.

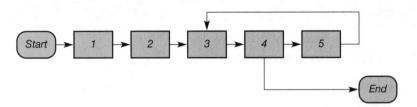

Figure 8.6
Execution phase

8.5.1 Reviewing the test object/infrastructure

Aim

The aim of this activity is to determine whether the delivered components of the test object and the infrastructure function in such a way that they can be tested properly.

Procedure

The procedure consists of the following:
● reviewing the infrastructure
● reviewing the test object
● executing the pre-test.

Reviewing the infrastructure

If this has not yet been done in the activity 'setting up the infrastructure' (see section 8.4.6), the infrastructure is checked for completeness with the aid of the checklist. Any missing components are reported by means of a defect report. These components must be made available as quickly as possible. The tests can be executed only when all required and specified components are present.

Reviewing the test object

The checklist is used to check the supplied test object for completeness. Here, any missing parts are reported by means of a defect report. After reaching agreement, the installation of the test object can be carried out.

Executing the pretest

After both the infrastructure and the test object have been installed fully, the pretest is executed on the basis of the test script. Successful completion of the pretest is a condition for the next activities in the execution phase. The defects from the pretest are registered and made available immediately to the suppliers concerned. This makes it possible to introduce quickly any adaptations or to take adequate measures to enable the pretest to be completed successfully.

Products

Defects. Operational and testable test object, including test infrastructure.

Techniques

Not applicable.

8.5.2 Setting up initial test databases

Aim

The aim of this activity is to construct the initial test databases required to perform the tests described in the test scripts.

Procedure

The files are filled with the 'initial situation', as described during the activity 'defining initial test databases' (see section 8.4.2). Constructing these initial test databases may occur in different ways. As soon as the initial test databases have been constructed and checked, a back-up is made to make it possible to restore the initial situation at any moment. Defects are registered in accordance with the procedures recorded in the test plan. Chapter 26 discusses the problems and the various alternatives that can be applied when constructing the initial test databases. Chapter 27 describes the resources that can be used when constructing the initial test databases.

Products

Defects. Initial test databases (physical).

Techniques

Not applicable.

8.5.3 Executing (re)tests

Aim

The aim of this activity is to obtain test results on the basis of which the assessment of the test object can take place.

Procedure

The procedure consists of the following:

- executing test scripts
- executing static tests.

Executing test scripts

The test scripts are executed in the sequence specified in the test scenario. Discipline is very important throughout the execution of the test. The tests should be carried out as they are recorded in the scenario and the test scripts. If the testers deviate from the test scripts, then there is no guarantee that the strategy recorded in the test plan will actually be carried out. If sufficient time is available, it is possible to perform extra tests on the basis of the 'test-specification technique' error guessing. Such tests should be documented, however, so that any defects can be analyzed and reproduced. In the case of mainframe applications, it is necessary to coordinate the planned execution of the test scripts relating to the batch components of the system with the system manager.

Executing static tests

It is recorded in the test strategy whether the quality characteristics that are to be tested statically, such as flexibility and continuity, belong to the 'scope' of the tests to be carried out. If this is the case, then these static tests are carried out on the basis of a checklist. The latter is used to try to gain insight into the quality aspect concerned. Any incidences are registered and processed using a defect procedure. The conclusion regarding the executed test is recorded in the periodic quality report.

Products

Test results.

Techniques

Checklists on quality characteristics (see Chapter 16).

8.5.4 Comparing and analyzing the test results

Aim

The aim of this activity is to establish the similarities and to analyze the differences between the test results obtained and the results forecast in the test scripts.

Procedure

The procedure consists of the following:
- comparing test results
- analyzing differences.

Comparing test results

The test results are compared with the results forecast in the test scripts. This is the most important activity of the entire test process. If any differences are overlooked at this stage, then there is no guarantee that these will be detected later. If no differences are found, then this must be recorded. If differences have been found, they must be analyzed further.

Analyzing differences

The differences found are analyzed during this activity. When establishing the cause of the deviation, there are various possibilities:

- a test execution error, which means that the test concerned must be executed again;
- a test specification error;
- a programming error;
- shortcomings in the test environment;
- an inconsistency or obscurity in the test basis.

Problems (defects) are registered formally in accordance with the established procedures. In the test scripts, the identification numbers of defects are registered with those test actions in which the defect was detected. This quickly makes it clear which test actions should be carried out again in the case of any retests. The test scripts, the defects and the test results are combined to produce a test report. Various test tools are available for comparing the test results and analyzing the differences, including comparators and query languages (see Chapter 27).

Products

Defects. Test reports.

Techniques

Not applicable.

8.5.5 Maintaining the test scenario

Aim

The aim of this activity is to keep the test scenario up to date so that it is clear at all times which test scripts must be executed and in which order.

Procedure

During the execution of the (re)tests, problems may be found that have consequences for the execution of the tests. Firstly, it has to be determined whether the testware must be adapted and the test must re-run. The re-run of the test is included in the test scenario. Any re-work with respect to the testware is initiated.

Secondly, defects nearly always lead to the inclusion of a retest in the test scenario. It is important, however, to determine how the retest should be executed. Full or partial re-execution of a test script depends on the following:

- the severity of the defects;
- the number of defects;
- the degree to which the previous execution of the test script was disrupted by the defects;
- the available time;
- the importance of the function.

Maintaining the test scenario is of great importance. Not only does it provide insight into the test scripts that still have to be executed, it also forms the basis for the changes that have to be introduced into the detailed schedule of the execution phase and the overall schedule of the test process.

Products
Adapted test scenario.

Techniques
Not applicable.

8.6 Completion phase

Introduction
The aim of the completion phase consists of a number of parts:

- conserving the testware so that it can be reused for subsequent tests;
- obtaining experience figures for the benefit of better control of future test processes;
- drafting the final report, informing the customer of the course of the test, and discharging the test team.

Preconditions
The execution of the tests must be completed, and the decision taken to not perform any more (re)tests before the completion phase can be started.

Procedure
A selection is made from what is often a large amount of testware, such as test cases, test results, descriptions of the infrastructure, and the tools that were employed. The objective is that in the event of modifications and corresponding maintenance tests, the testware merely needs to be adapted, therefore avoiding the need to design a completely new test. During the test process, an attempt will have been made to keep the test cases consistent with the specifications and the developed system. If necessary, the selected test cases must be brought up to date. The idea is that during the maintenance phase, the test cases remain consistent with the specifications of the system.

The test process is also evaluated. The statistics and evaluations collected are combined with the results of a final evaluation. The subject of the evaluation is not only the test process but also the quality of the product. It is advisable to also prepare a costs/benefits analysis of the test process. This is a difficult but fascinating and instructive activity. The often large number of statistics that become available are indispensable when planning future test processes and system development processes, and for organizing quality systems.

Following the preservation, evaluation and presentation of the evaluation report, the customer may discharge the test organization.

Activities

The completion phase consists of the following activities:

1   Evaluating the test object.
2   Evaluating the test process.
3   Preparing an evaluation report.
4   Preserving testware.
5   Discharging the test team.

Figure 8.7 indicates the sequence and dependencies of the various activities.

Figure 8.7
Completion phase

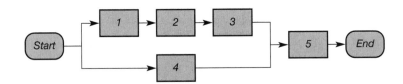

8.6.1 Evaluating the test object

Aim

The aim of this activity is to evaluate the quality of the test object and to draw up the final release advice.

Procedure

On the basis of the executed tests, the test reports and the (status of the) registered defects, the final release advice is drawn up. It is important to indicate which defects at the time of hand-over have not been solved ('known errors') and what risks evolve from this situation. This means that one should also point out any alternatives, such as postponement, providing a lower functionality level, etc. Use can be made of the checklist 'production release' for this evaluation.

Products

Release advice.

Techniques

Checklist 'production release' (see Chapter 17).

8.6.2 Evaluating the test process

Aim

The aim of this activity is to obtain insight into the way in which the test process proceeded, and to collect experience data for future test processes.

Procedure

The procedure consists of the following:

- evaluating the test process
- collecting experience data
- drawing up a costs/benefits analysis.

Evaluating the test process

At the end of the test, it is determined how the test process proceeded. The important aspects are the evaluation of the test plan, the test strategy, and the methods and techniques used. Use can be made of the checklist 'test project evaluation' for this evaluation.

Collecting experience data

Experience data are collected and combined on the basis of the completed test process. Within the framework of this activity, the following data are important:

- number of detected defects;
- duration per main activity;
- duration necessary for drafting a test specification in relation to the number of test points of the test unit concerned;
- duration necessary for the execution of a test in relation to the number of test points of the test unit concerned;
- number of retests.

An extensive list of the possible experience data to be collected is included in the checklist 'metrics test object' (see Chapter 23). In addition, Chapter 23 examines in detail the goal–question–metric method used for implementing metrics.

Drawing up a costs/benefits analysis

The costs of the test process are relatively simple to determine. These include the costs of the resources, people and means used. The benefits of the test process, on the other hand, are less easily established. One of the benefits is that no costs have been made because a defect did not occur. It is possible to approach this by relating the defect to possible repair costs after production has started. What would have been the cost if the defect had not been detected? For example:

- the cost of a shutdown of production and the non-activity of users;
- the cost of repairs of inconsistencies in the database that are noticed only after some time and that call for major repairs, regarding not only the software but also the production data;
- failure costs: not achieving (all) business objectives;
- the costs of a damaged image of the organization or the loss of clients.

Products

Test process evaluation. Experience data. Costs/benefits analysis.

Techniques

Checklist 'test project evaluation' (see Chapter 17). Checklist 'metrics test object' (see Chapter 23). Goal–question–metric method (see Chapter 23).

8.6.3   Preparing an evaluation report
Aim

The aim of the evaluation report is to inform the customer about the quality of the test object and the course of the test process.

Procedure

On the basis of the results of the evaluation of the test object and the test process, the evaluation report is drawn up. The final report should include at least the following aspects:

- *Evaluation of the test object.* The results of the evaluation of the test object are displayed. It is particularly important to list any unsolved defects and the related risks.
- *Evaluation of the test process.* The results of the evaluation of the test process are displayed. The following subdivision can be made:
  - Evaluation of the test strategy: To what degree has the chosen test strategy been deviated from? Was the chosen test strategy the correct one: which components of the system have been tested too much or too little?
  - Scheduling versus realization: To what degree has the schedule been realized? Have any structural deviations been detected?
  - Evaluation of resources, methods and techniques: To what degree have the selected resources been used? Have the selected methods and techniques been used correctly, and are there any defects relating to the methods and techniques?

The evaluation report is made available to the customer, and may also be presented.

Products

Evaluation report.

Techniques

Not applicable.

8.6.4   Preserving testware
Aim

The aim of this activity is to select and update the created testware in such a way that future tests can make full use of this testware.

Procedure

The procedure consists of the following activities:

- drawing up a testware packing list
- collecting and updating testware
- handing over testware.

Drawing up a testware packing list

After consultation with the future manager of the system, an inventory is made of the documents that will be made available. The objective is that in the event of modifications and corresponding maintenance tests, the testware is reusable and it will not be necessary to design a completely new test. The test products to be delivered are included in a 'packing list'. This list is a subcollection of the test products.

It is important to indicate how these test deliverables were produced so that future maintenance may be carried out properly. This refers in particular to the test-specification techniques, tools, etc. that have been used.

Collecting and updating testware

The testware to be handed over must be completed and adapted where necessary. Particularly during the final phase of execution, maintenance of the testware may be postponed. Before handing over to the future users, it should be ensured that any changes have been processed.

Handing over testware

Finally, the actual hand-over of the testware takes place. In accordance with the packing list, all selected components, both physical (in digital form and on paper) and logical (with regard to management), are handed over.

Products

Testware packing list. Testware.

Techniques

Not applicable.

8.6.5 Discharging the test team

Aim

This is the formal completion of the test process that provides the test team with a discharge statement.

Procedure

On the basis of the evaluation report and the testware that has been handed over, the customer is asked to officially terminate the test process and to provide the test team with a discharge. After receiving the discharge, the test team is disbanded.

Products

Discharge statement.

Techniques

Not applicable.

Lifecycle of low-level tests

9

9.1   Introduction

This chapter describes the phases of the low-level tests, noting the activities to be carried out for each phase. This practical approach makes it possible to provide more structure and better coverage in low-level testing. The description focuses on the differences from the high-level test lifecycle. Implementing the low-level test lifecycle requires knowledge gained from Chapter 8. For more information on low-level testing, refer to the British Standards Institute (1998b).

9.2   Characteristics of low-level testing

Low-level testing means carrying out tests using the knowledge of the internal structure of the system. Unit, program and module tests are performed from the moment that the system's first building blocks are created. The infrastructure and programming language used determine to what degree there are separate tests for units, programs or modules. Testers must check whether the elementary components or sets have been coded according to the technical specifications. In TMap, the only term used in this context is *unit test*. A unit test is a test executed by the developer in a laboratory environment, which should demonstrate that the program meets the requirements described in the design specifications.

Having established that the quality of the system's elementary components is satisfactory, larger sections of the system are tested in their entirety in the integration test. The emphasis here is on the data flow and the interaction between the programs up to the subsystem level. An *integration test* is a test executed by the developer in a laboratory environment, which should demonstrate that a logical set of programs meets the requirements set in the design specifications.

When low-level tests are compared with high-level tests, such as the system test and the acceptance test, a number of important differences can be distinguished.

- With unit tests in particular, the discoverer (tester) of defects is often the same person as the solver (developer) of the defects. This means that the communication on defects can be minimal.
- The aim of low-level testing is to solve all defects before the software is handed over. The low-level test report can therefore be more concise than high-level test reports.
- In low-level testing, it is often the developers who are doing the testing. A developer wants to show that the product works, while the tester wants to show the difference between the required and the present quality of the product (and to do so will actively search for defects). This difference in mindset means that comprehensive and/or in-depth low-level testing is at odds with the mentality of most developers, and hence evokes much opposition and/or results in carelessly executed tests.
- Unlike high-level tests, low-level tests are an integral part of the system-development process. More so than with high-level tests, the lifecycle of the test activities must therefore be interwoven and integrated with the activities of system development.
- In low-level tests, white-box techniques are used. By using the knowledge of the internal operation of the system, these techniques find different types of defects than black-box techniques, which high-level tests mostly employ. It can be expected of low-level tests, for example, that every statement in the program code has been run at least once. Such a degree of coverage is, in practice, difficult to achieve in high-level tests. It is therefore not easy to replace low-level tests with high-level tests.
- Low-level tests are the first test carried out, which means that all defects are still in the product. This requires cheap and fast defect-correction methods. To achieve this, a flexible environment with few procedural barriers is of great importance.

9.3 Is there more structure and depth of testing in low-level testing?

We often see in practice that low-level testing occurs in unstructured fashion: tests are not planned or prepared, no use is made of test specification techniques, and there is no insight into what has or has not been tested, or to what extent. This means that insight into the quality of the (tested) product is also lacking. Demanding, time-consuming and inefficient high-level tests are often carried out in order to obtain sufficient insight into this quality, and to provide the developers with the opportunity of raising the quality to an acceptable level. It is therefore clear that low-level testing should be more structured.

Below we explain why this does not happen, and why it is so important.

9.3.1 Arguments against
Time pressure/too expensive in relation to benefits
The development team is often under great time pressure. It is therefore very tempting to avoid carrying out those activities that the team will not be assessed on. A team is usually assessed on 'solid' criteria, such as time. Assessment on less solid criteria, such as quality, is more difficult and is rare in practice. The benefits of good testing are generally minor for the team of developers, even though the benefits of good testing for the project as a whole are many times greater.

Sufficient trust in the quality
In general, developers are proud of their products and feel that the quality is good. It therefore does not make sense for a developer to go to too much trouble to detect defects in their products.

Another good test has been scheduled
The subsequent stage, e.g. the system test, includes a more intensive test than low-level testing. Why should the low-level tester spend much time on low-level testing if it will be carried out on a much larger scale later?

9.3.2 Arguments in favor
The single most important argument for more structure and depth of testing in low-level testing is that it enables the developers to determine for themselves that the software is of sufficient quality to be handed over to the next stage, most likely the system test. Of course the meaning of 'sufficient quality' is open to interpretation. Sufficient quality has many advantages for the development team:
- Fewer repairs are necessary because the products that are handed over to the next stage are of a higher quality.
- Scheduling will improve because the often uncertain amount of repair work decreases.
- The overall project time of the development route is shorter.
- Repairs are cheaper at an early stage than at a later stage because all the knowledge of the developed product is still fresh in the memory, and because at a later stage staff may have left the development team.
- The analysis of defects that you find yourself is much quicker and simpler than the analysis of those found by others. The further away (both organizationally and physically) the finder is from the defect, the more difficult and time-consuming the analysis will often be. This is reinforced because the system as a whole ('black-box') is tested at a later stage so that the defect found may be in any one of many separate components.
- The developers receive quicker feedback about the defects they have made so that they may prevent such defects from occurrng more quickly and easily in other programs.

- Certain types of defects are best detected with low-level testing. For instance, how does the program handle a failure to write to a file? These issues need to be tested, but they are often not addressed in functional specifications. When low-level testing detects too few of these, this means that the high-level tests are forced to use inefficient techniques to provide a disproportionate amount (for the detection of such defects) of effort to achieve the same quality of the test object as when the low-level test had been carried out properly.

For the project as a whole, and even for the complete lifecycle of the system, these advantages are even greater because the later test stages also profit (and often even to a greater extent) from these advantages, e.g. because fewer retests are necessary.

In addition, there are recent developments that increase the need for a structured low-level test approach: the increasing complexity of information systems plus the higher demands on quality and shorter time to market mean that a late overall test (which indicates whether the system has the quality required) is no longer acceptable. The development process also increasingly makes use of components that have not been developed in-house. This means that when analyzing defects, it is more difficult to determine the cause.

The advantages of a more structured low-level test approach therefore amply outweigh the disadvantages. It is a necessary precondition for successful structuring of low-level testing that the various people involved, such as the project leader and the developers, are aware of the importance of a better test process. In their assessment of the developers' team, the project leader should focus more on quality than on only time and money. Chapter 24 examines the structuring process.

TMap distinguishes five phases in the test process: planning and control, preparation, specification, execution, and completion. Each phase consists of various activities that are to be executed (see Figure 9.1). On the basis of the differences discussed above, the approach of low-level testing must be adapted in relation to high-level testing. Low-level testing needs to adhere less strictly to formal procedures. For this reason, the five phases of TMap for low-level testing have been 'stripped'.

9.4 Planning and control phase

The planning and control phase consists of the following activities:
1 Formulating the assignment.
2 Establishing the test basis.
3 Defining the test strategy.
4 Specifying test deliverables and reports.
5 Setting up the organization.
6 Specifying the infrastructure.

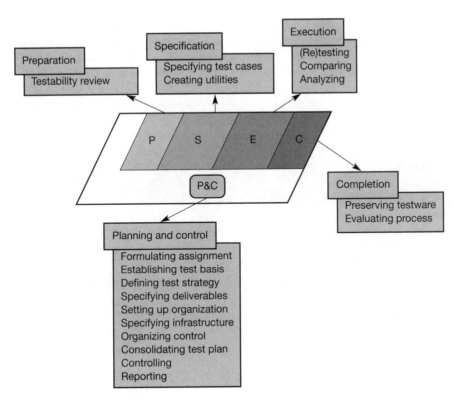

Figure 9.1
Lifecycle of low-level
testing

7 Organizing control.
8 Setting up schedules.
9 Consolidating the test plan.
10 Maintaining the test plan.
11 Controlling the test.
12 Reporting.

9.4.1 Formulating the assignment

This activity states the assignment, the customer (usually the project manager), the supplier (usually the development team leader) and the scope of the tests. Besides testing unit functionality and interfaces with other units, the scope may include the following:

- (not) testing certain interfaces with other systems
- (not) testing conversion software.

In addition, the assumptions and preconditions are described. The test process determines the assumptions for the rest of the project, while preconditions are imposed upon the test process from outside. These may be factors such as schedules and available resources.

9.4.2 Establishing the test basis

To perform low-level testing properly, and to meet the test assignment, it must be known in what way the system will be created. All (system) documents that describe this constitute the test basis. The test/development basis may consist of:

- functional design
- technical design
- program code
- change proposals
- system-management documentation
- standards.

9.4.3 Defining the test strategy

Aim

The aim of this activity is to determine what, how and to what depth tests should be executed. In fact, optimization takes place with the aim of distributing correctly the available resources over the test activities. The test strategy is also a tool for determining when testing can be stopped. Starting from the strategy, a reliable estimate of the required number of hours for the test process is made. The strategy definition is based on the strategy definition in the master test plan.

Procedure

The procedure consists of the following:

- define strategy for the unit test
- define strategy for the integration test
- setting up a budget (in hours).

Define strategy for the unit test

1   It is determined which quality characteristics are to be tested. Examples of quality characteristics on which low-level testing could focus include functionality, performance and maintainability. We use the word 'could' because low-level testing is not required for each quality characteristic.

2   On the basis of the development philosophy, system development environment and the programming language used, a subdivision is made, for instance into types of programs. This can include (groups of) programs for screen processing, data manipulation and calculations.

3   A degree of importance is attached to the combinations of the selected quality characteristics and the various programs, such as light, normal or thorough testing. The importance of certain programs for the customer plays a role here. As an option, this importance can be detailed further by establishing the criteria regarding the degree of coverage, such as the percentage of statements processed in the tests, or the percentage of program paths or of the composite conditions.

4   On the basis of the importance attached and the required coverage, the test techniques to be used and the desired verification are selected. Except for the degree of importance, the choice should also take into account what is feasible, seen from the point of view of both the tester and the technical environment.

Suitable formal test specification techniques for low-level testing include the algorithm test and the decision table test. An informal technique such as error guessing can also be used. If necessary, the techniques can be combined with the boundary value analyses (see also Chapter 15). Checklists are often used, e.g. to test graphical user interfaces (GUIs). Some more techniques can be found in British Standards Institute (1998b).

In addition to these, a test method can be used in which nothing is recorded on paper (in fact, this is often the case today). A disadvantage of this is that there is no insight into the depth and the completeness of the test, and therefore no insight into the quality of the test object. Other and later tests will consequently still have to show that the test object is of sufficient quality. Nevertheless, possible reasons to choose this form are that other techniques require more time and capacity, and add little additional quality in relation to the risks run, and that it is preferable for the improvement of low-level testing to occur in small steps. It will always remain the responsibility of the developer to supply a correct and properly working program or system.

Table 9.1 shows an example of the allocation of techniques to the quality characteristics and types of programs.

Quality characteristic	Type of program		
	Online screens	**Calculation modules**	**Reporting functions**
Functionality	Algorithm test	Algorithm test, decision table test (demand: 100% statement coverage)	Free (= undocumented)
Performance	Not tested	Real-life test	Not tested
Maintainability	Checklist maintainability	Checklist maintainability	Checklist maintainability

Table 9.1
Unit test strategy matrix

Define strategy for the integration test
There are many possible variants for the strategy of the integration test. One extreme is that all programs are integrated simultaneously, after which everything is tested as a whole. Myers (1979) describes this as 'big-bang testing'. The

other extreme is that all programs are integrated one by one, and a test is carried out after each step (incremental testing). Between these two extremes, there is a range of variants.

The first has the advantage that all programs are finished before integration testing. There is no need for simulating (as yet unfinished) programs. One disadvantage, however, is that in general it is difficult and time-consuming to trace the cause of defects found with this late integration. In fact, the system test starts immediately after the unit test. Another disadvantage is that many defects are not found because too many interfaces are difficult to access for testing and are therefore skipped.

The last variant has the advantage that the defects are found early when it is relatively easy to detect the cause. A disadvantage is that it can be a time-consuming activity because stubs and drivers (see Chapter 27) have to be developed and used in the test before the actual programs can be used.

As well as the integration steps, there are various possibilities for the program integration procedure:

- *Top-down.* Testing takes place from top to bottom, following the control flow (e.g. working from the menu). Programs are substituted by stubs.
- *Bottom-up.* Testing takes place from the bottom of the control flow upwards (e.g. data manipulation followed by the accompanying screen). Programs are substituted by drivers.
- *Available components first.* Integration is on the basis of the order in which the programs are delivered. Because no planning is needed, this is often a popular strategy. However, because important programs may not be available to the test team when they need them, it often results in chaos.
- *Function by function.* Integration on the basis of the functions, as recorded in the functional design.
- *Data-oriented.* Integration on the basis of some global data element, often used in object orientation strategy.

The best integration sequence and how many integration steps are required depends on the location of the high-risk components in the system. The best choice is to start integration with those programs that are expected to cause most problems. Doing so prevents major problems at the end of the integration test, which would result in the need to adapt part of the information system.

The strategy development for the integration test proceeds like that for the unit test. The steps and the main differences with the strategy development of the unit test are:

1   Selection of the quality characteristics to be tested. This step focuses mainly on the quality characteristic functionality because the aim of the integration test is to show that the programs work together in a functional way.
2   Dividing into integration steps. A division of the system takes place in integration steps instead of in types of programs.

3   Establishing test importance per quality characteristic/integration step.
4   Assigning the techniques and measuring instructions to be used.

Different techniques apply to the integration test than to the unit test, e.g. the program interface test. The degree of coverage of such techniques concerns the number of entities, functions or interfaces that occur in the tests (in relation to the total number). Table 9.2 is an example of the strategy matrix for the integration test.

Quality characteristic	Integration step	
	A	**B**
Functionality	Program interface test, with boundary values	Program interface test
Security	Checklist implementation authorization functionality	Checklist implementation authorization functionality

Table 9.2
Strategy matrix for integration tests

Setting up a budget (in hours)
On the basis of the strategy and taking into account the available resources, a well-founded budget is drawn up for the test process. In general, experience figures are used, e.g. a certain percentage of the total development efforts. The required and available time is divided up among the programs or integration steps to be tested.

9.4.4 Specifying test deliverables and reports
The aim of this activity is the definition of the test deliverables to be supplied and the way in which reports should be made. Depending on the chosen test techniques, the following testware results:
*   test cases, checklists, etc.
*   test results in the form of completed checklists, logging reports, screen dumps, etc.

An important choice to be made is the desired degree of test verification. How much certainty should there be that tests have indeed been carried out according to the agreed strategy? And how much time and money is one prepared to allocate to this verification? Increasingly, external parties, such as supervisory bodies, make demands on the verification that is to be provided. Possible forms of verification, which can often be combined, are:
*   *Marked test basis.* Ticking off that which has been tested in the test basis (e.g. the technical design) without specifying how the test has been carried out.

- *Test cases.* The test cases drawn up (with the aid of a certain specification technique).
- *Test cases + test reports.* The same as the previous case, plus a compiled report stating which test cases have been carried out and what the results were.
- *Test cases + test reports + proof.* The same as the previous case, plus proof of the execution of the test in the form of screen and database dumps, overviews, etc.
- *Test coverage tools (tools for measuring the degree of coverage achieved).* The output of such tools shows what has been tested, such as the percentage of the code or the interfaces between modules that has been covered.
- *Automated test scripts.* Carrying out such scripts shows quickly whether the software supplied is the same as the software that has been tested, and whether the installation was completed successfully.

It must also be agreed on what form the reports should take. It is possible that a separate test report will be supplied, but the report can also be part of the regular development reports.

9.4.5 Setting up the organization

Low-level testing requires a structured organization. The primary test tasks and the responsibility for the test process should be set. Often, the development project leader is responsible for the low-level test process, and often each programmer is also a unit tester. The unit test can be carried out by the author of the program or by another developer, but this decision depends strongly on the definition of the test strategy.

The advantage of the developer carrying out the test is that they are familiar with the internal operation of the program. This is the most efficient procedure because there is no training time and practically no overheads in terms of communication. The advantage of the test being carried out by a fellow developer is that this person is more likely to discover defects that the original developer failed to see because of his/her blind spots. A variant of this is that the developer tests their own program but using a test prepared by another developer.

Instead of the development project leader, an application integrator (AI) may assume responsibility for the integration test. An AI is responsible for both the progress of the integration process and the quality of the product delivered. Because the AI does not have the same multitude of tasks and responsibilities as the project leader, testing, and therefore quality of the test object, receives more attention (see also Chapter 19).

A thorough knowledge of the system with sufficient knowledge of testing is required for low-level testing. In practice, this knowledge of the system is usually sufficiently present, but test knowledge is often lacking. Means to raise the level of this knowledge include:

- training in test techniques and management, as well as test awareness;
- support and coaching by a test specialist.

The deployment of testers without any knowledge of the system must be avoided in low-level testing.

9.4.6 Specifying the infrastructure

Although low-level testing is normally a part of the development process as a whole, testing may impose specific demands on the infrastructure. The infrastructure includes the test environment, test tools and the office environment. The aim of defining this is to make these demands clear at as early a stage as possible so that suitable measures can be taken. A test environment must, for example, be thought of as the necessary test databases or the ability to manipulate the system date.

Test tools may offer support to the test activities with respect to the construction of initial test databases, execution of the tests and assessments. Well-known test tools for low-level testing are stubs and drivers, compilers, query languages, test coverage tools, debuggers, and static analysis tools (see Chapter 27). In addition to commercial tools, system-specific utilities developed in-house are often particularly useful. It is possible that such software is already available within the organization, but it is also possible that activities must be scheduled in order to develop it (and test it).

9.4.7 Organizing control

Control is defined as the control of the test process, the infrastructure and the test deliverables. This is considered to be part of the regular development activities. The only deviation is defect management. In high-level tests, the administration of each defect is sacred because the content of this administration is used to gain insight into the progress and the activities still to be carried out (retests), to draft reports, to collect metrics and to analyze trends. Although this is also possible in the case of low-level tests, it is far less of a necessity. When a unit tester finds a defect but the defect is solved and retested, the defect need not be administrated (unless the program is already used elsewhere). In this way, the programmer avoids their programming defects becoming public knowledge, and does not lose time administrating. A disadvantage is, of course, that there is less insight in the quality of the low-level tests. In the case of doubts concerning the cause or lack of clarity about the test basis, the defects will be described because these are presented to the designer within the development team. From the moment that the test object is accepted, all known defects and any defects found from then on must be administrated.

9.4.8 Setting up schedules

Working on the basis of the budget (hours) set, the available means and resources, the development schedule and the delivery schemes of the various parties involved, a global schedule for the remainder of the test procedure is set up. Usually, schedules for unit tests are not drawn up separately but constitute parts of the programming activities. The schedule of the integration (test), however, is usually drawn up separately. This schedule should contain at least the following aspects:

- activities to be carried out
- time to be spent per activity
- available overall project time
- products to be delivered
- employee(s) involved.

It is recommended to detail this overall schedule periodically to a detailed schedule, indicating for the short term who should test what and when.

9.4.9 Consolidating the test plan

Having carried out the activities discussed above, the test plan is composed, coordinated with the customer, reviewed and approved.

9.4.10 Maintaining the test plan

During the rest of the low-level testing process, it is the responsibility of the supplier of the low-level test process to keep the test plan and the scheduling up to date, and to report any deviations, in particular those relating to the agreed test strategy.

9.4.11 Controlling the test

In compliance with the procedures recorded in the test plan, three different forms of control are carried out: control of the test process, infrastructure control, and test deliverables control.

9.4.12 Reporting

Periodically, and upon request, reports are provided on the progress of the (test) process and the quality of the test object. The progress and quality reports, are often combined into a single report included in the progress reports which must be provided within the system development process. This report should contain at least the following aspects:

- total number of test cases
- number of test cases still to be executed
- number of successfully completed test cases.

The final report should consist of:

- evaluation of the test object, stating what has been tested, and listing the known errors, i.e. defects that have not been solved (yet);
- evaluation of the test strategy, possibly including communication to the customer of any deviations of the test strategy originally agreed upon.

9.5 Preparation phase

The preparation phase consists of a testability review of the test basis.

9.5.1 Testability review of the test basis

In the development review, it is decided whether development can take place on the basis of the initial documentation (the design). Parallel to (and preferably integrated with) this review, a review is also made with the aim of determining the testability of the documentation. Testability means the completeness, consistency and accessibility of the test basis and the ability to translate these into test cases.

9.6 Specification phase

The aim of the specification phase is to derive for each program and/or integration step the test cases on the basis of the test specification techniques assigned, and to prepare the execution of the test.

The following activities are distinguished in the specification phase:

1 Specifying tests (drafting test specifications, defining initial test databases, drawing up test scripts, drawing up a test scenario).
2 Creating utilities.

9.6.1 Specifying tests

The creation of test cases is done per program and/or integration step on the basis of the test techniques that have been assigned. It is also possible that no technique has been prescribed for a particular program. In this case, the tester has the task of simultaneously designing and executing the test cases during the execution phase of the test, without documenting it in a specific way. Not prescribing a technique does not mean that testing can be skipped. It simply means that the test cases need not be designed and executed according to a prescribed procedure.

It is possible that during this activity shortcomings and/or obscurities will be detected in the test basis. Obviously, it is important to record these as quickly as possible so that they can be improved and/or clarified. The registration and notification of these defects should be done by means of the general procedures described during the development process.

This activity requires relatively less time compared with high-level tests, because the test cases do not have to be described in great detail.

9.6.2 Creating utilities

To be able to execute properly the test of a program or an integration step, it is often necessary to create stubs or drivers. Stubs replace programs that are called by the software to be tested. Drivers replace programs that call the software to be tested.

The communication between the software to be tested and the stubs and drivers takes place by means of an interface. The stubs and drivers must be such that these interfaces contain realistic values and are consistent with the ultimate, actual interfaces between the various programs. The stubs and drivers themselves also qualify for testing. In certain cases, tools are available that generate stubs and drivers automatically.

9.7 Execution phase

The execution phase commences when the test environment has been completed, the test tools are available, and the test object is ready for testing. Two activities are distinguished:
1   Executing (re)tests.
2   Comparing and analyzing the test results.

9.7.1 Executing (re)tests

Discipline is very important throughout the execution of the test. The tests should at least be executed as determined in the test strategy. If the testers deviate from this, it should be reported to the customer so that measures can be taken. If, for example, a specific error is expected to have been made in several more programs, then it is possible to execute additional (non-documented) tests.

9.7.2 Comparing and analyzing the test results

The test results are compared with the expected results (as documented in the test scripts, if at all). This is the most important activity of the entire test process. If any differences are overlooked at this stage, then there is no guarantee that these will be detected later. The cause may be a programming error. If the programmer carries out the unit test, any programming errors are corrected immediately until all test cases run properly. But other causes are also possible: obscurities in the test basis, defects in the test environment, or defects in the test cases. All defects outside the immediate responsibility of the programmer/unit tester and in certain situations even the programming errors are registered formally according to the defect and/or configuration management procedures. After correction of a defect, the tests concerned are executed again until all tests have been completed and no more defects occur.

The test cases and the test results are combined into a test report.

9.8 Completion phase

The completion phase comprises two activities:
1 Preserving testware.
2 Evaluating the test process (optional).

9.8.1 Preserving testware

In this phase, it is determined which testware must be saved for future (re)tests so that these tests can be executed with minor adjustments. Possibly in consultation with the future manager of the system (or otherwise the customer), an inventory is made of the documents that will be made available. The test deliverables to be supplied are listed. The testware to be handed over must be completed and modified where necessary. Finally, the testware is handed over. An important deliverable of low-level testing is the testware of the integration test, as it is often suitable for regression testing during maintenance of an information system.

9.8.2 Evaluating the test process

At the end of the test, it may be determined how the overall test process went. The important aspects to be evaluated are the test plan, the test strategy, and the methods and techniques used. Results of the evaluation are input for subsequent test processes.

9.9 Coordination between low-level tests

When both the unit test and the integration test use the described procedure, it is a natural step to achieve some coordination between the two to ensure there is no unnecessary overlapping or gaps in the test coverage as a whole. We describe below a practical procedure that facilitates this coordination, clearly allocates the test responsibilities, and offers an easy first step towards structuring of the low-level test process.

In this approach, an application integrator (AI) is responsible for the progress of the integration process and for the quality of the product delivered. The AI discusses with their customer (the development project leader or team leader) the quality to be supplied: under which circumstances may the system or subsystem be released to the following phase (exit criteria)? The AI also requests insight into the quality of the programs entering the integration process (entry criteria) to establish whether the quality of these products is sufficient to carry out the integration process efficiently. A program is included in the integration process only if it meets the entry criteria.

A (sub)system is released if it can be demonstrated that it meets its exit criteria (see Figure 9.2). It may be clear that proper utilization of the exit and entry criteria will have great impact on the quality of the individual programs and the final system. Testing is very important in relation to these criteria as they may include such aspects as the quality characteristic to be tested, the desired degree of coverage, the use of certain test specification techniques, and the evidence to be supplied. The entry and exit criteria are therefore used to develop the strategy of the unit test and the integration test.

This procedure also applies when the integration process contains several

Figure 9.2
Entry and exit criteria

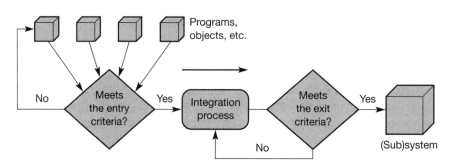

steps or when the system is under maintenance.

In order to prevent conflicts of interest, the AI should preferably not also have the role of designer or development project leader. This would create an area of tension between the AI, who is responsible for quality, and the development project leader, who is assessed particularly on aspects such as the supplied functionality, duration, and budget spent. The AI's role is described in Chapter 19.

Noticeable measures in the approach are:
- a conscious choice is made about the quality to be achieved and the tests to be carried out before delivery to the next phase can take place (which gives insight into quality);
- the tests carried out by the programmers become more transparent;
- in addition to the final responsibility of the development project leader or team leader, the responsibility for testing is assigned to one person within the development team.

A few implementations of this approach have already shown that later tests yield a significantly smaller number of serious defects. Another advantage of the approach is that earlier involvement of high-level tests is possible. Because there is better insight into the quality of the individual components of the system, the risks of executing certain tests at an earlier stage can be weighed up better. An example of this is that the acceptance test already assesses the screens on user-friendliness and effectiveness, while the integration test is still running. Such tests are useful only when there is a reasonable amount of trust in the quality of the screens.

Techniques   PART 3

Introduction to the techniques

10

10.1 The cornerstones

The four cornerstones of a structured test approach are a model related to the lifecycle of test activities, good organizational embedding, the right infrastructure and applicable techniques for executing activities. In this part of the book, we explain the 'techniques' cornerstone. Figure 10.1 relates the various techniques to the TMap lifecycle.

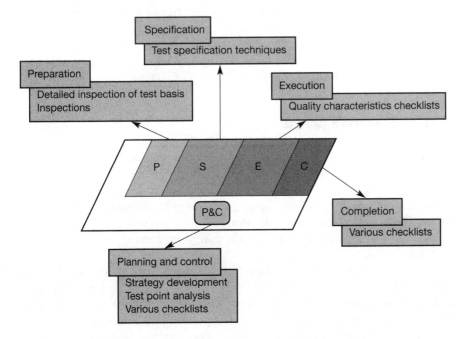

Figure 10.1
Test techniques and TMap

10.2 Planning and control phase

There are two techniques available for supporting the planning and control phase: development of test strategy (see Chapter 11) and test point analysis (TPA; see Chapter 12). The determination of the explicit test strategy is a tool to communicate with the customer about the organization and the strategic choices of the testing. The customer expects certain qualities of the system to be delivered, which may differ from case to case. It is important to be able to communicate with the customer about this and to make the manner by which testing will be performed comply with the customer's wishes. The technique 'development of strategy' offers a procedure to reach such an explicit test strategy.

Time pressure is the main pitfall. The tester usually does not have the necessary data to be able to indicate how much time they really need and which risks will be taken if less time is available. A well-founded estimation, that indicates clearly why a certain amount of testing time is needed is indispensable and makes it possible to indicate directly which risks will be taken if less time is spent on testing.

In order to meet this demand, TPA has been developed. TPA delivers a translation from the determined test strategy to the number of hours needed. By means of TPA, an estimate can be made for a system test or an acceptance test.

While drawing up a test plan, the checklists 'global study of information system', 'preconditions and assumptions', 'risks of test project' and 'test facilities' may be useful (see Chapter 17).

10.3 Preparation phase

The test basis is preferably formed by the documentation on which basis the tests will be prepared and specified. Although this kind of documentation is not always available, it is obvious that the review of what is available is an important precondition to guarantee good progress during the specification phase. The review is essentially the evaluation of the test basis to determine whether the documentation is sufficiently complete, accurate and consistent to function as a reference for the test.

There are two techniques for carrying out the review: the testability review of the test basis (see Chapter 13) and the inspection (see Chapter 14). The testability review of the test basis is an evaluation of the test basis, executed independently by the test team. With the inspection, the assessment is executed in a more formal approach together with various 'users' of the documentation, such as the end user, the development team, the accountant and of course the test team.

10.4 Specification phase

Important techniques are those by which the test cases will be derived from the test basis: the test-specification techniques. Test cases are determined based on information of what should be. A test case consists of a description of an initial situation, the actions to be performed, and the prediction of the result. A test case tests one or more quality characteristics of one or more functions of the information system. There is an abundance of test specification techniques for testing the various quality characteristics within the different test levels (see Chapter 15).

10.5 Execution phase

For the quality characteristics that are tested statistically, checklists are available (see Chapter 16). For each quality characteristic, the relevant measures are described that influence the quality level of the characteristic concerned. Moreover, a checklist is included that may be used while dynamically implicitly testing user-friendliness. Before giving a final release advice, a final assessment may be carried out if required. Here the checklist 'release to production' (see Chapter 17) may be used.

10.6 Completion phase

As support for the set-up of a final report and the evaluation of the test project, a checklist is available. The quality of the test project can be assessed during and in the completion phase of the testing process using the checklist 'evaluation of test project' (see Chapter 17).

Development of a test strategy 11

11.1 Introduction

A test strategy is a means of communicating with the customer matters such as the organization of testing and the strategic choices that go with it, and indicates how testing is to be carried out. In order to make the best possible use of resources and time, it is decided on which parts and aspects of the system the emphasis should fall. The test strategy forms an important basis for a structured approach to testing and makes a major contribution to a manageable test process.

The customer who commissions the test will expect specific qualities of the system when in production, and will want to know whether the released system will meet these requirements. If the system qualitatively does not meet the requirements, or meets them to only a limited extent, this implies high damage for the organization, for instance since high re-work costs will be needed or clients/users will be dissatisfied. Therefore this situation forms a risk for the organization. *A risk is defined as the chance of a failure[1] occurring related to the damage expected when this failure does occur.*

Testing covers such risks by giving insight into the extent to which the system meets the quality demands. When quality turns out to be insufficient, timely measures can be taken, e.g. re-work by developers. If the shipping of the system implies many risks for the organization, better testing is obvious as a solution. And the reverse also holds: *no risk, no test.*

Although we refer to quality and risks in a general sense, there may be big differences, depending on the situation. It is extremely important to discuss this with the customer, and to translate the customer's wishes into the way testing will be performed. Thus, the test strategy is directed toward finding the optimal balance between the test effort to be exerted and the coverage required for the risks (see Figure 11.1). To this end, the risks are specified up to the level of quality characteristics and separate subsystem. In doing so, it becomes possible to find a suitable test coverage for the assessed risks. Here, a higher test coverage usually results in more test effort. In order to be able to achieve a variation in

---

[1] Error = mistake, something done by a human. Fault or defect = the result of an error, residing in the code or documents. Failure = when a fault is executed, the result or manifestation of one or more faults.

test coverage, the use of more than one test-specification technique (test-design technique), each offering a specified test coverage, is crucial.

An analogy with insurance may clarify this. A person wants to cover a relevant risk and takes out appropriate insurance. This insurance takes a certain premium. If the person wants to pay less, they buy insurance with a lower cover. The consequence is that there will be no payment if the uncovered risk occurs. On the other hand, if cover were too large, then too much premium is paid since a situation has been insured that is unlikely to occur for this person.

Figure 11.1

The balance between budget and risk coverage

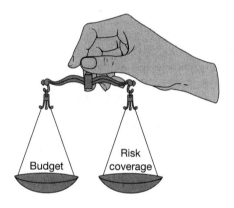

11.2 Risk assessment

Test strategy is based on risk assessment. This means assessing the damage of the consequences of defects undetected before the operation and occurring during operation. Risk assessment takes place on the basis of quality characteristics and subsystems. For instance, if the system is not user-friendly enough, what will be the negative consequences? And what will be the damage when the salary-calculation module in a payroll system does not work correctly?

In order to be able to perform this assessment well, the separate aspects of a risk are considered:

$$\text{Risk} = \text{chance of failure} \times \text{damage}$$

where chance of failure is related to aspects such as frequency of use and the chance of a failure occurring. In a function that is used dozens of times each day, the chance of a fault demonstrating itself is much bigger than with a function used once a year. For the assessment of the chance of faults, the following list may be helpful. It presents the locations where faults tend to cluster (based partly on Schaefer, 1996).

- complex functions;
- completely new functions;

- (especially frequently) adjusted functions;
- functions for which certain tools or techniques were employed for the first time;
- functions that were transferred from one developer to another during development;
- functions that were constructed under extreme time pressure;
- functions that had to be optimized more frequently than average;
- functions in which many defects were found earlier (e.g. in previous releases or during earlier reviews);
- functions with many interfaces.

The chance of failure is also greater with:
- inexperienced developers;
- insufficient involvement of users;
- insufficient quality assurance during development;
- insufficient quality of low-level tests;
- new development tools and development environment;
- large development teams;
- development teams with suboptimal communication (e.g. owing to geographical spread or personal causes);
- functions developed under political pressure, with unresolved internal differences in the organization.

If and when the fault manifests itself, what will be the damage for the organization? Aspects are costs of repair (of both the system and the consequences), foregone income, and loss of clients or confidence. Usually, the damage increases if the fault has an impact on other functions or systems. In the case of faults occurring in batch processes, it may be possible to prevent them from hampering users so that the eventual damage will be smaller than with similar online processes. Of course, this holds only if faults are detected on time.

Because of the complexity of the matter, it is impossible to assess risks with complete objectivity and in detail: it is a global assessment. It is therefore important for the risk assessment to be carried out not only by the test manager, but also by a large number of other people involved in the scheme, e.g. customer, users, development team, accountants and IT auditors. This not only increases the quality of the strategy but also has the advantage that the different parties are more aware of the risks and the extent to which testing contributes to making these risks manageable in a better way.

The developer of the test strategy should realize that users are the best people to assess the damage and the frequency of use when valuing the risks (end users, system managers and application managers, line management), whereas project team members are best to assess the chance of fault (project managers, designers, programmers, project quality staff, test manager).

The focus in risk assessment is on product risks, i.e. what is the risk for the organization if the product does not demonstrate the expected quality? In addition, there are (test) project risks. If the system must be in production on a certain date, if functional specifications are produced too late, if no experienced testers are available, or if the test infrastructure is not ready on time, then we speak of (test) project risks. These are not taken into account in determining the test strategy, but they do play a role in the test plan.

In developing a test strategy, the aim is to ensure that the test will be organized in such a way that with a certain extent of reliability:

- the most important defects will be found;
- the defects will be found in an early stage;
- the defects that require the most re-work time will be found first:
- efficient use is made of resources;
- accurate quality advice can be given eventually.

To summarize, *test strategy aims to find the most important defects as early as possible against the lowest costs*.

In practice, the development of a test strategy is often planned to coincide with preparing the budget, e.g. with the help of test point analysis (TPA; see Chapter 12). The advantage is that the consequences of the adopted strategy are translated immediately into time required for testing, and consequently the cost of testing, which makes the strategic choices manageable. If the time available for testing is more or less fixed, it is also possible to use test strategy combined with TPA to determine what can be achieved within the time limits. It is probably even more important to make it clear at this time which parts cannot be tested, or cannot be tested fully, and what risks will therefore be incurred.

11.3 Quality characteristics

Quality characteristics are the properties of an information system. These quality characteristics concern the information system as it is being used, but are also related to the maintenance and control of an information system.

- Does the system do all that is expected of it? Is the input processed correctly? Is everything processed, and is nothing processed twice? Is access to programs and/or data restricted to authorized people? Is the information in time for the activities and decisions for which it is required?
- To what extent is the system protected against faults? If a fault occur, how quickly and easily can it be corrected?
- How easy is it for users to (learn to) operate the system?
- How easy is maintenance and control, how quickly can it be carried out, and how much adaptation of the software is required? It is not merely a matter of adapting functionality but also of adapting the infrastructure and the interface to other systems. The reusability of (the design of) the software and the suitability of the infrastructure are also quality characteristics.

TMap distinguishes the following quality characteristics:
- connectivity
- continuity
- data controllability
- effectivity
- efficiency
- flexibility
- functionality
- (suitability of) infrastructure
- maintainability
- manageability
- performance
- portability
- reusability
- security
- suitability
- testability
- user-friendliness.

Appendix B gives a cross-reference between the quality characteristics of TMap and the quality characteristics of ISO 9126.

11.3.1 Connectivity

The ease with which a link with a different information system or within the information system can be made and modified. Connectivity is promoted greatly by using industry standards. It is tested by assessing the measures concerned with a checklist.

11.3.2 Continuity

The certainty that the information system will continue uninterruptedly, which means that it can be resumed within a reasonable period of time even after serious disruptions. The quality characteristic of continuity can be divided into characteristics that apply in this order for increasingly severe disruptions of the information system:

- *Operational reliability*. The degree to which the information system remains free from interruptions.
- *Robustness*. The degree to which the information system proceeds as usual, even after an interruption.
- *Recoverability*. The ease and speed with which the information system can be restored after an interruption.
- *Degradation possibilities*. The ease with which the core of the information system can continue after a part has failed.
- *Possibility of diversion*. The ease with which (part of) the information system can continue elsewhere.

Continuity is usually tested statically by assessing the set-up and existence of the continuity measures on the basis of a checklist, but it can also be tested dynamically implicitly by collecting metrics during the execution of dynamically explicit tests.

11.3.3 Data controllability
The ease with which the correctness and completeness of the information (in the course of time) can be checked. Well-known means to improve data controllability include check totals, quadratic counts and audit trails. Data controllability can be tested statically for the set-up of the measures concerned by using a checklist, or dynamically explicitly for the implementation of the measures concerned in the system.

11.3.4 Effectivity
The degree to which the information system meets the demands of the organization and the profile of the end users for whom it is intended, as well as the degree to which the information system contributes to the achievement of business objectives. An effective information system is reflected in increased efficiency of business processes. Will a new system work in practice? Ultimately, it is only the user organization that can answer that question. If the aspect of effectivity is recognized explicitly in the test strategy, then a separate test level must be set up to cater for it: the business simulation or test bed. During a business simulation, a random group of potential users tests the effectivity aspects of the product in an environment that resembles the 'natural' environment in which the system will be used as much as possible: the simulated production environment. The test takes place on the basis of a number of practice-oriented assignments or test scripts. Effectivity testing can therefore be qualified as dynamically explicit testing.

11.3.5 Efficiency
The relationship between the performance level of the system (expressed in the transaction volume and overall speed) and the number of resources (central processing unit cycles, disk access time, memory and network capacity, etc.) that are used. Efficiency is tested dynamically explicitly using the real-life test and/or dynamically implicitly by collecting metrics during the execution of tests aimed at functionality.

11.3.6 Flexibility
The degree to which the user may introduce extensions or modifications to the information system without changing the software itself. Or, the degree to which the system can be modified by the controlling organization without being dependent on the IT department for maintenance. Flexibility is tested by assessing the measures concerned with a checklist.

11.3.7 Functionality

The certainty that data processing is correct and complete, in accordance with the description in the functional specifications. The quality characteristic of functionality can be divided into correctness and completeness:

- *Correctness*. The degree to which the system processes the input and changes entered correctly, in accordance with the specifications, to produce consistent data sets.
- *Completeness*. The certainty that all inputs and changes are processed by the system.

In testing, achieving the specified functionality is often the most important criterion to proceed to acceptance of the information system. Various techniques can be used to test the functional operation dynamically explicitly.

11.3.8 Infrastructure

The suitability of hardware, network, systems software and database management system (DBMS) for the application concerned, and the degree to which the elements of this infrastructure inter-relate. This aspect can be tested in various ways (checklists, real-life test), but the tester's expertise with respect to the infrastructural elements concerned is always of major importance.

11.3.9 Maintainability

The ease with which the information system can adapt to new demands from the user, to changing external environments, or in order to correct defects. Insight in maintainability is gained, for example, by recording the average time (both elapsed time and hours of work time) it takes to solve a defect during testing. This is done by calculating the average effort (mean time to repair, MTTR) and deciding on its spread (if necessary per subsystem). Maintainability is also tested by assessing the internal quality of the information system by means of a checklist. Insight into the structure of the software (an aspect of maintainability) is obtained by carrying out static tests, preferably supported by static analysis tools.

11.3.10 Manageability

The ease with which the information system is maintained in its operational state. Manageability is aimed primarily at technical system control, often assigned to system management. Installability of the information system is part of manageability, as is de-installability in some cases. Manageability is measured by assessing the presence of measures and tools that facilitate control.

11.3.11 Performance

The speed with which the information system processes interactive and batch transactions. If this quality characteristic is chosen, it is often necessary to define special tests in which the performance can be measured in a representative way in a simulated production environment. Performance can be tested dynamically explicitly using the real-life test and/or dynamically implicitly by collecting metrics during the execution of tests aimed at functionality.

11.3.12 Portability
The diversity of the hardware and software platforms on which the information system can run, and how easy it is to transfer the system from one environment to another. Portability to a particular environment is quantified by expressing the adaptation costs as a percentage of the costs of rebuilding it for the new environment. The degree of portability is determined by using a checklist.

11.3.13 Reusability
The degree to which parts of the information system, or the design, can be reused for the development of different applications. If the system is based on reusable modules to a high degree, then this also benefits its maintainability. Reusability is tested by assessing the information system and/or the design by means of a checklist.

11.3.14 Security
The certainty that data can be viewed and changed only by those who are authorized to do so. Security can be explicitly tested dynamically by means of the semantic test specification technique, and statically by assessing the set-up and existence of the security measures on the basis of a checklist.

11.3.15 Suitability
The degree to which manual procedures match the automated information system and the fitness for use of these manual procedures for the organization. The aspect of timeliness is often included in suitability tests. Timeliness is defined as the degree to which the information is made available in time in order to take the measures for which this information was intended. Suitability is dynamically explicitly tested by means of the process cycle test.

11.3.16 Testability
The ease with which the functionality and performance level of the system (after each modification) are tested, and the speed at which this can be done. Testability in this case concerns the entire information system. The degree of testability of the documentation is measured statically by means of the 'review of the test basis' checklist during the preparation phase. There is also a checklist available to measure the testability of the information system as a whole.

11.3.17 User-friendliness
The ease with which end users use the system. This general definition is often divided into how easy it is for end users to learn to work with the information system and how easy it is for trained users to work with. It is difficult to find an objective and workable unit of measurement for user-friendliness. It is, however, often possible to express an (subjective) opinion in general terms concerning the

user-friendliness of the system. In the process of assessing the user-friendliness it is obvious that the end users play an important role. User-friendliness can be tested dynamically implicitly by collecting metrics during the execution of the functionality tests. After a certain test period, which concentrates in particular on semantic and syntactic tests, testers must complete a questionnaire on user-friendliness.

11.4 Procedure

In developing a test strategy we distinguish between a test strategy as part of a master test plan and as part of a test plan for a specific test level, e.g. acceptance test or system test. The procedure can be followed for both the development of new systems and the maintenance of existing systems. For the latter, however, it is best to make a few adjustments in the basic procedure (see section 11.4.4).

The development of a test strategy is not something that can be done purely methodically or formally. The experience and skills of the person performing this activity in the area of testing are a major success factor for a sound test strategy. The steps outlined below are aids and indicators.

One should also realize that test strategies arise as a result of iterative processes and in connection with other activities for a test plan. If the first test strategy produces an amount of necessary test effort or a time schedule that is unacceptable to the customer, the strategy should be adjusted. The lack of test skills or suitable infrastructure can also result in adjustments to the test strategy.

11.4.1 Strategy in master test planning
The steps to be taken for a test strategy in master test planning are:
1   Determine the quality characteristics.
2   Determine the relative importance of quality characteristics.
3   Assign quality characteristics to test levels.

Step 1: determine the quality characteristics
In close liaison with the customer and other parties involved, a selection of quality characteristics is made on which the tests must focus. In doing so, one should take into account risks for the business as well as aspects such as system requirements, business objectives concerning the information system, directions and standards set by system management. These quality characteristics are also used for reporting to the customer during test execution and completion.

During this activity, it is determined which of the quality characteristics mentioned above are included in the tests to be executed. Some characteristics are difficult to test. The customer may want the system to be user-friendly and flexible, for instance, but these wishes then turn out not to have been translated into measurable requirements. This is why a substantial part of the effort here is devoted to formulating – albeit afterwards – the relevant quality demands as measurably and unambiguously as possible. It is also the case that some quality characteristics demand a relatively large effort in testing. Since it is not useful to offer possibilities that cannot be fulfilled, it should be determined beforehand what the estimated effort needed for a decision to be made will be.

For non-IT people, the quality characteristics as described above may be hard to handle. The concepts must be livened up. This can be done by finding illustrative examples of failures that may occur in production and the damage that would be caused by such failure. This is one of the most difficult aspects of the formulation of a test strategy.

Step 2: determine the relative importance of quality characteristics

On the basis of the results from step 1, a decision is made about the importance of the selected quality characteristics in relation to one another. This is done in a matrix (Table 11.1) by weighting the relative risks per quality characteristic. Here, the relative importance is indicated (in percentages). Note that it is not important to have exact percentages: the objective is to arrive at a general picture of the relative importance of the various quality characteristics. Filling in the matrix helps to evaluate the risks.

The customer should be forced to make choices. Therefore, as a directive we stipulate five per cent as the minimum. The sum of all the percentages should not exceed 100.

Table 11.1

Matrix of relative importance of quality characteristics

Quality characteristic	Relative importance
Connectivity	–
Continuity	10
Data controllability	–
Effectivity	–
Efficiency	–
Flexibility	–
Functionality	50
(Suitability of) infrastructure	–
Maintainability	5
Manageability	5
Performance	5
Portability	–
Reusability	–
Security	5
Suitability	10
Testability	–
User-friendliness	10
Total	**100%**

Notice the high percentage for functionality in this matrix. This conforms with practical experience: generally 50 per cent or more of the importance is attributed to this characteristic. The reason for this is that risks are usually larger for incorrect performing systems (functionality) than for slow systems (performance) or awkward systems (user-friendliness).

Step 3: assign quality characteristics to test levels

As stated in Chapter 7, evaluations such as inspections and reviews can also be included in the scope of the master test plan, and hence the strategy development. Throughout this chapter, we use the term 'testing' to mean 'testing and evaluating'.

With the aim of making the total test effort as efficient as possible, it is decided during test strategy development which test level or combination of levels the various selected quality characteristics will be tested with. In this way, the various test levels within a project are brought into balance. It is obvious that the different responsibilities and authorities remain intact.

A plus sign in a matrix indicates whether the test strategy takes a quality characteristic into account; two or three plus signs indicate that relatively more attention is to be paid to the quality characteristic for the specified test level. It is obvious that one quality characteristic can be in effect for more than one test level, but depth will often vary. If structured test-specification techniques are used, the acceptance test, for example, may use results of previous tests levels, on the basis of which it may be decided to test with less depth. There is, of course, a relation between the relative importance and the number of plus signs given to a characteristic; however, this relation is subjective, not mathematical.

In Table 11.2, manageability has a relative importance of 5 and has five plus signs. Continuity has twice the relative importance (10) but only four plus signs. The two pluses given to the production acceptance test (PAT) means that extensive (and expensive!) testing of continuity is to take place, whereas most pluses for testing manageability are given to the far less time-consuming inspections.

	Inspection/ review of requirements	Inspection/ review of functional specification	Inspection/ review of technical design	Unit test	Integration test	System test	Functional acceptance test	Production acceptance test	Relative importance
Continuity	+		+					++	10
Functionality	++	++		+	+	+++	++		50
Maintainability		+				+			5
Manageability	+	+	++					+	5
Performance		+					+	+	5
Security	+	+	+				+	+	5
Suitability	+	++					++		10
User-friendliness		+					++		10
Total									**100%**

Table 11.2 Example of a test strategy for test levels

11.4.2 Strategy for a test level

The steps that need to be taken in order to arrive at a test strategy for a specific test level are as follows:

1   Determine the quality characteristics.
2   Determine the relative importance of quality characteristics.
3   Divide the system into subsystems.
4   Determine the relative importance of subsystems.
5   Specify test importance per subsystem and quality characteristic.
6   Establish test techniques to be used.

The strategy determination for a specific test level naturally has the master test plan strategy as a basis. If a master test plan, including a test strategy, is there, then step 1 can be omitted and step 2 will be an easy and quick activity. Nevertheless, all the steps are discussed below, so the description can be used for both the situation in which there is no master test plan and the situation in which there is a master test plan (including a test strategy). In the latter case, the strategy development, as indicated above, will be less extensive.

Step 1: determine the quality characteristics
In collaboration with the customer and perhaps other parties concerned, the quality characteristics are determined on which the test will focus in relation to business risks. The same instructions apply as for the corresponding step from the strategy development for the master test plan. During the test and in the completion phase, results are reported on the basis of these quality characteristics.

Step 2: Determine the relative importance of quality characteristics
Based on the results of step 1, the relative importance of the selected quality characteristics is determined by weighting the risks per quality characteristic (Table 11.3). In order to force the customer to make choices, a value of five per cent is the minimum.

Although Table 11.3 is based on the master test plan example, the relative importance given to quality characteristics will differ from the latter because not all quality characteristics of the master test plan will be tested at this test level, but the number still has to total 100%. Secondly, if two characteristics with the same relative importance in the master test plan strategy both have to be tested at this test level, they do not have to be tested with the same relative importance at this test level.

Table 11.3
Matrix of relative
importance of quality
characteristics for a
specific test level

Quality characteristic	Relative importance
Functionality	50
Performance	5
Security	5
Suitability	20
User-friendliness	20
Total	**100%**

Step 3: divide the system into subsystems

During this and the following steps, the test strategy is refined further. This implies that the quality characteristics and their relative importance as indicated in the matrix are to be broken down for the combination of test-specification technique and subsystem, and then for test-specification technique and test unit.

The information system is divided into subsystems. Although the term 'subsystem' is used here and in the remainder of this chapter, this division can also be made using terms such as 'components' or 'functional areas'. The bottom line is that quality demands are not the same for individual parts of the system. Moreover, the various subsystems may have different risks for the organization. In principle, the division in subsystems is the same as that given in the design documentation. If we deviate from this, we must clearly indicate the motivation for this. Examples of alternative divisions are on the basis of extent of risk or on the basis of order of release by the developer. If a conversion module is there, this is to be treated as a separate subsystem. Often, the subsystem 'total system' is distinguished. This serves the purpose of indicating that some quality characteristics can be evaluated effectively only with the help of an integral test, testing the coherence of the various subsystems. In a later stage, the various subsystems are divided further into independent test units. For example, in a logistics system the subsystem 'sales' may be divided into the test units 'quotations' (all functions regarding quotations) and 'orders'.

Step 4: determine the relative importance of subsystems

On the basis of the result of the previous step, the relative importance (in percentages) of the subsystems should be indicated in the matrix. This is done by weighting the risks for each subsystem (Table 11.4). It is a matter not of exact percentages but rather of getting a general image of the importance of the subsystems as seen through the eyes of the customer and other parties concerned. This step helps in asking people to form an opinion.

Subsystem	Relative importance
1	30
2	15
3	20
Conversion	15
System	20
Total	**100%**

Step 5: specify test importance per subsystem and quality characteristic

Finally, a refinement is made by assessing the importance of the combination of quality characteristics and subsystems. For example, a refinement may be that user-friendliness is important (relative importance of 20), but this holds predominantly for online subsystem 1 and not at all for batch subsystem 3. Again, it is emphasized that test strategy determination is not a mathematical affair: it is meant to get an image of the relative test importance of the various subsystems and quality characteristics. This is also the reason why we use plus signs as notational symbols, rather than opting for the pseudo-certainty of a mathematical formula. The matrix of weights may look something like Table 11.5:

	Subsystem 1	Subsystem 2	Subsystem 3	Conversion	Total system	Relative importance
Functionality	++	+	+	++	+	50
Performance	+		+			5
Security	+	+				5
Suitability	+	+	+		++	20
User-friendliness	++	+				20
Relative importance	30	15	20	15	20	**100%**

Step 6: establish test techniques to be used

The final step in test strategy involves the selection of the test-specification techniques that will be used to test the combination of the selected quality characteristics and subsystems. A high importance implies the use of techniques with a high coverage, or the use of more techniques; a low importance implies the use of techniques with a lower coverage, or the use of fewer techniques. The introduction to Chapter 15 discusses in detail the various depths of testing in relation to the test specification techniques. It also describes for each test-specification technique how the test coverage can be varied within a technique.

In addition to depth of testing, in choosing the techniques one should take into account various other factors, including:

- *Quality characteristic to be tested.* A technique is fit for testing one or more quality characteristics. Some quality characteristics are best tested with one set of techniques, while others are best tested with another one.
- *Area of application.* Some techniques are specifically suitable for testing the interaction (screens, reports, online) between the system and the users, while others are better used for testing the processing of systems (batch processes). There is a relation with the type of defect to be found with a technique, e.g. false input checks, incorrect processing or defects of integration. (See also the introduction to Chapter 15.)
- *Availability of test basis.* Each technique starts from a certain test basis. This may be the functional specification, the technical design, program code or descriptions of the end-user organization. The exact form of the test basis is also relevant to the choice of a technique, e.g. decision tables, pseudo-code, structured language or unstructured prose. (See also the introduction to Chapter 15.)
- *Extent of formality.* Informal test-specification techniques offer more freedom for the tester in making the test cases than do formal techniques, but they give fewer certainties on the test coverage achieved. (See also the introduction to Chapter 15.)
- *Use of resources.* The application of a technique requires a specific amount of resources, in terms of human and machine capacity. The use of resources has a direct relation with costs.
- *Required knowledge and skills.* Not every tester is able to use each technique. For the useful application of some techniques, much business knowledge is needed. For other techniques, more analytical talent is required. Therefore, the knowledge and skills of the test staff also influences the choice for techniques.

We distinguish three categories of techniques: dynamically explicit testing, dynamically implicit testing, and static testing.

Often, the way that the system functions is tested by means of specific test cases (dynamically explicit testing). There are various test-specification techniques available for this. Testing can also be done by collecting metrics during the development and test process (dynamically implicit testing) and/or by assessing the measures taken on the basis of a checklist (static testing).

Table 11.6 shows the techniques that are available for executing a test aimed at the quality characteristic. The aim should be to use a minimum set of techniques to cover all selected quality characteristics. For more information on the various techniques, refer to Chapters 15 and Chapter 16.

	AGT	CKL	DCoT	DCyT	DTT	ECT	EG	PCT	PIT	RLT	SEM	SP	STAT	SYN	TR
Connectivity		x													
Continuity		x								x			x		
Data controllability		x	x			x	x								
Effectivity							x					x			
Efficiency							x			x			x		
Flexibility		x													
Functionality	x		x	x	x	x	x		x	x				x	
(Suitability of) infrastructure		x							x						
Maintainability		x											x		
Manageability		x													
Performance							x			x			x		
Portability		x													
Reusability		x													
Security		x					x	x		x	x				
Suitability							x	x							
Testability		x													x
User-friendliness		x					x	x		x			x	x	

Table 11.6 Techniques available for executing tests

AGT, algorithm test; CKL, assessment using a checklist; DCoT, data combination test; DCyT, data cycle test; DTT, decision table test; ECT, Elementary comparison test; EG, error guessing; PCT, process cycle test; PIT, program interface test; RLT, real-life test; SEM, semantic test; SP, simulated production; STAT, assessment by collecting metrics; SYN, syntactic test; TR, testability review of the test basis.

In Table 11.6, error guessing appears to be an attractive technique because it can be applied to almost all quality characteristics. It should be noted, however, that this technique is merely unstructured testing on the basis of expert knowledge. Error guessing is therefore no more than a valuable complement to the structured test-specification techniques.

Although Table 11.6 shows that a large number of techniques is available, practice has shown that it is possible to make a quick selection of techniques by taking a number of factors into account. The knowledge and skills of the test manager are of great importance here. The selection of the test techniques must be made at an early stage of the test process. This makes it possible for the test team to be trained in the appropriate techniques if necessary, and for the required checklists to be adapted to the specific situation.

The result of this subactivity is the definition of the techniques to be used in the test for each subsystem. Optionally – in particular, in larger test projects – the test strategy is not specified in detail until the preparation phase by explicitly assigning techniques to test units. The order of priority of the tests to be executed is also determined, ensuring that the most important tests are executed at the earliest possible stage.

Example: test strategy for an acceptance test
The details of this test plan model are shown in Appendix A.

Quality characteristics
In collaboration with the assignor, the quality characteristics that are to be tested by the acceptance test of WOOF have been selected. The relative importance of these quality characteristics has been determined by weighting the risks per quality characteristic (Table 11.7).

Quality characteristic	Relative importance
Data controllability	5
Functionality	50
Performance	5
Security	10
Suitability	20
User-friendliness	10
Total	**100%**

Table 11.7
Relative importance of quality characteristics

Subsystems
Based on the general functional design and the test assignment, the following subsystems have been distinguished:
- Principal data, consisting of the processes:
  - maintaining factor (create, update, read);
  - authorization/removal of factor data;
  - maintaining age groups and tariff (create, update, read);
  - authorization/removal of age groups and tariff data;
  - reporting.
- Tax assessment data, consisting of the processes:
  - maintaining Grayhound citizen's data (create, update, read);
  - authorization/removal of Grayhound citizen's data;
  - create/report assessment register;
  - calculating the tax assessment;
  - viewing and deleting assessment register.

Based on the test assignment and the selected quality characteristics of the subsystems 'principal data' and 'tax assessment data', the 'entire system' is distinguished. This serves the purpose of indicating that some quality characteristics can be evaluated effectively only with the help of an integral test, testing the coherence of the various subsystems (Table 11.8).

Quality characteristic	Relative importance
Principal data	30
Tax assessment data	50
Entire system	20
Total	**100%**

Strategy matrix

In collaboration with the assignor, the relative importance within the information system is determined for each subsystem: a plus sign indicates that a particular quality characteristic is applicable for a particular subsystem, and two pluses indicate that relatively more attention is given to the combination of quality characteristic/subsystem.

Table 11.9 is the strategy matrix for the acceptance test of WOOF.

Quality characteristic	Principle data	Assessment data	Entire system	Relative importance (%)
Data controllability		++		5
Functionality	+	++		50
Performance		+	++	5
Security	++	+		10
Suitability			++	20
User-friendliness	+	++	+	10
Relative importance (%)	30	50	20	**100**

Test techniques per subsystem

Based on the strategy matrix, the characteristics of the various available test techniques and the characteristics of the distinguished subsystems, test techniques have been assigned to the subsystems (Table 11.10).

11.4.3 Strategy during the test process

The test strategy determined in advance will often be put under pressure in a later stage of the test project. In such a situation, the test manager is asked to perform fewer or shorter tests in order to conform to the adjusted schedule. The consequences are seen mainly in the last step of strategy development: suddenly, some tests must be cancelled or carried out in less depth. Using the test strategy as a basis, the test manager may discuss with the customer which tests can be dropped or where less thorough testing can be done. By indicating which parts are to be tested less in relation to the risks assessed (translated into importance levels in the strategy), the test manager can report in a solid fashion on the increased risks

Subsystem	Test techniques
Principal data	Checklist user-friendliness
	Data combination test
	Semantic test
Tax assessment data	Checklist data controllability
	Checklist user-friendliness
	Elementary comparison test
	Semantic test
	Statistics on performance
Entire system	Checklist user-friendliness
	Process cycle test
	Real-life test

Table 11.10
Test techniques
assigned to the
subsystems

after the testing phase. Therefore, it is essential not to change steps 1–5: the risks and the importance levels do not change. The result is that when testing is reduced, there will be more risks after the system has been implemented.

There is also the possibility that testing shows that part of the system contains an excessive number of (or excessively few) defects. Such a situation justifies adjustments in the test strategy, namely the increase or decrease of test effort. Contrary to the situation mentioned above, risks here will remain the same after implementation of the system. The correction can be summarized as follows: *testing should continue for as long as the costs for finding and correcting defects during testing are lower than the costs connected to the defect occurring in production.*

In finding and correcting defects, costs other than just test costs play a role, e.g. extensive costs may be concerned with the delay in shipping the product. For a defect occurring in production, one should also take into account the chance that the defect will actually occur: a defect that will never occur implies no risk.

11.4.4 Strategy during maintenance

The strategy-development technique described above can be used for new development without any reservation. The question that can be asked is to what extent these steps are useful during maintenance testing on an information system. This section discusses the (test) difference between new development and maintenance, and the consequences for strategy steps.

The main difference between the development of new systems and maintenance for the test strategy is the chance of a fault. In the case of maintenance, changes are made to an existing information system based on change proposals. These changes should be tested. During maintenance, there is a risk that new faults are introduced, with a decrease in quality for the system as a result. This phenomenon of quality degradation is called regression. It is also the reason for testing the parts of the system that have not changed.

This different chance of fault in the case of maintenance implies for the strategy that the relative importance of the subsystems may change: a subsystem that had a high importance when it was developed may be unchanged in maintenance. Since the chance of regression is the only risk in this case, the test importance is much lower. Therefore, test strategy development for a test level can be modified by changing the concept of 'subsystem' to 'change'. For each change, an analysis is carried out to discover which system parts were changed, which parts may have been influenced by the change, and which quality characteristics are relevant. There are various possibilities for testing each change, dependent on the risks:

- a limited test, focused only on the change;
- a complete (re)test of the function that had been changed;
- a test of the coherence of the changed function and the adjacent functions.

There should also be a regression test for the system as a whole. This test focuses on the integration between the changed and unchanged parts of the system, since the chance of regression is largest here. If the test strategy for the new developed system is available, then the importance levels attributed to the subsystems here can be of use. A regression test can be executed in part or in full, depending on the risks and the required test effort. The use of test tools is most effective in the execution of regression tests. The main advantage of automation of regression tests is that a full test can be executed each time with limited effort, and one need not decide which parts of the regression test will and will not be executed.

The decision to formulate the strategy either in terms of subsystems or change proposals is influenced by the number of change proposals and the part of the system affected by the changes. The more changes and the larger the part of the system affected, the stronger will be the preference to determine the test strategy at the level of subsystems rather than using change proposals. If a decision is made to use change proposals, the steps of the strategy development for a test level are as follows:

1 Determine changes (in the form of accepted change proposals and solved defects).
2 Determine the relative importance of changes and regression test.
3 Identify quality characteristics.
4 Determine the relative importance of quality characteristics.
5 Detail the test importance for each change/regression test and for each quality characteristic.
6 Determine the test techniques to be used.

Table 11.11 shows an example matrix for step 2. It shows that the regression test has been assigned a value of ten per cent because its importance is related to the test depth, not the test effort. It is true, however, that the total effort of this regression test is often much larger than the test effort required for detailed testing of the changes. The reason is that usually only a very small number of functions are changed during maintenance.

Table 11.11
Matrix of relative importance of changes and regression test

Change/regression test	Relative importance
Change proposal 1	20
Change proposal 2	20
Solved defect 1	20
...	30
Regression test of entire system	10
Total	**100%**

In addition to the changed chance of failure, there are other differences between new construction and maintenance. Although these do not affect the technique of strategy development, they do influence the final test strategy. Examples of other differences include:

- *Test basis is absent, incomplete, or not up to date.* This situation, which often occurs during maintenance, affects the selection of the test techniques.
- *Planned maintenance and emergency fixes.* Most of the maintenance can be planned, and the strategy development that has been described can be applied without restrictions. The situation is more difficult in the case of emergency fixes, when a production failure must be solved and the system should be operative again as quickly as possible. Formal strategy development is often too time-consuming here. It is possible, however, to develop a number of strategy scenarios beforehand: if program x fails and is being repaired, what should be tested then? These scenarios support the best possible test in the case of emergency fixes.

The steps do not change in the case of developing a strategy for a master test plan. In the assignment of the degree of importance, however, the different chance of failure is taken into account.

Test point analysis and estimation

12

12.1 Introduction

This chapter describes the test estimation technique known as test point analysis (TPA). TPA covers high-level testing. It can be used to objectively prepare an estimate for a system test or an acceptance test. An estimate for the test activities preceding high-level testing (i.e. activities during low-level testing) will already have been included in the estimate produced by function point analysis (FPA). FPA is a technique that calculates the functional size of an information system, and expresses the size in function points (FPs). The International Function Point User Group (IFPUG, 1994) developed a well-known method. Although sometimes an FPA also includes an estimate for high-level tests, this estimate is generally too rough. The huge difference between the estimates from TPA and FPA is that in TPA the risk-based test strategy is taken into account. In an FPA, high-level tests are included by increasing the productivity factor. This is like saying that testing takes $x\%$ of the development effort, regardless of the risks involved. To summarize, while the FPA productivity factor covers the program and integration testing, it lacks sufficient cover of system testing or acceptance testing.

TPA can also be used in cases where the test hour allowance has been predetermined. By performing a TPA, any risks involved can be identified clearly by comparing the objective TPA estimate with the predetermined number of test hours. With TPA, it is also possible to demonstrate the relative importance of the various functions, with a view to using the available testing time as effectively as possible.

There are estimation techniques other than TPA, and these are described at the end of this chapter. They may be used when there is no TPA available, or to check a TPA estimation. In order to get the best possible estimation, it is recommended that more than one test estimation technique is used in all cases.

12.2 Philosophy

When formulating an estimate for a high-level test, three elements are relevant: the size of the information system to be tested, the test strategy (selection of system components and quality characteristics to be tested and the coverage of testing), and the level of productivity. The first two elements together determine the volume of testing work to be undertaken (expressed in test points). If the number of test points is multiplied by the productivity (the amount of time needed to perform a given volume of testing work), then the result is a test estimate in hours. These three elements are considered in more detail below.

12.2.1 Size

For the purposes of TPA, the size of an information system is determined mainly by the number of function points assigned to it. However, a number of additions or adjustments need to be made because certain factors that have little or no influence on the number of function points are pertinent to testing. The factors in question are:

- *complexity*: this relates to the number of conditions in a function. More conditions almost always means more test cases, and therefore a larger volume of testing work;
- *interfacing*: the degree of interfacing of a function is determined by the number of data sets modified by a function, and the number of other functions that access those data sets. Interfacing is relevant because these other functions will require testing if the modifying function is changed;
- *uniformity*: it is important to consider the extent to which the structure of a function allows it to be tested using existing or slightly modified specifications, i.e. the extent to which the information system contains similarly structured functions.

12.2.2 Test strategy

During development or maintenance, quality requirements will have been specified for the information system. The test activities must determine the extent to which these requirements have been satisfied. In collaboration with the customer, the system and/or subsystem quality characteristics to be tested are identified and their relative importance determined. The importance of each characteristic influences the thoroughness of the related test activities. The more important a quality characteristic, the more exact and thorough the tests have to be, and the larger the volume of work. The importance of the various characteristics should be determined in consultation with the client when the test strategy is being formulated; the information can then be used as TPA input. In the course of the TPA process, the volume of testing work is calculated on the basis of the test strategy.

While certain general quality requirements apply to the information system as a whole, there are also differences between the various functions in terms of the requirements to be met. From the user's point of view, a data entry function that he or she utilizes throughout the day may be much more important than a batch processing function that creates a weekly report for management. For

each function, therefore, there are two (subjective) factors that influence the thoroughness of testing:
- user importance of the function
- use intensity.

As indicated previously, the importance attached to the various quality characteristics for testing purposes, and the importance of the various subsystems or functions, determines the test strategy. The test strategy specifies which quality characteristics are to be tested for each subsystem or function, and the relevant degree of coverage. Thus, TPA and strategy determination are related closely; in fact, in practice they are often performed at the same time.

12.2.3 Productivity
Productivity is not a new concept to anyone who has produced estimates on the basis of function points. In FPA, productivity is an expression of the relationship between the number of hours necessary for a task and the measured number of function points. In TPA, productivity relates to the time necessary to execute one test point. Productivity has two components:
- *Skill factor.* This is based on the knowledge and skill of the test team, and is therefore specific to the individual organization.
- *Environmental factor.* This indicates the degree to which the environment influences the test activities to which the productivity is related. Influential environmental considerations include, among other factors, the availability of test tools, the amount of experience the team has with the test environment, the quality of the test basis, and the availability of testware.

12.3 Global procedure

The TPA procedure is illustrated in Figure 12.1.

The number of test points necessary for testing the dynamically measurable quality characteristics is calculated for each function on the basis of:
- the number of function points assigned to the function;
- the function-dependent factors (complexity, interfacing, uniformity, user importance and use intensity);
- the quality requirements or test strategy for those quality characteristics that are tested dynamically.

The sum of the test points assigned to the individual functions is the number of dynamic test points.

The number of test points necessary for testing the statically measurable quality characteristics is calculated on the basis of the total number of function

Figure 12.1

Overview of test point
analysis

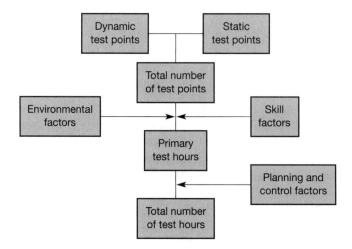

points for the information system and the quality requirements or test strategy
for those quality characteristics that are tested by means of static testing. This
produces the number of static test points.

The total number of test points is the sum of the dynamic and static test
points. The number of primary test hours can then be calculated by multiplying
the total number of test points by the calculated environmental factor and the
applicable skill factor. The primary test hours represent the volume of work
involved in the primary testing activities, i.e. the time required for completion
of the TMap phases preparation, specification, execution and completion.

Finally, the total number of test hours is obtained by adding an allowance
for secondary test activities (TMap phase planning and control) to the primary
number of test hours. The size of this allowance, which represents the volume
of work involved in the management activities, depends on the size of the test
team and the availability of management tools. The total number of test hours
is an estimate of the time required for all TMap test activities, excluding the
recording of the test plan.

12.4 Principles

In TPA the following principles apply:
- TPA is concerned only with the measurable quality characteristics that fall
  within the scope of acceptance testing and/or system testing. A characteristic is considered 'measurable' if an appropriate TMap test technique is
  available. Sufficient practical experience should already have been acquired
  using the test technique for the quality characteristic in question to allow
  the volume of work to be predicted reliably.

- The corollary of the first principle is that using the TPA technique in its present form, it is not possible to allow for all the quality characteristics that might be addressed by acceptance testing or system testing. The characteristics for which allowance cannot be made are those for which no predefined test technique exists (as yet), and those in relation to which insufficient practical experience has been acquired. It is likely that a subsequent version of the TPA system will cover more quality characteristics.
- TPA is, in principle, analyst-independent, i.e. if two people were to perform a TPA of the same information system, then they should obtain the same result. This is because clear rating definitions are provided for all factors that can be rated on an objective basis, while the customer determines all other factors.
- TPA depends on the availability of a function point count produced using IFPUG (1994). For TPA, the gross function point count is used as the basis for analysis.
- For TPA purposes, the test team's knowledge of the subject matter is not treated as a variable to affect the amount of work involved in the tests. Naturally, it is assumed that the team does have a certain amount of knowledge of the subject matter. Sufficient knowledge is thus a precondition that must be assumed at the test planning stage.
- TPA estimates are made on the assumption that, on average, one complete retest will be conducted. This implies that if one of the functions in a system needs more than one retest, this will have to be compensated for internally by other functions requiring no retest.

12.5 Test point analysis: details of the technique

12.5.1 Input and starting conditions

To conduct a TPA, one needs access to a functional design, consisting of detailed process descriptions and a logical data model, preferably including a create, read update and delete (CRUD) table. In addition, a function point count made using the IFPUG (1994) technique is necessary. A count made using either of these two techniques can be used as input for the TPA. However, when determining a skill factor from historical data, it is important that only one of these function point counting methods is used; different methods should not be combined. The choice for one of the function point counting techniques does not affect test point calculation, but it can influence the skill factor. For TPA purposes, the function point count is amended as follows:

- The function points for the various (logical) data sets defined within the function point count are assigned to the function(s) that provide(s) the input for those (logical) data sets.

- The function points for the various linked data sets defined within the function point count are assigned to the function(s) that use(s) those linked data sets.
- The number of function points for a clone-class FPA function is the same as the number of points assigned to the relevant original FPA function. A clone is an FPA function that has already been specified or developed within the same or another user function in the same project.
- The number of function points for a dummy-class FPA function is calculated if possible; otherwise, such functions are treated as being of an average complexity, and the corresponding number of function points is assigned. A dummy is an FPA function of which the functionality does not need to be specified or developed but which is nevertheless available because specification or development has been undertaken outside the project.

If no function point count is available but one is considered desirable (for TPA purposes), the time needed to carry out the count can be determined by counting the number of logical data sets, and multiplying by:

- 28 in the case of a system of low complexity (less than ten logical data sets);
- 35 in the case of a system of average complexity (10–25 logical data sets);
- 42 in the case of a highly complex system (more than 25 logical data sets).

This results in a rough estimation of the number of function points. The number is divided by 400 to obtain the number of days necessary for the count. (Note: it is generally considered possible to count 350–400 function points per day.)

12.5.2 Dynamic test points

The number of dynamic test points is the sum of the test points assigned to the individual functions. To calculate the test points for the individual functions, the influencing variables and factors are divided into two categories:

- function-dependent (D_f);
- quality requirements relating to the quality characteristics to be tested dynamically (Q_d).

The FPA function is used as the function unit. The calculation of user importance and use intensity is based largely on the user function as a means of communication. The importance that users attribute to the user function also applies to all underlying FPA functions.

Function-dependent factors

The various function-dependent factors and their associated ratings are described below. Listed ratings only should be selected; intermediate ratings are not allowed. If insufficient information is available to enable rating of a given factor, the nominal rating (that in bold type) should be assigned.

User importance
The user importance is an expression of the importance that the user attaches to a given function relative to the system's other functions. A useful rule of thumb is that about 25 per cent of functions should be placed in the 'high' importance category, 50 per cent in the 'normal' category, and 25 per cent in the 'low' category.

User importance is assigned to the functionality identified by the user. This means assigning user importance to the user function. The user importance of a function should, of course, be determined in close liaison with the sponsor and other representatives of the user organization.
Rating:
3   *Low*: the importance of the function relative to the other functions is low.
6   *Normal*: the importance of the function relative to the other functions is normal.
12 *High*: the importance of the function relative to the other functions is high.

Use intensity
Use intensity is defined as the frequency with which a certain function is processed by the users and the size of the user group that uses this function. As with user importance, use intensity is determined at a user function level.
Rating:
2   *Low*: the function is executed by the user organization a few times a day/week.
4   *Normal*: the function is executed by the user organization many times/ day.
8   *High*: the function is used continuously throughout the day.

Interfacing
Interfacing is an expression of the extent to which a modification in a given function affects other parts of the system. The degree of interfacing is determined by ascertaining first the logical data sets (LDSs) that the function can modify, then the other functions that access these LDSs. An interface rating is assigned to the function by reference to a table in which the numbers of LDSs affected by the function are ranged vertically, and the numbers of other functions accessing the LDSs are ranged horizontally (Table 12.1). When working out the number of other functions affected, a given function may be counted several times if it accesses several LDSs, all of which are maintained by the function for which the calculation is being made.

Table 12.1

Interface ratings

L, low interfacing;
A, average interfacing;
H, high interfacing.

LDS	Function		
	1	2–5	>5
1	L	L	A
2–5	L	A	H
>5	A	H	H

If a function does not modify any LDSs, it is given a low interface rating. A CRUD table is very useful for determining the degree of interfacing.

Rating:

2   The degree of interfacing associated with the function is low.
4   The degree of interfacing associated with the function is normal.
8   The degree of interfacing associated with the function is high.

Complexity

The complexity of a function is determined on the basis of its algorithm. The general structure of the algorithm may be described using pseudo-code, control flow diagrams or ordinary text. The complexity rating of the function depends on the number of conditions in the function's algorithm. When counting the conditions, only the processing algorithm should be considered. Conditions that are the result of database checks, such as domain validations or physical presence checks, are not taken into account, since these are included implicitly in the function point count.

Composite conditions such as 'IF a AND b, THEN' count twice, since without the AND statement, two IF statements would have been needed. Similarly, a CASE statement with *n* cases counts as *n*–1 conditions, since replacement of the 'CASE' statement with a series of 'IF' statements would result in *n*–1 conditions. To summarize, count the (simple) conditions, not the operators.

Rating:

3   The function contains no more than 5 conditions.
6   The function contains between 6 and 11 conditions.
12 The function contains more than 11 conditions.

Uniformity

Under the following circumstances, only 60 per cent of the test points assigned to the function under analysis count towards the system total:

● in the case of a second occurrence of a virtually unique function: in such cases, the test specifications can be largely reused;

● in the case of a clone function: the test specifications can be reused for clone functions;

- in the case of a dummy function (provided that reusable test specifications have already been drawn up for the dummy).

A uniformity factor of 0.6 is assigned in cases as described above; otherwise a uniformity factor of 1 is assigned. An information system may therefore contain functions that possess a degree of uniformity for test purposes, even though they are regarded as unique in the context of an FPA. In FPA, the term 'unique' applies to the following:

- a function that uses a combination of data sets that is not used by any other input function;
- a function that, although it does not use a unique combination of data sets, uses a unique processing technique (e.g. a unique method of updating a data set).

Conversely, an information system may contain functions that, although they are regarded as completely uniform in the context of an FPA and therefore do not warrant any function points, do count in TPA since they need to be tested. Clones and dummies come under this heading.

Method of calculation
The D_f factor is calculated by adding the ratings for the first four function-dependent variables (user importance, use intensity, interfacing and complexity) and dividing the sum by 20 (the nominal rating). The result should then be multiplied by the uniformity factor. A D_f factor is calculated for each function.

$$D_f = \frac{(Ue + Uy + I + C)}{20} \times U$$

Where D_f = weightings factor for the function-dependent factors, Ue = user importance, Uy = use intensity, I = interfacing, C = complexity, and U = uniformity.

Standard functions
If, as is often the case, the function point count includes the error report function, help-screen function and/or menu structure function, then standard numbers of test points can be assigned, as indicated in Table 12.2.

Function	FPs	Ue	Uy	I	C	U	D_f
Error message	4	6	8	4	3	1	1.05
Help screens	4	6	8	4	3	1	1.05
Menus	4	6	8	4	3	1	1.05

Table 12.2
Standard test points

Dynamic quality characteristics (Qd)

We now describe how the requirements relating to dynamically measurable quality characteristics are taken into account in the TPA process. In this context, a distinction is made between implicitly and explicitly measurable quality characteristics.

In TPA, four dynamically, explicitly measurable quality characteristics are recognized:

- functionality
- performance
- security
- suitability/effectivity (no distinction has (yet) been made between these characteristics, since there are no testing techniques available with this level of accuracy).

The importance of the requirements relating to each quality characteristic is rated. If necessary, this is done separately for each subsystem.

Rating:

0   Quality requirements are not important and are therefore disregarded for test purposes.

3   Quality requirements are relatively unimportant, but they do need to be taken into consideration for test purposes.

4   Quality requirements are of average importance (this rating is generally appropriate
when the information system relates to a support process).

5   Quality requirements are very important (this rating is generally appropriate when
the information system relates to a primary process).

6   Quality requirements are extremely important.

The dynamic, explicitly measurable quality characteristics have the following weightings factors:

Functionality	=	0.75
Performance	=	0.10
Security	=	0.05
Suitability	=	0.10

Where high-level tests are concerned, the elementary comparative test (ECT), data combination test (DCoT), semantic test (SEM) and syntactic test (SYN) are available for testing the quality characteristics of suitability. The SEM is available for testing security. The process cycle test (PCT), software usability measurement inventory (SUMI) (Kirakowski and Corbett, 1993), Use case techniques (Jacobson, 1992) and usability laboratory test (Nielsen, 1993) are available for testing suitability. The real-life test (RLT) is available for testing performance. Table 12.3 below shows how the choice for test-specification techniques is often related to the rating given to the quality characteristics.

Rating	3	4	5	6
Functionality				
Processing	DCoT and error guessing	DCoT	ECT and DCoT	ECT*
Screen checks	Error guessing	Sample SEM and error guessing	Sample both SEM and SYN	SEM and sample SYN
Performance	The thoroughness of the RLT is variable and will thus be determined by the rating and the amount of time that becomes available as a consequence			
Security	Error guessing	SEM sample user profiles	SEM user profiles	SEM user profiles and overall system**
Suitability	Error guessing and SUMI	Use cases or PCT and SUMI	Use cases or PCT and SUMI	PCT and usability laboratory test

Table 12.3
Choice of test-specification techniques according to the rating given to the quality characteristics

* ECT is a more thorough technique than DCoT, so testing all functions with ECT is more thorough than testing some functions with ECT and others with DCoT, as is done for rating 5.
** If the security characteristic is given a rating of 6, then the SEM should be used to examine the user profiles and associated access privileges for both the information system to be tested and the infrastructure or information network as a whole.

One has to determine which quality characteristics will be tested dynamically implicitly. A statement regarding these quality characteristics can be made by gathering data during test execution. ISO-9126 part 2 'External Metrics' can be used as a source of information or inspiration for this. For instance, performance can be tested explicitly applying the real-life test, or implicitly by gathering data and establishing metrics. The dynamic implicit quality characteristics need to be specified. Subsequently, the number of quality characteristics can be determined to which external metrics will be applied. Per characteristic a rating of 0.02 is applicable in the context of Q_d.

Method of calculation

The rating for each dynamically, explicitly measurable quality characteristic is divided by 4 (the nominal rating), then multiplied by the weightings factor. The ratings calculated for the four dynamically, explicitly measurable quality characteristics are then added.

If certain dynamically, implicitly measurable quality characteristics are to be included in the test, the appropriate weightings (0.02 for each characteristic) should be added to the result obtained for the dynamically, explicitly measurable quality characteristics. The figure calculated is the Q_d factor. Normally, a single Q_d factor can be calculated for the system as a whole. However, if different test strategies are to be used for the various subsystems, a separate Q_d factor calculation should be done for each subsystem.

Dynamic test point formula

The number of direct test points is the sum of the test points assigned to the individual functions. This can be calculated by entering the data obtained so far into the following formula:

$$TP_f = FP_f \times D_f \times Q_d$$

Where TP_f = the number of test points assigned to the function, FP_f = number of function points assigned to the function, D_f = the weightings factor for the function-dependent factors, and Q_d = the weightings factor for the quality characteristics.

12.5.3 Static test points

The static test point count depends mainly on the function point count for the system as a whole. The static test point count is also influenced by the requirements regarding the quality characteristics to be tested statically (the Q_s factor).

One has to determine whether the statically measurable quality characteristics are relevant for test purposes. A static test can be carried out using a checklist. In principle, all quality characteristics can be tested using a checklist. The standard number of test points for applying a checklist is 16 per quality characteristic. For example, security can be measured dynamically using a semantic test, and/or statically by evaluating the security measures with the aid of a checklist.

Method of calculation

If a quality characteristic is tested by means of a checklist (static test), the factor Q_s will have a value of 16. For each subsequent quality characteristic to be included in the static test, another value of 16 is added to the Q_s factor rating.

12.5.4 Total number of test points
The total number of test points assigned to the system as a whole is calculated by entering the data obtained so far into the following formula:

$$ TP = \sum TP_f + \frac{(FP \times Q_s)}{500} $$

Where TP = the total number of test points assigned to the system as a whole, $\sum TP_f$ = the sum of the test points assigned to the individual functions (dynamic test points), FP = the total number of function points assigned to the system as a whole (minimum value 500), and Q_s = the weightings factor for the statically measurable quality characteristics.

12.5.5 Primary test hours
The formula presented in section 12.5.4 produces the total number of test points assigned to the system as a whole. This total number of test points is a measure of the volume of the primary test activities. The primary number of test points is multiplied by the skill factor and the environmental factor in order to obtain the primary test hour count. The primary test hour count is the number of hours required for carrying out the test activities involved in the TMap phases preparation, specification, execution and completion.

Skill factor
The skill factor represents the number of test hours required per test point. The higher the skill factor, the larger the number of test hours required. The skill factor is a measure of the experience, knowledge and skill of the test team. It may vary from one organization to the next, or from one organizational unit to the next. Skill factors can be calculated by analyzing completed test projects, thus historical data on such projects are necessary for the determination of skill factors. In practice, the skill factor has shown to have a value between 0.7 and 2.0.

Environmental factor
The number of test hours required for each test point is also influenced by the environmental factor. A number of environmental variables are defined for calculation of the environmental factor. These, and the associated ratings, are described below. Again, one of the ratings given must be selected; intermediate ratings are not allowed. If insufficient information is available to enable rating of a given variable, then the nominal rating (in bold type) should be assigned.

Test tools
The test tools variable reflects the extent to which the testing activities are being supported by test tools. For the purpose of calculating this variable, the term 'test tools' covers tools that are used for the primary test activities.

The availability of test tools means that some of these activities can be performed automatically and therefore more quickly. However, the availability of test tools is no guarantee; effective use of these tools is what matters.

Rating:

1   During testing, a supporting tool for test specification *and* a test execution tool are used effectively.

2   During testing, a supporting tool for test specification is used effectively *or* a test execution tool is effectively used.

4   No test tools are available.

Preceding tests

This variable reflects the quality of preceding tests. If an estimate is prepared for an acceptance test, then the preceding test will have been the system test. If the estimate is for a system test, then the preceding tests will have been low-level tests. The quality of these preceding tests influences the amount of functionality that may require less thorough testing with less coverage, as well as the duration of the test activities – the better the preceding tests have been performed, the less likely one is to encounter problems during the test under consideration.

Rating:

2   A plan for the preceding test is available, and the test team is familiar with the actual test cases and test results.

4   A plan for the preceding test is available.

8   No plan for the preceding tests is available.

Test basis

The test basis variable reflects the quality of the (system) documentation upon which the test under consideration is to be based. The quality of the test basis influences the amount of time required for the preparation and specification phases.

Rating:

3   During system development, documentation standards and templates are being used. In addition, reviews are organized.

6   During system development, documentation standards and templates are being used, but their use is not checked in any formal way.

12   The system documentation was not developed using specific standards and templates.

Development environment

The development environment variable reflects the nature of the environment within which the information system was developed. In this context, the degree to which the development environment will have prevented errors and inappropriate working methods is of particular importance. If errors of a given type cannot be made, it is not necessary to test for them.

Rating:

2 The system was developed using a 4 GL programming language with an integrated database management system (DBMS) containing numerous constraints.

4 The system was developed using a 4 GL programming language, possibly in combination with a 3 GL programming language.

8 The system was developed using only a 3 GL programming language (such as COBOL, PASCAL or RPG).

Test environment

The test environment variable reflects the extent to which the test infrastructure – in which testing is to take place – has previously been tried out. In a well-tried test infrastructure, fewer problems and delays are likely during the execution phase.

Rating:

1 The environment has been used for testing several times in the past.

2 The test is to be conducted in a newly equipped environment similar to other well-used
environments within the organization.

4 The test is to be conducted in a newly equipped environment, which may be considered experimental within the organization.

Testware

The testware variable reflects the extent to which the tests can be conducted using existing testware. The availability of usable testware influences mainly the time required for the specification phase.

Rating:

1 A usable, general initial data set (tables, etc.) and specified test cases are available for the test.

2 A usable, general initial data set (tables, etc.) is available for the test.

4 No usable testware is available.

Method of calculation

The environmental factor (E) is calculated by adding together the ratings for the various environmental variables (test tools, development testing, test basis, development environment, test environment and testware) and subsequently dividing the sum by 21 (the sum of the nominal ratings). Normally, one environmental factor is worked out for the system as a whole, but separate factors can be calculated for the individual subsystems if appropriate.

Primary test hours formula

The number of primary test hours is obtained by multiplying the number of test points by the skill factor and the environmental factor:

$$PT = TP \times S \times E$$

Where PT = the total number of primary test hours, TP = the total number of test points assigned to the system as a whole, S = the skill factor, and E = the environmental factor.

12.5.6 Total number of test hours

Since every test process involves tasks that may be placed under the heading 'planning and control', allowance needs to be made for such activities. The number of primary test hours and the planning and control allowance together give the total number of test hours. The standard (nominal) allowance is ten per cent. However, the allowance may be increased or decreased in line with the following two factors:

- team size
- management tools.

Team size

The team size factor reflects the number of people making up the team (including the test manager and, where appropriate, the test controller).
    Rating:
3   The team consists of no more than four people.
6   The team consists of between five and ten people.
12   The team consists of more than ten people.

Management tools

The management or planning and control tools variable reflects the extent to which automated resources are to be used for planning and control.
    Rating:
2   Both an automated time registration system and an automated defect tracking system (including configuration management) are available and are applied.
4   Either an automated time registration system or an automated defect tracking system (including configuration management) is available and is applied.
8   No automated (management) systems are available.

Method of calculation

The planning and management percentage is obtained by adding together the ratings for the two influencing factors (team size and management tools). The allowance in hours is calculated by multiplying the primary test hour count by this percentage. Addition of the planning and control allowance to the number of primary test hours gives the total number of test hours.

12.5.7 Distribution over phases

The result of a TPA is an estimate for the complete test process, excluding the writing of the test plan. According to TMap, the test process is divided into five phases. Many customers will want to see estimates for the individual phases, as well as for the complete test process. The estimate for the planning and control phase will normally be the same as the planning and control allowance, i.e. the primary test hour count multiplied by the planning and control percentage. The primary test hours are then divided between the preparation, specification, execution and completion phases. The breakdown between the phases may, of course, vary from one organization to another, or even from one organizational unit to another. Suitable phase percentages can be calculated by analyzing completed test projects, thus historical data on such projects are necessary for breaking down the total estimate.

Experience with the TPA technique and TMap suggests that the following percentages are generally appropriate:

Preparation   =   10%
Specification   =   40%
Execution   =   45%
Completion   =   5%.

12.6 Test point analysis at an early stage

A test project estimate is often needed at an early stage. Until detailed functional specifications are obtained, however, it is not possible to determine factors such as complexity and interfacing. Nevertheless, a rough FPA can often be performed on the basis of very general specifications. If a rough function point count is available, a rough TPA can be performed as well.

For a rough TPA, a single function is defined of which the size is determined by the total (gross) function point count. All function-dependent factors (user importance, user intensity, complexity, interfacing and uniformity) are usually assigned the neutral value, so that D_f has a value of 1. A TPA can then be carried out as described in section 12.5. The environmental factor will often have to be based on assumptions; any such assumptions should be clearly documented and recorded on the test estimate when it is presented to the customer.

12.7 Test point analysis calculation example

In Appendix A, a complete TPA calculation has been included. The paragraph below gives only a small example.

An information system has two user functions and one internal logical data set:

Registration: 11 function points, broken down between the FPA functions as follows:

Input   3 function points
Update   4 function points
Delete   4 function points

Processing: 12 function points, broken down between the FPA functions as follows:

Output 1   5 function points
Output 2   7 function points

Seven function points are assigned to the internal logical data set 'data'; for the TPA, these are added to the input function.

12.7.1 Calculation of the dynamic test points

Calculating the function-dependent variables (D_f):

	Registration	**Processing**
User importance	6	12
User intensity	8	2
Interfacing	2	2
Complexity	3	6
Uniformity	1	1
$D_f =$	$19/20 \times 1 = 0.95$	$22/20 \times 1 = 1.10$

(In this example, it is assumed that the interface and complexity ratings are the same for the FPA functions within a given user function.)

Calculating the dynamically measurable quality characteristics (Q_d):

Functionality	5	$5/4 \times 0.75 = 0.94$
Performance	0	
Security	4	$4/4 \times 0.05 = 0.05$
Suitability	0	

Dynamic implicit testing (gathering metrics) is carried out for:

Efficiency	$= 0.02$
Maintainability	$= 0.02$
Performance	$= 0.02$

$$Q_d = 0.94 + 0.05 + (3 \times 0.02) = 1.05$$

Calculating the number of dynamic test points:

	FP_f	D_f	Q_d	=	TP_f
Registration	18	0.95	1.05	=	18
Processing	12	1.10	1.05	=	14
Total number of dynamic test points					32

12.7.2 Calculation of static test points

Static testing is carried out for:

Reliability = 16
Qs = 16

Calculation of the total number of test points:

$$TP = \Sigma\, TP_f \; + \; \frac{(FP \times Q_s)}{500}$$

$$TP = 32 + \frac{(500 \times 16)}{500} = 48$$

12.7.3 Calculation of the number of primary test hours

Skill factor:

The skill factor for this organization is 1.2.

Environmental factor:

The ratings given to the various environmental variables are as follows:

Test tools = 4	(no test tools)
Development testing = 4	(a system test plan is available)
Test basis = 3	(documentation template and inspections)
Development environment = 4	(4 GL (Oracle) in combination with COBOL)
Test environment = 1	(proven environment)
Testware = 4	(no usable testware available)

$$E = 20/21$$
$$= 0.95$$

$$PT = TP \times S \times E$$

$$\text{Primary test hours (PT)} = 48 \times 1.2 \times 0.95$$
$$= 54.72$$

12.7.4 Calculation of the planning and control allowance

Team size = 3   (the team consists of two people)
Planning and control tools = 4   (automated time registration is available)

Planning and control allowance = 7%.

12.7.5 Calculation of the total number of test hours

Primary test hours   = 55
P & C allowance   = 55 × 0.07 = 3.85 (rounded off to 4)

Total number of test hours = 55 + 4 = 59

12.8 Other estimation techniques

We present here a list of global test-estimation techniques. When applying these techniques, we make use of experience data. These data generally differ from one organization to the next. For a methodological approach to gathering experience data, refer to Chapter 23.

12.8.1 Time spent in design/development phase

In an organization with a standard approach to system development, the hours spent on functional design, construction and functional test over more than one project may turn out to be constant. When the number of hours spent on functional design is known, a first estimation of the test hours is feasible. When design and construction have been accomplished, a more precise estimation of the test hours can be carried out. This way of estimating may also be used in the case of maintenance for estimating the number of hours needed for testing the adjustments only.

12.8.2 Extrapolation

Extrapolation is a useful means of estimating if the test project has already started. If it is known how many functions there are to be tested, then the test specifications for one function are made. Suppose that this will take five hours and there is a total of 80 functions to be tested; then, 400 hours are needed for the complete test specification. On the assumption that test specification takes up 40 per cent of the total testing time, this produces a total of 1000 hours of testing time.

As soon as more data become available for these 80 functions (e.g. distribution in the three classes, light, average and heavy) and a few functions of each class have been specified, the estimate will become more reliable.

12.8.3 Quantitative data in test basis

In the event that no data are available on the hours spent during design, and there are no metrics, different ways of estimating are needed. In such cases it is possible to estimate the test project using the number of user requirements or even the number of pages of which the test basis consists or the number of words in the (functional) design. By measuring in practice how much time a test project takes for a given quantification of the test basis, an average test effort per unit test basis can be computed. This can be used for future test projects.

12.8.4 Data model

This method is derived from the previous one, and estimates on the basis of the number of entities and attributes in the data model. The number of test hours is related to the number of entities or attributes. This produces the number for the average test effort per entity or attribute, and can thus be used for future test projects.

12.8.5 Number of screens and fields

Another method derived from estimating on the basis of the data model is performing an estimate based on the number of screens and screen fields. This is a particularly convenient method for a user acceptance test.

12.8.5 Quantitative data in test object

If the application has been constructed, then the test project may be estimated from the number of kilo lines of code (KLOC). However, this is useful only if the application has been built before test activities commence. On the other hand, one can re-estimate halfway through the test project at the moment the KLOC data become available. There should be any empirical statistic from which test hours can be derived. This statistic may depend on the environment, such as the organization, development tools and test techniques used.

Testability review of the test basis

13

13.1 Introduction

During the planning phase, the test team determines which documentation to use as the test basis. During the preparation phase, the testability of this test basis is assessed using the review technique described in this chapter. Testability in this case means the completeness, unambiguousness and consistency of the documentation on which the test is based. Good testability is an important condition for successful progress during the actual specification of the tests. The review is, in fact, an audit of the test basis, in order to determine whether the quality of the documentation is sufficient to serve as a reference for testing.

Another important reason for carrying out a testability review is that potentially costly defects are found at an early stage of the development and test process. The test basis can be regarded as the technical specification of the system. Anything that is not included in the test basis is left to be solved by the development team, which develops the new information system on the basis of the documentation. This documentation may contain defects, which, if they are not discovered on time, may result in a large amount of costly correction work. The sooner a defect is found in a development process, the simpler it is to rectify. For example, if a specification defect is not discovered until the execution of the acceptance test, then rectification costs will be considerable; then not only will the software have to be adapted, but so will the technical and functional design.

13.2 Procedure

The following steps must be taken within the framework of a testability review of the test basis:

1   Selecting relevant documentation.
2   Composing a checklist.
3   Assessing documentation on testability.
4   Reporting.

13.2.1 Selecting relevant documentation

In principle, the test plan identifies the documentation to be used for deriving test cases. However, changes may have occurred since writing the test plan. At this point, the test team identifies the correct test basis. Finally, the various components of the test basis are actually collected.

13.2.2 Composing a checklist

To be able to check the documentation for testability, a checklist should be used. This is dependent on the selected test-specification techniques, the type of documentation, and the quality characteristics to be tested. In the remainder of the description of this technique, we will indicate which specific aspects may be reviewed for the various test-specification techniques and a number of dynamically testable quality characteristics. These checklists may be combined into a single checklist for the testability review of the test basis. It is also possible to use the general checklists for the high-level and low-level tests, which are also included in this chapter. Establishing one checklist prevents the same parts of the test basis from being reviewed more than once.

The diversity of types of documentation makes it impossible to compose one general checklist that applies to every test type. For each organization, and possibly each project, a checklist should be composed for each test type. The following description of checklists may be useful in this respect.

13.2.3 Assessing documentation on testability

On the basis of the composed checklist, the test team assesses the documentation and records test basis defects by means of a defect report. On the basis of the testability review, early defect detection will improve the quality of the test basis. It also creates a thorough insight into the nature and size of the information system. This justifies a relatively great effort.

13.2.4 Reporting

On the basis of the individual test basis defects, the test team writes a testability review report. This report provides a general summary with regard to the quality and/or the testability of the documentation. Possible consequences of insufficient quality should also be described. The following sections are distinguished in the testability review report:

- *Formulating the assignment.* Identification of the test basis, and descriptions of the client and the supplier, i.e. the people responsible for executing the assignment. The test manager is likely to be the supplier.
- *Conclusion.* The conclusion with regard to the testability of the reviewed documentation and any related consequences and/or risks: has the test basis sufficient quality to ensure that specifying tests will be useful?
- *Recommendations.* Recommendations with regard to the present documentation and any structural recommendations to improve the quality of future documentation.

- *Defects*. The defects found are described, or the related defect report is referred to.
- *Appendix*. The checklist used.

13.3 Test-specification techniques checklist

For a description of each test-specification technique, to chapter 15.

13.3.1 Algorithm test

The structure of an algorithm is tested in an algorithm test. The desired test basis is a flow chart, a decision table or a Nassi–Shneiderman diagram complemented by a description. The following checklist can be used to check the documentation:

- Have the (program) algorithms been described (e.g. in the form of a flow chart, decision table or Nassi–Shneiderman diagram)?
- Is the triggering event indicated clearly? (i.e. when should the algorithm be started)?
- Is it indicated clearly which data are being used, and what the source is?
- Is the result of the algorithm clear?
- Have the various decision points been described, including the accompanying conditions?

13.2.2 Data cycle test

The data cycle test focuses on the lifecycle of data. The create, read, update and delete (CRUD) matrix thus forms an essential part of the test basis. If this matrix is not present, it must be created to enable the drafting of the test specification within the framework of the data cycle test. The following checklist can be used to check the test basis for the data cycle test:

- Is a CRUD matrix present?
- Can every entity be entered, viewed, changed and deleted?
- Is it clear in which function(s) an entity can be entered, viewed, changed or deleted?
- Are all entities described?
- Is there an entity diagram (entity relationship diagram, ERD)?
- Have the relationships between the various entities been described?
- Have the referential relation checks for the relations been described?

13.3.3 Data combination test

As the data combination test is a less formal method, the demands on the test basis are also less strict. The following checklist can be used to check the specifications:

- Have the various screen and print layouts been described?
- Has the method of processing the functions been described, including the input, output and the decision paths?

- Have the relationships between the various functions been described?
- Is there a dialog design (screen sequences, menus)?

13.3.4 Decision table test

Using the decision table test, the processing of a program or function is tested in a highly formal manner. This test-specification technique demands a high-quality test basis. The following checklist can be used to check the design specifications:

- Have the triggering events of the process been indicated clearly (this concerns events originating from the user, an external system, or an internal function and/or program)?
- Has the processing method been described in such a way that the various processing paths can be recognized?
- Are the determinants (factors) that influence the process clearly recognizable, and have these been described?
- Is the output of the process clear, and is it possible to predict results?

13.3.5 Elementary comparison test

The elementary comparison test concerns the description of the (logical) processing of data. The description of processing may use pseudo-code and/or decisions tables. With respect to the elementary comparison test, the following checklist can be used to check the specifications:

- Has the processing method been described in such a way that the various processing paths can be recognized?
- Is it clear under which conditions each processing path must be taken?
- Has processing been described unambiguously, including input and output?
- Has processing been described for each input item?

13.3.6 Error guessing

A specific review on certain aspects of the test basis is not necessary in order to use the error guessing test technique. It is important that a thorough understanding of the (sub)system to be tested can be obtained from the documentation. This insight can also be gained from carrying out structured tests in connection with error guessing.

13.3.7 Process cycle test (suitability)

The test basis for the process cycle test consists mainly of descriptions of procedures and related forms. Preferably, flow charts should be added to the procedure descriptions. The following checklist can be used to check the procedure descriptions present:

- Have all manual procedures to be executed by users been described?
- Has the responsibility as well as authority for each manual task been described?

- Has a description been made of the individual tasks?
- Have the security aspects of this procedure been described?
- Is the triggering event indicated clearly? (i.e. when should the procedure be started)?
- Has it been indicated which data (forms) are to be used, and what their source is?
- Have the activities to be carried out been described, including exceptions and checks?
- Is the result of every procedure clear?
- Have the various decision points been described, including any related conditions?
- Has a distinction been made between end-user procedures and system-user procedures?
- Have the relationships between the automated and the non-automated parts of the information system been described?
- Is the (draft) user manual available?

13.3.8 Program interface test

The program interface test focuses on the interaction between two programs and/or modules. The basic principle is that the programs to be integrated should function properly independently of each another. In a program interface test, the simulated data flows are replaced by real data flows. The following checks can be carried out on the test basis within the framework of this test-specification technique:

- Has the processing of individual programs been described, including input and output?
- Have the locations of the interfaces been indicated?
- Has the relationship between the various programs been described?
- Has processing been described for each of the items entered?
- Has it been indicated which attributes belong to the entities involved in the interfaces?
- Has the domain of the data crossing the interface been described (type, range, values permitted, any special validity rules)?

13.3.9 Real-life test (including performance and efficiency)

All documentation regarding the operational use of the system is collected, including the system requirements specified during the various system-development phases. With regard to the real-life test, it should be assessed for the testability review of the test basis whether the system documentation that is present provides a sufficient degree of insight into the future use of the system. This includes the number of users, the intensity of use, and the daily, weekly and monthly cycles. The following questions may constitute an explicit part of the review within the framework of the real-life test:

- Has the expected frequency of use been described on a function level?
- Has it been described for each type of user which functions may be carried out?
- Has it been described for each function when it will be used (daily, weekly, annually, daytime, evening)?
- Is there insight into the relationship between the various batch procedures across the (sub)systems?
- Has the configuration for the production environment been described (hardware, network, system software, database management system (DBMS), etc.)?
- Have specific requirements been set for the performance of online functionality?
- Is a distinction being made between the response time when starting up a function and the screen change within a function?
- Have specific performance requirements been set for data retrieval and manipulation?
- Have specific performance requirements been set for batch functionality?
- Have specific requirements been set for memory use?
- Are there any requirements for the number of database calls per transaction?
- Are there any requirements for the maximum page and buffer sizes?
- Are there any requirements for the size of the application and/or the database?

13.3.10 Semantic test (including security)

The semantic test largely concerns documentation describing input checks on a function level, standards for error handling on (sub)system level, and requirements regarding access security for functions and/or data. The following checklist can be used to check the specifications:

- Have any standards for error handling been described at (sub)system level?
- Have the input checks (in particular the relation checks) – including any related error message – been described as part of the function description, and can these be implemented?
- Have any specific requirements been set for access security of functions and/or data?
- Have any user profiles been described with regard to security?
- Has it been described which requirements are set for identification (user ID) and authentication (password)?

13.3.11 Syntactic test

During the testability review of the test basis, the documentation that is necessary for the implementation of the syntactic test of the system is selected and assessed. This concerns screen layouts, screen descriptions, overview layouts, report descriptions, standards present at (sub)system level, and the data model. The following checklist can be used:

- Have any applicable standards been described at system level?
- Have any applicable standards been described at subsystem level?
- Have the layouts of the screens, menus and dialogs been described?
- In this context, has any attention been given to the following aspects:
  - field length of the items;
  - location of items on the screen;
  - distinction between input and output items;
  - primary input checks (not resulting from domain definition);
  - error handling;
  - mandatory and non-mandatory items;
  - possible function keys, help screens and selections?
- Have the screen items and/or attributes been included in the data model?
- Have the types (numeric, alphanumeric, date) and the domains of the input and output data been described?
- Are the specified mandatory and non-mandatory items consistent with the options from the data model?
- Do the described screen layouts comply with the standards?
- Have the layouts of the reports been described?
- In this context, has any attention been given to the following aspects:
  - field length of the items;
  - location of items in the report?
- Have the report items and/or attributes been included in the data model?
- Do the described report layouts comply with the standards?

13.4 High-level test checklists

13.4.1 General

- Is all of the documentation supplied sufficiently accessible?
- Have the relationships between the various documents been described sufficiently and clearly?
- Does the table of contents of the documentation supplied match the actual contents?
- Is a logical data model present?
- Has an implementation of the data structure been described?
- Has a division of the system into subsystems been made?
- Have any specifications of the interfaces been given?
- Have all functions and subfunctions been described?
- Are screen sequence diagrams (dialog design) present?
- Is error handling described?

- Have the input and output been described for each function?
- Are the layouts of the screens and lists present?
- Have any specifications of the necessary hardware and software been given?

13.4.2 Logical data model
- Is an entity relationship diagram present?
- Have all entities and relationships listed been included in the diagram?
- Have the relationships between the data models of the various subsystems been described?

13.4.3 Logical data structure
- Have all drawn entities and relationships been listed?
- Are descriptions present of all relationships included in the data model (also those with other (sub)systems)?
- Have the types of relationship been described?
- Has it been defined for all entities which attributes belong to them?
- Have all security and privacy aspects of the attributes been described?
- Are the key attributes defined for each entity?
- Have the domains (type, range, values permitted) and any particulars of the attributes been described?
- Have the integrity requirements of the attributes been listed?
- Have the desired access paths been indicated?
- Have potential problem areas been indicated, and have unresolved issues been described?

13.4.3 Division into subsystems and interfaces
- Does the description of the selected subsystems include a summary description of the functions to be carried out, the required processes, and the data?
- Has the implementation sequence been indicated?
- Have the locations of the interfaces been indicated?
- Is it clear who the owner of the interface is, and what the security requirements are?
- Is there a description of the (composition of the) interface?
- Is there a description of the physical construction?
- Have the activities that are still to be carried out for the physical construction been described and included in the schedule?

13.4.5 Function structure
- Have all functions been displayed, e.g. in the data flow diagrams?
- Has a short description of the function been given?
- Have the conditions that apply to the execution been listed, including their frequency?
- Has it been indicated whether functions are manual or to be automated?

- Has it been stated whether the functions that are to be automated should be carried out online or in batch?
- Have the security requirements been described?
- Have the measures taken within the framework of correctness and completeness of data been described e.g.
  - validations of input (relation checks, referential checks);
  - redundant input (check totals);
  - duplicate input;
  - programmed checks on the results of data processing;
  - sequential numbering of transactions and reports?
- Have the performance requirements been described?
- Has the relative importance of the function in relation to other functions been described?
- Is there a cross-reference between the functions and the screen sequence diagrams?
- Is there a short description of the data flows?
- Is there a cross-reference between the functions and the input and output flows?
- Have the sources of all input been listed and described?
- Have the destinations of all output been listed and described?
- Has it been indicated which organizational unit or which information system it concerns?
- Have all basic functions been included in a data flow diagram?
- Has processing been described?

13.4.6 Description of screen sequence, including layout
- Is there an overview of the relationships between functions and screens?
- Has the structure of the screen sequence been described?
- Do the screens comply with the applicable guidelines?
- Has the screen input been described?
- Has the screen output been described?
- Have the screen checks been described?
- Has the use of function keys been described?
- Is there a description of the use of the help functions?
- Has the use of attributes been described?
- Is there a description of the screen and print layout?

13.4.7 Specifications of the required hardware and software
- Has the necessary capacity for the production environment of hardware, system software, network and communication devices been stated (quantitatively)?

13.4.8 Quality requirements

- Have the quality requirements and/or performance requirements for the information system to be created been specified (this is especially important for the quality characteristics included in the test strategy)?
- Have the quality requirements been specified in such a way that they are measurable and may be used as acceptance criteria?

13.5 Low-level test checklists

13.5.1 General

- Is all the documentation supplied sufficiently accessible?
- Have the relationships between the various documents been described sufficiently? (If, for example, the documentation consists of detailed descriptions of input processes, processing and output processes, there is no overview of how everything is connected. Can a system generate an invoice before the order line has been executed?)
- Does the table of contents of the documentation supplied match the actual contents?
- Is there a description of the physical database?
- Is the system security described?
- Has the system structure been described?
- Do program descriptions exist?

13.5.2 Design of the physical database

- Have the arguments in favour of, and against, the solution chosen been described?
- Has the physical database been included in an entity relationship diagram (ERD)?
- Is there a description of record layouts and access paths?
- Has a comparison between the logical data model and the physical data model been included?
- Have the maximum, minimum and average sizes of each record format of the physical database been given?
- Has the organization around the physical database been described?
- Has the sequence (ordering) been described?
- Has the file organization been described?

13.5.3 System security

- Have the measures with regard to the following risk areas been described:
  - abnormal termination of a job
  - system failure
  - errors in the data set

- recoverability (restart and recovery)
- access security?
- Have measures been described regarding:
  - continuity
  - integrity
  - privacy
  - data controllability (audit trail)?
- Have the deviations from the normal procedures been described?

13.5.4 System structure
- Has the system structure of the subsystem been displayed on the basis of which a program division can be made?

13.5.5 Program division
- Have all programs been displayed in the form of a system flow?
- Have the following been described for all programs within the system flow:
  - the name of the program
  - the input and output
  - the processing?

13.5.6 Program description
Have the following aspects been described for the various program descriptions:
- the identification and the aim of the program;
- the description of the function/transaction(s);
- the description of the input and output flows;
- the description of the links to other programs and/or (sub)systems;
- the description of the buffers and files;
- the description of the key data;
- the description of the possible sorts;
- the description of the parameters (including the check);
- the description of logging;
- the schematic representation of the program;
- the description of the program that belongs to the diagram, containing the sections and paragraphs called, and the standard routines used?

13.5.7 Performance requirements
- Have the performance requirements been specified? (This is particularly important if testing performance is part of the test strategy.)
- Are the performance requirements measurable?

Inspections **14**

14.1 Introduction

In some organizations, the design specifications are evaluated before starting the next development phase. By merging various aspects from the testability review of the test basis into such an evaluation, some degree of synergy between evaluations and the testability review of the test basis is established. In this situation, one or more members of the test team participate in the evaluation process. They assess the testability of the design specifications. The testers may also take the initiative with the introduction of an evaluation process, thus making evaluation an integral part of the test approach. Of course, while executing test activities, the various checklists as described in the previous chapter may be used.

The most effective technique to perform evaluations is the inspection, although essentially each kind of evaluation by colleagues has an additional value (Paulk, 1999). The inspection technique includes the evaluation as a team of an (intermediate) product by detecting and registering of defects, aimed at the implementation of an incidental as well as a structural improvement of quality of products (Fagan, 1986).

Within inspection, a number of phases are distinguished, of which the preparation phase is the most important. During the preparation the members of the team – the various assessors of the document – look individually for as many unique defects as possible. The emphasis is on unique defects that will not be found by other participants. This is achieved by assigning one or more roles to each participant, e.g. a user may assess the functionality, an (internal) accountant the data controllability, and a representative of the test team the testability. The participants therefore assess the design specifications each from their own points of view.

The additional value of inspection may be increased by invoking a causal analysis meeting. The purpose of this is to analyze the causes of any defects that are found, e.g. the limited or erroneous involvement of users while drawing up the specification document. The causal analysis meeting is actually an impetus to process improvement aimed at preventing such defects in the future. While applying inspections in practice, it is important that the person who organizes and steers the inspection has some degree of independence. In order to achieve a high degree of effectiveness and efficiency, this person – indicated by the term 'moderator' in inspection literature – possesses a profound knowledge of the inspection technique.

This chapter focuses on the basic steps for performing an inspection. For more information about inspections, please see Gilb and Graham (1993).

14.2 Advantages

The use of inspections of products (documents) of the development process has various advantages:

- By detecting defects at an early stage, a relatively cheap improvement of quality of the products can be achieved.
- Because the product is assessed from different angles (the so-called 'roles'), more defects will be detected than with the use of traditional evaluation techniques.
- The evaluation of a product by a team has the additional advantage that there is an exchange of information between the participants (learning effect), including knowledge about system development such as specification and development techniques, quality, the quality system, and structured testing.
- Inspections are not limited to design documentation but can be used for all levels of documentation, such as management plans, development plans, test plans, user guides, manuals and program code. In addition, inspections may be performed at various deliverables of the test process, such as test specifications and test scripts.
- Finally, there is a general raising of awareness and motivation regarding the development of quality products.

In conclusion, inspection is a very suitable technique for improving the quality of products. This applies at first to the assessed products themselves. It is also important that the quality improvement of the products is not achieved once but is structural. The feedback from the inspection process to the development processes allows for process improvements, which in turn help to avoid other mistakes as much as possible.

14.3 Procedure

Steps to be taken for inspection are:
1 Checking on entry criteria.
2 Organizing the inspection.
3 Kick-off.

4   Preparation.
5   Defect registration meeting.
6   Discussion meeting.
7   Causal analysis meeting.
8   Performing of re-work.
9   Follow-up.
10 Checking on exit criteria.

14.3.1 Checking on entry criteria

The author of a product announces to the moderator that the product is ready for inspection. Before an inspection is started, however, the moderator checks whether the product meets the entry criteria, which should be met before a product is inspected. The entry criteria are designed to prevent time-wasting by the participants of the inspection, and to motivate the author to deliver a good product. Examples of entry criteria are:

- the (part of the) product to be inspected should be complete (no half-finished versions);
- the reference documentation should have been approved;
- the references should be correct and up to date;
- an initial quick scan executed by the moderator detects no more than x defects;
- the document should have been spell-checked;
- the document is produced according to the agreed standard.

14.3.2 Organizing the inspection

If the product to be inspected meets the entry criteria, then the moderator organizes an inspection. This means, among other things, that a team should be composed and roles should be assigned to the participants. Roles may be defined using the '1 to 4 model' (van Veenendaal, 1999):

- *Type 1 role*. Evaluation against the reference documentation (e.g. evaluating whether the design covers all requirements of the specification).
- *Type 2 role*. Evaluation against standards (e.g. internal consistence, clarity, nomenclature).
- *Type 3 role*. Evaluation against related documents of the same level (e.g. interfaces between the various subsystems).
- *Type 4 role*. Evaluation against the use (e.g. for a design document: testability, maintainability, developability).

Eventually, the author may come out with specific issues (roles) that should be involved during inspections. Finally, the documents, including related items such as reference documentation and standards, will be distributed among the participants, and planning appointments will be set regarding preparation and meetings.

14.3.3 Kick-off

The kick-off meeting is held before the actual inspection takes place. The meeting is optional, and may be organized by the moderator for the following reasons:

- If participants are invited who have not yet participated in an inspection, the moderator gives a short introduction to the technique and the procedure.
- The author of the product to be inspected gives an introduction on the product.
- If there are improvements or changes to the inspection procedure, a short explanation is given.

If a kick-off meeting is held, the documents are distributed and the roles may be explained. The kick-off meeting should last no more than half an hour.

14.3.4 Preparation

The preparation phase is the most important phase of the inspection. In order to make the meetings as effective and efficient as possible, good preparation is essential. During the preparation, participants look for as many *unique* defects as possible, i.e. defects that other participants will not find. This is achieved by using the role principle described earlier. A 'role' means that a product is assessed from a specific angle. No role has an exclusive area: everybody should register *any* defect they detect and mention it during the defect registration meeting.

It is important that the inspection (and thus the preparation) is concerned with looking for defects not only in the product to be inspected but also in all documents relevant to this product, such as reference documentation, inter-face documents and standards. Usually, about 25 per cent of the detected defects relate to documents other than the one to be inspected (Gilb and Graham, 1993).

14.3.5 Defect registration meeting

The purpose of the defect registration meeting is not only the logging of the defects detected by the participants during the preparation but also the detection of new defects during the meeting and the exchange of knowledge. As indicated before, attention should be paid to defects in the product to be inspected, as well as to defects 'outside' the product.

The moderator, the performers of the inspection, and the author attend the defect registration meeting. The moderator should take care that for each page of the product the detected defects are listed. These defects are registered by the minutes secretary (author) in a defect report. Cosmetic defects are not usually registered, but are handed to the author after the meeting. For the sake of effi-ciency, defects and their (possible) solutions are not discussed during the meeting. If any are essential, there may be limited opportunity to do so during a discussion meeting. The defect registration meeting should last for two hours at most, but usually about one hour. The duration of the meeting is also limited due to the size of the document to be inspected (10–15 pages at most).

14.3.6 Discussion meeting
The optional discussion meeting comes directly after the defect registration meeting. This meeting is intended to discuss the alternative solutions of a limited number of defects selected during the defect registration meeting (indicated in the defect report). Eventually, those people not involved specifically in the subject of the discussion may leave the meeting.

14.3.7 Causal analysis meeting
The causal analysis meeting is held selectively, and takes place after a limited number of representative defect registration meetings. The purpose of the causal analysis meeting is to analyze the causes of the most important defects. This is the first impetus towards structural improvement of quality aimed at preventing such defects in future. The causal analysis meeting is held in the form of a brainstorm session. An inventory is made of possible causes and corresponding solutions of a number of important defects selected by the moderator. This meeting is attended by the same people that attended the defect registration meeting.

14.3.8 Performing of rework
During the re-work phase, the author performs the adaptation of the assessed product. This adaptation occurs based on the defects stated during the defect registration meeting. Action should be taken on each registered defect. This means that any defect regarding the inspected document itself should be solved in that document. Defects made in any other document should be registered as a change proposal.

14.3.9 Follow-up
The follow-up is the last step in the inspection process, and serves as a check of the re-work. The role of the moderator here is to check whether action was taken on each registered defect. The moderator does not check whether such actions were done correctly. In order to give feedback to the participants, the version of the document may be circulated. Participants can check whether the defects detected by them have been solved in the right way, and may make additional remarks on the document if necessary.

14.3.10 Checking on exit criteria
Finally, the product can leave the inspection process provided that the exit criteria are met. The moderator performs the exit check. Examples of exit criteria are:
- re-work should be completed;
- the document has obtained a new version number;
- all changes should be recorded in the new version of the inspected product (change history);

- the change proposals to other documents are submitted according to the current change procedure;
- the inspection form is filled in and handed to the employee responsible for quality management, in order to collect statistics on the quality of the product.

On various occasions during the inspection process, data are collected on the effectiveness and efficiency of the inspection. These data are registered on an inspection form. The data of several sessions are processed to metrics, and analyzed by the quality management department. Based on this analysis, structural improvements in the inspection and/or development process may be applied (see Chapter 23).

Test-specification techniques   **15**

A test-specification technique is a standardized method of deriving test cases from reference information. In this chapter, we first explain why the use of test-specification techniques is so important, before describing the steps in test-specification techniques at the generic level. Then we will list the characteristics of the available techniques, and discuss the possible variations of coverage. These overviews simplify the selection of the appropriate test-specification technique when determining the test strategy. Lastly, we will deal in detail with the various techniques.

Each step of each test-specification technique is described in full detail so that the technique can be used independently. Some details are identical for different techniques, so the reader will find a certain amount of repetition in this chapter.

15.1 Why use test-specification techniques?

There are various arguments to indicate the importance of (the application of) test-specification techniques.

- Using techniques provides insight into the quality and coverage of the tests, based on solid implementation of the test strategy, which gives the correct coverage in the correct place.
- As a test-specification technique aims to find certain types of defects (e.g. in the interfaces, input validations or processing), such defects will be detected more effectively than in the case of randomly specified test cases.
- Tests can be reproduced because the order and content of the test execution has been specified in detail.
- The standardized working procedure makes the test process independent of the person who specifies and carries out the test cases.
- The standardized working procedure makes the test specifications transferable and maintainable.
- The test process can be planned and controlled more easily because the test-specification and execution processes have been divided into well-defined blocks.

15.2 Generic description of the steps

A generic plan consisting of discrete steps is used to describe the test-specification techniques. This makes it easier to compare test-specification techniques. A description of the steps is given below.

15.2.1 Identifying test situations

Each test-specification technique aims to find certain types of defects. The first step is to identify the situations that are to be tested in the test basis. The test basis may consist of the functional requirements, the user guide and/or the administrative procedures. The test basis is analyzed, and each situation that is to be tested is identified. The test-specification technique may state, for example, that the situations to be tested are all those that are formed by having all conditions both true and false, or that each entry field is tested with a valid and an invalid entry value. As the identification of test situations differs per test-specification technique, this step contains the greatest differences between the various techniques.

15.2.2 Specifying logical test cases

In some test-specification techniques, a series of situations to be tested is transformed into a logical test case. Such a test case passes through the test object concerned (e.g. a complex calculation function) from start to finish. This step is used when the individual test situations cannot be approached directly during the testing but only after other test situations have been passed through first, or when it is not possible to check the result of a certain test situation immediately but only after passing through a number of other test situations.

15.2.3 Specifying physical test cases

The next step is the creation of the physical test cases. Each test situation or logical test case is detailed to contain a starting situation, actions to be taken, and the result checks to be performed. The level of detail is such that when the test is executed at a later stage, this is done as efficiently as possible. The exact details of a physical test case are obviously based on the results of the previous steps, but they are also influenced by agreements on, for example, the use of boundary values (see below) or the use of certain initial data sets, such as a copy of the production database.

15.2.4 Establishing the initial data set

In order to execute physical test cases, a starting situation is usually necessary. The starting situations for several test cases often contain the same data. Such data are recorded once in an initial data set for the entire test and not with each individual test case. The initial data set is filled physically before testing begins.

15.2.5 Assembling the test script

The final step is to define the test script, which places the test actions and result checks of the individual test cases in the optimal sequence for test execution. The test script is thus the staged plan for the test execution, which also allows for progress monitoring. The physical test cases in conjunction with the initial data set form the basis for the test script to be created.

15.3 Characteristics

To make the selection of the test-specification technique easier, and to compare techniques, we describe a number of characteristics for each technique. We may distinguish the following characteristics:

- white-box or black-box
- formal or informal
- application areas
- the principle from which the test cases are derived
- the quality characteristic to be tested
- required type of test basis.

In addition, there is a large amount of literature on the test-specification techniques (see the bibliography at the end of this book).

15.3.1 Black-box or white-box

Black-box test-specification techniques are usually based on functional requirements, administrative procedures and quality requirements. In black-box testing, the system is considered in the form in which it will ultimately be used. White-box test-specification techniques are usually based on the code, program descriptions and technical design, i.e. explicit use is made of knowledge of the system's internal structure.

15.3.2 Formal or informal

We also make a distinction between formal and informal test-specification techniques. Informal test-specification techniques give the tester a freer rein when setting up test cases. This places more emphasis on the tester's creativity, and makes the quality of the test more dependent on the tester's (subject-specific) expertise. Informal test-specification techniques are less dependent on the quality of the test basis, but have the disadvantage that the degree of coverage in relation to the test basis is less clear.

15.3.3 Application areas

Some test-specification techniques are particularly suited to testing the interaction between systems and users (screens, reports, online), while others are more suited to testing the relationship between the administrative organization and the system or to test batch processing. Yet another group is used to test the integration between functions and/or data. The suitability of the various techniques is related to the type of defects that can be found with their aid, such as incorrect input validations, incorrect processing or integration defects.

15.3.4 Principles of test case derivation

Test-specification techniques use various principles to derive test cases, some of which are described below.

Processing logic

An important principle is to base test cases on detailed knowledge of the logic of the processing of the program, function or system to be tested. Processing here is seen as a composite set of decisions and actions. A decision consists of one or more conditions. The various combinations of actions and decisions that may be taken consecutively are referred to as paths. In this instance, a test case concerns the path to be taken, i.e. a part of the processing logic. Other terms used for this way of deriving test cases are logic testing (Myers, 1979; Kit, 1995), control flow testing, path testing, and transaction-flow testing (Beizer, 1990).

In the following example, a person who is married and has worked for five years will follow the path B1/A2/B2/A3, resulting in a salary of 7000.

Specification	Explanation
IF worked = Y AND number of years ≥ 10	Decision B1, consisting of conditions C1 and C2
THEN salary := 10 000	Action A1
ELSE salary := 5000	Action A2
IF married = Y	Decision B2, consisting of condition C3
THEN salary := salary + 2000	Action A3

The processing logic may be considered at various levels. In low-level tests, the focus is on the internal structure of programs. The statements in the program then constitute the decisions and actions. For high-level tests, the functional requirements could be regarded as the processing. The number of combinations of actions, conditions and paths that are tested determines the coverage of such tests. Well-known forms of coverage are listed in Table 15.1.

Coverage	Combination of actions, conditions and paths
Statement coverage	Each action (= statement) is executed at least once.
Decision coverage	Each action is executed at least once, and every possible result (True or False) of a decision has been completed at least once. This implies statement coverage.
Condition coverage	Each action is executed at least once, and every possible result of a condition is completed at least once. This implies statement coverage.
Decision/condition coverage	Each action is executed at least once, and every possible result of a condition and a decision is completed at least once. This implies both condition and decision coverage.
Modified decision/condition coverage (British Standards Institute, 1998b)	Each action is executed at least once, and every possible result of a condition determines at least once, independent of other condition results, the result of the decision. This implies decision/condition coverage. For a more detailed explanation of this coverage measure, see Section 15.8.
Multiple condition coverage	All possible combinations of results of conditions in a decision are completed at least once. This implies modified decision/condition coverage.
Path^n coverage, with $n = 1,2,...,$ also referred to as test measure n	All of the aforementioned types of coverage refer to discrete actions and decisions. In the case of path coverage, the focus is on the number of possible paths. The concept of 'test measure' is used to determine to what extent the dependencies between consecutive decisions are tested. For test measure n, all combinations of n consecutive decisions are included in test paths. The selection of a particular test measure has a direct effect on the number of test cases (and therefore the test effort), and the degree of coverage of the tests. Using the test measure parameter, we can choose the number of test cases that corresponds to the defined test strategy. For an example of this complex definition of the concept of test measure, refer to the description of the algorithm test in Section 15.4.

Table 15.1
Types of coverage

Equivalence partitioning

With this principle of deriving test cases, an investigation can be conducted into which classes of possible input values result in the same type of processing. These classes are referred to as equivalence partitions. Another term used for deriving by means of equivalence partitioning is 'domain testing' (Beizer, 1990).

A distinction is made between valid and invalid equivalence partitions. Input values from an invalid equivalence partition result in some kind of exception handling, such as generating an error message. Input values from a valid equivalence partition should be processed correctly. The principle of this division is that to make a test case, each value from such a partition has an equal chance of finding a defect, and testing with multiple values from the same partition barely increases the chance of finding defects. By basing test cases on this equivalence partitioning instead of on every possible input value, the number of test cases remains limited while still achieving a good coverage. The following example may serve as an illustration, where the input 'age' is subjected to the following check:

$$18 \leq age =\leq 65$$

There are now three distinct equivalence partitions for age:

- age is less than or equal to 18;
- age has a value in the range 19–65;
- age is greater than 65.

The test cases to be selected for age may then be 10 (invalid), 35 (valid) or 70 (invalid).

It should be noted that test-specification techniques that derive test cases on the basis of the processing logic often implicitly use equivalence partitioning.

Boundary value analysis

An important specialization of the above principle is the boundary value analysis. The values at and around the boundaries of an equivalence partition are referred to as boundary values. These are values in which a large number of defects occur in practice. When determining the test cases, values from near these boundaries are chosen so that each boundary is tested with a minimum of two test cases – one in which the input value is equal to the boundary, and one that is just beyond it. The application of the boundary value analysis leads to more test cases, but it increases the test's chances of finding defects compared with a random selection from within the equivalence partitions.

Take the example:

$$18 \leq age =\leq 65$$

The boundary values to be selected for age are 18 (invalid), 19 (valid), 65 (valid) and 66 (invalid).

Boundary value analysis includes the boundary values not only on the input side but also on the output side. Suppose a page in a price quotation may contain up to ten lines. This is then tested by printing an estimate containing ten lines (all lines on one page) and one with 11 lines (the eleventh line on the second page). A possible extension of the boundary value analysis is that three values instead of two must be chosen for a boundary. The extra value is then chosen just within the equivalence partition defined by the boundary value. Take the example:

$$age =\leq 18$$

The boundary values to be selected for age are then 17 (valid), 18 (valid) and 19 (invalid). If this comparison is incorrectly programmed as 'age = 18', it will not be found with two boundary values, but it will be found with the extra value 17.

Operational use

Test cases can also be derived on the basis of the expected use of the system in practice. The test cases simulate the different situations that may occur in production. For example, functions that are used frequently in practice will have a proportional number of test cases specified, regardless of the complexity or the importance of the function. Testing on the basis of operational use often results in a large number of test cases all belonging to the same equivalence partition, therefore offering little chance of finding new defects. Operational use is often applied when designing performance tests.

Create, read, update and delete

Test cases can also be based on the lifecycle of data (create, read, update and delete CRUD). Data emerge, are retrieved and changed, and eventually are often removed again. Test cases based on this principle investigate whether the functions interact correctly, and whether the referential relation checks (consistency checks of the data model) are complied with. This provides insight into the (completeness of the) lifecycle of the data or entities.

Other derivation methods

The principles discussed above are used in TMap test-specification techniques. In addition, there are various other principles, such as cause/effect graphing, state-transition and syntax testing. For a description of these principles, see Myers (1979) and Beizer (1990).

15.3.5 Classification of test-specification techniques

Table 15.2 shows the characteristics of TMap test-specification techniques. This table makes it easier to select the correct test-specification technique, because one can see at a glance the main characteristics of the techniques and compare them with one another.

TMap technique	White-box (WB) /black-box (BB), formal/informal	Test basis	Derivation principle (with coverage)	Quality characteristics	Application areas
Algorithm test	WB, formal	Internal structure, e.g. program code or technical design	Processing logic: decision coverage in combination with path coverage, optionally with additional test measure 2 or higher	Functionality	Processing
Data cycle test	BB, informal	Functional requirements	CRUD: on the basis of the lifecycle of data	Functionality	Integration between functions and data
Data combination test	BB, informal	Functional requirements	Equivalence partitioning	Functionality Data controllability	Processing, integration between functions and data
Decision table test	WB, BB, formal	Decision tables, both internal structure and (functional) specifications	Processing logic: decision coverage in combination with path coverage, optionally with additional decision /condition coverage and/or a higher test measure	Functionality	Complex processing
Elementary comparison test	WB, BB, formal	Internal structure (WB) or formal functional requirements (BB), e.g. pseudo-code or structured language	Processing logic: modified decision/ condition coverage	Functionality Data controllability	Complex processing
Error guessing	BB, informal	All types of test basis	Other: based on assumptions as to where the errors have been made	Security Data controllability Functionality User-friendliness Suitability Performance Efficiency	All

Table 15.2 Characteristics of test-specification techniques

TMap technique	White-box (WB) /black-box (BB), formal/informal	Test basis	Derivation principle (with coverage)	Quality characteristics	Application areas
Program interface test	WB, formal	Internal structure, e.g. program code or technical design	Equivalence partitioning	Functionality	Integration between programs
Process cycle test	BB, formal	Administrative Organizational procedures	Processing logic: decision coverage, standard with test measure 2, but the weight of this test measure can be increased or decreased as desired	Security Effectivity User-friendliness Suitability	Integration between the administrative organization and the system
Real-life test	BB, informal	All types of test basis	Operational usage	Security Continuity Infrastructure Performance Efficiency	Simulation of practical use
Semantic test	BB, formal	Functional requirements	Equivalence partitioning on the basis of the relationships between data and input	Security Functionality User-friendliness	Interaction (screens) between system and user, input validation, simple processing
Syntactic test	BB, formal	Functional requirements	Testing the layout of the screens and reports, and the primary data definitions (this latter is executed on the basis of equivalence partitioning)	Functionality User-friendliness	Interaction (screens, reports, online) between system and user, input validation

Table 15.2 continued

15.3.6 Variations within test-specification techniques

When determining the test strategy, varying degrees of importance are assigned to the different quality characteristics or parts of the system. Assigning a high degree of importance implies the application of techniques with a higher coverage and/or application of multiple techniques, while assigning a low degree of importance implies the opposite. The many test-specification techniques included in TMap assist the implementation of the strategy. In addition, most test-specification techniques offer the possibility of introducing variations to the test coverage. This greatly increases the selection options, making it possible to determine the optimum strategy. Table 15.3 shows examples of variations that can be used for the various test-specification techniques. These variations were created partly on the basis of a wide range of practical experience.

Table 15.3

Variations in coverage

Technique	Varying coverage by
Algorithm test	Using higher or lower test measures
	Using boundary values
Data cycle test	Less coverage by not using all 'Change' actions on data
Data combination test	Using boundary values
	Dependencies between concepts or considering equivalence partitioning
Decision table test	Using higher or lower test measures
	Using a higher or lower detailing measure
	Using boundary values
Elementary comparison test	Using boundary values
	Multiple condition coverage (instead of modified decision/condition coverage)
Error guessing	Varying the amount of time to be spent (time-boxing)
Process cycle test	Using higher or lower test measures
	Explicitly checking the result of the process (instead of implicitly checking that the next action can be executed)
Program interface test	Using boundary values

Table 15.3
continued

Technique	Varying coverage by
Real-life test	Varying the degree of the representativeness of the test and test environment in relation to the expected production situation, e.g. to test the system's performance to find out whether it can handle the expected 60 users simultaneously, one can either simulate 60 users or simulate 10 users and extrapolate the results to 60. However, use extrapolation with extreme care and get expert advice, as performance usually drops exponentially rather than linearly
	Limiting the test situations to the most common production situations (80% rule)
Semantic test	Using boundary values
Syntactic test	Writing out the test cases in detail or making use of a checklist: coverage is the same in both cases, but setting up a checklist requires less effort. It does, however, make higher demands on the knowledge and experience of the testers
	Testing the primary data definitions is not done for every screen (e.g. when 'date of birth_client' appears on two screens, the input check is tested only on the first screen)
	Many checks are possible on every primary data definition, e.g. test cases are possible for a numeric value on the lower boundary, the lower boundary − 1, the upper boundary, the upper boundary + 1, non-numeric characters, spaces, etc. Limitations can be set here
	Random testing
	Using boundary values

15.4 Algorithm test

15.4.1 Introduction

The aim of the algorithm test is to test the structure of a program. This means that the algorithm test is a structure test; the test cases are derived from the structure of an algorithm and/or a program, not from the related processing.

Every test case therefore consists of a group of consecutive actions that together follow a path through the algorithm. The algorithm test is pre-eminently a formal white-box test specification technique used to execute the unit test and/or the integration test.

15.4.2 Procedure

The following steps must be taken within the framework of an algorithm test:

1   Making an inventory of decision points.
2   Determining test paths.
3   Specifying test cases.
4   Establishing the initial data set.
5   Assembling the test script.

Making an inventory of decision points

The test basis – often the program design or the technical design – is studied for the algorithm test. In principle, there should be an overview of the structure of the algorithm present in the design, e.g. in the form of a flow chart, a decision table, or a Nassi–Shneiderman diagram. If it is not possible to gain insight into the structure of the algorithm on the basis of the design, then additional documentation should be created.

On the basis of the insight gained into the structure of the algorithm, the individual decision points and actions are coded uniquely (A, B, C, etc. for the decision points, and 1, 2, 3, etc., for the actions). Sequential actions between two decision points receive a common number.

Determining test paths

Depending on the chosen depth of testing, consecutive actions are combined to create test paths. The desired depth of testing should be translated into the desired test measure.

Test measures

The test measure parameter is used to decide to what extent dependencies between consecutive decision points are tested. In test measure n, all dependencies of actions before a decision point and after $n-1$ decision points are verified by including all possible combinations regarding the action concerned in test paths. The selection of paths is subject to the requirement that repetitions must be executed 0, 1 and 2 or more times.

The selection of a particular test measure has a direct effect on the number of test cases (and therefore the test effort), and on the degree of coverage of the tests. Using the test measure parameter, we can choose the number of test cases that corresponds to the defined test strategy.

The complex definition of the concept of test measure described here is best explained with the aid of an example. The following example, in which test measure 2 has been chosen, indicates how the test path can be determined. For every decision point found, the action combinations are determined. For test measure 2, this means that an inventory is made of all possible action combinations of two consecutive actions. An action combination in test measure 2 is therefore a link between one action before a decision point and one action after a decision point. All action combinations, i.e. all combinations of two consecutive actions with a decision point in between, are written out. Consider the flow chart in Figure 15.1.

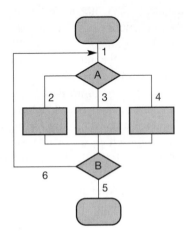

Figure 15.1
Flow chart showing the test path for test measure 2

The action combinations for the decision points are:
A: (1,2); (1,3); (1,4); (6,2); (6,3); (6,4)
B: (2,5); (3,5); (4,5); (2,6); (3,6); (4,6)

These action combinations must now be linked to create paths that run from the start to the end of the algorithm. In our example, each path starts with action 1 and ends with action 5. Each action combination must be included in at least one path, as follows:

1 Put the action combinations in ascending order: (1,2); (1,3); (1,4); (2,5); (2,6); (3,5); (3,6); (4,5); (4,6); (6,2); (6,3); (6,4).

2 Start with the first action combination that has not yet been included in a path, in this case (1,2). Subsequently, the first action combination that starts with a 2 and has not yet been included in a path is linked after the first, in this case (2,5). This creates the path (1,2,5) and the following path can be started.

3 The remaining action combinations are (1,2); (1,3); (1,4); (2,5); (2,6); (3,5); (3,6); (4,5); (4,6); (6,2); (6,3); (6,4).

4 Continue with the remaining action combinations. The first action combination that has not yet been included in a path is (1,3). The first action combination that starts with a 3 and has not yet been included in a path is (3,5). This creates the path (1,3,5) and the following path can be started.

5 The remaining action combinations are ~~(1,2)~~; ~~(1,3)~~; (1,4); ~~(2,5)~~; (2,6); ~~(3,5)~~; (3,6); (4,5); (4,6); (6,2); (6,3); (6,4).

6 Continue with the remaining action combinations. The first action combination that has not yet been included in a path is (1,4). The first action combination that starts with a 4 and has not yet been included in a path is (4,5). This creates the path (1,4,5) and the following path can be started.

7 The remaining action combinations are ~~(1,2)~~; ~~(1,3)~~; ~~(1,4)~~; ~~(2,5)~~; (2,6); ~~(3,5)~~; (3,6); ~~(4,5)~~; (4,6); (6,2); (6,3); (6,4).

8 The first action combination that has not yet been included in a path is (2,6). Because this action combination does not start at the beginning of the algorithm, a preceding action combination must be determined; (1,2) is selected for this. This has now been used twice, but that is clearly not a problem. Then continue with an action combination that starts with a 6 and has not yet been included in a path. Action combination (6,2) is selected. The test path is completed with combination (2,5), which creates test path (1,2,6,2,5).

9 The remaining action combinations are ~~(1,2)~~; ~~(1,3)~~; ~~(1,4)~~; ~~(2,5)~~; ~~(2,6)~~; ~~(3,5)~~; (3,6); ~~(4,5)~~; (4,6); ~~(6,2)~~; (6,3); (6,4).

10 The rest of the action combinations are included in test path (1,3,6,4,6,3,5), and all action combinations have now been included in the following paths:
Path 1: (1,2,5)
Path 2: (1,3,5)
Path 3: (1,4,5)
Path 4: (1,2,6,2,5)
Path 5: (1,3,6,4,6,3,5)

The selection of paths is subject to the requirement that repetitions (action 6) must be executed 0, 1, 2 or more times. In our example, the requirement of 2 or more has been met by means of path 5.

As may be gleaned from the procedure, the idea behind test measure 2 is that the execution of an (program) action may have consequences for the program (action) immediately after a decision point. In other words, it is not only the decision but also the execution of the previous action(s) that is important for an action.

Test measure 1 assumes that an action is affected only by the decision and not by previous actions. For test measure 1, the following action combinations arise:

– : (1)
A : (2); (3); (4)
B : (5); (6)

For these action combinations, we have the following path combinations:
Path 1: (1,2,5)
Path 2: (1,3,6,4,5)

Against the smaller number of test paths and the correspondingly smaller effort, there is of course a lesser degree of coverage.

Other test measures
In addition to test measures 1 and 2, there are higher test measures. When they are used, the assumption is that the execution of an action affects two or more subsequent actions. These test measures are usually chosen only for high-risk and very complex functions. In administrative automation, there is usually only a very limited number of functions that qualify for a test measure higher than 2. The choice between test measure 1, test measure 2 or a higher test measure is made per function or per subsystem.

Specifying test cases
During this step, the logical test paths are translated into physical test cases. This means that the test input must be determined for each test path to make sure that exactly the right path is run. In addition, a predicted output must be specified for every test input of a test path.

Finding the correct physical content is often a very complex process. The test input should be such that exactly the right path is run. This means that the test input for every decision point must be such that the right exit is taken, which in itself can be quite difficult. The greatest difficulty is caused by the fact that actions are being executed on the test input during the passage down the path. This means that all previous actions must be taken into account at every decision point. Variables and parameters that have no impact on the path (according to the design specifications) should receive a default value.

Establishing the initial data set
It is decided whether the test to be executed requires a specific initial data set. If this is the case, then a concise description of this set must be made. This description is added to the description of the test paths and the test cases.

Assembling the test script
The result of this step is the delivery of a test script. This describes the test actions and checks that need to be executed in the order indicated. The test specification constitutes the basis for the test script to be created. The test script

should also list any preconditions for the test script to be executed. Preconditions often concern the presence of an initial data set, the fact that the system date should have a certain value, or the availability of certain stubs and/or drivers (see also Section 27.5.4).

This last step is optional if the algorithm test is applied with a unit test. Whether or not a detailed test script will have to be created depends, in particular, on the organization of the test and the importance of testware for future maintenance purposes.

15.4.3 Test execution and assessment

The test is executed on the basis of the description of the test paths and test cases, possibly detailed in a test script. Assessment of the test is done in the first instance with the aid of the precalculated results. As the algorithm test is often applied as part of a unit test, the tester is often also the developer and/or programmer. If this is so, then assessing also means finding the cause of the defect, therefore a broader assessment occurs than if functions were separated.

Documenting the test results with a unit test is less important if testing and troubleshooting are carried out by the same person. However, creating test documentation can still be important for demonstrating that the required test coverage was achieved.

15.5 Data combination test

15.5.1 Introduction

The reference of a data combination test (DCoT) is, as its name implies, the data and their processing combinations. It is a test in which the processing by functions and the relationships between functions are tested. The DCoT is a test-specification technique that is used to test the functionality (the correctness and the completeness of the processing) within the framework of a high-level test, in particular the acceptance test. The DCoT is an informal test-specification technique. Although there are clear guidelines on how to select test cases (see below), the tester should use their intuition and understanding of the object to be tested when making the selection. This has the following advantages:

- Those who are not IT specialists can easily create a good test on the basis of their understanding of the information system.
- The quality of the test basis is of less importance.
- A good test specification and test scripts can be made with relatively little effort.

The disadvantage is the relative incompleteness of the test. As a result of the informal character, the quality of the DCoT that is executed depends on the quality of the tester. For a more formal and more complete test, the elementary comparison test-specification technique can be used.

The DCoT starts with an inventory of the input data for each main function before the values that influence the process flow are determined. On the basis of this, the test cases are created; then for each function it is determined which of these test cases must be executed. This constitutes the basis for the test. By placing the test cases and checks in the order in which they should be executed, and possibly adding preparatory actions, we arrive at a test script.

The DCoT offers good coverage with regard to the expected practical use of the functions. Defects found in the test are usually processing defects: Are the data manipulated correctly? Are calculations being performed properly? Are the various functions correctly inter-related?

15.5.2 Procedure

The steps that must be taken in order to arrive at a specification for a DCoT include:

1   Specifying test cases.
2   Establishing the initial data set.
3   Assembling the test script.

Specifying test cases

The result of this step should be a test specification. This describes the test cases and the way in which they were selected. Specifying test cases consists of several parts:

1   Establishing test situations.
2   Establishing test cases.
3   Establishing test actions.
4   Establishing checks.

To illustrate this, we will use an example in which a process (task) handles the submission and follow-up of price quotations. A quotation is entered by a representative, in which a quotation line is created for each item. Many variations are possible, including discounts, delivery and payment conditions. The representative's superior can approve the quotation. This means that there are separate functions. As soon as the quotation has been approved, it can be printed and sent. When the quotation has been printed, it can no longer be changed. An approved (not yet printed) quotation that is changed automatically receives the status of 'provisional' again. After some time, the client will either accept or reject the quotation.

Establishing test situations

Establishing the test situations starts with an inventory of the data that are used when executing the task. Each task usually has a *central concept*, which in this example is the quotation. For each task, the relationships of the central concept with other concepts that are important (the *marginal concepts*) are recorded. Establishing the central and marginal concepts constitutes the source of the DCoT, and must therefore be done with care. The central concept is usually quite obvious. If this is not the case, the task has probably not been specified properly. Before the marginal concepts are determined, the central concept must be reviewed for any necessary further subdivision. Then an inventory can be made in order to determine which marginal concepts affect the behaviour of the system.

With the central and related marginal concepts of the task to be tested in hand, it is time to determine the values for each concept in relation to the central concept. Emphasis should not be placed on finding all possible values for concepts such as currency (e.g. EUR, USD and CAD); it is much more important to focus on those concepts that control the decisions in the systems.

Sometimes, a marginal concept may be so important that it has to be detailed further, such as the quotation line in the example below.

Test situations

Central concept	Marginal	Values
Quotation	–	Provisional, approved, printed, accepted, rejected
	Customer	Known or not known in the system
	Quotation address	Yes/no present
	Quotation line	Quantity: 0, 1 or more screens
	Discount	Yes/no fill in
	Payment conditions	Yes/no default from customer data
	Delivery conditions	Yes/no default from customer data
Quotation line	–	Quantity: 0, 1 or more screens
	Price	Yes/no default
	Line discount	Yes/no present
	Line text	Yes/no enter

Establishing test cases

On the basis of the test situations described above, test cases are established. When establishing the test cases, one must make sure that all test situations (values) occur at least once. An important restriction is the fact that the different test situations often exclude one another. When in doubt, it is often useful to add test cases in advance, to prevent having to do this during test execution.

Test cases

Test case	Quotation-1	Quotation-2	Quotation-3
Quotation:			
Customer	CUS_1	New	CUS_2
Quotation address	Present	Enter	Enter
Discount	Enter	Enter	Not
Payment conditions	Default	Enter	Over-ride default
Delivery conditions	Default	Enter	Over-ride default
Quotation line:			
Item quantity	0	1	More screens
Price	–	Yes	Yes/no default
Line discount	–	Yes	Yes/no present
Line text	–	No	Yes/no enter

Establishing test actions

When the test cases have been established, the test actions can also be described. A test action is a predefined action that can be successful or can fail (the actual test). Each concept must be reviewed to see which functions apply. This includes issues such as entering, changing, removing, viewing, printing and modifying the status. Also, pay attention to the functions that are related to the time cycle (day/week/month/year balancing). The test actions must be established from the concepts in combination with the possible functions.

Test actions

1.	Enter	
001	Enter quotation 1	
002	Enter quotation 2	
003	Enter quotation 3	
2.	Change	
004	Status provisional	It should be possible to change a provisional quotation
005	Status approved (not printed)	
006	Status printed*	It should be impossible to change a quotation that has been printed
007	Status accepted*	
008	Status rejected*	
3.	View quotation	
009	View quotation	

4.   Print quotation
010   Status provisional*
011   Status approved
012   Status printed*
013   Status accepted*

5.   Report quotation
014   Report quotations after entry
015   Report quotations with mixed status

6.   Approve quotation
        From status   To status
016   Provisional   Approved
017   ...

A * indicates that an error message should follow the action concerned.

Establishing checks
A description must be given on how to check whether processing has been successful. The various results may be precalculated in this step.

Checks

C01   Total amount of quotation on the screen with line input, change and deletion
C02   Completeness when printing
C03   Increase quotation number in control data
C04   ...

Establishing the initial data set
It should be decided whether it is necessary to have an initial data set established for the test. If necessary, then a description of this set must be made. This description indicates, for the benefit of (future) testware control, which test cases each specific data item relates to. The description should be added to the test specification. With regard to our example, the following can be noted:

Initial data set

Customers:
 – CUS_1 for test case Quotation 1
 – CUS_2 for test case Quotation 3
 Items:
 – ...

If the initial data set contains data that can be used for only a limited time, e.g. as a result of a deadline, this should be stated separately. In a subsequent acceptance test, it should then be checked whether these time-dependent data are still valid, and whether the initial data set therefore needs to be adapted.

Assembling the test script

The result of this step should be a test script, which describes in the correct order the test actions and checks that must be executed during the actual test. The test specifications containing descriptions of the test cases form the basis for the test script to be drawn up. Creating a test script is relatively simple. It mainly entails putting the information gathered into the right order. When doing so, ensure that all test actions and all checks are executed at least once.

The test script should also list any preconditions. The preconditions of a test script are the conditions (e.g. the existence of a particular quotation) with which the initial data set must comply before the test script can be executed; usually, these conditions are completed by another test script. The results of one test are often the preconditions for another test. The rule of thumb is that the number of preconditions should be minimized so that tests can be executed more independently of each other. The preconditions can be used to determine the order in which the tests are to be executed.

15.5.3 Test execution and assessment

The test is executed on the basis of the test scripts, which should be executed in the correct order. The execution order is recorded in the test scenario. Possible shortcomings with regard to the test specification, the test script or the initial data set should be recorded. For the following test cycle, the initial data set should be reset, adapted and saved.

Assessment of the data combination test is not a trivial matter, despite the explicit checks that have been done. Unexpected defects often occur, which should be investigated. It is of great importance that the test can be repeated and hence the test results reproduced.

The test results can be recorded in the test script. For this purpose, two columns are included in the test script: 'OK' and 'Note'. The test results are marked in the 'OK' column, with either 'yes' (no defect found) or 'no' (defect found), while the 'Note' column can be used to indicate the number of the accompanying defect report. A short overall assessment regarding the test script that has been executed can also be included in the test script.

15.5.4 Example: data combination test for the function, report tax register

In this example, the data combination test is applied for the function, report tax register of the WOOF system (see Appendix A). The selection criteria that can be used are the citizen's code and the tax assessment date. At least one of these criteria has to contain a value.

Test situations

Concept	Related to	Values
Tax register	Citizen's code	Empty, existing value, not existing value
	Date tax assessment	Empty, existing value, not existing value

Test cases

	001	002	003
Citizen's code	Not existing value	Empty	Existing value
Date tax assessment	Empty	Existing value	Not existing value

Test actions and checks

A01   Enter selection criteria according to test case 001.
A02   Enter selection criteria according to test case 002.
A03   Enter selection criteria according to test case 003.
C01   Message 'Nothing selected' appears.
C02   Report containg all complying tax registers is created.
C03   Message 'Nothing found' appears.

Initial data set

Grayhound citizen

Code	0001	0002	0003
Surname	Jones	Mackay	Tyler
Initials	O.N.E.	T.W.O.	T.H.R.E.E.
Prefix	Mr	Mr	Prof
Street	Onelane	Twolane	Threelane
Number	1	2	3
Postcode	AB1 2CD	AB1 2CD	AB1 2CD
City	Grayhound	Grayhound	Grayhound
Income	10 000	20 000	30 000
Date of birth	18-10-1964	18-2-1890	18-6-1910
No. of dogs	1	1	1
Approved	Y	Y	Y

Age group

Age group code	A	B
Age from	0	66
Age to	65	100
Approved	Y	Y

Tariff

Tariff code	1
Tariff income from	0
Tariff	300
Tariff income to	90 000
Approved	Y

Factor

Age group	A	B
No. of dogs	1	1
Factor	1.5	2
Approved	Y	Y

Citizen's code	Date tax assessment
1	30-12-1991
1	30-12-1992
3	30-12-1992

Test script

ID	Description	OK	Remarks
A01	Enter code 0002 (Mackay), no date	Y/N	
C01	Message 'Nothing selected' appears	Y/N	
A02	No code and tax assessment date 30-12-1992	Y/N	
C02	Report containing tax assessment register of code 0001 and 0003	Y/N	
A03	Enter code 0003 (Tyler) and date 30-12-1991	Y/N	
C03	Message 'Nothing found' appears	Y/N	

15.6 Data cycle test

15.6.1 Introduction

The data cycle test is a test-specification technique used to test the lifecycle of data. Data emerge, are retrieved and changed, and eventually are often removed again. During the data cycle test, it is verified whether sequences of functions process the data correctly, and whether the referential integrity checks (consistency checks of the data model) are complied with. The aim of the data cycle test is therefore not to test the functional checks as they are described in the function description. This means not only that the online viewing function is used to check whether the data have been processed correctly, but also that the limitations set by the data model during entry, changing and/or deletion are tracked down and tested. In addition, all functions that make use of the data – according to the CRUD matrix – will be checked to see whether they actually work.

A CRUD matrix is a matrix in which the horizontal axis displays the entities and the vertical axis displays the functions. Where a function carries out a particular action on an entity, this is indicated in the matrix by means of C(reate), R(ead), U(pdate), and/or D(elete). This provides insight into the (completeness of the) lifecycle of data and/or entities.

The data cycle test is a black-box test-specification technique that is often used during the acceptance test. During the data cycle test, nearly the entire information system is usually dealt with. This technique is therefore often used during one of the last stages of the acceptance test: testing the system integration.

There are two variants of the data cycle test. We will discuss first the data cycle test that focuses on the control functions of the master data and/or basic tables. A control function is defined here as a function that performs all elementary actions (creating/entering, reading/viewing, changing/updating, and deleting). The other functions of the information system in principle view only the data set concerned. Sometimes, a single attribute of the data set is updated by another function, e.g. the updating of the latest invoice number. Control functions are often constructed as a whole and supplied to the test team. It is therefore possible and sensible to combine all aspects of such a function in a single test. For this variant of the data cycle test, a CRUD matrix may be desirable but is not necessary.

For the second variant, i.e. the data cycle test at the system level, the CRUD matrix is indispensable. This variant of the data cycle test is often a test that affects several parts of the information system. The lifecycle of the data concerned (often the core data of the information system) is determined by a multitude of functions.

15.6.2 Procedure

The steps that must be taken to arrive at a data cycle test include the following:
1   Making an inventory of the CRUD matrix and relationship checks.
2   Preparing test cases for each entity.
3   Establishing test actions and checks.
4   Establishing the initial data set.
5   Assembling the test script.

Making an inventory of the CRUD matrix, and relationship checks

The test basis is studied with the aim of determining which control functions are present. For each function that is recognized, it is determined which elementary actions are executed by the function concerned and with regard to what entities. The presence of a CRUD matrix makes this activity much simpler. In principle, the first section of this activity produces a CRUD matrix (Table

15.4). Even if the CRUD matrix is not used by the test team, setting up such a matrix is still useful. Thinking about the design of an information system often starts with the functions; for each function, a description is given of the data used. When setting up a CRUD matrix, thinking starts from the data, and for each entity a description is given of the functions and the way in which they use the entity concerned. Setting up such a matrix sometimes reveals uncertainties and/or instances of incompleteness that would otherwise not be found with a function-oriented approach.

	Entity 1	**Entity 2**	**Entity** n
Function 1	R	C, U, D	–
Function 2	C	C, R, D	–
Function n	C, R, D	–	–

Table 15.4
A CRUD matrix

Generally, only a very limited number of entities are maintained simultaneously by a single control function. The CRUD matrix provides a simple view of these functions. In most other cases, a more extensive CRUD matrix is required because there are more functions.

After setting up the CRUD matrix, the test basis is studied again, this time with the aim of determining the places where the referential integrity checks take place within the information system. Referential integrity checks are checks between multiple entities, e.g. if a CLIENT is deleted, then the related CLIENT_ADDRESSES must also be deleted, or the validity period of a CLIENT_ADDRESS may not overlap with the validity period of another CLIENT_ADDRESS.

Preparing test cases for each entity
Test cases are created for each entity. In principle, the actions are placed in the following basic order:
1 Create, read.
2 Update, read.
3 Delete, read.

A test case therefore consists of:
1 Entering data (one test case for each creation option).
2 Changing (one test case for each change option).
3 Deleting data (using each delete function).
4 Checking the data after each action using the view option.

Further additions and variants will emerge from the referential integrity checks.

Establishing test actions and checks

The processing check is integrated in each test case as a read action is listed after each create/update/delete action. The data are created, and then read by each view function, to check whether the data have been created correctly and completely. After the data have been changed once using each change option, they are viewed in order to check whether the change has taken place correctly by means of a function that is marked as R(ead) in the CRUD matrix. Finally, the data are deleted using every possible delete function, and a check is performed using a read function.

During the test of the entities regarding the control function(s), a check is performed with at least one other function to see whether the data are usable elsewhere in the information system. A short test is executed on these functions. This often consists only of read actions. It is important that reading consists not only of checking whether the data has been processed correctly but also whether:

- all restrictions (consistency checks of the data model) on entering, changing and/or deleting have been identified, described, and tested, e.g. a country code can be deleted only if there are no longer any accounts payable or receivables that make use of that country code;
- a test action has been defined with respect to all functions (including the batch functions) that make use of the entity according to the CRUD matrix.

Establishing the initial data set

It is decided whether it is necessary for an initial data set to be present for the test that is to be executed. If it is necessary, then a description must be given that indicates for which test case particular data have been specified in the initial data set. This description is added to the test specification drawn up earlier. If the initial data set contains data that can be used for only a limited time, e.g. as a result of a date item, then this should be stated explicitly. In a subsequent test, it will then be checked whether these time dependent data are still valid and, on the basis of this, whether the initial data set needs adapting.

Assembling the test script

The result of this step is the delivery of a test script. This describes the test actions and checks that need to be executed in the order indicated. The test specification constitutes the basis for the test script to be created. The test script should also list any preconditions. The preconditions of a test script are the conditions (e.g. the existence of a particular quotation) with which the initial data set must comply before the test script can be executed. Usually, these preconditions are fulfilled by another test script, i.e. the results of one test are often the preconditions for another test.

As a rule of thumb, the number of preconditions should be minimized. This way, tests can be executed more independently of each other. The preconditions can be used to determine the order in which the tests are to be executed.

15.6.3 Test execution and assessment

The tests are executed according to the test scripts. Assessing the test results of a data cycle test for control functions is simple. The check is often done on screen during the execution of the test. If the contents of the files cannot be viewed with a viewing function or a report function, then a tool (e.g. SQL) must be used to view and check the contents of the database.

The test results can, if so desired, be recorded in the test script. For this purpose, two columns have been included in the test script: 'OK' and 'Note'. The test results are marked in the 'OK' column with either 'yes' (no defect found) or 'no' (defect found), while the 'Note' column can be used to indicate the number of the accompanying defect report.

15.7 Decision table test

15.7.1 Introduction

The decision table test is a formal test-specification technique, hence the test cases are derived from the test basis according to set rules. The decision table test is dependent on two parameters. One (test measure) indicates to what extent dependencies *between* different decision points are tested, while the other (detailing measure) indicates to what extent dependencies *within* decision points are tested. Depending on the choice of parameters, this technique provides many or few test cases, and a higher or lower degree of coverage. One of the strengths of the decision table technique is that the parameters can be used to adapt the test to the test strategy. As soon as the parameters have been determined, the procedure for the decision table test is unequivocally set.

The decision table test focuses on the completeness and correctness of processing, and therefore the quality characteristic of functionality. This technique was developed in principle for white-box testing, but it can also be applied to black-box testing.

15.7.2 Procedure

The steps that must be taken to arrive at a decision table test include the following:
1 Defining logical test columns.
2 Specifying logical test cases.
3 Specifying physical test cases.
4 Establishing the initial data set.
5 Assembling the test script.

Defining logical test columns

In this step, one or more decision tables are created for each process. A decision table is used to unequivocally represent the logical processing of a process, and constitutes a link for the tester between the test basis and the logical test cases. The aim of creating the decision tables is threefold:

- explicitly establishing the logical processing of the processes to ensure that no obscurities occur during subsequent phases;
- identifying any imperfections in the test basis (e.g. incomplete descriptions of situations);
- obtaining the initial situations for the logical test cases.

Creating the logical test columns occurs in three substeps:
1   Distilling events.
2   Establishing determinants.
3   Creating decision tables.

This will be illustrated by an example in which a process (task) calculates salaries to be paid. The process is started as part of the monthly processing.

The person whose salary is being calculated is identified by means of a number; the salary program checks whether the number is valid, which indicates that the person is on the payroll. If the number is not valid, then the system generates an error message.   (1)

The salary is calculated as follows:

$$\text{IF worked = Y AND number of years} \geq 10 \tag{2}$$
$$\text{THEN salary := } 10\,000$$
$$\text{ELSE salary := } 5000$$
$$\text{IF (married = Y OR living together = Y) AND country = 'Netherlands'} \tag{3}$$
$$\text{THEN salary := salary + } 5000$$
$$\text{ELSE}\qquad \text{IF age} \geq 18 \text{ AND age} \leq 60 \tag{4}$$
$$\text{THEN salary := salary + } 4000$$
$$\text{ELSE salary := salary + } 3000$$
$$\text{IF worked = Y AND department = 'production' AND age} \geq 18 \tag{5}$$
$$\text{THEN salary := salary + } 1000$$

Distilling events
This first substep tracks the events (the activities that start the process). A process can be started by the user, an external system or an internal function. Each process has one or more events. In our example there is one event: the monthly processing.

Establishing determinants
In the second substep, the determinants are established. These are the characteristics that affect the processing of the process. Here, we should pay attention not only to the characteristics of the event but also to those of the processing. A determinant can be both negative and positive. A determinant is negative if the process always generates an error message as soon as the determinant is true; a determinant is positive if it is not negative. This substep tracks the determinants and determines whether they are negative or positive. In the salary calculation example, there are five determinants:

0	Monthly processing	(event)
1	Person's number absent	(negative determinant)
2	Indication worked/Number of years of service	(positive determinant)
3	Civil status/Country	(positive determinant)
4	Age	(positive determinant)
5	Worked/Age/Department	(positive determinant)

Creating decision tables
In the third substep, the decision tables are created on the basis of the determinants. The general form of a decision table (with hypothetical values) is shown in Table 15.5.

Logical test column	1	2	...	*n*
Event	1	1	...	1
Determinant 1	0	1	...	1
Determinant 2	–	–	...	...
Determinant 3	–	–	...	...
Determinant 4	–	–	...	...
Result 1	X	Imp	...	
Result 2	–	–	...	...

Table 15.5
General form of a decision table

Each column of the decision table constitutes a logical test column. The part above the double line constitutes the event and the situation description, while the part below the line states the consequences and/or results. A decision table therefore describes the proper results for all possible situations. The choice of the number of situations described is determined by the test strategy.

The cells above the double line contain the values 0, 1 or –. The value 1 means that the determinant is true, the value 0 means that the determinant is false, and the value – means that the determinant's value is irrelevant. The applicable event always has the value 1; the determinants can have the values 0, 1 or –. Below the double line, the cells contain a cross or 'Imp', or are empty. If there is a cross, the result concerned will occur; if a cell is empty, the result concerned will not occur in that situation; 'Imp' implies that the situation is not possible, e.g. because certain values of determinants exclude each other. We distinguish the following possibilities:

- all combinations of determinants, i.e. all possible situations, are tested;
- the minimum number of situations is tested, in which each determinant is at least 0 once and 1 once;
- the number of situations tested is between these extremes.

This method of combining is applied only with positive determinants. The negative determinants are not tested in combination with each other. The negative determinants must take the value True one by one. During the other tests, these determinants are therefore false.

As an example, a decision table is created for a process in which an inventory yields one event and five determinants. Of the five determinants, three are positive and two are negative. On the basis of the test strategy (function is of extreme importance), it is decided that all combinations of the (positive) determinants are to be tested (i.e. all situations). Firstly, a decision table is created for the negative determinants (Table 15.6).

Table 15.6
Decision table for a process with one event and five determinants

Logical test column	1	2	3–10 (see Table 15.7)
Event	1	1	1
Determinant 1	1	0	0
Determinant 2	–	1	0
Error message	X	X	–

The first logical test column describes the situation in which determinant 1 is true. As determinant 1 is a negative determinant, this means that the result is an error message independent of the values of the other determinants. The second logical test column describes the situation in which determinant 1 is false and determinant 2 is true. This is an error message independent of the values of the other determinants. Because the correct operation of determinant 1 has been verified with the first logical test column already, and the second logical test column is meant to verify the correct operation of determinant 2, then determinant 1 gets the value False. This process is continued until all negative determinants have been true once. During subsequent processing of the positive determinants, no more attention is being paid to the negative determinants, i.e. in our example after logical test column 2, all negative determinants are false.

Then we create the rest of the decision table in which the positive determinants are described (Table 15.7). In principle, the last column of the negative decision table must be added to every logical test column. As in our example, it was decided to test all possible situations.

Table 15.7
Decision table for the positive determinants in our example (see text for details)

Logical test column	3	4	5	6	7	8	9	10
Event	1	1	1	1	1	1	1	1
Determinant 3	0	1	1	0	0	1	1	0
Determinant 4	0	0	1	1	0	0	1	1
Determinant 5	0	0	0	0	1	1	1	1
Result 1	X				X	X		
Result 2		X	X	X	X		X	X

It is relatively simple to check whether all possible situations of the determinants have been recorded in the table. A total of ten logical test columns arise for this process. This means 100 percent coverage at the logical specification level, with the disadvantage of the large number of logical test columns and therefore test cases. The effort that must be made to complete the test is therefore great.

For processes of lesser importance, a different procedure must be used to restrict the number of logical test columns, while retaining a reasonable degree of coverage. To provide a solution, the test measure parameter is introduced.

A test has the test measure n if the table for each group of n determinants contains all possible combinations, i.e. if a decision table has the test measure n, then there are 2^n situations in the decision table for each group of n determinants. Again, we will use an example. The decision table from the previous example has the test measure 3, as this contains all possible combinations of the three determinants. The following decision table for the same example has test measure 2 (Table 15.8).

Logical test column	4	5	6	7
Event	1	1	1	1
Determinant 3	0	1	1	0
Determinant 4	0	0	1	1
Determinant 5	1	0	1	0
Result 1	X			
Result 2	X	X	X	X

Table 15.8
Decision table for our example (see text), with a test measure of 2

For each group of two determinants, all combinations are included in the decision table.

On the basis of this, it can be concluded that it is possible to calculate the number of logical test columns per test measure with a given number of positive determinants, and hence the achieved degree of coverage. It is therefore possible with a given number of determinants to choose a test measure that on the one hand best suits the desired degree of coverage on the basis of the test strategy, and on the other hand does not exceed the budgeted test effort. The results of such a calculation are displayed in Tables 15.9 and 15.10 for processes with a maximum of ten positive determinants.

Table 15.9 shows the number of logical test columns (in the positive part of the identification table) per test measure with a given number of positive determinants.

Test measure:	1	2	3	4	5	6	7	8	9	10
1 determinant	2	2	2	2	2	2	2	2	2	2
2 determinants	2	4	4	4	4	4	4	4	4	4
3 determinants	2	4	8	8	8	8	8	8	8	8
4 determinants	2	5	8	16	16	16	16	16	16	16
5 determinants	2	6	10	16	32	32	32	32	32	32
6 determinants	2	7	12	22	32	64	64	64	64	64
7 determinants	2	8	14	29	49	64	128	128	128	128
8 determinants	2	9	16	37	72	107	128	256	256	256
9 determinants	2	10	18	46	102	172	228	256	512	512
10 determinants	2	11	20	56	140	266	392	476	512	1024

Table 15.10 shows the degree of coverage per test measure with a given number of positive determinants.

Test measure:	1	2	3	4	5	6	7	8	9	10
1 determinant	100	100	100	100	100	100	100	100	100	100
2 determinants	50	100	100	100	100	100	100	100	100	100
3 determinants	25	50	100	100	100	100	100	100	100	100
4 determinants	13	31	50	100	100	100	100	100	100	100
5 determinants	6	19	31	50	100	100	100	100	100	100
6 determinants	3	11	19	34	50	100	100	100	100	100
7 determinants	2	6	11	23	38	50	100	100	100	100
8 determinants	1	4	6	14	28	42	50	100	100	100
9 determinants	0.5	2	4	9	20	34	45	50	100	100
10 determinants	0.2	1	2	5	14	26	38	46	50	100

Tables 15.9 and 15.10 are used to make the right choice regarding the test measure, after which the decision tables can be created. With regard to the salary calculation example we used earlier, we can distinguish the following decision tables:

Table 15.11 shows the decision table for the negative determinant of 'person's number'. The rest of the decision table (the positive part), in which the positive determinants are described, is shown in Table 15.12. The last column of the negative decision table must be added to every logical test column. A test with test measure 2 was chosen.

Logical test column	1	2–6
Event: monthly processing	1	1
Determinant: 'person's number unknown'	1	0
Error message	X	

Logical test column	2	3	4	5	6
Monthly processing	1	1	1	1	1
Indication worked/Years of service	0	1	1	0	1
Civil status/Country	0	0	1	1	1
Age	1	0	– (1)	– (0)	– (0)
Worked/Age/Department	1	0	0	0	1
Salary	X	X	X	X	X

Table 15.12
Decision table for the positive determinants described in our example (see text for details)

A dash in the Table 15.12 indicates that the combination is impossible according to the processing logic.

Specifying logical test cases

Decision tables contain logical test columns. Each logical test column indicates which results should occur if the determinants have the values specified in the column. During the test, it must be verified whether those results actually occur in the situation concerned. A logical test column is similar to a logical test case. The difference is that the decision table test technique demands that the logical test cases have been unequivocally defined, whereas this is not the case for the logical test columns. This is because the determinants may be complex. If a determinant consists of several simple determinants (e.g. $X \geq 0$ AND $Y = 3$), then the complex determinant may be true or false in several ways. The situation is therefore not unequivocally set.

Only if all determinants are simple is the situation unequivocally set and the logical test column is equal to the logical test case. In all other cases, the combinations of the determinants must be broken down into combinations of simple determinants.

Just as the test measure indicates to what extent combinations *between* the different determinants are tested, the detailing measure indicates to what extent combinations of simple determinants *within* a complex determinant are tested.

There are various detailing measures available to break down a complex determinant. A high degree of detailing leads to a relatively large number of test cases and therefore a relatively high test effort. The importance of the process is decisive for the detailing measure that is chosen. We distinguish the following detailing measures:

- multiple condition coverage
- decision coverage
- condition coverage
- decision/condition coverage
- condition/determination coverage.

The meaning and operation of the various detailing measures are explained by means of an example: V is a complex determinant that contains the simple determinants A, B and C (V = A AND (B OR C)). The complex determinant V has the truth table shown in Table 15.13.

Number	A	B	C	V
1	0	0	0	0
2	0	0	1	0
3	0	1	0	0
4	0	1	1	0
5	1	1	0	1
6	1	1	1	1
7	1	0	0	0
8	1	0	1	1

Table 15.13 indicates the first detailing measure, the *multiple condition coverage*. In such coverage, all possible combinations within a complex determinant are tested. This is the highest degree of detailing. This detailing measure produces a very large number of test cases, but produces 100 percent coverage at the logical level. The number of test cases increases rapidly, however, if the complex determinant consists of a large number of simple determinants (2^n test cases for n simple determinants).

The second detailing measure is *decision coverage*. This measure tests the correctness of the complex determinant by allowing the complex determinant to be true once and false once. This could produce the truth table shown in Table 15.14.

Number	A	B	C	V
1	0	1	1	0
2	1	1	1	1

The detailing measure of decision coverage always produces only two test cases. Obviously, the degree of coverage achieved with this detailing measure is low. If the above test cases were to be applied and V = A AND B was implemented instead of V = A AND (B OR C), then this defect would not be found.

The third detailing measure is *condition coverage*. This detailing measure tests the correctness of the complex determinant by allowing each simple determinant to be both true and false at least once. In our example, this may yield Table 15.15:

Number	A	B	C	V
1	0	1	1	0
2	1	0	0	0

An important difference from the previous implementation is that condition coverage allows the various test cases to have the same value for the complex determinant. This measure produces only two test cases and an equally low degree of coverage. If the above test cases were to be applied and V = A AND B AND C was implemented instead of V = A AND (B OR C), this defect would not be found.

The fourth detailing measure is *decision/condition* coverage. This measure tests the correctness of the complex determinant by allowing the complex determinant to be true once and false once, on condition that every simple determinant is also both true and false at least once. In the example, this may yield Table 15.16.

Number	A	B	C	V
1	1	1	1	1
2	0	0	0	0

Table 15.16
Truth table for our example (see text for details)

As was the case with both of the previous detailing measures, this measure produces only two test cases, and the degree of coverage is also very low. If the above test cases were to be applied, and V = (A OR B) AND C was implemented instead of V = A AND (B OR C), this defect would not be found.

Finally, the fifth detailing measure is *condition/determination coverage*. This measure tests the correctness of the complex determinant by letting every simple determinant determine the value of the complex determinant (at least) twice: true once and false once. In our example, this may yield Table 15.17.

Number	A	B	C	V
1 (A is determining)	0	1	1	0
2 (B and C are determining)	1	0	0	0
3 (A and C are determining)	1	0	1	1
4 (A and B are determining)	1	1	0	1

Table 15.17
Truth table for our example (see text for details)

This detailing measure may produce up to $(3/2 \times n) + 1$ test cases, where n is the number of simple determinants. The degree of coverage of this detailing measure is relatively high, with a relatively limited number of test cases. It is actually quite difficult to provide an example of an incorrect implementation of simple determinants in the complex determinant, which is not found by the previous test cases.

With regard to the salary calculation example, we will apply decision coverage for the complex determinants. There are four complex determinants for salary calculation:

2   Indication worked/number years of service
3   Civil status/Country
4   Age
5   Worked/Age/Department.

Application of the decision coverage detailing measure for determinant 2 (IF worked = Y AND number of years ≥ 10) produces Table 15.18.

Table 15.18
Applying decision coverage for determinant 2

Determinant 2	Indication worked	Number of years
Determinant 2 = true	1	1
Determinant 2 = false	1	0

Application of the decision coverage detailing measure for determinant 3 (IF (married = Y OR living together = Y) AND country = 'Netherlands') produces Table 15.19.

Table 15.19
Applying decision coverage for determinant 3

Determinant 3	Married	Living together	Country
Determinant 3 = true	1	0	1
Determinant 3 = false	0	1	0

Application of the decision coverage detailing measure for determinant 4 (IF age ≥ 18 AND age ≤ 60) produces Table 15.20.

Table 15.20
Applying decision coverage for determinant 4

Determinant 4	Age ≥ 18	Age ≤ 60
Determinant 4 = true	1	1
Determinant 4 = false	0	1

Application of the decision coverage detailing measure for determinant 5 (IF worked = Y AND department = 'production' AND age ≥ 18) produces Table 15.21.

Table 15.21
Applying decision coverage for determinant 5

Determinant 5	Indication worked	Department	Age ≥ 18
Determinant 5 = true	1	1	1
Determinant 5 = false	1	0	1

If all complex determinants are described according to the selected detailing measure, then there are two possibilities to transform the logical test columns into logical test cases: splitting and including. In *splitting*, each logical test column is split into several logical test cases. The advantage is that when a possible defect occurs, the cause can be found quickly. A disadvantage is that the number of logical test cases increases. In *including*, the various test cases that result from breaking down the complex determinants are included within the logical test columns. The advantage of this is that it provides a 1 : 1 transformation (one logical test column is transformed into one logical test case), which requires little effort. The disadvantage is that the cause of a defect is not always immediately clear.

The difference between the two transformation techniques is illustrated by an example. The decision table shown in Table 15.22 together with test measure 2 constitute the starting point.

Logical test column	1	2	3	4	5
Event	1	1	1	1	1
A ≥ 0	1	0	0	0	1
B = 6	0	1	0	0	1
C = 2 AND D = 4 AND E =5	0	0	1	0	1
F ≤ 0 OR G ≥ 0	0	0	0	1	1
Result 1	X				X
Result 2		X	X	X	X

Table 15.22
Decision table for our example (see text for details)

The detailing measure used is condition/determination coverage. This results in Table 15.23 for the third determinant:

Number	C = 2	D = 4	E = 5	Result
1 (C, D and E are determining)	1	1	1	1
2 (E is determining)	1	1	0	0
3 (D is determining)	1	0	1	0
4 (C is determining)	0	1	1	0

Table 15.23
Applying condition/determination coverage for determinant 3

Condition/determination coverage is also applied to the fourth determinant, producing Table 15.24.

Number	F ≤ 0	G ≥ 0	Result
1 (F and G are determining)	0	0	0
3 (G is determining)	0	1	1
4 (F is determining)	1	0	1

Table 15.24
Applying condition/determination coverage for determinant 4

Splitting produces the logical test cases shown in Table 15.25.

Table 15.25
Logical test cases
after splitting

Logical test case	1a	1b	1c	2a	2b	2c	3	4a	4b	4c	5a	5b
Event	1	1	1	1	1	1	1	1	1	1	1	1
A ≥ 0	1	1	1	0	0	0	0	0	0	0	1	1
B = 6	0	0	0	1	1	1	0	0	0	0	1	1
C = 2	1	1	0	1	1	0	1	1	1	0	1	1
D = 4	1	0	1	1	0	1	1	1	0	1	1	1
E = 5	0	1	1	0	1	1	1	0	1	1	1	1
F ≤ 0	0	0	0	0	0	0	0	0	1	1	0	1
G ≥ 0	0	0	0	0	0	0	0	1	0	0	1	0
Result 1	X	X	X								X	X
Result 2				X	X	X	X	X	X	X	X	X

Splitting the logical test columns thus produces 12 logical test cases, which means an increase of no less than seven logical test cases compared with the number of test columns.

Applying including according to the selected detailing measure produces the logical test cases shown in Table 15.26.

Table 15.26
Logical test cases after
including

Logical test case	1	2	3	4	5
Event	1	1	1	1	1
A ≥ 0	1	0	0	0	1
B = 6	0	1	0	0	1
C = 2	1	1	1	0	1
D = 4	1	0	1	1	1
E = 5	0	1	1	1	1
F ≤ 0	0	0	0	0	1
G ≥ 0	0	0	0	1	0
Result 1	X				X
Result 2		X	X	X	X

In general, including is chosen for the transformation of logical test columns into logical test cases; only in special cases (a very great importance and/or risk) is splitting preferred. Usually, the maximum detailing measure is chosen that can still be included in the existing logical test columns. This restricts the number of logical test cases and hence keeps the test effort to a minimum. In our example, the condition/determination coverage detailing measure can just be included in the existing columns. The multiple condition coverage detailing measure, on the other hand, needs at least seven columns, of which the third determinant is false and these seven columns are absent. The condition/

determination coverage detailing measure is therefore the highest feasible detailing measure that can be included.

The final step with regard to our salary calculation example that is detailed consists of transforming the logical test columns into logical test cases. Including the logical test columns described above in logical test cases produces the results shown in Table 15.27.

Logical test case	1	2	3	4	5
Event	1	1	1	1	1
Determinant 1 Person's number	1	0	0	0	0
Determinant 2 Worked = Y	1	1	1	1	1
Determinant 2 Number of years ≥ 10	0	1	1	0	1
Determinant 3 Married = Y	0	0	1	1	1
Determinant 3 Living together = Y	1	1	0	0	0
Determinant 3 Country = 'Netherlands'	0	0	1	1	1
Determinant 4 Age ≥ 18	1	0	–	–	–
Determinant 4 Age ≤ 60	1	1	–	–	–
Determinant 5 Worked = Y	1	1	1	1	1
Determinant 5 Department = 'production'	1	0	0	0	1
Determinant 5 Age ≥ 18	1	0	1	1	1
Error message	X				
Salary		10 000	13 000	15 000	16 000

Table 15.27 Including the logical test columns

When including the logical test cases, a problem arises with determinant 5 in test case 2 if the accompanying value is taken directly from the decision coverage table. This is because there is another dependency with the value of age from determinant 4. This shows that translating logical test columns into logical test cases and then into physical test cases requires a certain degree of accuracy: it is not merely a matter of copying directly from the data already present.

Specifying physical test cases

The next step consists of translating the logical test cases into physical test cases. During this step, each logical test case is translated into a detailed description of how coverage of the logical test case should be obtained during the execution of the test. This step results in a description of the physical test cases.

Number

Each physical test case is numbered in such a way that it is possible to determine exactly from which logical test case it has been derived. This occurs by maintaining the same number but replacing the letters LTC (logical test case) by PTC (physical test case). Numbering can occur on the basis of the location of the test case in the decision table, and/or it can be a reference to the test basis from which it was derived.

Determinants
The test case is determined by the value of the determinants of the test case concerned. These values must be detailed and, in particular, described in concrete terms. Sometimes, however, a determinant's value is determined by an action or the event. In such cases, a detailed description should be made of the action that is to be executed.

Result
The expected result is determined and, if applicable, calculated. The expected result must be described in such a way that it can be checked, i.e. it should say not only *what* should be checked, but also *how* it must be checked.

Establishing the initial data set
In order to be able to execute the physical test cases, certain data are required. Some of these data have been indicated explicitly by the physical specification of the determinants. On the other hand, it is often necessary to define certain master data along with the data that are primarily required for the test. For reasons of control and reuse, it is wise to define these data in advance and have them at hand, instead of creating them during the test. During this step, initial data sets are described. These data should be given a meaningful name to make it easy to identify the test case to which they belong. If there are time-dependent data, this must be stated explicitly so that it can be taken into consideration at a later stage during retests.

Assembling the test script
The sequence in which the physical test cases must be executed must be recorded in the test script. In doing so, the aim should be maximum efficiency. This means that within the space available, one must choose the sequence that results in the least number of changes (such as logging on and off under different user IDs, or resetting the initial databases), because such activities are time consuming. It is impossible to provide general rules for this. The presence of explicit test expertise is therefore indispensable.

15.7.3 Test execution and assessment
The tests are executed according to the test scripts. We can obtain a good insight into the progress of the test by keeping an account of how many test cases have been defined, how many have been tested, and how many of these have found a defect. Assessing the results of a decision table test is highly variable. It is not always immediately clear what the defect is. This depends mainly on the number of determinants that has been tested by means of a certain test case.

The test results can be recorded in the test script. For this purpose, two columns have been included in the test script: 'OK' and 'Note'. The test results are marked in the 'OK' column, with either 'yes' (no defect found) or 'no' (defect found), while the 'Note' column can be used to indicate the number of the accompanying defect report. An overall assessment regarding the test script that has been executed can also be included in the test script.

15.8 Elementary comparison test

15.8.1 Introduction
In the elementary comparison test (ECT), the processing is tested in detail. The test verifies all functional paths of a function. This is done by making an inventory of all functional conditions that are subsequently translated into lines of pseudo-code. Then the test cases are defined for the various functional paths that can be distinguished within the function. The ECT guarantees a reasonable degree of completeness, but it is labor intensive. For this reason, it should be used primarily to test very important functions and/or complex calculations. This technique can be applied in both a batch and online environment

15.8.2 Procedure
ECT involves the following steps:

1 Analyzing function description.
2 Establishing test situations.
3 Establishing logical test cases.
4 Establishing physical test cases.
5 Establishing test actions.
6 Establishing checks.
7 Establishing the initial data set.
8 Assembling the test script.

To illustrate this, we will use an example of a sports club subscription:

```
IF   (system date – date of birth) <= 18 years
     THEN subscription := 0
     IF NOT
          subscription := 200
          IF date of birth >= 1-1-1964 AND income ≤ 45 000 AND
            indication defaulter = 0
                    THEN subscription := subscription – 50
          END-IF
          IF date of registration ≤ 1-1-1988 AND membership type = 'general'
            AND indication defaulter = 0
            AND (type of player = 'comp' OR player level = 'c')
                    THEN subscription := subscription + 50
          END-IF
END-IF
```

Analyzing function descriptions

A section on processing has been incorporated in the function description, which should describe unambiguously the decision paths and related aspects. This may already have taken place by means of the pseudo-code, as in this example. If the description was made by means of a different technique, e.g. using decision tables, the ECT can also be applied. The main point is the presence of an unambiguous description of the processing paths.

Before deciding which situations are to be tested, the processing, described in pseudo-code in our example, must be analyzed. This includes finding the conditions, which are often recognized by terms such as 'DO', 'IF', 'REPEAT', etc. These are singled out one by one, and provided with a unique identification tag, after which the situations to be tested are defined. This applies only when the IF or DO part is driven by means of data input. In 'DO as long as counter $\leq$ 10', for example, the DO part is driven internally and not by means of explicit data input. Such lines of pseudo-code are not taken into consideration when defining test situations within the framework of ECT.

```
C1 IF (system date – date of birth) <= 18 years
        THEN subscription := 0
        ELSE
            subscription := 200
    C2      IF date of birth >= 1-1-1964 AND income ≤ 45 000
            AND indication defaulter = 0
                THEN subscription := subscription – 50
            END-IF
    C3      IF date of registration ≤ 1-1-1988 AND membership type =
                'general' AND indication defaulter = 0 AND
                (type of player = 'comp'
                OR player level = 'c')
                THEN subscription := subscription + 50
            END-IF
    END-IF
```

Establishing test situations

After the conditions have been identified (indicated in the example above with tags C1, C2 and C3), the situations to be tested for each condition must be determined. It is very important to differentiate between simple and complex conditions. Simple conditions consist of only one comparison, the *elementary comparison*. An example is the C1 condition. Complex conditions are conditions that contain multiple comparisons, connected by AND or OR relationships. An example is the C2 condition.

Before we look at our example in greater detail, we must first introduce some fundamentals of Boolean algebra. The (simple) condition IF (system date – date of birth) $\leq$ 18 years is either true or false. There are no other options. Simple conditions result in either of two situations, namely the situation in which the comparison is true and the situation where the comparison is false. In the present example, this leads to the test situations shown in Table 15.28.

Test situation	1	2
C1	True	False
System date – date of birth	$\leq=$ 18 years	$\geq$ 18 years

Table 15.28
Test situations for our example (see text for details)

The same applies to complex conditions. Compare the following complex conditions:

IF date of birth $\geq=$ 1-1-1964 AND income $\leq$ 45 000

IF date of birth $\geq=$ 1-1-1964 OR income $\leq$ 45 000

This type of condition is also either true or false, but the truth value of a complex condition depends on whether the constituent simple conditions are true or false. In addition, the conjunction between the simple conditions also plays an important role: are the conditions joined by the conjunction AND or OR? In Boolean algebra, a zero (0) is used to indicate that something is false, and a one (1) is used when something is true. Starting from two conditions, this provides the following possible combinations:

$$\begin{vmatrix} 0 & 0 \\ 0 & 1 \\ 1 & 0 \\ 1 & 1 \end{vmatrix}$$

In the 0–0 situation, both statements are false. In the 0–1 situation and the 1–0 situation, only one of the two statements is true. In the 1–1 situation, both statements are true. But what is the final result for the complex condition, given the type of conjunction incorporated? The following table lists all possible combinations:

$$\begin{vmatrix} (0 \text{ AND } 0) \rightarrow 0 \ (0 \text{ OR } 0) \rightarrow 0 \\ (0 \text{ AND } 1) \rightarrow 0 \ (0 \text{ OR } 1) \rightarrow 1 \\ (1 \text{ AND } 0) \rightarrow 0 \ (1 \text{ OR } 0) \rightarrow 1 \\ (1 \text{ AND } 1) \rightarrow 1 \ (1 \text{ OR } 1) \rightarrow 1 \end{vmatrix}$$

This shows that there are crucial differences. In the case of an AND situation, the end result of two conditions is only true if the two individual conditions are true. In all other cases, the end result is false. In the case of an OR situation, the opposite is the case: the end result is only false if both conditions are false. In all other cases, the end result is true.

A complex condition that contains three separate conditions provides the following eight possible combinations:

$$\begin{vmatrix} 0 & 0 & 0 \\ 0 & 0 & 1 \\ 0 & 1 & 0 \\ 0 & 1 & 1 \\ 1 & 0 & 0 \\ 1 & 0 & 1 \\ 1 & 1 & 0 \\ 1 & 1 & 1 \end{vmatrix}$$

The number of possibilities increases exponentially. With six elementary comparisons, there are already 64 (2^6) possibilities. The ECT is based on the fact that it is not useful to identify all these possibilities as situations to be tested, but that an adequate coverage can be achieved with a much smaller number of test situations. With an ECT, the test situations in the case of complex conditions are selected in such a way that a change in the value of any one of the elementary comparisons changes the value of the complex condition. This means that for an OR relationship the situation true–true, and for the AND relationship the situation false–false, is not tested. The chances of finding a defect here that has not already been observed in the true–false or false–true situations are minimal.

If we write 0 for false and 1 for true, we can summarize as follows: *for a complex condition consisting of multiple comparisons between which there is an AND relationship, those situations will be tested in which each elementary comparison has a truth value of 1, as well as all those situations in which only one elementary comparison has a truth value of 0 while the rest are 1. The opposite applies to a complex condition consisting of OR, i.e. the only situations that are tested are the one in which each elementary comparison has a truth value of 0, plus all situations in which just one elementary comparison has a truth value of 1 and the rest are 0. This reduces the number of test situations to the number of elementary comparisons plus 1 (= no change).*

This is shown in Table 15.29 for condition 2 of our example (note that an AND conjunction can also be displayed as '&' and an OR as '|').

Test situation	C2.1	C2.2	C2.3	C2.4
C2 (= C2a & C2b & C2c)	1 (111)	0 (011)	0 (101)	0 (110)
C2a date of birth ≥ 1-1-1964	≥=1-1-1964	≤ 1-1-1964	≥= 1-1-1964	≥= 1-1-1964
C2b income ≤ 45 000	≤ 45 000	≤ 45 000	≥= 45 000	≤ 45 000
C2c indication defaulter = 0	0	0	0	1

Table 15.29

Test situations for condition 2 of our example (see text for details)

For complex conditions with only AND or OR relationships, the test situations are easy to find. It becomes more difficult when the complex condition consists of a combination of one or more AND and OR relationships, such as in the C3 example. In such cases, we use a matrix (Table 15.30). In the first column, we put each elementary comparison. The second column shows how the truth value true (1) for the complex condition can be arrived at in such a way that a change in the value of the elementary comparison on the row in question (its value is underlined for the sake of clarity) would change the value of the complex condition to false (0). The third column does the same for situations in which the truth value of the complex condition is false. Obviously, the only difference between the second and third columns is to be found in the underlined values. Note that a dot in the format makes sure that the various groups that constitute the complex condition are easy to recognize.

After crossing off the repetitive test situations in the matrix, we are left with the logical test situations. It is advisable to copy the underlining in the value against which a test situation is being crossed off, as this facilitates checks being performed.

C3 (= C3a & C3b & C3c & (C3d I C3e)	1 (subscription := subscription + 50)	0 (subscription := subscription)
Date of registration ≤ 1-1-1988 (C3a)	$\underline{1}$.1.1.01	$\underline{0}$.1.1.01
Membership type = 'general' (C3b)	1.$\underline{1}$.1.01	1.$\underline{0}$.1.01
Indication defaulter = 0 (C3c)	1.1.$\underline{1}$.01	1.1.$\underline{0}$.01
Type of player = 'comp' (C3d)	1.1.1.$\underline{1}$0	1.1.1.$\underline{0}$0
Player level = 'c' (C3e)	1.1.1.0$\underline{1}$	1.1.1.0$\underline{0}$

Table 15.30

Test situations for condition 3 of our example (see text for details)

Note that there is no particular reason why on rows 2 to 4 the constituent complex condition (C3d I C3e) is chosen to be 01 rather than 10 (but it could not have been 00, as the outcome should evaluate true, or 11, as this situation is not tested). If we now cross off the repeated values, we are left with the test situations shown in Table 15.31 (note that this is the number of comparisons plus 1).

Table 15.31
Test situations
remaining for condition
3 after repeated values
have been crossed out
(see text for details)

C3 (= C3a & C3b & C3c & (C3d l C3e)	1(subscription := subscription + 50	0 subscription := subscription
Date of registration ≤ 1-1-1988 (C3a)	1.1.1.01	0.1.1.01
Membership type = 'general' (C3b)	~~1.1.1.01~~	1.0.1.01
Indication defaulter = 0 (C3c)	~~1.1.1.01~~	1.1.0.01
Type of player = 'comp' (C3d)	1.1.1.10	1.1.1.00
Player level = 'c' (C3e)	~~1.1.1.01~~	~~1.1.1.00~~

This gives us the logical test situations shown in Table 15.32.

Test situation	C3.1	C3.2	C3.3	C3.4	C3.5	C3.6
C3	1 (11101)	1 (11110)	0 (01101)	0 (10101)	0(11001)	0(11100)
Date of registration	≤ 1-1-1988	≤ 1-1-1988	>= 1-1-1988	≤ 1-1-1988	≤ 1-1-1988	≤ 1-1-1988
Membership type	General	General	General	General	General	General
Indication defaulter	0	0	0	0	1	0
Type of player	≠comp	comp	≠comp	≠comp	≠comp	≠comp
Player level	c	≠c	c	c	c	≠c

Table 15.32 Logical test situations for condition 3 of our example (see text for details)

Establishing logical test cases

Establishing the logical test cases means finding the functional paths in which each situation of each condition should be completed at least once. In doing so, one should take into account the possibility that the same comparison may occur in more than one condition. An example of this is the comparison 'indication defaulter = 0' in conditions 2 and 3. When selecting the path combinations, one should also ensure that the expected end result is as unique as possible for the chosen path combinations. In our example, C2 = true and C3 = true gives the same result as C2 = false and C3 = false, because the subscription remains the same (namely 200). Test cases with C2 = true and C3 = false, or vice versa, have a unique end result and are therefore better test cases.

To help find test cases, and to check whether all situations in the test cases have been recorded, a matrix can be used (Table 15.33). All defined test situations are listed in the first column. The second column lists the value of the condition in this situation, and the third column gives the next condition to be processed. The test cases are then listed. If the test cases have been defined properly, all situations to be tested will be ticked off at least once. To cover all test situations in our subscription example, seven test cases have been defined.

For larger matrices, an additional column can be included for greater clarity, in which the total number of ticks for a test situation is filled in. This may not be zero.

Test situation	Value	To	Test case: 1	2	3	4	5	6	7	Check
C1.1	1	End	X							1
C1.2	0	C2		X	X	X	X	X	X	6
C2.1	1	C3		X				X		2
C2.2	0	C3			X				X	2
C2.3	0	C3				X				1
C2.4	0	C3					X			1
C3.1	1	End		X						1
C3.2	1	End			X					1
C3.3	0	End				X				1
C3.4	0	End						X		1
C3.5	0	End					X			1
C3.6	0	End							X	1

Table 15.33 Matrix to check whether all situations in the test cases have been recorded

Some situations will be tested several times. This is often unavoidable, and should be seen not as a waste of time but as an opportunity: by varying the input for that situation, more thorough testing is achieved.

Establishing physical test cases

The next step is to convert the logical test cases that have been found into physical test cases (Table 15.34). Note that the system date is a determining factor here.

Test case	1	2	3	4
Path	C1.1	C1.2, C2.1, C3.1	C1.2, C2.2, C3,2	C1.2, C2.3, C3.3
Date of birth	25-10-1990	1-1-1964	31-12-1963	1-1-1964
Income	44 999	44 999	44 999	45 000
Date of registration	31-12-1987	31-12-1987	31-12-1987	1-1-1988
Membership type	General	General	General	General
Indication defaulter	1	0	0	0
Type of player	Recreational	Recreational	Comp	Recreational
Player level	C	C	A	C

Test case	5	6	7
Path	C1.2, C2.4, C3.5	C1.2, C2.1, C3.4	C1.2, C2.2, C3.6
Date of birth	1-1-1964	1-1-1964	31-12-1963
Income	44 999	44 999	44 999
Date of registration	15-7-1987	31-12-1980	31-12-1987
Membership type	General	Honorary	General
Indication defaulter	1	0	0
Type of player	Recreational	Recreational	Recreational
Player level	C	C	A

Table 15.34 Converting logical test cases into physical test cases

Establishing test actions

When the test cases have been established, the test actions can also be established. A test action is a predefined action that can be successful or can fail (the actual test). For this purpose, all relevant subtasks (functions) are listed first. Usually, this concerns issues such as creating, changing, approving, displaying, deleting, etc. The question is whether this example contains test actions. This depends on how the subscription is calculated. This may take place after entry of a person, i.e. after entering personal data, the system will calculate the subscription. A second possibility is that a batch process calculates the subscription for all people at once.

For the former test actions will have to take place in which personal data are entered. After all, checks can take place only after a person has been entered. In the second situation, it will be sufficient to create the initial data set. Personal data entry occurs once, after which the data set is saved as a test set. Every time the batch must be tested again, the test set is loaded and the batch is run. Then the results of this are checked. For this example, we will assume that there is a batch that calculates the subscription for all people at once.

Test actions

This concerns a batch job (see the specification of the initial data set).

Establishing checks

It is necessary to describe what should be checked so that we can determine whether processing has been successful. The various results are precalculated in this step:

C01	Test case 1	Subscription:= 0
C02	Test case 2	Subscription:= 200
C03	Test case 3	Subscription:= 250
C04	Test case 4	Subscription:= 200
C05	Test case 5	Subscription:= 200
C06	Test case 6	Subscription:= 150
C07	Test case 7	Subscription:= 200

Establishing the initial data set

It should be decided whether it is necessary for the initial data set to be present for the test that is to be executed. If it is, then a description must be given that indicates for which test case data have been specified in the set. This description should be added to the test specification that was drawn up at an earlier stage. Entering the initial data occurs during the setting up of the initial test database (execution phase). With regard to our example, the following can be noted:

Initial data set

Table Persons/members:
- according to test cases 1–7 (test cases are based on any random system date between now and 24-10-2009).

Table Membership type:
- – 'general' for test cases 1, 2, 3, 4, 5 and 7;
- – 'honorary' for test case 6.

Table Type of player:
- – 'recreational' for test cases 1, 2, 4, 5, 6 and 7;
- – 'comp' for test case 3.

Table Player level:
- – 'c' for test cases 1,2,4,5 and 6;
- – 'a' for test cases 3 and 7.

If the initial data set contains data that can be used only for a limited time, e.g. as a result of an end date or a system date as in our example, this should be stated explicitly. In a retest, it should then be checked whether these time-dependent data are still valid and, on the basis of this, whether the initial data set needs to be adapted. Time dependencies should be prevented if possible, as they make retesting more time consuming and error prone.

Assembling the test script

A test script is assembled on the basis of the test cases in which the test actions and checks that are to be executed are described in the correct order. The test script lists any pre- and post-conditions. A precondition for test script X could be, for example, that test script Y has been completed or that the system date has a certain value.

As our example concerns batch processing, the test script remains relatively simple. It lists only the start-up of the batch concerned and the checks that must be performed subsequently.

15.8.3 Test execution

The tests are executed according to the test scripts. One obtains a good insight into the progress of the test by keeping an account of how many test cases have been defined in total, how many have been tested, and how many of these found a defect.

15.8.4 Assessment

Assessing the results of the elementary comparison tests is often difficult. Many conditions in the paths render it hard to isolate any suspicious conditions in the case of deviating results. Reporting can be by means of the test script. For this purpose, two columns have been included in the test script: 'OK' and 'Note'. The test results are marked in the 'OK' column, with either 'yes' (no defect found) or 'no' (defect found), while the 'Note' column can be used to indicate the number of the accompanying defect report, if applicable. An overall assessment regarding the test script that has been executed can also be included in the test script.

15.9 Error guessing

15.9.1 Introduction

Error guessing is unstructured testing. Its value lies in the unexpected: tests are executed that would otherwise not have been considered. It is a valuable complement to the structured test-specification techniques. The error guessing technique is used in particular with high-level testing and can focus in principle on all possible quality characteristics.

The experience of the tester plays an important role here. The tester has complete freedom to invent test cases on the spot and try them out. The essence of error guessing is that the tester tries to find those cases that always cause problems – trying out these cases is the way to test them.

In principle, the only starting condition for error guessing is that the tester has a thorough understanding of the system to be tested. In addition, a certain degree of stability of the system to be tested is desirable. Error guessing is eminently suitable for the final stage of the test process.

However, it must not be used as the only technique. The benefit of structured testing is the relative completeness that is achieved. It is also not advisable to apply error guessing to a relatively unstable system: because of the nature of this technique, repeatability and hence the reproducibility of the defects found are small.

15.9.2 Procedure

Preparation for error guessing includes the activity identifying weaknesses.

Identifying weaknesses

This is performed before execution of the error guessing test. During this activity, it may also be determined that it is necessary to construct a certain starting situation (e.g. an initial data set) for the test.

The weaknesses often stem from errors in the mental processes of others and issues that have been forgotten. These aspects constitute the basis for the test that is to be executed. Examples are:

- error handling, e.g. error upon error, or interruption of a process at an unexpected moment;
- illegal values, e.g. negative numbers, null values, values that are too great, names that are too long, or empty records;
- parts of the information system that were subject to change requests during the project;
- security;
- claiming too many resources.

A plan is made for the error guessing test on the basis of identified weaknesses. A tester is given the assignment to perform error guessing regarding a specific part of the aspect during a certain period of time.

15.9.3 Test execution

The execution of the test depends on what you wish to test: a relationship, the processing of a certain function, or a screen layout. It may be necessary to construct certain starting situations, as indicated above. You will need to decide whether to document the test specifications and test execution. If the test is not documented, then the initial data set must be removed after completion of the test, to prevent noise. However, if any defects are found, the corresponding test cases should be documented. This can be done in a test script, but also as part of the description in the defect report. It is also important to check the test documentation that is already present. It is, after all, possible that the defect would have been found on the basis of the test cases already present, but that the accompanying test script is only executed at a later stage.

The second condition that must be met as well as possible is the reproducibility of the test. It is possible that during error guessing defects are found while the starting situation or test actions are unknown.

If a tester is using error guessing on a test unit that is the responsibility of another tester (a recommended practice), then any defects found should be handed over to the tester, who then carries out a structured test on that specific test unit. There must be an accurate description of the starting situation and the test actions that gave rise to that particular defect. The tester who is responsible then assesses the extent to which their test documentation needs to be adapted.

15.10 Process cycle test

15.10.1 Introduction

The aim of the process cycle test (PCT) is to check whether the automated part of the information system fits within the administrative organization (AO) procedures, paying particular attention to the interfaces between the automated processes and the manual procedures. It is assumed here that the automated processes in themselves work in accordance with the specifications. The PCT verifies whether the automated processes and the manual procedures match each other. This should provide answers to the following questions:

- Do the automated processes provide sufficient information in order to perform all manual procedures?
- Does the output of the manual procedures provide sufficient data in order to start all automated processes?
- Do employees have sufficient authorization to perform the procedures?

The PCT is used mainly to establish suitability. If necessary, the test can also focus on the quality characteristics of user-friendliness and security.

The PCT differs from other test-specification techniques on a number of points, e.g. it is not a specification test but a structural test. The test cases derive from the structure of the procedure flow (just as in a unit test, the test cases derive from the structure of the algorithm), not from the design specifications. Every test case therefore consists of a sequence of actions that together form a path through the procedure flow.

Contrary to other test cases that are created with the aid of other test-specification techniques, no (explicit) checks are related to these actions. The (implicit) check on a certain action is simply that the subsequent action can be executed. It is therefore sufficient to check whether the sequence of actions can actually be executed.

Another difference is that execution requires more than just the technical test infrastructure upon which the automated part of the information system runs. The manual procedures must usually be performed by different types of employees, which means that more testers are needed. It is also possible to have the test executed by a single tester who has several user IDs and who logs in and out several times during the execution of the test. Finally, only some of the necessary data are in the database of the automated part of the information system; the rest are outside, e.g. in forms that have been filled in.

When the various steps are specified, a distinction is made between the in-depth PCT and a 'normal' PCT. The selection between the two is made on the basis of the importance of suitability of the quality characteristic in the test strategy. The difference between the two tests can be reduced to the difference in test measure.

The test measure is used to decide to what extent dependencies between consecutive decision points are tested. In test measure n, all dependencies of actions before a decision point and after $n-1$ decision points are verified by including all possible combinations regarding the actions in test paths. One works on the basis of test measure 2 with an in-depth PCT and test measure 1 with the 'normal' PCT.

A detailed description of the in-depth process cycle test (test measure 2) is given first, followed by a description of the 'normal' process cycle test (test measure 1).

15.10.2 Procedure of the process cycle test for test measure 2

The steps to be taken in order to arrive at a specification for a process cycle test for test measure 2 include:

1   Making an inventory of decision points.
2   Establishing path combinations and paths.
3   Specifying test cases.
4   Establishing the initial data set.
5   Assembling the test script.

Making an inventory of decision points

The test basis for the test concerned is read. This is a description of the AO procedures for the PCT. Within these AO procedures, the decision points (decision
processes or decision procedures) must be tracked down. In an ideal situation, if the
AO procedures are displayed in the form of a procedure flow, this is a simple activity, and concerns merely searching for the (rhombus-shaped) decision symbols.

Establishing path combinations and paths

For every decision point found, the path combinations must be determined. A
path combination is a link between an action before a decision point and an
action after the same decision point. When creating path combinations, it is
wise to number the actions first. Sequential actions between two decision points
receive a common number. All path combinations, i.e. all combinations of two
consecutive actions with a decision point in between, must be written out. This
is illustrated in the following example (Figure 15.2).

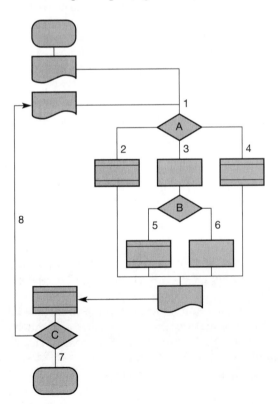

Figure 15.2
Flow chart showing path
combinations

In the client registration department, modification forms come in concerning the name and address data of customers. The head of the department
receives the modification forms and passes them on to an employee of the

department. Depending on the type of modification (changing, entering or deleting), a maintenance function for the name and address data is started. If it concerns a new client (modification type = entering), then a certain continuation screen is filled in depending on the country code.

After the modification has been performed, the employee provides the head of the department with a written report of completion, who then checks the modification using the function of approval of name and address data. If the modification is correct, it is approved and the procedure is ended. If a defect is detected, the modification is returned to the employee concerned.

Path combinations for decision point A: (1,2); (1,3); (1,4); (8,2); (8,3) and (8,4).
Path combinations for decision point B: (3,5) and (3,6).
Path combinations for decision point C: (2,7); (4,7); (5,7); (6,7); (2,8); (4,8); (5,8) and (6,8).

These path combinations must now be linked to create paths that run from the start of the procedure flow to the end of the procedure flow. In our example, each path starts with action 1 and ends with action 7. Each path combination must be included in at least one path, so the path combinations are (1,2); (1,3); (1,4); (2,7); (2,8); (3,5); (3,6); (4,7); (4,8); (5,7); (5,8); (6,7); (6,8); (8,2); (8,3) and (8,4).

1   Start with the first path combination that has not yet been included in a path, in this case (1,2). Then link the first path combination that starts with a 2 and has not yet been included in a path, in this case (2,7). This creates the path (1,2,7), after which the next path can be started. The remaining path combinations are (1,2); (1,3); (1,4); (2,7); (2,8); (3,5); (3,6); (4,7); (4,8); (5,7); (5,8); (6,7); (6,8); (8,2); (8,3) and (8,4).

2   Continue with the remaining path combinations. The first path combination that has not yet been included in a path is (1,3). The first path combination that starts with a 3 and has not yet been included in a path is (3,5). The first path combination that starts with a 5 and has not yet been included in a path is (5,7). Another path is created: (1,3,5,7). The remaining path combinations are (1,2); (1,3); (1,4); (2,7); (2,8); (3,5); (3,6); (4,7); (4,8); (5,7); (5,8); (6,7); (6,8); (8,2); (8,3) and (8,4).

3   The first path combination that has not yet been included in a path is (1,4). The first path combination that starts with a 4 and has not yet been included in a path, is (4,7). Another path is created: (1,4,7). The remaining path combinations are (1,2); (1,3); (1,4); (2,7); (2,8); (3,5); (3,6); (4,7); (4,8); (5,7); (5,8); (6,7); (6,8); (8,2); (8,3) and (8,4).

4   The first path combination that has not yet been included in a path is (2,8). Because this path combination does not start at the beginning of the procedure flow, another path combination must be placed in front of it: (1,2) is selected. This has now been used twice, but that is not a problem. Then continue with the search for the first path combination that starts with an 8

and has not yet been included in a path: (8,2). Because there are no more path combinations that start with a 2 and have not yet been included, a path combination is selected that starts with a 2 but has already been included: (2,7) is chosen, which results in the path (1,2,8,2,7). The remaining path combinations are ~~(1,2)~~; ~~(1,3)~~; ~~(1,4)~~; ~~(2,7)~~; ~~(2,8)~~; ~~(3,5)~~; (3,6); ~~(4,7)~~; (4,8); ~~(5,7)~~; (5,8); (6,7); (6,8); ~~(8,2)~~; (8,3) and (8,4).

5   The first path combination that has not yet been included in a path is (3,6). Because this path combination does not start at the beginning of the procedure flow, another path combination must be placed in front of it: (1,3) is selected. Then search for the first path combination that starts with a 6 and has not yet been included in a path: this is (6,7), creating the path (1,3,6,7). The remaining path combinations are ~~(1,2)~~; ~~(1,3)~~; ~~(1,4)~~; ~~(2,7)~~; ~~(2,8)~~; ~~(3,5)~~; ~~(3,6)~~; ~~(4,7)~~; (4,8); ~~(5,7)~~; (5,8); ~~(6,7)~~; (6,8); ~~(8,2)~~; (8,3) and (8,4).

6   The first path combination that has not yet been included in a path is (4,8). Because this path combination does not start at the beginning of the procedure flow, another path combination must be placed in front of it: (1,4) is selected. Then search for the first path combination that starts with a 8 and has not yet been included in a path: this is (8,3). Because there are no more path combinations that start with a 3 and have not yet been included, a path combination is selected that starts with a 3 but that has already been included: this is (3,5). Again, there are possible unused path combinations: (5,8); (8,4) and finally (4,7), which has already been used. This provides the path (1,4,8,3,5,8,4,7). The remaining path combinations are ~~(1,2)~~; ~~(1,3)~~; ~~(1,4)~~; ~~(2,7)~~; ~~(2,8)~~; ~~(3,5)~~; ~~(3,6)~~; ~~(4,7)~~; ~~(4,8)~~; ~~(5,7)~~; ~~(5,8)~~; ~~(6,7)~~; (6,8); ~~(8,2)~~; ~~(8,3)~~ and ~~(8,4)~~.

7   The last remaining path combination, (6,8), is included in a path that is as simple as possible: (1,3,6,8,2,7). This means that all path combinations have been included in the following paths:
Path 1: (1,2,7)
Path 2: (1,3,5,7)
Path 3: (1,4,7)
Path 4: (1,2,8,2,7)
Path 5: (1,3,6,7)
Path 6: (1,4,8,3,5,8,4,7)
Path 7: (1,3,6,8,2,7)

In Table 15.35, the path combinations have been set out against the paths. It is wise to make such a cross-reference table: by doing so, it becomes clear that each path combination has been included in a path at least once. This table is easily automated in a simple spreadsheet using the formula =IF(ISERR(SEARCH(R1C, RC1, 1)), '', '1') plus the completeness check formula as bottom row: =IF(SUM(C)=0,'X','). (Thanks, Mark Fewster!)

Path/Combination	12	13	14	27	28	35	36	47	48	57	58	67	68	82	83	84
127	X			X												
1357		X				X				X						
147			X					X								
12827	X			X	X									X		
1367		X					X					X				
14835847			X			X		X	X		X				X	X
136827		X		X			X						X	X		

Table 15.35 Cross-reference table setting out path combinations against the paths

Specifying test cases

The paths through the procedure flow must be provided with a definite content in this step. As we have said before, this means that for each path, a sequence of actions must be described in such a way that the correct path is taken when these actions are executed. This is an activity that requires a certain amount of inventiveness and is therefore quite difficult to describe in general terms. We will restrict ourselves to giving an example.

The actual content of path 4 = (1,2,8,2,7) may look like this:

P4-1   The supervisor provides the employee with a modification form containing a modification assignment for customer data (action 1).

P4-2   The employee determines the type of modification on the basis of the modification form in the decision process A (modification type is change).

P4-3   The employee performs the customer modification, making a deliberate error, and then submits a written completion report to the supervisor (action 2).

P4-4   The supervisor of the department checks whether the modification has been entered properly in decision process C (the supervisor must discover the error).

P4-5   The supervisor returns the modification form to the employee with a request to enter the modification again (action 8).

P4-6   The employee determines the type of modification on the basis of the modification form in the decision process A (modification type is therefore Change again).

P4-7   The employee carries out the customer modification, this time correctly (action 2).

P4-8   The supervisor of the department checks whether the modification has been entered properly in decision process C (the supervisor discovers no error now).

P4-9   The supervisor approves the customer modification (action 7).

Establishing the initial data set

It should be decided whether it is necessary for the initial data set to be present for the test that is to be executed. As mentioned before, this concerns data not only in the database of the automated part of the information system but also informs that have been filled in. In the example of path 4, at least one customer must be present in the database of the automated system and there must be a form filled out to contain the original modification order.

Assembling the test script

The result of this step should be a test script. This test script is used to execute the tests. This means that the actions from the paths must be made concrete (i.e. not 'make a change', but: 'change the address for the customer with customer number 827 from 37 High Street to 47 Lower Street'). For each action to be executed, a short description is given. If a work instruction or a user manual is available, a reference to this is included. This makes it possible during testing to perform the action according to the descriptions in the user manual or work instruction, allowing any errors or obscurities to be detected. Including these documents in the PCT makes the quality characteristic of user-friendliness an aspect of this test.

In the test script, the actions are often linked to the user ID of an official who is authorized to perform the activity concerned. Defining user IDs per function group, including the future authorization, makes it possible to test security by using these user IDs. By expanding the test script with user IDs and the link with the user manual or the work instruction, the scope of the PCT can also be expanded in a relatively simple way with the quality characteristics of user-friendliness and security.

The test script should also list any preconditions. Preconditions often refer to the initial data set or to the fact that a system date should have a certain value. A precondition for test script X may be that test script Y has been executed completely.

15.10.3 Procedure of the process cycle test for test measure 1

The steps to be taken in order to arrive at a specification for a PCT for test measure 1 include:

1 Making an inventory of decision points.
2 Determining test paths.
3 Specifying test cases.
4 Establishing the initial data set.
5 Assembling the test script.

The approach to be taken with steps 1, 3, 4 and 5 is, in principle, the same as with test measure 2, so we will not describe these again. The difference between the two types of PC2 is in step 2, determining test paths.

Determining test paths

The test paths are the various possibilities for the process flow to be run. The following rules apply:

- A test path always starts at a starting point and continues to an end point.
- All separate activities must occur at least once in a test path.
- The aim is to have as few test paths as possible, but to include all possible activities.

When determining the test paths, the starting point is the start symbol of the first process. Then the first decision point is found. A decision point is indicated in the process flow with a rhombus. A decision point indicates an intersection, where the procedure is split into several paths. From the decision point, a path must be chosen. The easiest way is to first choose the shortest possible path. The path is followed through the subsequent decision points until an end symbol is reached. The entire sequence of following the paths from the starting symbol to the end symbol constitutes the first test path.

The next test path takes the same path as the first test path until the last decision point. A different direction is chosen at this point. The determination of the test paths is continued from the last decision point until all paths after the decision point have been included in a test path. The same is done from the second to last decision point. This procedure is followed until all possible paths from all decision points have been dealt with.

By working your way back from the last decision point, the test paths are determined in a structured way and the completeness of the test can be ensured. If a different direction is taken at the first decision point, we could possibly end up with fewer test paths, but ensuring completeness would be a much more complex activity, with the risk that a path was overlooked.

The procedure is applied to the procedure flow that has previously been displayed schematically with the description of the process cycle test on the basis of test measure 2. Starting from the starting symbol and consistently choosing the path with the lowest number from the decision point creates the first test path: 1,2,7.

Then we start to detail the path from the last decision point (C). Instead of taking path 7, we take path 8. At decision point A, path 3 is chosen, and at decision point B, path 5 is chosen. This creates the second test path: 1,2,8,3,5,7.

As the last decision point has been specified in full, the next step is to start from the second to last decision point (B). Instead of path 5, which already appears in test path 2, path 6 is chosen. At decision point C, the choice is, in principle, indifferent, although as path 4 has not yet been included, and we must try to have a minimum number of test paths, path 8 is chosen for decision point C. The third test path therefore looks like this: 1,3,6,8,4,7. Now, all activities have been included in the following test paths:

Path 1: (1,2,7)
Path 2: (1,2,8,3,5,7)
Path 3: (1,3,6,8,4,7)

The number of test paths has now been reduced from seven with the PCT with test measure 2 to three with the PCT with test measure 1. Obviously, this means a lower degree of coverage with the PCT with test measure 1, but this was a conscious choice in the test strategy.

When determining the test paths, one must make a note of the activities that have already been dealt with. The simplest technique for this is to tick off the paths on the procedure flows. In our example, the first test path already involves paths 1, 2 and 7. This leaves paths 3, 4, 5, 6 and 8. As a test path always runs from a starting symbol to an end symbol, it is necessary that paths 1 and 7 occur several times in the test paths.

15.10.4 Test execution and assessment
The tests are executed according to the test scripts. Assessing the test results of a process cycle test is usually straightforward. The check can take place immediately because it consists merely of checking the feasibility of the next action. Reporting can be by means of the test script. For this purpose, two columns have been included in the test script: 'OK' and 'Note'. The 'OK' column shows the test result, e.g. 'yes' (no defect found) or 'no' (defect found). The 'Note' column may show the number of the accompanying defect report. A short total assessment regarding the test script that has been executed can also be included in the test script.

15.11 Program interface test

15.11.1 Introduction
The program interface test (PIT) is a test-specification technique used to test the interfaces between the various programs and/or modules. Before a PIT can be started, the programs to be integrated must have been tested independently of each other using simulated data flows. If all programs to be integrated function properly independently of each other when driven by simulated data flows, this technique is used to verify whether the programs still function correctly after integration. If this is the case, the programs are then driven with 'real' data flows instead of simulated ones. The PIT is used mainly in the integration test.

15.11.2 Overall operation
The outline of the PIT is shown in Figure 15.3:

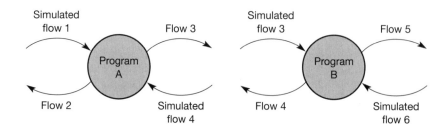

Programs A and B have already been tested by means of simulated data flows. The input of program A has been simulated by flows 1 and 4, while the output of Program A (flows 2 and 3) is collected and checked for correctness. A similar explanation applies to program B: the input has been simulated by flows 3 and 6, and the output (4 and 5) was collected and checked for correctness.

During the PIT, it must be verified whether program B still functions correctly when the simulated input flow 3, is replaced by the 'real' flow 3, and whether program A still functions correctly when the simulated input flow 4 is replaced by the 'real' flow 4.

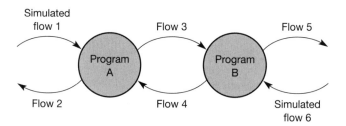

Figure 15.4 shows the interface between programs A and B. Input from other programs is still simulated (flows 1 and 6), and the output to other programs is still siphoned off prematurely. The other interfaces will be dealt with at a later integration step. Programs A and B are then viewed as one program, with flows 1 and 6 as input and flows 2 and 5 as output, and the interface of the composite program with the other programs is tested. This means that the simulated flows 1 and 6 are replaced by data flows from new programs to be integrated.

The aim of the PIT is to check whether the various programs interpret the data flows in the same way. It is here that defects often occur because the data flows between two programs have been described in several places. Flow 3, for example, has been described as an output flow for program A and an input flow for program B. Obviously, there has been coordination between those involved and agreements have been made about the format of the data flows, but these agreements may have been interpreted or implemented differently. If this is the case, it was not noticed during earlier tests because the tests were executed on the basis of a single description. These types of misinterpretations and incorrect execution are dealt with during an integration test in which the PIT technique is used as a tool. The PIT focuses in particular on the interfaces, not explicitly on the correctness and completeness of processing.

We can distinguish two types of data flows: direct and indirect data flows. With a *direct data flow*, the sender program transports the data directly to the receiving program without storing them in a file. With an *indirect data flow*, the sender program stores the data in a file and the receiving program collects the data from this file. Both types of data flows can be tested using the PIT. The data cycle test is also available for testing indirect data flows.

15.11.3 Procedure

The following steps must be taken within the framework of a PIT:

1   Identifying the data flows.
2   Establishing equivalence partitions.
3   Establishing test cases.
4   Establishing test actions and checks.
5   Establishing the initial data set.
6   Assembling the test script.

Identifying the data flows

The first thing to do during this step is to identify the data flows (direct and indirect) that are involved in the integration. These data flows are then observed at the attributes level. The domain of each attribute is determined, as well as the validity rules for other attributes that are present.

Establishing equivalence partitions

In general, it is not possible to include all possible values of attributes from the domains in test cases. Therefore, the domain for each attribute is split into equivalence partitions. An equivalence partition is a subcollection of a domain containing the attribute values that are equal (equivalence) for the purposes of the test. Clearly, an attribute value can belong to only one equivalence partition.

The division of an attribute's domain into equivalence partitions depends mainly on the format of the attribute (numeric, alphanumeric or date). There are general and format specific rules:

- Each attribute value from a domain must be included in an equivalence partition.
- Each attribute value can occur in only a single equivalence partition.
- If an attribute is not mandatory for the sender program, then the empty set is also an equivalence partition.
- If the domain of an attribute contains only a few values, then each value is an equivalence partition (consisting of a single element). This means that there are no equivalence values.

- If the domain of the attribute contains a large number of numeric values, then the following equivalence partitions are taken:
  - the smallest number;
  - the greatest number;
  - 0 (if within the domain);
  - a number with the greatest number of positions (both before and after the decimal point);
  - a number with the smallest number of positions (both before and after the decimal point);
  - the remaining numbers.

  If these numbers coincide (e.g. the greatest number of the attribute domain is the number with the greatest number of positions, or the smallest number in the attribute domain is 0), then the equivalence partitions are combined.
- If the domain of the attribute contains a large number of alphanumeric values, then the following equivalence partitions are taken:
  - a value with the minimum number of positions;
  - a value with the maximum number of positions;
  - the other values.

When these steps have been executed, the test cases for the PIT are described at the logical level.

Establishing test cases

This step consists of two parts. First, a representative from each equivalence partition must be chosen. If an equivalence partition consists of a single attribute value, there is no choice. If an equivalence partition contains several attribute values, then a choice must be made. In principle, it does not matter which attribute values are chosen as representatives. Preferably, choose an attribute value that borders on another equivalence partition to be the representative.

When a representative has been chosen from each equivalence partition, the representatives must be combined into test cases. These test cases will almost always also be the physical test cases. The validity rules must be taken into account here because these state that certain combinations of attribute values are not permitted. The representatives should be included in as few test cases as possible. Each test case requires a certain amount of processing time, and the test cases are merely a means to test the representatives.

Establishing test actions and checks

For each test case, a description must be made of the accompanying test action(s) and measurable check(s). This means that for each test case, it must be determined which actions the tester must perform on the sender program, i.e. how should the sender program be started, so that a data flow with the correct contents (in conformance with the test case) is sent to the receiving program? This can be a complex activity. It requires working retroactively from the output (the test case) in order to determine what the input should be. To achieve this, one needs at least to be familiar with the sender program's functionality, but it also requires inventiveness and creativity.

For each physical test case, one must also determine the expected result and how the output of the program can be checked to see whether the expected result has occurred. Working from the input (the test case), it must be determined what the output of the receiving process should be. This also requires knowledge of the functionality of the receiving program.

Establishing the initial data set

In order to execute the physical test cases, i.e. the actions on the sender program and the checks on the receiving program, certain data are required. For reasons of control and reuse, it is wise to define these data in advance once and have them at hand (instead of creating them during the test). During this step, the initial data sets are described. It is recommended to give these data a meaningful name, to make it easy to identify the test case to which they belong. If there are time-dependent data, these must be stated explicitly so that they can be taken into consideration during retests.

Assembling the test script

The sequence in which the physical test cases must be executed is recorded in the test script. In doing so, the aim should be maximum efficiency. This means that within the space available, one must choose the sequence that results in the least number of changes (such as logging on and off under different user IDs, or resetting the initial databases) because such activities are time consuming. It is impossible to provide general rules for this. The presence of test expertise is therefore indispensable.

15.11.4 Test execution and assessment

The test is executed on the basis of the description of the physical test cases that have been put into an executable sequence in a test script. Assessment of the test is done in the first instance with the aid of the precalculated results. As the PIT is usually applied as part of an integration test, the developer and/or the programmer often executes the tests. In such a set-up, assessment also means detecting the cause of the defect and therefore making a broader assessment than when there is a case of functions being separated.

15.12 Real-life test

15.12.1 Introduction

The aim of the real-life test, often performed in the form of shadow production, is to discover defects that are related to the final size of the information system. The test must imitate the actual situation as much as possible with regard to the number of processing actions, the number of users, and the information system load over a period of time. When the system is put into action, it often appears that a number of things do not work. Real-life testing prevents such surprises. Defects found during real-life testing are generally related to the resource use of the system:

- the response times are unsatisfactory;
- the batch processing speed is unsatisfactory;
- the available memory or disk space is too small;
- the printer capacity is unsatisfactory;
- the data communication network cannot cope with the load.

Another aspect that can be monitored with a real-life test is the relation with the environment, i.e. the actual functioning of the interfaces with other information systems in the production environment. The real-life test may focus on quality characteristics such as performance, infrastructure suitability or continuity. Often, the real-life test is used in the production acceptance test, when the information system already functions.

15.12.2 Procedure
The steps that must be taken to perform a real-life test are:
1 Operational profile of system use.
2 Specifying test cases.

Operational profile of system use
As the aim of the real-life test is to discover defects that are related to the final size of the information system, the actual situation must be imitated as much as possible during this test. Hence, an operational profile of the actual and (future) expected system use in production should be drawn up during the specification phase. This operational profile outlines actions (functions) that are executed during a certain period and lists the number of active users. A daily cycle consists of logging in, intensive use, lunch, intensive use, logging out, back-up, and daily batches. In addition, there can also be comparable weekly, monthly and annual cycles and specific processes such as back-up and recovery. An important consideration when setting up an operational profile is the degree of detail.

A larger and more detailed operational profile of the system use will obviously provide a better representation of reality, but it will also lead to an increase in the test effort for the specification and creation of test cases and the execution of the real-life test. In the operational profile, all system resources must be used realistically. It is pointless to simulate a greater use than will be the case in reality, because the result of such a test would be useless. If the system is too slow under such circumstances, this does not mean that the system will not suffice. If the system is not too slow, this just means that the system is overconfigured, without it being clear to what degree.

On the basis of the operational profile, one can decide to perform a real-life test on a number of essential elements of system use, e.g.

- *Intensive use*. The number of interactive users is the maximum. Under these circumstances, starting certain 'heavy' functions such as reports may be prohibited.
- *Normal use*. Average number of users: reports and a number of small batch functions can be started.
- *Daily batches*. A small number of interactive users, in combination with relatively 'heavy' batch jobs (daily processing and synchronization).
- *Recovery*. The system should recover from software and/or hardware defects.

Specifying test cases

The next step is to describe in detail those parts of the system use to be tested, and to specify the test cases for the real-life test. Again, the actual situation must be imitated as much as possible. For further detailing of those parts of the system use that are to be tested, the following activities need to be executed:

- *Identify user groups*. This can be done by using AO descriptions, analysis of the output target groups, or security reports at the function level. User groups are often related strongly to organizational functions and tasks. For back-up and recovery processes, system administrators should be included.
- *Report of tasks per user group*. A task is identified as a number of sequential actions that a user carries out, interacting with the information system and with a specific aim. The functional specifications are probably the main source of information for this activity. Alternatives are AO descriptions, the user manual, a prototype of the system, and possibly a previous version of the information system. It is advisable to perform this activity by means of direct contact (interviews) with the users. Involving users during this activity is often clarifying and provides a variety of additional information.
- *Determine the task frequency per unit of time*. Many testers who specify a real-life test on the basis of system use for the first time expect this task to be the most difficult one. In practice, however, it usually proves easier than expected. Often, data are already present from previous systems with a comparable functionality. If this is not the case, data should be collected, e.g. by monitoring how often a particular function is started and/or executed in the present system, or by interviewing users. It is important to realize that these are estimations of the frequency, not an accurate measuring.
- *Determine the relative frequency*. The relative frequency is determined by dividing the occurrence of a certain task in a unit of time by the total number of occurrences of all tasks that are executed in that period, e.g. during intensive use of a financial system, approximately 1000 tasks are executed per hour, distributed as follows:

Tasks	Frequency (hourly)	Relative frequency
Entering invoices	200	0.20
Entering payments of accounts receivable	500	0.50
Entering bank statements	100	0.10
Entering cash transactions	50	0.05
...	...	...
	1000	1.0

The test cases are created in accordance with the tasks and the relative frequency. If 'intensive use' of the financial system in the example means 100 users, and the relative frequency of 'entering invoices' is 0.20, then this would mean that 20 percent of the test cases relate to 'entering invoices'. One should also, in principle, ensure that each task is represented at least once.

For real-life testing, the exact content of the test cases is less relevant than for most other test-specification techniques. The only criterion is that reality is approached as closely as possible in terms of volume and frequency. For this reason, it is very useful if an operational system already exists from which a representative test set can be drawn. For some parts of the system use, the test cases can be created by preparing a daily production set (after processing) as real-life input. However, make sure that privacy aspects are considered.

15.12.3 Test execution and assessment

Performing the real-life test is usually a bigger problem than with other tests. If the number of end users is large, which is often the case, system use has to be simulated with the aid of tools. With these types of tools, one should consider carefully which system components are not being used. Often, terminal communication lines are not used or are used differently in the final production environment. Another limitation of simulation lies in the fact that it is often not possible to execute certain functions simultaneously. In an environment where the number of end users is small, one can perhaps get everybody to do overtime during a weekend in order to execute a previously determined test scenario.

It must be determined beforehand what and how one should measure during the real-life test. Measuring itself sometimes constitutes a load of the system, which may lead to a distortion of the results. On the other hand, one must have sufficient data to be able to perform a proper analysis afterwards.

Assessing a real-life test is very difficult. In particular simultaneous tests may have a negative effect on repeatability. It is for this reason that one must ensure that the test is not executed on unstable software. If the system has logging and monitoring facilities, one can use these to detect the causes of possible defects.

15.13 Semantic test

15.13.1 Introduction

The aim of a semantic test is to verify the relations between data during entry. These relations may be between the various data within a screen, between data in different screens, or between (input) data and data already present in the database.

Semantic testing starts with an inventory of the data relations and corresponding validations. These validations are analyzed into conditions and paths, i.e. what happens under what circumstances. These conditions are tested one by one (per screen). This test-specification technique is used mainly when testing online systems in the context of a system test or acceptance test.

In addition to functionality, the semantic test can focus on the quality characteristic of security. The check on access security can be seen as a relation check on the security definitions (authorisations) present in the system and the entry of user IDs and passwords.

In addition to the semantic tests, syntactic tests can be executed on the human–computer interface. The aim of this is to discover defects in the layout and the primary validations (including domains) with regard to the fields. Syntactic tests can be executed parallel to the semantic tests. The test scripts can possibly be combined.

15.13.2 Procedure

The steps that must be taken to arrive at a semantic test include:
1   Making an inventory of data relations.
2   Detailing data relations.
3   Establishing test actions and checks.
4   Establishing the initial data set.
5   Assembling the test script.

Making an inventory of data relations

The selected test basis for the test concerned is read. During this step, the points within the system are determined at which data relations (on screen level) are validated. All checks must receive a unique ID insofar as this has not already been done in the system documentation. In the 'WOOF' example, when registering a new citizen of Grayhound, the combination of surname, initials, prefix, street and house number must be unique.

Detailing data relations

The inventory of the data relations is written out in the form of a simple comparison (one comparison per data relation). In simple comparisons, only terms such as IF, THEN and ELSE occur, as opposed to complex comparisons in which terms such as AND and OR may occur. A data relation in the form of 'A AND B' is written out as:

```
IF A
    THEN    IF B
                            THEN correct entry and/or action
                            ELSE error message
    ELSE error message
```

A data relation in the form of 'A OR B' is written out as:

```
IF A
    THEN correct entry and/or action
    ELSE    IF B
                            THEN correct entry and/or action
                            ELSE error message
```

Whether the checks are written in the form of comparisons depends on the complexity of the data relations and the unambiguousness of the test basis. The distinct test cases for each data relation are also indicated. In the case of any lack of clarity in the test basis, it is important that coordination occurs with the team of developers.

As an example, the following text was added to a function description: 'The starting date of the change of address entered must be after the end date that is indicated for the previous address of the retirement beneficiary. If this is not the case, then an error message follows.' Within the framework of testing, this provides the following comparison:

```
IF 'end date old address' ≥= 'starting date new address'          (a)
    THEN error message                                   (test path 1)
    ELSE correct entry                                   (test path 2)
```

In this example, two test paths are distinguished: test path 1 in which condition A is true (end date ≥= starting date), and test path 2 in which statement A is false (end date ≤ starting date).

An example with multiple paths is the next check:

```
IF minimum stock code is equal to S(ignal)                        (a)
    THEN    IF number minimum stock is equal to zero               (b)
                            THEN error message103        (test path1)
                            ELSE correct entry           (test path 2)
    ELSE correct entry                                   (test path 3)
```

If the minimum stock code is not equal to S, then no further checks take place (test path 3). If the minimum stock code is equal to S, and the number of minimum stock is zero, then an error message follows (test path 1). If the minimum stock is not equal to zero, condition A is true and condition B is false, then no error message follows (test path 2).

The application of these rules to the WOOF example renders the following:

```
IF        surname exists                                    (a)
THEN    IF    initials exist                                (b)
        THEN IF      prefix exists                          (c)
             THEN IF      street exists                     (d)
                  THEN IF      number exists                (e)
                       THEN Error message          (path 1)
                       ELSE  correct input         (path 2)
                  ELSE  correct input              (path 3)
             ELSE  correct input                   (path 4)
        ELSE  correct input                        (path 5)
ELSE    correct input                              (path 6)
```

Establishing test actions and checks

By writing out the various data relation validations in (simple) comparisons, the test cases are recognized automatically on the basis of the test paths. Testing of the test paths occurs when the test actions are executed. In principle, each test path generates an accompanying test action and possibly a check. When describing the test action, the concrete values that apply when the test is executed should be used. Items that are not important for the test should receive the correct value if necessary. A check is described if more needs to be checked than just whether an action runs correctly (valid) or incorrectly (invalid).

A comprehensive and detailed description of the test actions is of particular importance when validations between items (data) on different screens are tested. It is then indicated which data should be filled in on previous screens to make it possible for the test to be executed. Testing data relations between items (data) within a screen is usually much easier.

After this step, the test specification is, in principle, complete. The test specification contains at least the data relations – including the accompanying test paths, and preferably in the form of comparisons – and a description of the test actions and checks. If there are a large number of data relation validations, it is advisable to include a cross-reference table of data relation validations, test paths and test actions so that it can be determined whether the test actions are present for all data relations and the accompanying test paths.

With regard to the example of the stock system, the following test actions can be distinguished:

A01   Enter minimum stock code S and number minimum stock 0.
A02   Enter minimum stock code S and number minimum stock 250.
A03   Enter minimum stock code B.

When entering action A01, it is checked whether the correct error message appears:
C01   EM 103: 'for stock code S, enter minimum stock number'.

The WOOF example contains the following test actions and checks:

A01   Register citizen with an existing combination of surname, initials, prefix, street and number.
A02   Register citizen with an existing combination of surname, initials, prefix and street but unique number.
A03   Register citizen with an existing combination of surname, initials and prefix already exists but unique street.
A04   Register citizen with an existing combination of surname and initials already exists but unique prefix.
A05   Register citizen with an existing surname but unique initials.
A06   Register citizen with a unique surname.

C01   Error message: 'Combination of surname, initials, prefix, street and number already exists'.
C02   Confirmation of registration.

Establishing the initial data set
It should be decided whether it is necessary for the initial data set to be present for the test that is to be executed, in which case a description of this set must be made. It is indicated here for which test case a data item has been recorded in the initial data set. This description should be added to the test specification.

The presence of an initial data set and a good description of the latter are of particular importance to test cases regarding the data relations that apply between screen items and (initial) data already present in the system.

In the example above regarding the entering of address data, where the entered address data is checked there must be a retirement beneficiary present in the initial data set, with address data and an end date.

If the initial data set contains data that can be used for only a limited length of time, e.g. as a result of an end date, this should be stated separately. In a subsequent test, it will need to be checked whether these time-dependent data are still valid, and whether the initial data set needs to be adapted.

In the initial WOOF data set, a citizen is present fulfilling (at least) the following criteria:

Surname: Tester
Initials: T.O.
Prefix: The
Street: Doglane
Number: 32

Assembling the test script
The result of this step should be a test script describing the actions that should be executed with the actual test execution in a particular temporal sequence. The test specifications containing a description of the test cases constitute the basis

for the test script that has to be drawn up. A test script is assembled on the basis of the test cases, in which the actions that are to be executed should be described in the correct order. The test script should also list any preconditions. A precondition for test script X may be that test script Y has been executed completely.

A test script for the WOOF example might look like this:

Function:	Register citizen of Grayhound
Test-ID:	SEM-01
Preconditions:	Initial data set is installed (conform specifications)
Version:	1.00
Date:	21-08-2000

ID	Description	Check	Ok	Notes
A01	Register citizen with:			
	Surname:	Tester		
	Initials:	T.O.		
	Prefix:	The		
	Street:	Doglane		
	Number:	32		
C01	Combination of surname, initials, prefix, street and number already exists	Error Message	Y/N	
A02	Register citizen with:			
	Surname:	Tester		
	Initials:	T.O.		
	Prefix:	The		
	Street:	Doglane		
	Number:	31		
C02	Conformation of registration		Y/N	
A03	Register citizen with:			
	Surname:	Tester		
	Initials:	T.O.		
	Prefix:	The		
	Street:	Catlane		
	Number:	32		
C02	Conformation of registration		Y/N	
A04	Register citizen with:			
	Surname:	Tester		
	Initials:	T.O.		
	Prefix:	Prof.		

ID	Description	Check	Ok	Notes
	Street:	Doglane		
	Number:	32		
C02	Conformation of registration		Y/N	
A05	Register citizen with:			
	Surname:	Tester		
	Initials:	T.P.		
	Prefix:	The		
	Street:	Doglane		
	Number:	32		
C02	Conformation of registration		Y/N	
A06	Register citizen with:			
	Surname:	Bester		
	Initials:	T.O.		
	Prefix:	The		
	Street:	Doglane		
	Number:	32		
C02	Conformation of registration		Y/N	

15.13.3 Test execution and assessment

The tests are executed according to the test scripts. One may obtain a good insight into the progress of the test by keeping track of how many checks have been defined, how many have been tested, and how many defects were detected. Assessment of the semantic test is usually straightforward: checks can occur immediately within the function. Reporting may be done with the aid of the test script. For this purpose, two columns have been included in the test script: 'OK' and 'Notes'. The test results are marked in the 'OK' column, with either 'yes' (no defect found) or 'no' (defect found), while the 'Notes' column can be used to indicate the number of the accompanying defect report. An overall assessment regarding the test script that has been executed can also be included in the test script.

15.14 Syntactic test

15.14.1 Introduction

The aim of the syntactic test is to discover defects in the layout of screens (windows) and reports, and in the primary input validations regarding them. Applicable standards can be used as testing criteria and specific descriptions of screens and reports in the functional specification. This can be done by relating all (screen) items to the attributes in the data model, and using these to determine the size and type of (screen) items and the restrictions that apply for the item itself. Also, an inventory is made of the available options, and related to the screens and screen items. Their testing is relatively straightforward.

This test-specification technique is particularly suitable for online systems, but the syntactic test can also be applied to batch systems for checking the produced reports.

In addition to the syntactic tests, semantic tests can be executed on the human–computer interface. The aim of this is to discover defects in the consistency between the entered fields or screens, and the information already present in the system. Semantic tests can be executed parallel to the syntactic tests. It is advisable to combine the test scripts of both test-specification techniques.

15.14.2 Procedure
The steps that must be taken to arrive at a syntactic test include:
1   Creating a checklist regarding screens and reports.
2   Establishing the screens and reports to be tested.
3   Assembling test scripts.

Creating a checklist regarding screens and reports
This step should be executed during the test-specification phase. As a result of this, two checklists are produced. It should be determined which syntactic checks need to be performed regarding the various screens (including items) and reports. These checks are described in general terms in the two checklists (one for the screens and one for the reports). First, the test basis is observed. The following must be distilled from the test basis:
●   What types of items are there: numeric, alphanumeric, date, logical, etc.?
●   What options are possible for each screen and/or each item: question mark selection, function keys, Help functions, etc.?

Then the checks for each item type must be determined. One should guard against wanting too much. Because of the large number of items, the number of checks may expand rapidly. In addition, the severity of the defects found with syntactic testing is usually not great, although they will often inconvenience users. The recognized (standard) checks regarding the items are part of the checklist for the screen test.

The other syntactic checks, e.g. validating the domain of an item, can be recognized in the same way. These checks together form the two checklists (one for the screens and one for the reports). We have included some examples of possible syntactic checks at the end of the description of this technique.

One could take into consideration the inner workings of the application when creating the checklist. If, for example, a standard date routine is used, it is pointless to check each date item for an invalid date. The chances of finding a defect here are so slight that it does not weigh up against the effort that testing requires.

Based on the functional design and the development methodology used, the following general checklist has been drawn up for the WOOF example:

- Enter no input in each field.
- Enter numeric and non-numeric values.
- Enter non-existing dates.
- Enter too many characters.
- Enter negative values.
- Enter legal values.
- Do the correct help screens appear when using function key F1?
- Is the default value for approval 'N'?
- Is the layout in accordance with the specifications?

Establishing the screens and reports to be tested

After the checklists have been drawn up, a number of screens and reports should be selected upon which the checks can be performed. It is advisable to apply the checklist based on use frequency, because the severity of the defects found in the syntactic test is usually very low. If a large number of defects are found during the execution of the test, then you may consider expanding the number of screens and/or reports upon which the checklists are applied.

In the WOOF example, when registering a new Grayhound citizen, the screen contains the following fields:

Field	Optional?	Definition	Length
Code (generated)	No	Numeric	6
Surname	No	Alphanumeric	20
Initials	No	Alphanumeric	10
Prefix	Yes	Alphabetic	7
Street	No	Alphanumeric	20
Number	No	Alphanumeric	6
Postcode	No	Alphanumeric	7
City	No	Alphabetic	20
Income	No	Numeric	6.2
Date of birth	No	Ddmmccyy	8
No. of dogs	No	Numeric	2

Function key	Result
F1	Help
F8	Save
F10	End

Assembling test scripts

The result of this step is the delivery of a test script. As stated above, a test script for a syntactic test can often be combined with a test script for a semantic test.

If the previous two steps – creating a checklist for the screens and reports, and establishing the screens and reports to be tested – have been executed in full, it may be sufficient to expand the test script of the semantic test already present. An action is added to the test script concerned, which states that the checks listed in the checklist should be performed on the screen or report concerned. For example:

AOX   Perform checks on screen xxx in accordance with syntactic screen checklist

The following test script is used for the syntactic test in the WOOF example:

ID	Description	Check	OK	Remark /issue
1	Enter no surname	EM-322.1	Y/N	
2	Pressing F1 results in the correct help screen?	Legal	Y/N	
3	Enter too many characters into surname (≥20)	Illegal	Y/N	
4	Enter legal value into surname (Graham)	Legal	Y/N	
5	Enter no initials	EM-322.2	Y/N	
6	Pressing F1 results in the correct help screen?	Legal	Y/N	
7	Enter too many characters into initials	Illegal	Y/N	
8	Enter legal value into initials (D.O.T.)	Legal	Y/N	
9	Pressing F1 results in the correct help screen?	Legal	Y/N	
10	Enter numeric values into prefix	EM-322.25	Y/N	
11	Enter too many characters into prefix	Illegal	Y/N	
12	Enter legal value into prefix (''=empty)	Legal	Y/N	
13	Enter no street	EM-322.3	Y/N	
14	Pressing F1 results in the correct help screen?	Legal	Y/N	
15	Enter non-numeric values into number	EM-322.22	Y/N	
16	Enter too many characters into street	Illegal	Y/N	
17	Enter legal value into street and number	Legal	Y/N	
18	Enter no area code	EM-322.4	Y/N	
19	Pressing F1 results in the correct help screen?	Legal	Y/N	
20	Enter too many characters into area code	Illegal	Y/N	
21	Enter a legal value outside of Grayhound into area code	Illegal	Y/N	
22	Enter a legal value into area code	Legal	Y/N	
23	Pressing F1 results in the correct help screen?	Legal	Y/N	
24	Default value city = 'Grayhound'		Y/N	
25	Enter no city (clear the field)	EM-322.5	Y/N	
26	Enter numeric values into city	EM-322.16	Y/N	
27	Enter too many characters into city	Illegal	Y/N	
28	Enter a value not equal to 'Grayhound' into city	EM-322.16	Y/N	
29	Enter a value equal to 'Grayhound' into city	Legal	Y/N	

30	Enter no date of birth	EM-322.7	Y/N
31	Pressing F1 results in the correct help screen?	Legal	Y/N
32	Enter non-numeric values into date of birth	EM-322.14	Y/N
33	Enter too many characters into date of birth	Illegal	Y/N
34	Enter illegal value into date of birth (29-02-1999)	EM-322.14	Y/N
35	Enter legal, future value into date of birth	EM-322.14	Y/N
36	Enter legal value into date of birth	Legal	Y/N
37	Enter no no. of dogs	EM-322.8	Y/N
38	Enter non-numeric values into no. of dogs	Illegal	Y/N
39	Pressing F1 results in the correct help screen?	Legal	Y/N
40	Enter too many characters into no. of dogs	Illegal	Y/N
41	No. of dogs = 0	EM-322.19	Y/N
42	Enter legal value into no. of dogs	Legal	Y/N
43	Enter no income	F322.10	Y/N
44	Pressing F1 results in the correct help screen?	Legal	Y/N
45	Enter non-numeric values into income	F322.18	Y/N
46	Enter too many characters into income	Illegal	Y/N
47	Enter a negative value into income	Illegal	Y/N
48	Enter legal value into income	Legal	Y/N
49	Is the layout in accordance with the specifications?		Y/N
50	Press F4	Illegal	Y/N
51	Pressing F8 results in 'Saved'	Legal	Y/N
52	Press F7	Illegal	Y/N
53	Pressing F10 results in 'End'?	Legal	Y/N

15.14.3 Test execution and assessment

The tests are executed on the basis of:

- the test scripts;
- the checklist of the aspects to be checked per screen (item type) and report;
- the system documentation and/or test basis.

Keeping track of the number of items that must be tested, the number that have already been tested, and the number of defects that were detected provides a good insight into the progress of the test. Assessment of a syntactic test is usually straightforward. The checks can occur immediately within the function. The test results can be recorded in the test script. For this purpose, two columns have been included: 'OK' and 'Note'. The test results are marked in the 'OK' column with either 'yes' (no defect found) or 'no' (defect found), while the 'Note' column can be used to indicate the number of the accompanying defect report. An overall assessment regarding the test script that has been executed can also be included in the test script.

15.14.4 An alternative procedure

A different procedure, which is slightly more pragmatic, is the following: Step 1 (creating the checklist) as previously described, is skipped. A section is added to the test script of the selected screens and reports, describing a number of syntactic checks that are performed specifically for the screen or report concerned. This means that after the test script for the semantic test has been drawn up, a brainstorming session is used to draw up a limited number of syntactic checks that can be performed on the specific screen or report. These checks are described and added to the test script.

15.14.5 Syntactic checks

This section gives a detailed description of the checks that may be performed in a syntactic (screen) test. The three categories that can be distinguished are:

- layout check
- functional use check
- item check.

For each check category, we indicate what can be tested and what the check pertains to (a screen or a report).

Layout check

The layout check may apply to each screen and/or report. The screen is checked on the basis of the screen layout from the functional specifications, and the reports on the basis of the report layout. With respect to the layout, the following checks can be performed:

Headers
Check whether the headers comply with the standards. A requirement for all screens and reports may be that the following items are present:

- screen name or report name
- system date
- version number.

The requirements with respect to the header will often be described under the (sub)system standards regarding the human–computer interface. For the items concerned, checks may be run to see whether they are in the proper locations on the screen or the report, and whether they contain the correct values.

Items
The following checks can be performed with respect to the items present in the screen or the report:

- Presence (are any items absent and/or are there any items in the screen that should not be there?).
- Do items have the correct names?
- Is the location of the items on the screen or in the report correct?

Function key check

The checks with respect to function keys apply only to the screens. Such checks can be performed on the basis of a test script. The latter should state what should be tested for the function key concerned (including possible options, selections, etc). A possible format could be the following:

Fxx: Condition1[Action1], Condition2[Action2], ...

where Fxx: is the name of the function key, Condition1 is the condition under which the action is executed, e.g. the position of the cursor in a particular item, and Action1 is the action to be executed.

Item check

This check can be performed for both screens and reports on the basis of the descriptions of the screens and reports from the system documentation.

Screen item check

For each item on the screen, the following checks may be performed:

- *Input/output (I/O) check:*
  - for all possible input items (I), test whether input into the item concerned is possible;
  - for all possible output items (O), test whether there is any output to the screen, and whether the output is correct. Also check whether input is prohibited;
  - For all input/output items (I/O), check both the input and output, as above. In addition, check whether the correct default values are presented if this applies to the item concerned.
- *Field definition check:*
  - enter numbers in numeric fields and check whether the entry of letters is prohibited;
  - enter letters and/or number in alphanumeric fields;
  - enter letters in alpha (non-numeric) fields, and check whether the entry of numbers is prohibited;
  - enter valid dates in date fields, enter invalid dates, and check that no letters can be entered;
  - if domains have been specified, checks may be performed on these.

When the checks to be performed in the framework of the field definitions are determined, equivalence partitioning can be used. An equivalence partition is a subcollection of a domain containing the attribute values that are equal (equivalence) for the test. Clearly, an attribute value can belong to only one equivalence partition. The division of field definitions and attributes domains into equivalence partitions depends mainly on the format of the attribute (numeric, alphanumeric or date). There are both general and format specific rules. For a description of the various rules relating to equivalence partitioning, refer to section 15.3.4.

- *Checking mandatory items.* Report each screen as being completed without entering data in items. In the case of mandatory items, a message should appear on the screen. Then complete the first item, and report the screen as completed. Complete the next mandatory item and report as completed, etc.
- *Help check.* If any help texts should be present for a particular item, check whether these actually display, whether they display correctly, and whether the help text is correct for the item concerned.

Report item check
With respect to the reports, the item level check can be restricted to the observation that the output displays correctly in the report. Check on the basis of the descriptions of the reports whether all described items actually display in the report.

Checklists for quality characteristics

16

16.1 Introduction

This chapter includes checklists for the quality characteristics that are evaluated by means of static testing. In addition, a checklist is included that can be used during dynamic implicit testing of user-friendliness. For each checklist, the attributes are described that are relevant for the quality characteristic at issue. The measures with a positive influence are indicated with a '+', and those with a negative influence are preceded by '–'. On the basis of the results, an experienced tester will formulate a conclusion as to this quality characteristic. The measures described are divided into a number of attention areas:

- production organization
- user organization
- functional system architecture
- technical system architecture
- data infrastructure
- physical security measures
- development environment
- production environment.

The organization of the development process has not been included in this list since measures in this area are process measures directed towards the effectiveness and efficiency of the resulting process. Testing, by definition, focuses on determining the quality of products, and is in principle not interested in the way in which – or the process with which – the various products have come about.

It is not always possible to investigate a specific quality characteristic in a given organization using a standard checklist. Therefore, the checklists in this chapter serve as references and as examples for organization-independent – or even project-independent – checklists.

The checklists in this chapter are concerned with the following quality characteristics:

- connectivity
- continuity

- data controllability
- flexibility
- (suitability of) infrastructure
- maintainability
- manageability
- portability
- reusability
- security
- testability
- user-friendliness.

16.2 Connectivity

Connectivity is the ease with which a link with a different information system or within the information system can be made and modified.

Functional system architecture

+ Has use been made of a general reference model?
+ Has the choice for subsystems been argued?
+ Does the documentation state which measurements are available to prevent faulty user input and user actions?
+ Does it state how recovery of faults should be done?
+ Is the interaction between user and system written down, and are the user's responsibilities and authorities specified well?
+ Is the interaction between the system and other systems specified enough?

Technical system architecture

+ Has use been made of applied (inter)national standards, e.g. to exchange data via networks (Transmission Control Protocol/Internet Protocol (TCP/IP)), of applications in the IBM environment, or of a standard programming language that can be compiled on a wide variety of hardware?
+ Has a standard machine interface been used?
+ Is it possible to secure additional critical or essential functions?
+ Have the systems to which data will be exchanged been specified?
+ Has a generalized subsystem (interface) been specified for the interaction of data with other systems?
+ Have standards (nomenclature, coding, structure) been used for the interaction of data?
+ Have standards been used for the connection between hardware and infrastructure components?
+ Maintainability influences the connectivity regarding the technical system architecture (see checklist for maintainability).

Data infrastructure

+   Does a organization-wide data model exist in which the system data are integrated with the company data?
+   Is the logical data model specified?
+   Do the data match the data model at the organizational level?
+   Is the data model normalized?
−   Is the data model parameterized?
−   Is the data encrypted?

Production environment

+   For the benefit of the internal connectivity, have infrastructure components been used that are geared to infrastructure already in use?
+   Is a current infrastructure in use?

16.3   Continuity

Continuity is the certainty that data processing will continue uninterruptedly, which means that it can be resumed within a reasonable period of time even after serious interruptions. The quality attribute 'continuity' is divided into sub-attributes, for which separate checklists exist.

16.3.1 Operational reliability

Operational reliability is the degree to which the information system remains free from interruptions.

Production organization

+   Is an efficient production scheme set up with a balanced regulation of priorities between the applications and with the supporting functions, such as the back-up procedure?
+   Are well-trained substitutes on stand-by within the production organization?

User organization

+   Are well-trained substitutes on stand-by within the user organization?
    Has the security within the user organization been arranged (see checklis-for security)?

Functional system architecture

+   Will the input be checked?
+   Are passwords being used?
+   Will attempts for access be checked?
+   Has the choice for subsystems been argued?

Technical system architecture

+ Has use been made of applied (inter)national standards, e.g. to exchange data via networks (TCP/IP), of applications in the IBM environment, or of a standard programming language that can be compiled on a wide variety of hardware?
+ Is a specific application present and in use for security?
+ Are the input, output and processing implemented separately?
+ Has data consistency been taken care of by use of checkpoint/restart utilities?
+ Will the data processing be done dually?
+ Has the data processing been split into subtransactions?
+ Is the operator able to supply status information?
+ Have check processes ('watchdogs') been applied?
+ Are the subsystems decentralized?
+ Are the program modules being reused?
− Is use made of technical actions in interfaces?
− Are the programs parameterized?
− Are the algorithms optimized, i.e. for performance reasons?
− Will user input be completed automatically?

Data infrastructure

+ Will a periodic check be done on the consistency of the database and data sets?
+ Is the data storage decentralized?
− Is the data encrypted?

Physical security measurements

+ Is access to the organization grounds and buildings controlled?
+ Is access to the computer center restricted to the people who belong there?
+ Is the computer center housed in a building that is secured against lightning, fire, electricity failure and water damage?

Development environment

+ Are 4GL facilities used?

Production environment

+ Have hardware, network, PCs, system software and database management system (DBMS) been chosen that are geared to one another and to the applications?
+ Have hardware suppliers been chosen who will offer adequate support during the lifecycle of the information system?
+ Has the definition of the requisite processing and data storage capacity for the information system (centrally and decentrally) to comply with all functional and quality requirements been made objectively?
+ Will a diagnosis of the hardware, network, etc. be made periodically?
+ Is a dual set of hardware, etc. available for alternate use?

16.3.2 Robustness

Robustness is the degree to which the information system proceeds as usual, even after an interruption.

Production organization

+ Are well-trained substitutes on stand-by within the production organization?

User organization

+ Are well-trained substitutes on stand-by within the user organization?

Functional system architecture

+ Are the essential functions of the information system shielded in a separate subsystem?

Technical system architecture

+ Are automatic alternate facilities built in?
+ Have check processes ('watchdogs') been applied?
+ Will the data processing be done dually?
+ Is the operator able to supply status information?
+ Has the consistency of data been taken care of by use of checkpoint/restart utilities?

Production environment

+ Have hardware, network, PCs, system software and DBMS been chosen that are geared to one another and to the applications?
+ Is a dual set of hardware, etc. available for alternate use?

16.3.3 Recoverability

Recoverability is the ease and speed with which the information system can be restored after an interruption.

Production organization

+ Are well-trained substitutes on stand-by within the production organization?

User organization

+ Are well-trained substitutes on stand-by within the user organization?
+ Is there insurance against the risk of damage caused by faults or disruptions in the information services?

Functional system architecture

+ Has the choice for subsystems been argued?
+ Are utilities available for incidental queries or reports?

Technical system architecture

+ Has use been made of applied (inter)national standards, e.g. to exchange data via networks (TCP/IP), of applications in the IBM environment, or of a standard programming language that can be compiled on a wide variety of hardware?
+ Does a back-up and recovery system containing procedures and executables exist for:
  - the periodic saving of a coherent set copies of data sets;
  - logging of all transactions starting from the last generation;
  - the reprocessing of all logged transactions?
+ Will the recovery procedure be tested periodically?
+ Have check processes ('watchdogs') been applied?
+ Has the consistency of data been taken care of by use of checkpoint/ restart utilities?
+ Are the subsystems decentralized?
+ Is the essential functionality stored in separate modules?
+ Will the data processing be done dually?
+ Are automatic alternate facilities built in?
+ Does an actual overview of all used programs, including version numbers, exist?
+ The recoverability is influenced considerably by the maintainability regarding the technical system architecture (see checklist for maintainability)

Data infrastructure

+ Is the data storage decentralized?
+ Are utilities available for analysis and reorganization of the database?
+ Does an overview of all used data sets exist?
− Has the database access been optimized?

Physical security measurements

+ Are the back-ups of vital data stored in a special, extra-security location, preferably outside the computer center?

Production environment

+ Is a dual set of hardware, etc. available for alternate use?

16.3.4 Degradation possibilities

Degradation possibilities are the ease with which the core of the information system can continue after a part has failed.

Production organization

+ Have provisions been made so in the event of serious disturbances or disasters the information services may continue as much as possible?
+ Has a similar production environment been reserved, e.g. in a different computer center, including accompanying procedures for alternate use?
+ Have manual procedures been prepared in order to substitute (parts of) the automated information services?

Functional system architecture

+   Have the functions been modelled in coherence with the company business process model?

+   Has the choice for subsystems been argued?

+   Is the data processing functionally structured in such a way that it is possible to continue the processing of data when some non-essential parts of the information system are shut down?

Technical system architecture

+   Is the essential functionality stored in separate modules?

+   Are the subsystems decentralized?

Data infrastructure

+   Is the data storage decentralized?

–   Has the database access been optimized?

16.3.5 Possibility of diversion

The possibility of diversion is the ease with which (part of) the information system can continue elsewhere.

Processing/user organization

+   Have provisions been made so in the event of serious disturbances or disasters the information services may continue as much as possible?

+   Is a plan for disasters available?

+   Is the user organization's level of dependency on the information system stated (critical, sensitive, non-sensitive)?

+   Has the maximally tolerable time of breakdown been stated?

+   Has it been determined what constitutes a disaster?

+   Has a coordinator been assigned in case a disaster occurs, and are the authorities and responsibilities determined for such situations?

+   Have the emergency procedures and the alternate procedures for a possible transition period been described? (Among other aspects, attention needs to be paid to procedures handling unfinished transactions at the moment of breakdown.)

+   Does the plan for disasters include possible alternate hardware?

+   Is, as part of the plan for disasters, a plan for an alternate location available?

+   Have the organizational aspects been described, including the procedures for an alternative location?

+   Has it been established which functionary is authorized to decide to make use of alternative computers?

+   Has a similar production environment been reserved, e.g. in an alternate computer center, including accompanying procedures for alternate use?

+   Does the (external) executive organization responsible for the implementation of the alternate use have an up-to-date plan for alternate use?

+ Is the plan for disasters known within the relevant organization departments? Will the plan for alternate use be tested periodically (at least once a year)?
+ Will the findings of the test of the alternate computer use lead to amendments in the plan for alternate use?
+ Will a test of the plan for alternate use take place after a major change in the system architecture?
+ Have manual procedures been prepared in order to substitute (parts of) the automated information services?

16.4 Data controllability

Data controllability is the ease with which the correctness and completeness of the information (in the course of time) can be checked.

Functional system architecture

+ Do programmed checks on the results of the data processing exist, such as control totals and square counts?
+ Will transactions be numbered subsequently, and are these transaction numbers referred to in the mutation logs?
+ Will report pages be numbered subsequently, mentioning the total number of pages?
+ Will historical data and mutation records be recorded and saved?
+ Do retrieval functions with sufficient selection possibilities exist regarding the historical data?
+ Do possibilities exist related to an audit trail?
+ For the benefit of the audit trail, will mutations be recorded, including who did it and using which function?

Technical system architecture

+ Do functions exist to check the correctness of the data?
+ Do functions exist to check the completeness of the data?
+ Will all transactions be registered, i.e. logged?

Data infrastructure

+ Do possibilities exist for a (periodic) check of the data consistency?

16.5 Flexibility

Flexibility is the degree to which the user may introduce extensions or modifications to the information system without changing the software itself.

Technical system architecture

+ Have the programs been parameterized?
  Are logical values used instead of hard coded values?
+ Has the data processing been separated from the data retrieval?
+ Is it possible to modify (combinations of) input functions in order to change a method of working?
+ Is it possible to modify (combinations of) control functions in order to change a method of working?
+ Is it possible to modify (combinations of) processing functions in order to change a method of working?
+ Is it possible to modify (combinations of) output functions in order to change a method of working?
+ Is it possible to tune menu structures?
+ Is it possible to change the contents of the input screens?
+ Is it possible to change the layout of the input screens?
+ Is it possible to create a selection of output data?
+ Is it possible to change the layout of the output?

Data infrastructure

+ Has the data model been parameterized?
+ Has the data model been normalized?
+ Has the normalized data model been implemented without changes?
+ Do several search keys exist for each entity?
+ Does a meta data model exist?
+ Has a relational data structure been used?
+ Is it possible to specify different search trails?

Development environment

+ Are 4GL facilities used?
+ Can the user organization define reports easily?

16.6   (Suitability of) infrastructure

The suitability of infrastructure is the suitability of hardware, network, systems software and DBMS for the application concerned, and the degree to which the elements of this infrastructure interrelate.

Development environment

+ Have one or more 3GL or 4GL programming environments been selected that are appropriate for the application concerned and that fit to the rest of the infrastructure?

Production environment

+ Have hardware, network, PCs, system software and DBMS been chosen that are tuned to each other and to the applications?
+ Has an objective definition been made for the quantity of processing capacity needed by the information system (centrally or decentrally) to match all functional and quality requirements?

16.7   Maintainability

Maintainability is the ease of adapting the information system to new demands from the user, to changing external environments, or in order to correct defects.

Functional system architecture

+ Has the choice for subsystems been argued?
+ Has a general reference model been used?
+ Have the functions been modeled in coherence with the company business process model?
+ Is open, consistent and up-to-date functional documentation available?

Technical system architecture

+ Have standards for development been used (e.g. standard scheme techniques, standards for structured programming, standards for database approach, recognizable nomenclature, and standards for the use of user interfaces)?
+ Have applied (inter)national standards been used, e.g. to exchange data via networks (TCP/IP), applications in the IBM environment, or a standard programming language that can be compiled on a wide variety of hardware?
+ Are the routine actions built into the interface consistent?
+ Have check processes ('watchdogs') been applied?
+ Is the operator able to supply status information?
+ Is the data processing split up into subtransactions?
+ Have the input, the processing and the output been implemented separately?
+ Have possible machine dependencies been implemented in separate modules?
+ Has the essential functionality been stored in separate modules?
+ Have I/O operations been classified in separate modules in order to separate the retrieval of data from the processing of data?
+ Have the programs been structured, and are they easy to understand?
+ Is open, consistent and up-to-date technical documentation available?
− Have the programs been parameterized?
− Will technical actions within the interface be used?
− Are the subsystems decentralized?
− Will data processing be done dually?
− Have the algorithms been optimized?

Data infrastructure
+   Is the data model normalized?
−   Are the data encrypted?
−   Has the approach of the database been optimized?

Development environment
+   Is an integrated test facility available?
+   Will 4GL facilities be used?
+   Will an integrated functional development environment be used (work-bench (CASE tool), text processor etc.)?
+   Will an integrated technical development environment be used (DBMS, 4GL)?
+   Will a code or system generator (ICASE) be used?

16.8   Manageability

Manageability is the ease with which the information system is maintained in its operational state.

Processing organization
+   Has it been determined whether additional education is required to operate the new or changed information system?
+   Does an adequate procedure exist in case of disturbance?
+   Is the hardware, etc. insured?
+   Is a plan for disasters available?

Functional system architecture
+   Is a short functional description available?
+   Has the choice for subsystems been argued?
+   Do guidelines exist for the restriction of the access to the applications?
+   Are passwords being used?
+   Will the attempts for access be checked?

Technical system architecture
+   Will back-ups be made automatically?
+   Have check processes ('watchdogs') been applied?
+   Are the input, output and processing implemented separately?
+   Is the operator able to supply status information?
+   Has the consistency of data been taken care for by use of the checkpoint/restart utilities?
+   Have applied (inter)national or company standards been used, e.g. to exchange data via networks (OSI, TCP/IP), applications in the IBM environment (SAA), or a standard programming language?
+   Has a standard machine interface been used?

+ Are the routine actions built into the interface consistent?
+ Is there a description of the user applications and standard modules (including version numbers) required at installation?
+ Have standards for nomenclature been used?
+ Is it possible to perform each function (including the non-logical) at least once?
+ Does a back-up and recovery system containing procedures and executables exist for:
    • the periodic saving of a coherent set of copies of data sets;
    • logging of all transactions starting from the last generation;
    • the reprocessing of all logged transactions?
+ Does the back-up procedure determine when the data sets and database need to be secured and how long these back-ups should be kept?
+ Is it possible to restart an application after a system breakdown?
+ Is it possible to restart an application after an application breakdown?
+ Is a description of the required authorizations available?
+ Is a procedure for the maintenance of the authorizations available?
+ Is a specific application present and in use for security?
+ Do specific standards and norms exist for input, batch processing, online processing, output and security?
+ Are these specific standards and norms met?
+ Are all transactions registered, i.e. logged?
– Will the data processing be done dually?
– Are the subsystems decentralized?
– Are the programs parameterized?

Data infrastructure
+ Does documentation exist about the data model, and is this documentation consistent?
– Are the data encrypted?
– Is the data storage decentralized?

Physical security measures
+ Is access to the organization grounds and buildings controlled?
+ Have measures been taken to prevent, signal or take care of technical disturbances and disasters?
+ Are the back-ups of vital data stored in a special, extra-security location, preferably outside the computer center?
+ Is access to the computer center restricted to the people who belong there?

Production environment
+ Is a dual set of hardware, etc. available for alternate use?
+ Is there a description of the hardware and software components for the infrastructure?

+ Do specific standards and norms from the processing organization exist for resource use, external memory and performance?
+ Are these specific standards and norms met?
+ Does a production manual exist?
+ Does the production manual contain the following components:
    - an introduction, with a summary of names, identifications and characteristics of the functionality of the system and subsystems;
    - a scheme of the system structure;
    - a relational scheme of the run structure with, for each run the time, the programs, indicatives per program and the estimate of time;
    - the data of the contact people (name, department, telephone number);
    - for each run to be executed, the following data: name, identification, characteristics, system flow scheme and/or subsystem flow scheme, by which the data flows are related to parts of the configuration and from which the interfaces with the systems or subsystems that do not belong to the run can be derived;
    - receipt and preparation containing:
        type, source and time of receipt;
        reception activities and checks;
        data conversion, instructions and checks;
        destination and actions at delivery of input media;
        destination and the actions at delivery of basic documents;
    - preparation of production containing:
        time schedule;
        description of the working procedure ('jobstream');
        schemes for handling removable disks and storage instructions;
        deliverance of input;
    - service manual containing:
        general service workbook;
        service, check and error displays, together with the accompanying instructions;
        possibilities for interruption;
        instructions for restart at unplanned interruptions;
    - production manual containing:
        handling of removable disks;
        checks and reports;
        completion activities
        delivery and distribution;
        ultimate time of delivery.
+ Has the planning for production been changed, based on the new or updated information system?
+ Has it been determined how to request for and plan incidental batches?
+ Is an integrated test facility available?

+   Is a current infrastructure in use?
+   Has a detailed analysis been made of the processing capacity, storage capacity, data communication hardware and system applications?

16.9   Portability

Portability is the diversity of the hardware and software platforms on which the information system can run, and how easy it is to transfer the system from one environment to another.

Technical system architecture
+   Have the programs been parameterized?
+   Have applied (inter)national standards been used, e.g. for the exchange of data via networks (TCP/IP), applications in the IBM environment, or a standard programming language that can be compiled on a wide variety of hardware?
+   Has a standard machine interface been used?
+   Have possible machine dependencies been implemented in separate modules?
–   Have the algorithms been optimized?
–   Are the subsystems decentralized?

Data infrastructure
–   Has the approach of the database been optimized?
+   Is the construction of the data programs (rules of integrity) independent of a specific DBMS (applied with client/server systems)?

Development environment
+   Have 4GL facilities been used?
+   Have common used tools for development been used?
+   Will a commonly used infrastructure be adopted?
+   Has a standard programming language been used that can be compiled on a variety of machines?

Production environment
+   Has an infrastructure (hardware, network, etc.) been selected that is upwards compatible within a certain range?
+   Has a commonly used infrastructure been adopted?

16.10 Reusability

Reusability is the degree to which parts of the information system, or the design, can be reused for the development of different applications.

Functional system architecture

+   Has a general reference model been used?
+   Have the functions been modeled with a company business process model?
+   The reusability is influenced considerably by the maintainability of (part of) the information system (see checklist for maintainability).

Technical system architecture

+   Have applied (inter)national standards been used, e.g. to exchange data via networks (TCP/IP), applications in the IBM environment, or a standard programming language that can be compiled on a wide variety of hardware?
+   Have the programs been parameterized?
+   Has the data processing been split up into subtransactions?
+   Have the input, the processing and the output been implemented separately?
+   Have possible machine dependencies been implemented in separate modules?
+   Have I/O operations been arranged in individual modules in order to separate the retrieval of data from the processing of data?
+   Has a standard machine interface been used?
+   Have standard actions been built consistently into the interface?
+   Have program modules been reused?
−   Have the algorithms been optimized?

Data infrastructure

+   Do the data match the organization data model?
+   Has the data model been parameterized?
−   Has the approach of the database been optimized?

Production environment

+   Is a current infrastructure in use?

16.11 Security

Security is the certainty that data can be viewed and changed only by those who are authorized to do so.

Processing organization

+   Has the processing of confidential data (e.g. the salary run) been classified in separate procedures that may be processed only by authorized people?

User organization

+   Are jobs, authorities and responsibilities in the organization of the information services separated clearly?
+   Has a classification of documents been made, consisting of a number of classes of confidentiality?

+   Has a limitation (and registration) of the circulation of classified documents to dedicated functionaries been arranged based on this classification?
+   Does a procedure exist for authorization of important documents that leave the organization?
+   Does a check exist on behalf of the internal accountants on the processing of the procedures based on information produced afterwards?
+   Will attention be paid to both the written and automated fixed data?
+   Will the functional separation be continued when authorizing personnel? Will authorization be given based on the 'need to do' or 'need to know' principle? (Does the logical access match the existing schemes for the AO?)
+   Has job separation been arranged between:
    *   the person who has the authority to use functions in an information system for retrieval or updating data (end users);
    *   the person who decides who has access to specified functions (data) and to whom account must be given about the access possibilities implemented;
    *   the person who is responsible for the actual authorization of the employees to functions (data)?
+   Will a distinction be made between the responsibilities for input, processing, correction and checking at the granting of authorization?
+   Will a distinction be made between creating, reading, updating and deleting of data at the granting of authorization?
+   Will the requirements for logical security access be taken into consideration at the distribution of data (to third parties) and at external data communication?
+   Does a specific security procedure exist for functionaries who are in charge of internal control or security (i.e. the system administrator)?
+   Is the way in which the logical security access is constructed written adequately?
+   Does a procedure exist with the several actions to be carried out based on the access logging or the reports made?
+   Does the information system comply with legal commitments?

Functional system architecture
+   Does the product documentation contain the possibilities regarding security?
+   Is it stated explicitly:
    *   what the strategy is to security, based on aims and treatments;
    *   which security employees are there;
    *   which procedures regarding the security must be followed in order to utilize the functionality optimally?

Technical system architecture
+   Are the possibilities that exist to restrict the access to the system software, documents and data sets utilized as best as possible?
+   Within the security access, are functionality for identification, authentication, authorization, logging and reporting distinguished?

+   Is it possible to make a difference between the responsibilities for input, processing, correction and checking at the granting of authorization?
+   Is it possible to make a difference between input, change, query and removal of data at the granting of authorization?
+   Has consideration been made for the requirements of the (logical) security access with external data communication?
+   Will the users maintain their own passwords, and are they responsible for the use of their user IDs and passwords?
+   Does a (technical) procedure exist for the changing of passwords periodically?
+   Is the length of the password at least six characters, and is it possible to enter each keyboard character?
+   Is there a restriction on the number of attempts to log in?
+   Are the input and storage of passwords conducted in such a way that third parties cannot recognize them?
+   Will the security access be violated by the use of query languages?
+   Will any unsuccessful attempts for use be logged?
+   Have measures been taken for the restriction of the period for free access to the terminal (i.e. automatic log-off)?
+   Is a specific application present and in use for security?
+   Will the memory be cleared after processing?
−   Are the subsystems decentralized?
−   Will the data processing be done dually?

Data infrastructure
+   Are the data encrypted?
+   Will the data that are sent over the network be encrypted?
−   Is the data storage decentralized?

Physical security measurements
+   Is access to the organization grounds and buildings controlled?
+   Is access to the computer center restricted to the people who belong there?

Production environment
+   Will a different identification (user ID) and authentication (password) be used for the test environment and the production environment?

16.12 Testability

Testability is the ease with which the functionality and performance level of the system (after each modification) can be tested, and how fast this can be done.

User organization
+ Is the resulting testware completed and preserved for the benefit of future tests?
+ Do tools for planning and defect management exist in support of the test process?

Functional system architecture
+ Has the choice for subsystems been motivated?
+ Is open, consistent and up-to-date functional documentation available?
– Does a strong interaction or effect exist between the several functions?

Technical system architecture
+ Have standards for development been used (e.g. standard scheme techniques, standards for structured programming, standards for database approach, recognizable nomenclature, and standards for the use of user interfaces)?
+ Have check processes ('watchdogs') been applied?
+ Is the operator able to supply status information?
+ Is the data processing split up into subtransactions?
+ Have the input, processing and output been implemented separately?
+ Have possible machine dependencies been implemented in separate modules?
+ Has the essential functionality been stored in separate modules?
+ Have I/O operations been classified in individual modules in order to separate the retrieval of data from the processing of data?
+ Are program modules reused?
+ Have the programs been structured, and are they easy to understand?
+ Is open, consistent and up-to-date technical documentation available?
– Are the subsystems decentralized?
– Will the data processing be done dually?
– Have the programs been parameterized?
– Have the algorithms been optimized?
– Can test data be restored easily?

Data infrastructure
– Are the data encrypted?
– Has the data storage been decentralized?
– Has the data model been parameterized?
– Has the approach of the database been optimized?

Development environment
+ Is an integrated test facility available?
+ Will test tools be used, e.g. for test execution or test planning and control?
+ Is it possible to perform queries regarding the data sets?
+ Will 4GL facilities be used?
+ Does a separate test environment exist?

+   Will an integrated functional development environment be used (e.g. work-bench (CASE-tool), word processor).
+   Will an integrated technical development environment (DBMS, 4GL) be used?
+   Will a code or system generator (ICASE) be used?

16.13 User-friendliness

User-friendliness is the ease with which end users use the system. If and when the quality attribute 'user-friendliness' is chosen as part of the test strategy, this generally gives problems, because the characteristic is very subjective. A possible way of going about this is to create a questionnaire – it is wise to supply enough space on this checklist for additional comments. This questionnaire will be filled out by both testers and users, after which the test manager or test team leader will have insight into the user-friendliness of the information system. This procedure will remain subjective in some way, so it is recommended that this is combined with semantic or syntactical tests.

Possible questions in this questionnaire include:
*   What is your general opinion regarding the screen layouts?
    – Unacceptable
    – Acceptable with adjustments
    – Acceptable
*   Did you notice screens in a negative manner?
    – No
    – Yes
*   What is your opinion about terminology on the screens?
*   What is your opinion about the use of icons (if relevant)?
*   Are the error messages clear?
    – Yes
    – No
*   Are the help screens and help texts clear, and what is your opinion on the use of them?
*   What is your opinion about the use of the mouse?
*   What is your opinion about the user documentation i.e. to what extent does the user documentation really support working with the information system?
*   What is your opinion about the start-up procedure?
*   What is your opinion about the use of the function keys and buttons?
*   Do you want more standardization for menu screens, function screens, function keys, buttons, etc.?
*   What is your opinion about the menu structure? Do you want user menus?
*   Are the function names clear to you?

- To what extent do the functions meet the way of working and the structure of the user organization?
- What is your general opinion about the layout of the reports?
  - Unacceptable
  - Acceptable, with adjustments
  - Acceptable
- Did you notice reports in a negative manner?
  - No
  - Yes
- Do the reports contain the information wanted (are there too many or too few details)?
- What is your opinion about the standards regarding the headers and footers of reports?
- What is your opinion about the print facilities?

The survey may be concluded with a question to give a general evaluation of the user-friendliness in terms of a score (from 1 to 10, 10 being excellent), thus the user-friendliness of the system is quantifiable in some way.

Other checklists **17**

17.1 Introduction

Checklists are useful for preparing and executing the test activities. Of course, it is not possible to evaluate a specific situation in a specific organization using a standard checklist. The standard checklists described in this chapter are meant as an example for constructing organization-dependent and sometimes even project-dependent checklists. No distinction has been made as to whether questions have a positive or negative effect, as this is obvious in most cases. The following checklists have been included:

- *Test project evaluation.* This checklist can be used during and after completion of the test project to evaluate the quality of the project. Based on the results of an intermediate evaluation, risks may be recognized in time, allowing adequate measures to be taken.
- *Global investigation of the information system.* This checklist can be used to support the global review and study activity from the planning and control phase.
- *Preconditions and assumptions.* Preconditions and assumptions are determined when the test plan is being written. This checklist contains some examples of possible preconditions and assumptions.
- *Test project risks.* In writing the test plan, the risks regarding the test project must be made explicit. The checklist contains a number of possible risks.
- *Structuring.* Before introducing structured testing in an organization, the current situation of testing should be assessed. The checklist can be used to facilitate this assessment.
- *Test facilities.* This checklist contains points that could be important when organizing and setting up the test infrastructure, the test organization, and test control during the planning and control phase.
- *Production release.* Before a system is given a release advice for production, this checklist can be completed. Here, attention is given to completeness of the product, completeness of test activities, production preparations and production operations.

17.2 Test project evaluation

This checklist can be used during and after completion of the test project to assess the project quality. Its use during the test project may be a good way to prevent problems.

- Has the production release checklist been completed?
- Is the test project running under pressure of time? If so, are concessions being made towards the original test strategy?
- Are the users involved in the test project on time?
- Do the users believe that the acceptance test is given sufficient time?
- Are concessions being made during the test project with respect to the planned test volume and intensity?
- Is the test team receiving support from experienced (external) advisors and test specialists?
- Is there sufficient subject knowledge available in the test team?
- Has defect handling been organized properly, and does version control work adequately?
- Are the connections to existing systems and the organization receiving sufficient attention?
- Is there sufficient coordination with other projects?
- Does the prescribed test method, as established in the test handbook, provide enough information and support in the case of any problems?
- Is there a check as to whether the guidelines are being observed?
- Is there a procedure for possible deviations from these guidelines?
- Has a test plan been created according to the regulations?
- Is there a critical end date when testing must have been completed?
- Has the test plan been specified in greater detail and/or maintained during the execution of the test?
- Are the requested supporting aspects (tools, appliances, etc.) being made available in sufficient quantities and on time?
- Is it possible to complete the intended test plan within the limits set?
- Is the test plan clear, and can it be executed by the members of the test team?
- Are scheduling techniques and tools being applied?
- Is there adequate monitoring of the test activities and test progress?
- Are the reasons for adjustment of the schedule documented clearly, and have these been made known to those involved?
- Is it possible to indicate clearly one's position in relation to the schedule?
- Is there a constant good relation between the test schedule and the overall project schedule?
- Do the standard techniques and tools suffice?
- Is there sufficient contribution in the test team of:
  - system designers
  - system administrators

- – system management staff
- – subject matter experts
- – end users
- – accounting department staff?
- Is the management involved sufficiently in the testing process?
- Is there a proper and unequivocal division of tasks?
- Is version control of application components to be tested being applied?
- Is there a need for any special training with regard to hardware, software and/or testing?
- Are the members of the test team universally deployable?
- Is the test lifecycle being used as prescribed?
- Are all system functions being completed during testing?
- Are any test cases other than those of the test basis being carried out?
- Do users assess the quality of the test method used by the development team?
- Does the development team provide complex test cases to the acceptance testers?
- Is error guessing being used?
- Are utilities being tested?
- Is the back-up/restore software being tested?
- Is the conversion software being tested?
- Have provisions been made for a regression test at the end of the test?
- Are automated tools being used for the creation of test cases?
- Are all scheduled test scripts being carried out?
- Are the administrative organizational procedures relating to the new system being tested?
- Are any available checklists being used?
- Are the consultation structures successful, both those within the test team and those with the developers?
- Is there a sufficient amount of documentation discipline?
- Is the testware completed systematically?
- Are the causes of defects in the test approach, scheduling and techniques always documented properly?
- Is the budget sufficient?
- Is there enough time for test activities and consultation activities?
- Is the office environment as it should be?
- Are sufficient test tools, terminals, printers, etc. available?
- Is sufficient capacity available on the (central) computer?
- Is the available space for files sufficient?
- Is there enough personnel?
- Are the test results being made available quickly enough?
- Are checks being carried out on the execution of the tests (random checks)?
- Is the content of each test document in accordance with the agreements?
- Is the content of each test document complete?
- Is the test documentation accessible for users?

17.3   Global investigation of the information system

These checklists include the possible investigation aspects of the global review and study activity from the planning and control phase.

Organizational information
- Business aims
- Culture
- Organization diagram (including information services)
- Possible bottlenecks.

Project information
- Customer
- Supplier
- Aim (assignment, strategic importance)
- Agreements (contracts)
- Standards and guidelines (development methods, etc.)
- Requirements study (including description of existing situation)
- Documentation from the basic design phase
- Development infrastructure (hardware, tools and systems software)
- Project organization, including personnel
- Reporting lines
- Activities and time schedules
- Financial planning
- Preconditions set for the test that is to be carried out
- Risks and measures.

Application information (in particular for a maintenance test process)
- Input and output (numbers and peaks)
- Number of changes
- Processes to be distinguished
- Data sets (storage techniques and size)
- Data model
- Operational infrastructure
- Links with other information systems
- Testware already present:
  - test specifications
  - test scripts
  - test scenarios
  - test infrastructure
  - test tools
  - metrics
  - evaluation report of previous tests.

17.4 Preconditions and assumptions

This checklist contains a number of possible preconditions and assumptions. Preconditions and assumptions are determined when the test plan is being written. In principle, preconditions are imposed upon the test project from outside. In general, these concern limits and conditions with regard to the required resources, people, budget and time. The test team, on the other hand, determines assumptions.

- *Fixed deadline.* The test should be completed no later than the fixed deadline.
- *Project plan.* During the execution of the various test activities, the current project plan acts as a precondition.
- *Deliveries of test units.* It is imperative that the development team delivers the software in functionally usable and testable units, in accordance with the development plans. In addition to the software, the user manuals must also be supplied. These functional units must have been submitted to a unit test and a system test, in accordance with the plan of action for the system test.
- *Insight and changes of development plans.* A previously agreed period of time before delivery of the subsystem, the test team should know the development team's schedule. Changes in the development schedule must be passed on to the acceptance test team before implementing these.
- *Participation in development schedule.* Via the project management, the test team will be given the possibility to influence the development and delivery sequence and the units that are to be delivered. This influence is necessary to be able to determine the sequence of the test specification, and to obtain stable and usable functions at an early stage in order to construct the initial data sets.
- *Quality of the production acceptance test.* System management carries out the production acceptance test on the quality characteristics and objects that have been assigned to it, first at subsystem level and lastly at the system level.
- *Quality of the system test.* The development team performs the system test on the designated quality characteristics and objects.
- *Insight in system test.* The acceptance test team may request insight into the following deliverables of the system test to be able to take system test quality and results into consideration if the test management feel it is necessary and useful:
  - scheduling
  - test strategy
  - test cases
  - test results
- *Scope of test basis.* The acceptance test team receives insight into all system documentation, including documents that are not part of the test basis. This concerns, in particular, the technical documentation in order to be able to translate the logical test cases into physical test cases.

- *Changes in test basis*. The test team must be informed immediately of any changes that are to be and have been carried out in the test basis.
- *Quality of test basis*. If the quality of the above-mentioned test basis does not allow specification or execution of tests, the shortcomings must be reported to the customer immediately in order to be rectified or completed.
- *Availability of test team*. The test team should be available in accordance with the test schedule. Its members should meet the profile described in terms of knowledge and experience. It is emphasized that any training of the test team is not part of the test project, and that methodological supervision should be available.
- *Support of development team*. During the execution of the test, structural support must be available from the development team in order to correct any defects in areas where progress of the test is a primary condition.
- *Support by user organization*. For support regarding the subject matter expertise, there is always the option of relying on the expertise present within the user organization.
- *Support by system management*. During the execution of the tests, structural support by system management should be available in order to correct any defects and shortcomings in the test environment.
- *Definition and maintenance of the test environment*. The definition of the acceptance test environment and the system test environment occurs in consultation between the development and the acceptance test team. If possible, the same or a similar set of control instruments is used. The technical organization, as well as maintenance and control, is carried out by system management.
- *Availability of test environment*. The technical infrastructure (hardware, software and required files) that is necessary for the test should be controllable for the test management and available in accordance with the schedule. System management provides structural assistance, according to conditions still to be agreed. There is a simulated production environment available in which the decentralized infrastructure can be tested.
- *Installation of test environment*. Installation of new and/or repaired software and files in the test environment occurs only after (written) permission from the test management.
- *Use of test tools*. The acceptance and system tests make use of the same test tools. To this end, a final list of test tools is established, as well as a well-founded proposal for the acquisition of such tools in the period agreed.

17.5 Test project risks

The risk section in the test plan lists the risks that have been identified. For each risk, the consequences and, if possible, the solutions and/or measures that can be taken should be indicated. The checklist contains a number of possible risks that can be identified with respect to a test project that is to be carried out. Risks can also be recognized during the project by using the test project evaluation checklist.

- Absence of a detailed schedule of the development team for the various subsystems.
- The previously determined deadline can have an influence on the execution of the test activities as a whole, as mentioned in the test plan.
- The test basis not being available on time (AO procedures, user manual and design specifications).
- Insufficient quality of the test basis.
- The function point count not being available on time, as well as their unreliability. Both aspects lead indirectly to an unreliable test schedule when applying test point analysis (TPA).
- The availability of test personnel (capacity, suitability in terms of test experience and expertise).
- Growth of the size, expressed in function points, of the information system to be tested.
- Making available and operation of the desired test environment.
- The manageability of the test environment and all elements (software and data) contained within it.
- The introduction of a new test approach with which the organization has no experience.

17.6 Structuring

If structured testing is introduced in an organization, the present status with respect to testing should be determined first. This requires a brief investigation called a test inventory. The checklist described below can be used to carry out the test inventory.[1]

Test lifecycle
- Which test levels do we distinguish (unit test, system test, acceptance test, etc), and what is tested by each test level?
- What is the connection between these test levels?
- To what extent do the test levels complement each other, and/or do the test levels overlap?
- Is testing phased for each individual test level (scheduling and control, preparation, specification, execution, and completion)?

---

[1] Such an inventory should preferably be carried out with the aid of the test process improvement (TPI) model described in Chapter 25 rather than this checklist. Because the TPI model is too large to publish in full in this book, the checklist has been retained.

Planning and control phase
- Is there a master plan from which the underlying test plans are set up?
- Are test plans set up?
- Does the test plan contain a description of the assignment, defining the responsibilities, scope, assumptions and preconditions?
- Is the test basis established in the test plan?
- Has a test strategy been set up on the basis of the desired degree of coverage and acceptance criteria?
- Is the test strategy determined in the framework of setting up the test plan?
- Has the test infrastructure been defined in the test plan, and have agreements been made concerning control?
- Has a procedure for reporting defects been described in the test plan?
- Does the test plan describe which deliverables are to be supplied during the test?
- Does the test plan describe the parts of the testware, and how control of the testware has been arranged?
- Does the test plan describe which (test) functions are distinguished, including the division of tasks, responsibilities and authorities?
- Does the test plan describe the various reporting lines from the test team?
- Does the test plan include a schedule of activities, and financial and personnel planning?
- Has a well-founded budget been set up for testing? (Is this done on the basis of a method, such as TPA?)

Preparation phase
- Is a review carried out on the test basis for each test level?
- Is a well-considered selection being made of the test techniques to be used?

Specification phase
- Are test specifications being set up?
- Are test specification techniques being used for this? If so, which ones?

Execution phase
- Is there formal defect control?
- How are test files constructed and controlled?
- Are there retests?

Completion phase
- On completion of the test, is the testware stored for the benefit of maintenance tests?
- Does a formal hand-over/release take place?

Test techniques
- Are there any techniques available to determine test strategies?
- Are there any test-budgeting techniques?

- Are there any test-specification techniques? If so, which ones?
- Are these techniques also being used?

Test organization

Project organization
- How is the test project organization set up?
- How are authorities and responsibilities distributed?
- Who carries out the tests?
- Have agreements been made regarding reporting?
- Are there any procedures for defect control?
- How do reviews and hand-over occur?
- Who is authorized to release a tested system?

Line organization
- Are there any standards for testing?
- If so, are these standards used?
- Is the use of the standards checked?
- Are any experience figures collected regarding testing?
- Is there any subject matter support available for testing?
- Is testing coordinated across all test projects?
- Has there been training in the field of testing?
- What level of knowledge do the employees have in the field of testing?

Infrastructure and test tools
The questions below must be answered for each individual test level:
- Is there a separate test environment for testing? Who is the owner of this test environment?
- Is the set-up of the test environment comparable with the production environment?
- Are there any procedures regarding version and configuration control for the test environment?
- Are there any back-up and recovery procedures?
- Are the organization of, and access to, the test environment separated from the development and production environment?
- Are there any test tools available for:
  - test management (planning, time registration, progress monitoring)
  - test specification
  - defect management
  - test budget
  - test execution (record and playback, test drivers, etc.)
  - file management.
- Are there any other (digital) resources available, such as checklists and standard documents?

Development environment
- What hardware is present?
- What system software is installed on it?
- How do database manipulation and control take place?
- Which programming languages are being used?
- How does system development take place (method)?
- Are any CASE tools being used?
- Are there any other automated tools that are important for the inventory? If so, which ones?

17.7   Test facilities

This checklist contains points to be noticed that could be important when organizing and setting up the test infrastructure, the test organization, and test control during the planning and control phase.

Workspace
- Rooms
- Meeting area
- Furniture (chairs, desks, tables, cabinets)
- Copy facilities
- Office supplies
- Forms
- Diskettes.

Hardware
- PCs, laptops and/or terminals
- Input and output media, such as printers, displays, personal identification number (PIN)/card readers
- Communication lines
- Storage space (tapes, disk space)
- Mainframe capacity
- Communication servers, network administration hardware
- Servers, collectors
- Interfaces; switches, modems; converters, adapters
- Connections to public networks (e.g. Datanet-1, telephone network or the Internet)
- Storage media, such as tapes, cassettes, disks and diskettes
- Power supply, cooling and cabling.

Software
- Operating systems
- Database management system (DBMS)

- Communication software
- Word-processing package
- Planning and progress-monitoring package
- Mainframe utilities
- Test tools
- Back-up and recovery
- Logging
- Authorization and security
- Accounting/statistics
- Assemblers, compilers
- Workbenches
- Prototyping, simulation
- (other) utilities (e.g. for dump, trace, job scheduling, etc.).

Training
- Introductory course on testing
- Course on test techniques
- Elementary understanding of functional design
- Elementary understanding of technical design
- Job Control Language (JCL).

Logistics
- Tea and coffee facilities
- Lunch facilities
- Rules for expenses claims
- Overtime regulations
- Access security outside office hours.

Staff

- Test team
- System control
- Users
- Production supervision
- Management.

Procedures
- Production control
- Hand-over from development team to test team
- Version control of the test object, the test environment and the testware
- Maintenance of the initial data sets
- Defect procedure
- Back-up/recovery, alternatives
- Security.

- Test instructions
- Schedule monitoring
- Test consultation
- Configuration management
- Data control
- Defect reporting and handling, restart
- Authorization and security.

Documentation
- Regulations or even a handbook for testing
- User documentation
- Generic input and control data, e.g. client, policy, article, rates, price, currency, location.

17.8   Production release

Before a system is given a release advice for production, the following release checklist can be completed. If all of the tests have been completed successfully, the majority of the questions will have been processed in these tests.

Completeness of deliverables
- Is a regression test available for maintenance?
- Has the necessary input and conversion software been delivered, tested and approved?
- Has control software been developed for occasional file corrections?
- Is the necessary help, emergency and correction software available?
- Are the measuring instruments for system performance available, and have they been tested?
- Are the required system documentation, user documentation and production documentation available, complete, accessible and consistent?
- Have the required restart facilities been implemented?
- Is there a scenario for system and data conversion?

Completeness of test activities
- Have the interfaces between the various programs been tested and approved?
- Have the interfaces between the various subsystems been tested and approved?
- Have the interfaces with other systems been tested and approved?
- Have the interfaces with decentralized applications been tested and approved?
- Have the interfaces with decentralized devices been tested and approved?
- Have the interfaces with the operating systems been tested and approved?
- Have the interfaces with the manual procedures been tested and approved?
- Have the data transmission facilities been tested and approved?

- Has the testware been completed?
- Has the testware passed the required quality check?
- Did the volume tests run as expected?
- Have the network connections been tested and approved?
- Have the required performance demands been met?
- Is there a checkpoint recovery, and does it work?
- Have all restart options been tested successfully?
- Does file access occur within the applicable (security) demands?
- Does the program also work with empty input files?
- Does the system respond adequately to extremely incorrect input?
- Have the various forms been tried out at least once?

Production preparation

- Are the new users familiar with the new system and any new hardware?
- Is software naming in accordance with the regulations?
- Do the demands on the system remain within the standards set?
- Are the defects that still exist at the time of going into production known (also to the user)?
- Is it known how any remaining defects must be dealt with?
- Is it possible to return to the previous situation in the case of insurmountable problems in production?
- Are the storage periods of files known?
- Is the prescribed processing sequence in the case of reconstruction known?
- Has sufficient consideration been given to the possibilities of the output media to be used?

Production implementation

- Is it known to what extent the capacity of the system is used (processing time, peripherals, personnel, etc.)?
- Have the user and control functions been separated sufficiently?
- Is the troubleshooting procedure clear and workable?
- Is adequate quality control possible on the system output by applying special checking techniques?
- Is a report produced after each process, mentioning the time, medium, number and version?
- Is the system output provided with a start and end indicator for the sake of a completeness check?

Organization   PART 4

Introduction to the organization

18

18.1 Test organization

The ensemble of various functions within one organization, such as sales, production and human resources management, determines the extent to which the objectives of the organization can be met. Information services is one of these functions. Testing is a set of activities within information services, just like the creation of functional specifications, the solving of a defect or the input of name–address–residence data of a new customer. For all these activities there are standards and procedures, and as long as they contribute sufficiently to the success of the organization, they will act as a cog in the machinery. People, infrastructure, methods and techniques should be made available, together with an organizational structure. Within this structure the various activities can take place.

This part of the book deals with the organizational structure of testing, and the allocation of test roles and tasks within a given organization. It is possible to note the test roles and some models for the organizational structure of the test processes. Depending on various parameters, the optimal organization for testing may be implemented at a strategic, tactical and operational level, both in the line organization and in a project setting.

18.2 Strategic level

At a strategic level in the organization, the quality aims should be determined, and the possibilities that can enable these goals to be met should be indicated. The translation of this, the quality policy, is the basis for the structuring of testing and the facilities that should be available.

Testing should be organized in the bigger picture. It is part of the quality system, the organizational structure and the facilities to bring about good quality management. Quality control is an instrument of quality assurance, the complex of actions needed for meeting the quality requirements. Testing is part of this checking mechanism, and focuses mainly on the end products of system development. It is important to keep an eye on this strong relationship when setting up the test organization.

18.3   Tactical level

Just like any other process within information services, testing requires regulations and assessments on the application and applicability of these. These regulations indicate on what preconditions, and according to what rules and standards, people, resources and methods should be deployed in order to achieve the strategic goals. They describe how the organization should give content to the four cornerstones under a structured testing approach: lifecycle, techniques, infrastructure and organization.

The roles test regulation, and controlling must be incorporated into the organization at a tactical level: an undesirable mix with the operational test processes should be avoided, and good tuning with the practical experiences and results should be guaranteed. Thus, they are genuine staff functions. Because of function separation, controlling is preferably set apart from regulation.

18.4   Operational level

The roles in the operational test process can be divided into roles for setting up and assessing regulations and pure operational roles. Roles for setting up and assessing regulations, for instance, are the supporting roles in the methodological, technical and functional areas. Testing and test management are genuine operational roles. Test activities are usually carried out in a matrix organization, partly within a project and partly in the line.

From the viewpoint of process management, the pure project organization is the ideal for each test manager. Testing demands a mixture of expertise in the subject matter, the information system, the infrastructure, the test tools and, of course, testing. It is a challenge for test management to obtain these disciplines sufficiently, in good time and at the required level; that is why a special (project) organization type is often opted for temporarily. The activities can then be carried out in a project more or less in isolation but supported strongly by, and dependent on, line functions. This requires much organizational talent and diplomacy from all parties concerned. The interests and responsibilities of project and line are all too often in conflict. This is an inherent feature of testing to which test management should pay attention. After all, testing is done for, or on behalf of, the line, and it is there that the interests of test management lie.

There is no such thing as a boundary after which the test process is handed over from the project to the line organization. This happens gradually: acceptance testing, for instance, often implies the introduction of the test process into the administration organization.

Maintenance testing of operational systems is usually carried out in the line organization. In such cases, there is a structural organization for testing, which performs ad hoc tests as well as the better planned test activities. All test roles are implemented in line functions in such a set-up, often performed in combination with roles such as system administration, maintenance programming or help-desk activities. For bigger maintenance releases, however, a test project is usually set up, the staffing of which is borrowed from the line organization. This requires sound agreements and strict organization, the main problem being the availability (or non-availability) of staff and infrastructure for the test project. The project has to engage in a competition, of which the winner will be known beforehand: production always comes first!

18.5 Note

This book describes the building stones for the organization for both test roles and test management and the organizational structure. Only in a small number of situations will all building stones described be used in the way and to the extent to which they are presented here. Depending on factors such as test level, the size of the test object and the exact nature of the organization, the optimal mixture of test roles, staff and management means will be chosen.

For a sound execution of high-level tests (system or acceptance tests), a large part of the described components will be needed in many instances. For low-level tests, it usually suffices to use a derivation of part of these components. The wide range of building stones offers the test manager the possibility of a careful selection and an optimal implementation of the test organization for high-level and low-level tests. As with each selection, there also exists a danger of too much or too little: beware of overabundance and bureaucracy on the one hand, but a lack of control on the other. The primary goal should be a quick, good test at the lowest possible cost.

18.6 Set-up of the organization

TMap offers tools that support the choice for the organizational structure. For operational test processes, read Chapters 7–9 and 21. For the arrangement of a structural organization, read Chapters 24 and 25. The various organizational aspects are dealt with in Chapters 19, 20, 22 and 23.

Test roles   **19**

In order to have the right testing personnel at the right moment, it is necessary to have a good understanding of the responsibilities and tasks involved in testing, as well as the required knowledge and skills. Various responsibilities in testing are described in that context in this chapter. We attempt to provide as broad as possible coverage of responsibilities and tasks. The following roles are considered:

- testing
- team leader
- test management
- methodology support
- technical support
- subject matter support
- intermediary
- control
- test regulation
- monitoring
- coordination and advice
- system management support
- application integrator
- test automation architect
- test automation engineer.

19.1   Testing

The role testing contains the primary testing tasks, i.e. the core of the test process. The testing tasks are the most creative, but also the most labour intensive. In the framework of the TMap lifecycle, testing is active from the testability review in the preparation phase through preserving testware in the completion phase.

19.1.1 Possible tasks
- *Review of the test basis (specifications).* To investigate the testability of specifications by means of reviewing.

- *Specification of logic and physical test cases and initial datasets*. By means of test specification techniques, to design and construct test cases as defined by the functional requirements.
- *Setting up initial databases*. On the basis of the specified initial datasets, to set up the various files essential for the execution of testing.
- *Execution of test cases (dynamic testing)*. To expose the test object to the test cases specified and compare the results obtained with the predicted results.
- *Static testing*. To test statically the components of the test object that are allocated for static rather than dynamic testing.
- *Registration of defects*. Following the relevant procedures, to keep a record of defects and (during the retesting) corrections of previously reported ones.
- *Preserving testware*. To collect, select and optimize the testware (the aggregate of test cases, results of testing and for example, description of test files and infrastructure applied).

19.1.2 Required competence and skills

Specific testing skills
- General knowledge of the TMap testing lifecycle.
- Skills in reviewing and test-specification techniques.
- Skills in using checklists in static testing.

Information engineering skills
- General knowledge and experience in the field of IT.
- Broad knowledge of system-development methods.
- Skills at interpreting functional requirements.

General
- Knowledge of the subject matter and the line-and-staff organizations.
- The capability to learn quickly how to use test tools.
- Knowledge of project organization and working practices in the framework of a project.
- Word processing and spreadsheet processing skills.
- Creativity and accuracy.

19.2   Team leader

A team leader provides guidance to a team of two to four testers. Team leading takes about 20 per cent of a team leader's time. In the framework of the TMap lifecycle, the role of team leader is active from the testability review in the preparation phase through to preserving testware in the completion phase.

19.2.1 Possible tasks

- *Creating detailed plans.* Test management spreads the workload over the teams. The team leader comes up with detailed planning of the activities allocated to the team.
- *Spreading workload over team members and monitoring the progress.*
- *Securing facilities.* To take care of the availability of test basis, test object, test techniques, infrastructure, support, etc.
- *Keeping record of the progress and allocating the (time) budget.*
- *Reporting on the progress and quality.* Test management is kept informed, periodically as well as on demand, on the progress and the allocation of (time) budgets, quality of the test object and any bottlenecks.
- *Bringing up solutions for bottlenecks, and implementation of such.* One may expect from a team leader that they bring up alternative solutions to every bottleneck.
- *Guidance and support for testers.* Where support facilities merely provide a general assistance, to complement it on the daily basis with individual coaching within their team.
- *Assessment of team members.* In appropriate situations, the team leader has to assess test team members and discuss their performance with them.

19.2.2 Required competence and skills
Specific testing skills

- Advanced knowledge of the TMap testing life-cycle.
- Specialist skills in reviewing and test-specification techniques.
- General knowledge of test tools.

Information engineering skills

- Extensive knowledge and experience in the field of IT.
- A good knowledge of system-development methods.
- Knowledge in the field of architectures and system-development tools.
- General acquaintance with hardware, software and data communication facilities.
- Skills at interpreting functional requirements.

General

- Skills in managing a project.
- Knowledge of the subject matter and the line-and-staff organization.
- The capability to learn quickly how to use test tools.
- Knowledge of project organization and working practices in the framework of a project.
- Word processing and spreadsheet processing skills.
- Creativity and accuracy.
- Good communication skills and motivating capacity.
- Good power of expression, and speaking and writing skills.

19.3   Test management

Test management is responsible for the planning, management and execution of the test process within the framework of schedules and budgets, and according to the quality requirements. Test management keeps a record of the progress of the test process and the quality of the test object, subject to the test plan. The role is active during the whole lifecycle of TMap.

19.3.1 Possible tasks

- *Creating, getting approval, and maintaining the test plan*:
  - risk assessment and defining a test strategy;
  - set up schedules and budgets;
  - to determine organization and infrastructure requirements;
  - to determine procedures, standards and norms.
- *Executing the test plan according to the schedule and within the budget*:
  - to set up the organization;
  - to implement the testing tasks and procedures according to the way they are described in the test plan;
  - to hire staff and assess their performance;
  - daily control of the testing activities: allocate tasks, determine detailed plans, progress control;
  - to chair internal meetings (the test manager acts as the chairperson for meetings of the test team);
  - to take part in project meetings, etc. (testing requires much communication with the project team, line and staff, etc.);
  - to maintain external contacts (the test manager is supposed to build and maintain an effective network);
  - internal quality management (the progress and the quality of the test process can be assured by means of periodical risk analysis and audits; on this basis the appropriate corrective or preventive steps will be taken as necessary);
  - to identify, anticipate and report any risks related to the project.
- *Reporting on the progress of the test process and the quality of test object:* during testing reports will be given periodically (e.g. weekly and monthly) on the progress of the testing activities as related to the schedule, and on the quality of the test object in terms of defects per severity class. Also, the trends will be indicated and measures to be taken recommended (if any):
  - giving release approval advice (on the basis of the quality indications observed during the test process and the actual state of affairs, test management gives advice on the quality of the test object);
  - evaluating the test process (test management evaluates the test process, e.g. from the viewpoint of the following: implementation of schedules, productivity, anticipated number of defects, experiences of the customer, testers and other participants).

19.3.2 Required competence and skills

Specific testing skills
- Comprehensive experience in applying the TMap lifecycle and techniques.
- Experience as a team leader, as an intermediary, and in support tasks.
- General acquaintance with test tools.

Information engineering skills
- Comprehensive knowledge and experience in the field of IT, acquired in various organizations.
- A good knowledge of system-development methods.
- Competence in the field of system architecture and system-development tools.
- General acquaintance with hardware, software and data communication facilities.

General
- Extensive experience in managing a project.
- Experience in use of planning and progress management tools.
- Basic knowledge of the subject matter and line and staff.
- Excellent communication skills and motivating capacity.
- Excellent power of expression, and speaking and writing skills.

Special skills
- A critical attitude ensuring that arguments are taken at their real value.
- Tact, resistance to panic, and the ability to endure criticism.
- The ability to settle conflicts and proficiency in negotiating techniques.
- Being capable of bringing together academic and technological solutions, as well as practical consequences of both.

19.4   Methodology support

The role of methodology support (MS) is to provide assistance concerning the methodology. It refers to all testing techniques and all members of the testing team, as well as, for example, strategy development by the test management as test case specification by a tester. The MS role may be active during the whole lifecycle of TMap.

19.4.1 Possible tasks
- *Establishing testing techniques.* The testing techniques that have been selected from the standard TMap arsenal for the specific test are (if necessary) adjusted to the test basis.
- *Developing new testing techniques.*

- *Making test regulations*. The regulations are usually released and distributed in the form of a handbook, which is subsequently maintained. A record is kept of the distribution of regulations.
- *Developing relevant training courses*. In the event that techniques or products are adjusted or updated, the training material should also be updated.
- *Teaching and tutoring*. To act as a teacher and tutor during the introduction of regulations
- *Giving advice and assistance in implementation of all possible testing techniques*:
  - test strategy development
  - test point analysis
  - testability review of test basis
  - formal inspection
  - test specification
  - others.
- *Giving advice to management*. To act as advisor (in the broadest sense) to the test management in daily affairs.

19.4.2 Required competence and skills

Specific testing skills
- Specialist experience in applying the TMap lifecycle and techniques.
- General acquaintance with test tools.

Information engineering skills
- Comprehensive knowledge and experience in the field of IT.
- Specialist knowledge of, and experience in, development and construction of information systems.
- Knowledge in the field of architectures and system-development tools.
- General acquaintance with hardware, software and data communication facilities.

General
- Knowledge of the subject matter and line and staff.
- The capability of getting familiar with the use of (test) tools.
- Knowledge of project organization and working practices in the framework of a project.
- Proficiency in word processing and working with spreadsheets.
- A creative, punctual and strictly methodical approach to work.
- Good communication skills and motivating capacity.
- Good power of expression, and speaking and writing skills.

Special skills
- A critical attitude ensuring that external requirements are taken at their real value.

- Being able to open the eyes of the organization to the importance of quality management and testing, and being able to ensure, as necessary, the improvement of testing activity.
- Capability of settling conflicts and negotiating, as well as proficiency in presentation, reporting and meeting techniques.
- Being capable of bringing together academic and technological solutions, as well as practical consequences of both.

19.5 Technical support

The role of technical support (TS) is to provide assistance concerning the technology. This role is responsible for the high-quality test infrastructure being continuously available to the test process. The supervision over and operability of test environments, test tools and the office space will also be secured. The TS role may be active during the whole lifecycle of TMap.

19.5.1 Possible tasks
- *Establishing test infrastructure*. Takes care of making available and maintaining the test infrastructure and the test environments, test tools and office environment, required for an adequate test process.
- *Supervising the test infrastructure*. Responsible for availability, supervision over and maintenance (including the change management) of the following:
    - test environments (hardware and software administration procedures);
    - networks for test environment and the office space;
    - technical office environment;
    - test tools.
- *Physical configuration management*. Physically stores the testware, test documentation and (if appropriate) test basis and test object.
- *Technical trouble shooting*. Takes care of solving technical problems, with the progress of the test having the highest priority.
- *Ensuring reproducibility of the tests*. The tests will be reproducible from the viewpoint of the technical infrastructure.
- *Creation, transformation, maintenance and administration of job control*. Takes care of the system management procedures and components bearing on software, databases and hardware, as well as system software and network components (JCL, scheduling, authorization, etc.).
- *Giving assistance and advice on the following topics:*
    - hardware and software, network and data communication, storage of test data;
    - determination of the consequences of changes in the infrastructure;
    - making test plans and detailed plans;
    - technical system supervision and application management;

- security, error handling, and calamities;
- test-related procedures and tools bearing on configuration management, change management, release management, production management, generation control, etc.;
- determination of profits and losses;
- development of test techniques for technical test cases;
- requirements for and execution of technical tests;
- defects in the technical infrastructure.

19.5.2 Required competence and skills

Specific testing skills
- Acquaintance with the TMap lifecycle and techniques.
- Extensive knowledge of test tools.

Information engineering skills
- General technical knowledge in the field of hardware, software and data communication facilities.
- Specific acquaintance with the hardware, software and data communication facilities within the organization relevant for the test.
- Comprehensive knowledge and experience in the field of IT.
- Acquaintance with methods of development and construction of information systems.
- Competence in the field of system architecture and system-development tools.
- Competence in operation of, and technical supervision over, information systems.
- Proficiency in managing hardware, software and data communication facilities.
- Advanced knowledge of supervision tools.

General
- Knowledge of the subject matter and line and staff.
- Capability to become familiar with the use of (test) tools.
- Knowledge of project organization and working practices in the framework of a project.
- Good communication skills and motivating capacity.
- Good power of expression, speaking and writing skills.

Special skills
- Creativity in analyzing and eliminating failures in the technical facilities.
- A critical attitude, ensuring that the external requirements are taken at their real value.
- Being capable of bringing together technological solutions and their practical application.

19.6   Subject matter support

The role of subject matter support (SM) is to provide assistance to the test process concerning the functionality. The role is responsible for availability of the subject matter knowledge and the knowledge of how the subject matter is functionally specified. It provides support in carrying out the activities where the functionality issues can be of importance. Those activities may include test strategy development or risk reporting by test management, as well as the testability review or specification of test cases by a tester. The SM role may be active during the whole lifecycle of TMap.

19.6.1 Possible tasks
Providing assistance and advice on the functionality of the test object in the following situations:

- strategy development and budgeting;
- adjustment and development of test-specification techniques;
- specification and implementation of test tools;
- training;
- review of the test basis (specifications);
- specification of test cases and basic data;
- carrying out test cases (dynamic testing);
- carrying out static tests;
- analysis of results of testing and defects;
- interpretation of statistics and creating risk reports.

19.6.2 Required competence and skills
Specific testing skills
General acquaintance with the TMap lifecycle and techniques is required.

Information engineering skills
- Comprehensive knowledge and experience in the field of IT.
- Competence in interpretation of functional requirements.

General
- Specialist (functional) knowledge of the subject matter and line and staff;
- Good communication skills and motivating capacity.
- Good power of expression, and speaking and writing skills.

Special skills
Being capable of bringing together functional solutions and their practical application.

19.7   Intermediary

In relatively large high-level test teams, it is advisable to introduce a separate role for the purpose of communicating adequately the defects and corresponding solutions. On these subjects, the intermediary maintains contact on the operational level between the test team and other parties. All defects and their solutions will pass via the intermediary. The most important purposes for which the role may be introduced are to:

- provide insight into defects and solutions;
- reduce the overhead costs. There is just one (critical) filter for the changes. Before being passed on along the communication channels, the defects undergo analysis for redundancy and value. At the same time, only 'real' solutions are accepted. This prevents excessive discussions and extra work.

Thanks to their central role in the traffic of defects and solutions, the intermediary plays an important part in risk reporting. In the framework of the TMap lifecycle, the role intermediary is active from the testability review in the preparation phase through preserving testware in the completion phase.

19.7.1 Possible tasks
- Sets requirements for procedures and tools for registration of defects.
- Collects defects and the respective background information.
- Checks the integrity and correctness of defects. Analyzes, classifies and evaluates the categories of urgency.
- Reports the defects to the appropriate entities using the procedures available.
- Takes part (as necessary) in communications with regard to the analysis and taking decisions.
- Collects relevant information for the testers about defects and problems available from other parties.
- Checks solutions for integrity and takes care of controlled implementation of the solutions. Reports availability of solutions for retesting.
- Keeps a record of the status of defects and solutions in respect to the actual test objects.
- Renders assistance to the test management in creating (on demand) risk reports.

19.7.2 Required competence and skills
Specific testing skills
General acquaintance with the TMap lifecycle and techniques is essential.

Information engineering skills
- Comprehensive knowledge and experience in the field of IT.
- Competence in interpretation of functional requirements.

General
- Specialist (functional) knowledge of the subject matter and line and staff.
- Excellent communication skills and motivating capacity.
- Excellent power of expression, and speaking and writing skills.

Special skills
- A critical attitude ensuring that arguments are taken at their real value.
- Tact, resistance to panic, and the ability to endure criticism.
- The ability to settle conflicts, and proficiency in negotiating techniques.

19.8 Control

Control is an administrative, logistic role. It is responsible for registration, storage and making available all the objects within the test process that require control. In some cases, controllers carry out the duties themselves; in other situations, they set up and manage a controlling body. The allocation of operational control duties depends strongly on the environment and the type of test process (scope, project or line-and-staff, new development or maintenance). How deeply control tasks are embedded in the organization is certainly as important. In relatively large projects the objects of control are allocated in the following way:
- *Control*:
  - hours and budgets
  - test documentation
  - defects and statistics
  - test basis and test object (for internal purposes)
  - testware, including files (registration).
- *Methodology support*:
  - test regulations.
- *Technical support*:
  - testware, including files (physically)
  - test basis, in an automated form (physically)
  - release management of the test object
  - test environment, test tools
  - technical work stations.

The role control is active throughout the whole TMap lifecycle.

19.8.1 Possible tasks

- *Progress control.* Registration, control and storage of, and making available, progress indicators. Time and budget accounting; control of product delivery and conformance to the deadlines.
- *Test documentation control.* Registration and storage of written communication, memos, reports, directives, accounts, etc.
- *Keeping record of defects and collecting statistics.* This task is fulfilled in close cooperation with the intermediary, whose task is to manage defects and statistics with respect to content.
- *Logical control of (parts of) the test basis and test object, exposed to the test process.* The task of supervising the test basis and the test object goes beyond the scope of the test process. Only the material that is (temporarily) available to the test process should be supervised.
- *Logical control of testware, including files.* Registration of and making available testware, including test files. Physical control is a technical support responsibility.
- *Premises and logistics.* Operational test teams change quite frequently in composition and number. This requires appropriate control of working premises and related matters. The control over technical aids is a technical support task.
- *Control of the delegated supervising duties.*

19.8.2 Required competence and skills
Specific testing skills
General acquaintance with the TMap lifecycle and techniques is essential.

Information engineering skills
General knowledge and experience in the field of IT is essential.

General
- Knowledge in the field of operation and control of information systems.
- Extensive knowledge of control tools.
- Knowledge of line and staff.
- Good communication skills.
- Excellent administrative skills.

19.9   Test regulation

Test regulation is active when testing is embedded completely or partially in the line organizational structure. 'Partially embedded in the line organization structure' means anything between the role of test regulation implemented as a full-time function and the role of test regulation included in a function containing all roles except the testing role. As far as the test regulation tasks are concerned, the role is similar to methodology support. Test regulation may be active during the whole lifecycle of TMap.

19.9.1 Possible tasks

- *Setting up and maintaining test regulations*. To select and adopt test regulations. These occur mostly in the form of a handbook, which should be maintained in a systematic way.
- *Distributing test regulations*. To ensure that up-to-date regulations are available to test personnel at any time. A record of the distribution will be kept.
- *Developing new test techniques and procedures*. On the basis of evaluation of new trends (in the market), new techniques and procedures are developed or acquired as required.

19.9.2 Required competence and skills

Specific testing skills

- Specialist experience in applying the TMap lifecycle and techniques.
- General acquaintance with test tools.

Information engineering skills

- Comprehensive knowledge and experience in the field of IT.
- Specialist knowledge of, and experience in, development and construction of information systems.
- Knowledge in the field of architectures and system development tools.
- General acquaintance with hardware, software and data communication facilities.

General

- Advanced knowledge of the subject matter and line and staff.
- Knowledge of project organization and working practices in the framework of a project.
- Proficiency in word processing and working with spreadsheets.
- A creative, punctual and strictly methodical approach to work.
- Good power of expression, and speaking and writing skills.

Special skills

- A critical attitude ensuring that external requirements are taken at their real value.
- Being capable of bringing together academic solutions and their practical applications.

19.10 Monitoring

Monitoring is active when testing is embedded completely or partially in the line organizational structure. 'Partially embedded in the line organization structure' may mean anything from the role of monitoring implemented as a full-time function, to the role being included in a function that contains all roles except the testing role.

Monitoring fulfills certain tasks of the roles of test management, intermediary and control. For the sake of separation of tasks, it is advisable to make a clear boundary between monitoring and test regulation. Monitoring could involve working for:

- test management
- accounting and IT auditing
- test regulation
- information management
- project management.

Monitoring may be active during the whole lifecycle of TMap.

19.10.1 Possible tasks

- *Monitoring for compliance to the test regulations*.
- *Monitoring for suitability of the test regulations*. Reviews and audits of test processes and products are carried out periodically as well as on demand in order to control the compliance to and suitability of the test regulations.
- *Reporting results*. The results of audits and inspections are reported to the client.

19.10.2 Required competence and skills

- Extensive knowledge and experience in application of auditing and reviewing techniques.
- Extensive knowledge of test regulations.
- Comprehensive knowledge and experience in the field of IT.
- The capability of working punctually and strictly methodically.
- Good power of expression in writing.
- Critical attitude.

19.11 Coordination and advice

Coordination and advice (C&A) is active when testing is embedded completely or partially in the line organization structure. C&A operates as a facilitating unit that provides support to the test processes. The role incorporates many supporting duties that usually occur in an operational test team. It should be mentioned that this role is of a strictly supporting nature and will never engage with operational testing.

Tests are carried out again and again, therefore it is not worthwhile reinventing the wheel for each individual project. As soon as it is established, the C&A role automatically receives questions regarding testing. In this context, the task of C&A is to consolidate testing expertise and experience to offer to the various test processes. Of course, C&A will be engaged directly in the maintenance of the test regulations.

In addition, C&A plays an important role in the collection and assessment of testing statistics. One of the major problems in testing is that it becomes clear whether the object has been tested properly only when testing is over. In order to be able to learn from this, the data on the progress of the test and production behaviour will be recorded and compared as far as possible. This will create an opportunity for a better evaluation of risks and better planning of test processes in subsequent projects.

As desired, C&A may check up the contents of various test plans with respect to planning aspects and competing test infrastructure requirements. C&A may, as necessary, fulfill the task of coordination.

The C&A role:

- collects information from all sources on which to base its advice and test project information;
- may take care of training, either by providing that itself or by means of out-sourcing;
- may be active during the whole TMap lifecycle.

19.11.1 Possible tasks

- *Making the master test plan of test processes*. Adjusts the competing testing activities within the project, as well as on the level of the organization.
- *Support in creating (detailed) test plans*:
  - risk assessment and strategy development;
  - planning and budgets;
  - determination of organization and infrastructure;
  - determination of procedures, standards and norms.
- *Support in setting up the test organization*. Functions and procedures are implemented subject to the structure determined by the test plan.
- *To hire staff and assess their performance.*
- *To develop and maintain training programs in testing*. Various testing staff roles and test regulations require training programmes. To the extent that those are not readily available, the new ones will be developed and maintained.
- *Teaching and tutoring*. Act as teacher and tutor during the introduction of regulations.
- *Intermediary for external training programs*. Where internal training programs in testing fall short of the demand, external facilities will be used. Often one systematically prefers external training for the sake of efficiency. C&A may play a cost-saving, coordinating role.
- *Advice and support on application of test techniques*. Provide advice and assistance in implementation of various testing techniques:
  - strategy development
  - test point analysis
  - testability review of the test basis

- – inspections
- – test specification
- – use of checklists
- – others.
- *Management advice*:
  - – in appropriate situations, act as an advisor for test management in the broadest sense;
  - – collect and evaluate testing statistics;
  - – during the operational test processes, information is generated concerning the progress of the testing and the quality of test objects. This information will be collected, systemized, and made available to the management.
- *Advice on engagement of external expertise*. Due to its corporate nature, the role of C&A acquires insight into the availability and quality of external expertise, as well as the respective charges.

19.11.2 Required competence and skills

Specific testing skills

- Comprehensive, specialist experience in applying the TMap lifecycle and techniques.
- Experience in test management and support tasks.
- General acquaintance with test tools.

Information engineering skills

- Comprehensive knowledge and experience in the field of IT.
- Specialist knowledge of, and experience in, system design and construction.
- Competence in the field of system architecture and system development tools.
- General acquaintance with hardware, software and data communication facilities.

General

- Knowledge of subject matter and the line and staff.
- Knowledge of project structure and affinity to the project approach.
- Being creative, punctual and able to approach work methodically.
- Good communication skills and motivating capacity.
- Good power of expression, and speaking and writing skills.

Special skills

- Being able to open the eyes of the organization to the importance of quality management and testing. Being able to ensure, as necessary, the improvement of respective testing activity.
- Skills in negotiating techniques, conflict handling, techniques of presentation, reporting and conferencing.

- Being capable of bringing together academic solutions and their practical application.

19.12 System management support

This line-and-staff role provides support for test processes, as far as technical aspects are concerned, as well as infrastructure supervision and maintenance. System management support fulfills the responsibilities of system management for testing. It is active when testing is embedded completely or partially in the organization structure. We should stress that this role has a purely facilitating nature, and therefore under no circumstances can it directly affect the critical path of the test process. Due to the required flexibility and prompt response, it is desirable that this kind of support is separated from the regular production activities one way or another. The role may be active during the whole TMap lifecycle.

The tasks and required skills coincide with those of the role technical support; only the place in the organization is different.

19.13 Application integrator

The application integrator (AI) is responsible for the integration of separate parts (programs, objects, modules, components, etc.) into a correctly functioning system. The AI reports to the project leader of development on the quality of the test object and the progress of the integration process, according to the plan of the integration test. To avoid a conflict of interests, the AI will not have the role of project leader of development. In this way, an area of tension is deliberately created between the AI, who is responsible for the quality, and the project leader of development, whose work is assessed largely on the basis of the functionality supplied, time and budget.

It is highly desirable to have an AI with a developer background. The AI should know much more about the internal operation of the system and be better equipped for finding the cause of a defect than a high-level tester. The AI should also have more knowledge and understanding of testing than other developers. Good contacts with developers are essential for the proper functioning of an AI.

19.13.1 Possible tasks
- Writing, getting approval for, and maintaining the plan of the integration test.
- Writing the entry criteria with which the separate programs, objects, modules, components, etc. will comply in order to be admitted to the integration process.
- Writing the exit criteria with which an integrated part of the system will comply in order to be approved for the following stage.

- Facilitating and supporting programmers in execution of unit tests.
- Integrating stand-alone programs, objects, modules, components, etc. into user functions or subsystems.
- Administering the plan of integration test according to the planning and the budget.
- (Enforcing) configuration and release management.
- (Enforcing) internal defect management.
- Role as a mediator with the customer's organization during subsequent test levels.
- Reporting about the progress of the integration process and the quality of the test object.
- Issuing release authorization.
- Assessing the integration process.

19.13.2 Required competence and skills
Specific testing skills
- Experience in applying the TMap lifecycle and techniques.
- Experience as a team leader and mediator, and in support tasks.

Information engineering skills
- Acquaintance with the method of system design.
- Knowledge of architecture and system-development tools.
- Acquaintance with hardware, software and data communication facilities.

General
- Basic knowledge of subject matter and the line and staff.
- Good communication skills and motivating capacity.
- Good power of expression, and speaking and writing skills.

Special skills
- A critical attitude ensuring that external requirements are taken at their real value.
- Tact, resistance to panic, and the ability to endure criticism.

19.14 Test automation architect

A test suite consists of the combination of test tools, test cases, test scripts and observed results. The test automation architect is responsible for the quality of the automated test suite as a whole, as well as for achieving the automation goals set for the respective test suite. The architect translates the goals, the approach selected and the features of the test object into a test suite architecture. Special attention is paid to the design and construction of the suite.

19.14.1 Possible tasks
- Administering a quick scan for a test automation assignment.
- Writing, getting approval for, and maintaining the action plan for construction of the test suite.
- Designing the test suite.
- Being in charge of design and construction of the test suite.
- Reporting about the progress and quality of the construction of the test suite.
- Enforcing or administering test tool selection.
- Training the users in applying the automated test suite.

19.14.2 Required competence and skills
Specific testing skills
- Experience in applying the TMap lifecycle and techniques.
- Experience as a team leader.
- Excessive knowledge of (the capacity of) test tools.
- Experience in test process automation.

Information engineering skills
- Good knowledge of methods of system design.
- Knowledge of architecture and system-development tools.
- Acquaintance with hardware, software and data communication facilities.
- Acquaintance with structured programming.

General
- Good communication skills and motivating capacity.
- Good power of expression, and speaking and writing skills.
- Good conceptual and analytical skills.
- The capability to learn quickly how to use a test tool.

Special skills
A critical attitude to ensure that the external requirements are taken at their real value is essential.

19.15 Test automation engineer

The test automation engineer is responsible for the technical side of the automated test suite. The engineer translates the test suite design into the modules to be constructed within the test tool. He or she constructs the test suite by means of new and existent test tools. Within the framework of the test automation architect's directions, the engineer administers the detailed design, construction and implementation of test suites.

19.15.1 Possible tasks

- Constructing, testing, supervising and maintaining a test suite.
- Providing support in designing a test suite.

19.15.2 Required competence and skills

Specific testing skills

- Experience in applying the TMap lifecycle and techniques.
- Knowledge of (the capacity of) test tools.
- Acquaintance with test process automation.

Information engineering skills

- Acquaintance with methods of system design.
- Knowledge of architecture and system-development tools.
- Acquaintance with hardware, software and data communication facilities.
- Experience in structured programming (preferably in the programming language of the tool).

General

- Good analytical skills.
- Creativity and punctuality.
- The capability to learn quickly how to use a test tool.

Special skills

A critical attitude to ensure that the external requirements are taken at their real value is essential.

Staff and training **20**

Testing requires a great variety of expertise. Chapter 19 lists the distinct roles and tasks, as well as the required knowledge and skills. This chapter examines the human resources and training aspects that are important within this context. Test management is responsible for allocating the right person to the right position, preferably in close consultation with the human resources management (HRM) department. A careful recruitment and training of testing staff is required. It is important to plan training courses as close as possible to the moment of practical application. The best results are achieved with a short theoretical introduction, followed immediately by thorough supervision during the execution of the actual work (i.e. training on the job). Suitable and experienced testing personnel are scarce; offering a career perspective to professional testers may be a solution.

20.1 Staff

It is important to have the proper combination of expertise within a test organization. Testing requires expertise in the fields of:

- the subject matter
- the developed system
- the infrastructure (test environment, developing platform, test tools) testing
- test management.

The low-level testers are usually developers, and the necessary test expertise concerns primarily the developed system and the development infrastructure. High-level testing involves developers, users, managers and/or testers: the required expertise is shifted more towards subject matter and test knowledge.

In addition to the usual problems relating to staff, the provision of staff for testing is characterized by a few peculiarities, that must be considered during selection, introduction and training:

- *Incorrect idea of testing, and hence also of the necessary testing staff.* Testing is usually carried out alongside regular activities, and designers or users temporarily take on the task of testing. In practice, there is insufficient test expertise in the test team. Few organizations value test functions equally highly as comparable development functions, despite the fact that 30 percent of the IT budget is spent on testing.

- *Testing requires a testing attitude and special social skills.* Testers set out to (dis)approve of their colleagues' work after those colleagues have pushed themselves to provide the best possible product. A more subtle way of expressing their 'approval' is for testers to enable others to add quality to their product. Testing thus also requires tact.

- *Testers must be thick-skinned because they are criticized from all sides:*
  - they overlook defects (100 percent testing is impossible);
  - testers are nit-pickers;
  - testers stay on the critical path too long, hence testing takes too long;
  - the test process is too expensive: can it not be cheaper and with fewer staff?
  - testers are too emphatically present. We do not construct in order to test!
  - when a system displays defects, it is often the testers who are blamed. When a system functions well, it is the system developers who receive praise;
  - not all tests are completed and test advice is often ignored. A tester must be capable of dealing with this;
  - testers are often inexperienced because (structured) testing is a new service to them;
  - testers must be talented in the field of improvization and innovation. The test plans are usually thwarted by delays incurred in previous processes.

- *Difficulty of planning the recruitment and outflow of testers.* The start, progress and completion of test processes are difficult to predict. A test process is characterized by underutilization, extra work and unexpected peaks in the workload. The suppliers of human resources want to know long beforehand who should be available and when. This causes conflicts, disappointments, decline in quality and a planning void.

- *Test training is regarded as superfluous.* Testing is often looked on as something that anyone can do.

The test manager would be wise to engage a professional in the field of personnel management. Experience has shown that personnel officials are happy to help, especially when it involves role descriptions and training demands as described in this book. Ensure that there is good insight into the needs, with regard to both the jobs and the planning (of the inflow of staff). If external expertise is required, which is regularly the case in test processes, there must be insight into the available budget.

20.2　Training

Great demands are made on testers. They are expected to have wide-ranging competences (IT knowledge in general, and social skills) as well as thorough knowledge (test methods and techniques). Training can be helpful here. It should create a bridge between the demands and the knowledge and skills available among the selected testers. A training program for testers includes a large number of topics. Test-specific training may include:

- Test methods and techniques:
  - importance of (structured) testing;
  - test lifecycle model, planning;
  - test-specification techniques;
  - techniques for reviews and inspections.
- Test environment and test tools:
  - automation of the test process;
  - test tools.
- Test management and control:
  - staff and training aspects;
  - test planning, test budget;
  - techniques for risk assessment and strategy development;
  - control procedures;
  - improving the test process.
- Reporting and documentation techniques.
- Quality management:
  - quality terminology;
  - standards;
  - auditing.
- Test attitude, i.e. social skills.

General training may include:

- General knowledge of IT:
  - information services, policy, planning;
  - organization of information services.
- Methods and tools for system development:
  - lifecycle models;
  - modeling techniques;
  - computer-aided software engineering (CASE), object orientation, 4GL, workbenches and component-based development.
- Planning and progress monitoring techniques:
  - planning tools;
  - function point analysis.

- Oral and written social skills, and personality:
  - reporting and presentation;
  - social skills.
- System administration and operation:
  - knowledge of information systems management;
  - configuration management and change management;
  - operational aspects such as production control, Job Control Language (JCL) and security.
- Technical infrastructure:
  - hardware: mainframes, PCs, etc.;
  - software: operating systems, middleware, database management system (DBMS), packages;
  - communication: servers, local area networks (LANs), wide area networks (WANs);
  - graphical user interfaces, client/server, Internet, etc.
- Spreadsheets and word processing.
- Subject matter and organizational knowledge:
  - functionality;
  - organization structure;
  - business objectives.

It is advisable to have the test training course constructed and made available in a modular fashion (Figure 20.1). Depending on the role and the employee's expertise, training can then be carried out more or less individually per (sub)topic.

Figure 20.1
Structure of test training courses

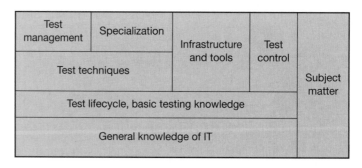

One usually has to rely on third parties for training courses, hence the requirements with respect to modularity and training strategy indicated here are, in fact, requirements for the training institutes.

Independent certification of a tester is performed by the Information Systems Examinations Board (ISEB), a section of the British Computer Society. ISEB offers three certificates of increasing difficulty for testers.

20.3 Career perspectives

20.3.1 Introduction

To professionalize testing within an organization, a career perspective must be offered. This section provides a methodology for the specification of test career paths. Essential components include training, gaining work experience, and a supervision program. These are shown per function and level in the 'career cube' (Figure 20.2). This cube helps the human resources manager match the available knowledge, skills and ambition of the professional testers with the requirements of the organization. The three dimensions of the career cube are defined as follows:

- height = functional growth
- width = functional differentiation
- depth = knowledge and skills.

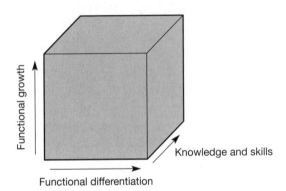

Figure 20.2
Dimensions of the career cube

20.3.2 Functional growth

Functional growth is the function progress that an employee may make, e.g. from tester to test manager (Figure 20.3). A distinction is made here between vertical and horizontal growth. When further vertical growth is no longer an option, there is the possibility for horizontal growth. Vertical growth means a higher function level; horizontal expansion means a higher performance level within the same function level. Improvement of the conditions of employment can be achieved in this structure by reaching either a higher function level or a higher performance level.

20.3.3 Functional differentiation

Three differentiations are distinguished in TMap (Figure 20.4):

- *Team and project leadership.* Employees who are capable of and interested in leading a test project choose this direction.
- *Methodological advice.* This direction is meant for employees who want to give test advice, e.g. when a test strategy is being established, in the selection of test-specification techniques, or organizing control.

Figure 20.3
Functional growth

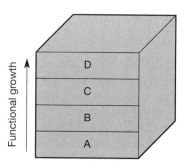

- *Technical advice*. Individuals who feel attracted to the technical side of testing opt for technical (test) advice. This includes the organization and utilization of test tools, or the set-up and management of a test infrastructure.

Figure 20.4
Functional differentiation

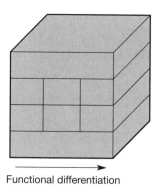

Functional differentiation

Figure 20.5 shows examples of function levels, with the function name indicated for each direction. At level A, there is no clear demarcation of columns. At this level, people gain a wide knowledge of test execution in all its aspects. At function levels B and C, differentiation applies. At function level D, differentiation does not apply. Employees at this level are expected to be capable of implementing successfully, and/or managing, each of the three differentiations.

Figure 20.5
Examples of function
levels

D	General test management		
C	Test project leadership	Methodological test advice	Technical test advice
B	Test team leadership	Methodological test specialization	Technical test specialization
A	Test execution		

20.3.4 Knowledge and skills

Building up knowledge and skills is represented by the third dimension of the career cube. The following components are distinguished:

- (test) training
- social skills
- experience
- coaching and support.

Coaching and support are essential conditions for a sound career path, in particular in the case of (a start in) one of the lower function levels. Each employee receives support in various ways. This is implemented by the test manager, the personnel official and/or experienced employees. Testers who have just started receive extra attention from a coach who supervises all aspects and developments. As the function level increases, the importance of practical experience and social skills training also increases considerably in relation to (test) training and coaching and support. The relationship between the required knowledge and skills is shown in Figure 20.6.

Finally, the full career cube is completed on the basis of the above (Figure 20.7). It shows the required knowledge and skills for each function (differentiation).

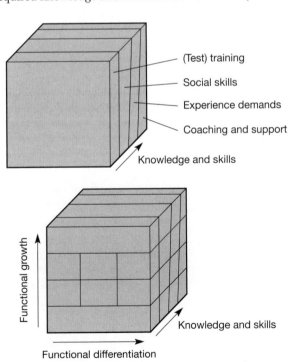

Figure 20.6
Knowledge and skills

Figure 20.7
Complete 'career cube'

Organization structure   **21**

21.1   Synergy

The combination of test roles, test facilities and test activities requires structure, i.e. a framework in which the test process takes place. This structure must be more than the sum total of all roles, so there must be synergy. The organization structure must be a unit in which the relationships between the various parts are of primary importance. Changing any of the parts implies changing the entire organization structure. This requires a great deal of attention in a sector that demands commitment from many disciplines and that depends to a great extent on changing circumstances.

21.2   Test roles and tasks

Operational roles and tasks with respect to testing include:
- *testing*: review, test specification, test execution and completion;
- *team leader*: managing test teams of two to four testers;
- *test management*: managing, planning, progress and quality monitoring, and reporting;
- *methodology support*: supporting test techniques and training;
- *technical support*: supporting the test infrastructure;
- *subject matter support*: supporting the functionality of the test object;
- *intermediary*: registration, assessment and routing of incoming and outgoing defects and solutions;
- *control*: controlling the test project, test infrastructure and testware;
- *application integrator*: (low-level testing) integration and (support of) testing, quality monitoring and reporting;
- *test automation architect*: designing test suites, quality monitoring and reporting;
- *test automation engineer*: developing, testing and controlling test suites.

Tasks related to creating and assessing regulations include:

- *test regulation*: design, fixation, execution and maintenance of test regulations;
- *monitoring*: testing execution and usability of the test regulations;
- *coordination and advice*: master test planning, collection of statistics, training and advice;
- *system management support*: controlling test facilities such as testware, test infrastructure.

21.3   A universal organizational structure?

It is impossible to establish a single universal organization structure for testing. The project organization is preferred for the operational test process. In the case of repeated testing in combination with scarce (test) knowledge, the structural test organization discussed later in section 21.4.4 can be used. The line organization is preferred for the roles of creating or assessing regulations. In general, the structure of the test organization should match that of the accompanying process of system development.

In addition, there are a large number of influencing factors that have their own effect on the selection of an organization structure. It is impossible to indicate absolute choices per parameter, as the individual weights of the influencing factors determine the organization structure. We list here some of the most important influencing factors:

- *Test level and test type.* Is it a low-level or high-level test, a system or an acceptance test, a functionality or a performance test? For high-level tests, the preference is for project organization.
- *Newly constructed or maintenance.* Is there existing testware, or does a completely new set testware have to be specified? Is there a strong relationship with the primary process of the organization? For all plannable activities, the preference is for project organization.
- *User involvement.* Will the user organization perform the acceptance test, or is it hardly involved? Will system management or functional management be participating? For maximum involvement, the preference is for project organization.
- *Organization of the development process.* Will development take place in a project or line organization, internal or external, against a fixed price or on the basis of calculations carried out afterwards? Organize the test organization in accordance with that of the development process.
- *Type and size of the organization.* How important are the information services for the organization? Is work done pragmatically or dogmatically? How many disciplines and employees are involved in the test process? How (quickly) do the decision-making processes usually take place? What powers will a test team have? Organize the test organization as much as possible in accordance with customs prevailing in the organization, with a preference for project organization.

- *Maturity of IT within the organization.* Does the organization have formal methods and techniques, workbenches, architectures, corporate data management? A high degree of formalization makes the organization structure less important.
- *Size and complexity of the test object.* Number of function points or test points, number of external interfaces; diversity of components (e.g. software, hardware, networks, documentation, administrative procedures, organization), overall project time in relation to the test effort; number of developers; number of testers? Organize the test organization in accordance with that of the development process.

21.4 Models and considerations

21.4.1 Operational test team

The operational test roles can be combined to create a structure that can be used to carry out the test process more or less independently (Figure 21.1). This can be in a line or project organization, or in a combination of the two.

Usually a test team operates within a project organization and is more or less self-supporting. The test team has its own functions with the supporting roles, and works as a project within a project.

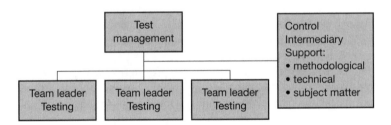

Figure 21.1
Operational test organization, the test team

21.4.2 Relation with project organization

The project management is responsible for implementing the preconditions for the test process, such as making sure that the staff, resources, schedules and test basis are available on time. Much of this administrative work can be assigned to the test management. Contact with the customer and the steering committee is maintained by the project management. Usually, there are weekly reports to the project management on progress and quality.

Upon request, advice is sometimes given directly to the steering committee and/or the customer concerning the quality, either periodically or on completion of the tests. In this context, acceptance test managers are advised to periodically report directly to the steering committee and/or the customer because test advice may conflict with the project management's interest.

Figure 21.2

Project organization
with test team

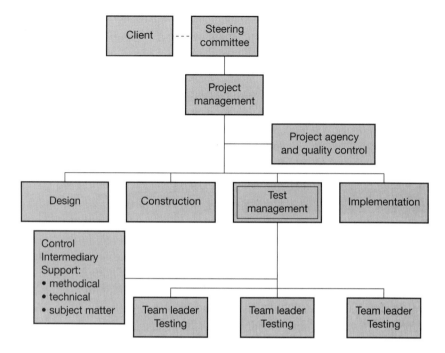

Figure 21.2 shows the organization of a high-level test team. Generally, the acceptance test team is part of the project organization, as indicated here, while the system test team is part of the construction team. In larger projects, there are sometimes two or more test teams, e.g. one for the system test, one for the functional acceptance test, and one for the production acceptance test. If the integrated system and acceptance test has been chosen, there will be only one team. The low-level tests are organized within the construction team.

21.4.3 Relation with line organization

The roles of creating and assessing regulations are usually embedded in functions in the line organization as a separate discipline or as part of a larger framework. Some operational test roles, such as methodical, technical and subject matter support and control, are also suitable for full or partial separation from the operational test processes.

Figure 21.3 shows where the roles for creating and assessing regulations could be placed in functions in the line organization of an imaginary company. Test regulations could be placed:

A. in the quality management department at company level because of the importance throughout all company units;

B. in the quality management department in the staff of information services throughout the three departments;

C. as part of the management function of the department information services.

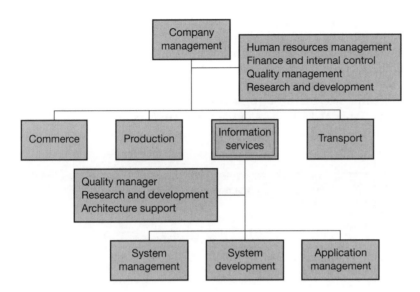

Figure 21.3
The line organization of
company X

Monitoring could be placed:

- in a function containing the role of test regulation;
- in the internal control (IC) department at company level;
- in a staff function of the department information services.

Coordination and advice could be placed:

A. in a staff function at company level;
B. in a staff function of information services;
C. as a general and technical office within one or more line departments within the department information services (separating infrastructure, development and functional aspects);
D. as an independent line function under information services. The coordination and advice role could be combined with the general and technical services support role into one function within the department information services.

System management support could be placed:

A. in a staff function in the department information services;
B. as a general and technical office within one or more line departments within information services (separating infrastructure, development and functional aspects);
C. in an independent line function under information services.

The system management support role could be combined with the coordination and advice role into a function within the department information services.

As indicated earlier in this chapter, the selection of the set-up of the organization depends on a large number of factors. A standard organization does not exist. Nevertheless, a rough indication has been included here based on experience and the size of the information services department in number of employees (Table 21.1). The size of the organization is shown vertically, and the roles are indicated horizontally; 'A', 'B', 'C' and 'D' indicate the preferred place in the organization.

Table 21.1
Organizational set-up depending on the size of the information services department

Size (number of employees)	Test regulations	Monitoring	C&A	System management support
≤25	C	A	B	A
≤100	B	A/C	B	B/C
≥=100	A	B	A/D	B/C

In situations in which testing is done not in the form of a project but in the line, operational test tasks are usually carried out in several places:

● System management: production acceptance test.
● System development: low-level and system tests.
● Application management/user organization: (functional) acceptance test.

It is advisable in such situations to have adequate coordination and control of the test processes, and to coordinate the test activities in a master plan.

21.4.4 TSite: the test factory

A test process is set up in the regular project test approach for the duration of the project. This means that the organization of the test process must be repeated for each new project. The project must be staffed, the infrastructure must be ordered and installed, and often control and work procedures, forms of planning and reporting, etc. will have to be set up. Expertise in the field of structural testing, test infrastructure and tools is often a scarce commodity within the organization. Because employees are often assigned to the project only temporarily, the learning effect is limited and much of the knowledge and experience gained is often lost again at the end of a project. The test environment that was set up with so much effort is eventually dismantled. This is certainly not the best situation in terms of controlling cost, time and quality.

Solution: a TSite

A special type of test organization that eliminates these disadvantages of a project approach is a test organization that is set up as a line department. This type of organization is often known by terms such as 'test factory', 'test service center', 'test laboratory' or 'test competence center'. In this book, we use the term 'TSite®', an abbreviation that stands for 'test site'. The test process in this form is separate from specific assignments, projects or systems, and is part of a permanent test organization.

The test process in a TSite can be compared with a factory with permanent staff (testers), machines (infrastructure and tools), standardized work procedures, etc. Different customers (departments, projects, systems) can commission their test assignments to this test organization. The customer comes to the test organization with their work assignment, which is scheduled in the form of work assignments for the staff, the infrastructure is set correctly, the assignment is carried out, and the customer collects the deliverables (reports, advice and possible defects on the tested object) at the agreed time. The quality standards of the test organization guarantee the customer a consistently high quality of testing.

This process is much more efficient and can be carried out in a much shorter space of time than when the organization has to be constructed each time from the bottom up (i.e. per project) because:

- the process is roughly the same for every assignment;
- there are experienced personnel trained in the factory;
- there is a reusable infrastructure.

Another advantage is that the often-scarce expertise in the field of structured testing, test environment and tools is used to the full.

The emphasis in a TSite is much more on the long-term aspects of the test process (efficiency, quality) than on a one-off project aspect such as supplying a quality advice within the agreed time and amount. A great deal of attention is paid, for example, to the reusability of testware, flexibility of the infrastructure, test automation and evaluation, and the optimization of standardized procedures. To obtain a basic staff of professional testers, personnel must be educated and trained in testing. In order to obtain and keep motivated employees, personnel management organizes test functions, and TSite offers its employees a career perspective in testing. In short, testing is a profession.

Application possibilities

The TSite type of organization is applied mainly in situations in which new system releases must be tested repeatedly, such as maintenance tests, large-scale projects or special development environments such as rapid application development, object orientation or components.

An organization may have several TSites, each of which may be geared towards a certain development environment, hardware platform and/or group of clients (projects, systems or departments). A TSite is also the obvious choice when the development process is arranged as a line organization or takes place externally.

Although the TSite usually belongs to the same organization as its clients, it is possible that organizations contract their test assignments to an external TSite.

Success factors

Although the advantages of TSites are evident, we should not ignore the project approach. There are several factors that influence the successful application of the TSite concept:

- The first, and perhaps most important factor, is whether testing is carried out according to a structured test approach. Without such an approach, a high quality and control of the test process cannot be guaranteed, successful test automation is impossible, and there is no standard procedure that can constantly be improved.
- There must be a sufficient supply of work in the form of test assignments to permanently occupy the TSite.
- For every assignment, there must be sufficient knowledge of the system and the subject matter. This knowledge is obtained from the project or from other departments. Often permanent TSite personnel may have insufficient or obsolete knowledge.
- There must be proper agreements and communication lines with the customers who supply their products for testing (customer, developers, users).
- There must be a permanent test infrastructure available, which can be set up quickly and adapted for specific assignments. Usually, this requires indirectly a certain standardization within the organization concerning the development environment, infrastructure and system development methodology.

21.5 Consultation structures

21.5.1 Testing and consulting

Testing requires consultation. This may be to agree on the appropriate test strategy or to have the right personnel on time, or may involve consultations about the hand-over of the test object and about the defects. The consultation structure is described in the test plan. Usually, some consultation structure has already been established around the test process, and testing must adapt to this. It is then the task of the test management to create the proper delegation and, in particular, to guard against a too extravagant consultation culture, i.e. avoid redundant meeting agendas in which the same subjects are discussed over and over again. The frequency and location of the meetings require the test management's attention; too many and too far costs too many valuable testing hours. It is advisable to maximize the available meeting hours in the test plan. This creates a monitoring mechanism. In all this, however, one should not underestimate the required informal and ad hoc meetings.

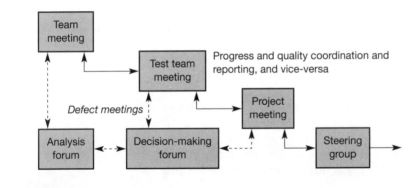

Figure 21.4
Test consultation
structure in the project
organization

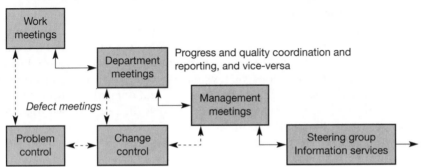

Figure 21.5
Test consultation
structure in the line
organization

21.5.2 Consultation structure in project and line

Figures 21.4 and 21.5 show the recommended consultation structure around a high-level test process for both the project and the line organization. From the test floor (team meetings, work meetings), there is coordination and information transfer to the steering committee and beyond. For the handling of the defects, separate consultation is provided for analysis and decision making.

21.5.3 Consultation characteristics

Team meetings/work meetings

These meetings are set in larger test teams or departments (more than five testers). Several test groups are operating within the context of a test team or a test department. This requires regular meetings about the activities.

Aim: coordination and progress monitoring.
Frequency: ad hoc to every fortnight.
Participants:
– permanent: testers, team leader, group leader;
– optional: methodical, functional and technical support, general and technical services support, intermediary.
Agenda: includes notifications, test activities, progress.
Reporting: to the test team/department meeting.

Test team meeting/department meeting
The test team meeting is the primary coordination consultation for the test process.

Aim: coordination and progress monitoring.
Frequency: ad hoc to every fortnight.
Participants:
- permanent: test manager/test leader, team leaders, leaders control/support;
- optional: intermediary.

Agenda: includes scheduling and progress monitoring, activities, monitoring of hours, quality, defects, changes, reporting vice versa.
Reporting: to project meeting/management meeting.

21.5.4 Related meetings
In the project meeting or management meeting, testing is usually represented by the test management. There is coordination of the test process and the quality of the test basis and test object. Monitoring of the complete project schedule is clearly important. It provides the test management with the opportunity to obtain insight at an early stage into the favorable and unfavorable aspects of the development process. This early information allows the test manager to anticipate future events by taking certain measures. The test management does not usually take part in the steering committee, where they are represented by the project or line management.

For analysis forum/defect control and decision forum/change control, see section 22.5.

Test control **22**

22.1   Introduction

There are three forms of control in a test process: control of the test process itself, control of the test infrastructure, and control of the test products. The test process involves the following control objects and/or aspects:

- progress
- quality
- statistics
- reports.

The test infrastructure involves the following control objects and/or aspects:

- test environment
- (test) tools
- office environment.

The test deliverables involve the following control objects and/or aspects:

- test basis
- test object
- testware
- test documentation
- test regulations.

Control of these objects is embedded in the TMap regulations. This chapter deals with a number of important control procedures:

- test deliverables control
- defect management
- quality management for testing.

As a consequence of government regulations, it is becoming more and more important to prove that testing has been done and to indicate what has been tested. Showing what has been tested is achieved with configuration management tools (showing which test cases refer to which part of the test basis). Proof that testing has been carried out must be provided by explicit reports.

In an increasing number of organizations, the following rule applies: if there is no proof of testing, then testing did not take place. Furthermore, it is often demanded that proof is provided that defects have been dealt with. These demands are expected to increase. In order to meet strict demands of traceability and burden of proof, test deliverables control, defect management and quality management must be tailored to this.

Test control should be set up in such a way that the traceability and/or burden of proof can be followed with every step. This means:

- the test specifications must indicate clearly from which part of the test basis they have been derived;
- in the execution of the test, proof must be provided about which test cases have actually been executed;
- insight must be given into which test cases have led to which defects;
- the proof during retesting must be recorded, i.e. which defects have been solved and proven to be so in a retest.

22.2   Control of the test process

Test process control focuses on managing the test process and controlling the quality of the test object. The following main tasks have been defined:

- registration, administration, storage and interpretation of:
  - progress and utilization of budget and time;
  - quality indicators;
  - test statistics;
- reports.

22.2.1 Progress and utilization of budget and time

Aim

During all TMap phases, progress must be monitored, with the data being recorded throughout the test process. On the basis of the collected data, it is possible to determine the progress of the test project as a whole and on a detailed level. This information offers control possibilities for test management in order to keep the test process controllable. If necessary, timely measures can be taken to correct negative trends. Periodic (preferably weekly) reports on progress are submitted to the customer.

Organization

This includes the organization and implementation of the following:

- identification of activities and deliverables;
- registration of progress data;
- creating and interpreting progress statistics and trends;
- periodic progress reports.

Objects

The activities and deliverables in the test planning are related to hours, resources, project time and dependencies. Within this framework, information is collected in order to gain insight into the degree to which the test planning has been and can be effected.

For a test process, the activities and deliverables listed in the lifecycle model are used as a reference for progress. For example:

- *Review of the test basis*: test basis defects.
- *Test specification*: test scenarios.
- *Setting up test databases*: test databases.
- *Test execution*: test results.
- *Comparing and analyzing results*: defects.
- *Preserving*: testware.

The degree of completion of the test deliverables provides insight into the progress. The following are registered for each activity:

- progress status (not started, processing, interrupted, percentage completed, completed);
- hours and resources (planned, spent, still to go, over/underspending).

The customers or project managers must be offered structural insight into the progress of the test process. For this, it is important to be able to report on the progress at the level of deliverables of the test process. It is recommended to add detail to the registration and the reports on the level of test levels and test units. When registering progress, one can differentiate between management and support and primary activities. For reasons of efficiency, it is recommended not to administrate explicitly all small activities. Their usefulness should be reviewed periodically (in consultation with the customer). For example, management and support activities can be administered separately only if their size is significant (more than day per week).

Interpretation and reporting

The collected data for test management are noted and compared with the actual planning, preferably in the form of a periodic report. Recognized trends or (potential) bottlenecks are listed explicitly. The data are subjected to statistical analysis (see section 22.2.3).

Procedures and tools

There should be a (possibly automated) procedure available for the registration and administration of the data and deliverables to be controlled. In most cases, monitoring and checking of the hours spent are usually done using a separate hour registration system. This must be complemented with budgets for each activity/deliverable. In addition, testing personnel must report on the spending on a weekly basis. The procedures and tools used here are usually available at the project and/or organization level, so use them!

Responsibilities

The tasks to be carried out in this framework are part of the control role and/or the system management support role. Monitoring progress is part of the test management role.

22.2.2 Quality indicators

Aim

The test activities provide information on the quality of the test object from the review of the test basis in the preparation phase up to the preservation of the testware in the completion phase. The defects found constitute the main measure of quality. All defects found are recorded. This provides a structural and almost immediately available insight into the quality of the supplied software, the environment(s), and other test objects. This information is used for periodic and ad hoc reports, for the compilation of a release advice, and for statistical purposes. The information is used to take action to improve the quality or possibly to modify the test strategy and/or the test effort.

Organization

This includes the organization and implementation of the following:
- identification of the quality indicators;
- recording of defects and solutions;
- creating and interpreting quality statistics and trends;
- periodic quality reports.

Objects

Defects can be observed in the test basis, the test object, the resources and the regulations. The following quality indicators can be recorded:
- *Number of defects still open per category of severity at a certain time.* A snapshot of the quality of the product. This indicator is easy to supply and has an immediate impact.

- *Number of solved defects per category of severity in a period*. The number of defects solved in a certain period.
- *Number of reported defects per category of severity in a period*. The number of reported defects per category of severity in a certain period.
- *Stability of the system*. An indication as to whether the product is stable, which means that it is no longer subject to change, based on the number of solved defects versus the number of reported defects per category of severity in a certain timeframe.
- *The number of recorded defects per category of severity per test day or week*. An indication of the amount of time needed to find a defect (if the number of defects per test day/week is high, then it is advisable (necessary) to continue testing).
- *Number of retests*. Number of retests with the hours spent per test unit.
- *Recovery time per defect*. The time elapsed from the moment a defect has been recorded to the moment when delivery occurs again per type and category of severity. This indicator can also be used to say something about the maintainability of the system concerned.
- *Test basis defects per subsystem*. Insight is provided into the number of functional shortcomings.
- *Lost and underutilized hours*. Registration in hours per event associated with inadequately available preconditions, quality or facilities, such as:
  - test basis cannot be used for testing;
  - test infrastructure is not available;
  - test object arrives too late or is incomplete;
  - personnel are unavailable.
- *Number of defects not yet found*. This estimate is based on the total number of defects found up to any given moment in connection with the number of defects from a recent period.
- *Mean time between failures (MTBF)*. The purpose of this indicator is to provide insight into the quality of the system, expressed in MTBF, subdivided into categories of severity. In the context of testing, the MTBF provides an estimate of the time per tester that elapses between the occurrence of two defects.

Interpretation and reporting

The collected data are made available to the test management, preferably in the form of periodic reports. Recognized trends are reported explicitly. The data are subjected to statistical analysis (see section 22.2.3).

Procedures and tools

All defects are recorded according to the defect management procedure (see section 22.5).

Responsibilities

The tasks to be carried out in this framework are part of the control role and/or the system management support role. Depending on the test type or the set-up of the organization, the tasks of recording and interpreting the quality indicators are part of the intermediary role.

22.2.3 Test statistics

Aim

During the entire test process, statistical information is recorded in order to be able to provide both test management and the customer with detailed insight into the status of the test process and the quality of the object. The method of establishing which data should be measured (metrics) is described in detail in Chapter 23. We describe below a possible set of statistical data.

Organization

This includes the organization and implementation of the following:
- determining which statistics are to be created;
- collecting the progress and quality information;
- creating, accumulating and interpreting statistics and trends;
- creating reports.

Objects

The statistics are created from data on the progress and utilization of the budget and time, and from quality indicators. The statistics can be compiled on the level of the test unit or they can be aggregated. A test unit can be a subsystem, function or program, or even a component of the test infrastructure. The statistical data that are collected depend on a number of factors, such as need of information, availability, size and type of the test object, and representativeness. The set of statistics to be collected must be determined during the setting up of the test plan, in consultation with the customer and any other parties concerned.

Statistics regarding the budget and cost of the test process, and budget utilization include:
- budget used in the time per test unit per test activity (test unit, period, hours spent differentiated into review, test specification, first test, retest(s), unforeseen, and overheads);
- budget used in the time per test unit per test function (test unit, period, hours spent on the categories of test management, support and testing, or even more detailed);
- cost of retests per test unit (test unit, period, number of retests, number of hours per retest).

Statistics required regarding the quality of the test object, and defects include:

- defects per test unit (test unit, period, number per category of severity, and test unit, period, status (still open, dealt with) per category of severity);
- defects and causes (test unit, period, number per type of defect, e.g. test basis, test object, infrastructure, test defect);
- defects per type of function (test unit, period, number per type of function, e.g. registration function, print function, screen presentation, batch processing);
- test defect per type (test unit, period, (tester) number per type of error, e.g. specification error, environment error, execution error; assessment error);
- defect recovery time (test unit, defect, category of severity, test number, time of announcement, time of recovery);
- defects per function point (test unit, function points, number of defects per category of severity);
- defects per test point (test unit, test points, number of defects per category of severity).

Interpretation and reporting

The statistical information is available continuously throughout the test process. Together with the most recent data on progress and quality, it is made available to test management, preferably in the form of periodic reports. Identified peculiarities are reported explicitly. The statistical information is also interesting after the test process has been completed. It is made available in the evaluation report, which is drawn up during the completion phase. In many cases, there is great interest in these evaluations. In addition to the customers, there is usually interest from disciplines such as quality management, issuing of rules, control, accountancy, methods and techniques, and even personnel and organization. The aim is quality improvement in various aspects. It is important to note that the information can be distributed only after permission from the owner, i.e. the customer who ordered the test.

Procedures and tools

The procedures and tools used for the registration of progress and quality are also used, as much as possible, to collect and maintain the statistics.

Responsibilities

The tasks to be carried out relating to statistics are part of the control role and/or the system management support role. Depending on the test type or the set-up of the organization, the tasks of recording and interpretation of the quality statistics may be part of the intermediary role.

22.2.4 Reports

Periodically, and ad hoc upon request, reports are provided on the progress of the test process and the quality of the test object. The test plan should list the frequency of the reports (TMap advice: weekly) and the content (form). It is important to report to the customer periodically from the beginning of the test process, i.e. from the moment the test plan is set. During the preparation and specification phases, management is inclined to be indifferent towards testing. There is only interest in progress during the execution of the tests, when testing is on the critical path of the project.

Trends are discovered during all phases of the test process. It is of importance to discover trends at the earliest possible stage. This allows corrective measures to be taken in time. This is almost always better, cheaper and faster.

A well-known trend is symbolized in the demonic quadrangle, with time, money, functionality and quality as cornerstones (Figure 22.1). At the start of a project, there is a certain balance between the cornerstones. It is safe to predict unforeseen events that may occur within the project, putting the quadrangle under pressure. Certain activities will experience a delay (time) and/or cost much more than planned (money). The project manager sometimes corrects this by cutting down on the other cornerstones (quality and functionality).

Figure 22.1
The demonic quadrangle

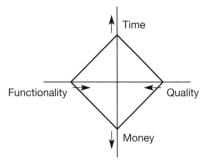

On the basis of the quadrangle, the test manager indicates the consequences of the project manager's decisions, e.g. are decisions always directed towards restricting quality and functionality? It is particularly difficult to identify this trend in time, which is all the more reason to assign a professional test manager. Depending on your point of view, the test manager is the project manager's conscience or pain in the neck! This role requires a high degree of professionalism because the test manager must deal carefully with the various interests within and outside the project.

The reports should give information on the most recent reporting period and the accumulated data of the test process as a whole. The subjects of progress and quality are combined in a single periodic report. In addition to the presentation in figures, the periodic report should also offer textual insight into the activities, the deliverables, the trends and possible bottlenecks.

22.2.5 Draft content of periodic reports

A periodic report should contain at least the following:

- agreements made in the previous period;
- activities of the previous period;
- the status of the (test) deliverables to be supplied, e.g. percentage completed;
- overview of hours spent (cumulative) per test unit:
  - number of hours planned (1);
  - number of hours spent in this period;
  - number of hours spent (2);
  - number of hours still to be completed (3);
  - total number of hours (2+3);
  - number of hours deviating (2+3–1);
  - planned end date;
  - expected end date;
- trends and remarks regarding progress;
- faults that have occurred in the test infrastructure, causes, recovery times and impact;
- overview (cumulative) of quality indicators:
  - number of defects per category in this period;
  - total number of defects per category;
  - number of solved defects per category in this period;
  - total number of solved defects per category;
  - recovery time per defect;
  - average recovery time per defect;
  - stability, e.g. percentage of defect-free test units;
  - number of retests per test unit;
- trends and notes on quality;
- bottlenecks (hard, serious obstructions);
- discussion points (potential bottlenecks);
- activities in the next period.

22.2.6 Risk reports

There will be requests for reports on quality that are independent of the regular reports at various points, including:

- reaching a milestone in the project;
- completing the system or acceptance test of (part of) the full system;
- a meeting of the steering committee or management;
- a request from the internal accountants service.

A test manager must be able to draw up a report within 24 hours. This should pay attention to the following aspects:

- How much of what was indicated in the test plan has been tested?
- What still needs to be tested?
- What are the trends and statistics on the quality of the test object?
- Advice on possible alternatives, such as postponement, making available less functionality, fewer retests, etc.

Here are a few tips regarding the compilation of risk reports:
- Always report completely and correctly, as nobody benefits from matters being made to look better than they are. Note that only rarely will testers report the situation to be worse than it really is.
- Report precisely, and ensure that the figures are well-founded.
- Try to report in terms of the risks that the customer runs, not just in the number of defects.
- Relate the reports to the test basis.
- Never answer questions such as 'can I go into production?' or 'can it be accepted?' with 'no': always say, 'yes, provided ... '.

22.3 Control of the test infrastructure

During the early phases of TMap, the test infrastructure is specified and ordered. After the installation, intake and acceptance, the test management is responsible for control. The test infrastructure is divided into three groups of facilities:
- test environment
- test tools
- office environment.

These aspects can be divided into two groups:

- *Technical control:*
  - test environment (hardware, software, control procedures);
  - test files (physical);
  - networks for test environment and office environment;
  - technical office organization;
  - test tools.
- *Logistical control.* The non-technical component of the office environment, such as canteen facilities, transport, admission passes, etc.

The tasks to be carried out in the framework of logistical control are part of the control and/or facilitary services support roles. These tasks are not discussed in this book.

The technical control tasks to be carried out are a part of the technical support role. When these tasks are carried out, support may be offered by the supplier or system management. The most important control tasks of the technical support role are:

- organization
- provision
- maintenance
- configuration management
- troubleshooting.

These tasks are described in more detail in Chapter 19.

22.3.1 Test environment and test tool changes

During the project, the infrastructure is subject to changes because of a variety of internal and external causes, including:

- phased delivery and changes in the infrastructure;
- delivery or redelivery of (parts of) the test object;
- new or changed procedures;
- changes in simulation and system software;
- changes to hardware, protocols, parameters, et cetera;
- new or changed test tools;
- changes in test files, tables, etc., e.g:
  - converting test input files into a new format;
  - reorganizing test files;
  - changes in naming convention.

Changes in the technical infrastructure may be introduced only after permission from the test management (possibly delegated to the technical support official). The manager registers the changes with the aid of the test control procedure. Depending on the type and size of the change, these will be communicated generally to the test team.

22.3.2 Availability of the test environment and test tools

The technical support official is responsible for creating regular back-ups of the infrastructure and must be capable of repairing the infrastructure by means of a recovery procedure. The tester must report faults in the test environment and the test tools to the technical support official, who will then analyze the fault and, depending on the severity, remedy it immediately. For those faults that cannot be remedied immediately, the tester must write a formal defect report. The technical support official provides data, periodically and on request, for reports on the availability of the test environment and test tools and (possibly) the progress and duration of the fault that has occurred.

22.4   Control of test deliverables

It is important to differentiate the various test deliverables, and to manage and control them unequivocally. In this process, we distinguish external and internal deliverables. External deliverables include the test basis and the test object. Internal deliverables include testware, the test basis (internal), the test object (internal), the test documentation and test regulations. Most test deliverables can be controlled with the aid of the test deliverables control procedure.

22.4.1 External deliverables

Control of external deliverables is an external responsibility. It is not advisable to try to record this from the test project. Control must occur at the source or it is doomed to fail. At the same time, it is often the test project that suffers the most from a lack of external control of the test basis and test object. It is therefore important to set demands (in the preconditions and assumptions of the test plan). For example, incoming deliverables must be identifiable (including their version and date), and the test project must have an influence on the prioritization process in the implementation of changes. The relation between the test object and the test basis must also be guarded well.

22.4.2 Internal deliverables

Testware

Testware is defined as all test deliverables that are produced during the test process. One of the requirements is that these products must be capable of being used for maintenance purposes and must therefore be transferable and maintainable. Testware includes the following:

- *Test plan(s).* Contain both master test plans and other test plans.
- *Logical test specifications.* The logical specifications contain the logical descriptions of the test cases.
- *Physical test specifications.* The physical test cases contain the physical descriptions of the test cases. The term 'physical' means that the test cases can be executed and verified. The physical test cases derive from the logical test cases and constitute the test scripts.
- *Test scenario.* A collection of test scripts indicating the order of the tests to be carried out.
- *Traceability matrix (or cross-reference matrix).* A matrix indicating the link between the (user) requirements (from the test basis) and the actual test cases. The situations to be tested from the test basis are listed vertically, and the test cases are listed horizontally.
- *Test input files.* In the test input files, created on the basis of the test scripts or the test scenario, the following must be described (in summary form):
  - aim;
  - physical name;

- creation date;
- short description of the contents;
- type of file and other relevant characteristics;
- reference to the test scripts or the test scenario.
- *Test output.* The output to be delivered may consist of printed output, hard copies of screens, hard-copy files and output files. The tester provides the manager with the output produced after completion of the test. The test documentation of the output to be provided contains:
  - reference to the physical name;
  - production date;
  - short description of the contents;
  - type of file and other relevant characteristics;
  - reference to the test scenario.
- *Basic documentation.* A description of the test environment, test tools, test organization and initial databases.
- *Test specification dossier.* The test specification dossier contains:
  - logical test specifications;
  - physical test specifications and test scripts;
  - description of the input files;
  - description of the output files;
  - test scenario.
- *Test execution dossier.* The test execution dossier contains:
  - description of the test infrastructure;
  - description of the test tools;
  - test results (including the defects) and reports;
  - information on defects and changes;
  - hand-over and version documentation.

The test deliverables control procedure (see section 22.4.3) can be used to control the testware.

Test basis (internal)
The documentation marked as test basis is saved in its original form and class. Control provides duplicates for the test activities and registers the assigned version numbers, etc. To prevent redundancy, maximum use will be made of external control procedures that are relevant to the test process. If necessary, the test deliverables control procedure (see section 22.4.3) fulfills this requirement.

Test object (internal)
Usually a test object consists of software, hardware and documentation. The software and hardware are controlled (by the technical support official) by procedures and other means available, and are often prescribed within the organization. The documentation may be managed in the same way as the test basis, i.e. possibly also with the aid of the test deliverables control procedure.

Test documentation
During the test process, various documents are received or written, including:
- project plans
- reports from the meetings (with decisions and activities lists)
- correspondence, both on paper and in electronic form (email)
- memos
- standards and guidelines
- test, review and audit reports
- progress and quality reports.

The control and/or system management support role ensures proper storage and supply of this documentation. The test deliverables control procedure (see section 22.4.3) may provide support here. Procedures and resources on the project and/or organizational level are usually available for this purpose.

Test regulations
The test regulations, such as lifecycle model, test techniques and documentation standards, must be unequivocally recorded, maintained and (in the case of changes) made available. The test deliverables control procedure can be used for this.

22.4.3 Test deliverables control procedure
The aim of this procedure is to manage the internal deliverables:
- testware
- test basis (internal)
- test object (internal)
- test documentation
- test regulations.

Responsibilities
The tasks to be carried out in this framework are part of control and/or system management support roles. The specific control of changes in the test regulations is often a task for the methodical support official. In this procedure, we use the term 'deliverables'. This includes all relevant parts of a deliverable. These may be documents, physical files or other materials.

With regard to security, it is advisable to appoint someone with the control role as being responsible for making copies of the (most crucial) deliverables and structurally storing these in a different building. The (changed) material should be refreshed on a weekly basis. Setting up such a security procedure depends on the size and the impact of an information system. Beware of excess! In the case of electronic storage, the controller is also responsible for back-up and recovery procedures.

The test deliverables control procedure consists of four steps:

1. *Delivery*. The testers supply the deliverables that must be controlled to the controller. The delivered files should preferably be placed in a separate directory. The deliverables must be supplied as a whole, e.g. it should contain a version date and a version number. The controller checks for completeness. Items that can be checked include:
   - name of author;
   - type of document (also in name of document);
   - final version and version date;
   - correctness of references to other documentation (the test deliverables must refer clearly to the corresponding test object and the corresponding test basis);
   - overview of changes, including overview of the versions, version dates and reasons for changes, as well as the name of the person who introduced the changes.

   Deliverables in electronic form must be supplied with their permanent names, which includes the version number.

2. *Registration*. The controller registers the deliverables in the administration on the basis of data such as the name of the supplier, name of the deliverables, date and version number. In addition, it is advisable to indicate how the document was created (e.g. the word processor used). It is also recorded how long the deliverables concerned should be kept. In certain cases, it may be necessary to record information on related deliverables for the deliverable to be registered. This is the case in organizations in which traceability is an important issue, e.g. because of legal obligations. When registering changed deliverables, the controller should ensure consistency between the various deliverables.

3. *Archiving*. A distinction is made between new and changed deliverables. Broadly speaking, this means that new deliverables are added to the archive and changed deliverables replace previous versions.

4. *Distributing*. Providing project team members or others with deliverables occurs by means of a copy of the required deliverable. The controller registers the version of the deliverables that has been passed on, and to whom and when.

This procedure may be supported by means of configuration management tools (see Chapter 27).

22.5 Defect management

The set-up of defect management depends on the type of organization or the type of test project. The defect procedure must match the defect form with its accompanying defect administration. The procedure makes demands on the selected type of administration and the defect form (make sure that no information is registered in the defect administration that is not processed further). The defect administration is a very useful source for collecting metrics (see Chapter 23). It is obvious that the degree of detailing of the defect administration determines the degree to which certain metrics can be recorded, e.g. if no difference is indicated as to the test type or test environment in which the defects occur, then it is logical that no reliable statements can be made on the costs/benefits of the development test compared with the acceptance test.

22.5.1 Defect procedure

Two types of defects are found during testing:

- *Internal (a test defect):*
  - test specification error
  - (own) test environment or test tool error
  - execution error
  - judgment error
  - other.
- *External (the defect is outside the test):*
  - test basis (specification, demands)
  - test object, e.g. software, documentation
  - test environment and test tools
  - other.

Figure 22.2 shows the relationship between deliverables and defects. A deliverable is tested after an order to do so has been received. The center column contains the primary flow of the test, from supply to the status 'completed'. The column 'internal repair' represents the feedback to the tester: (internal) decision-making and repairs on test products such as test scripts and files, and retests after test execution errors. The column 'external repair' represents the analysis procedures and decision-making procedures between the tester, supplier (programmer), system management and customer, as well as the repairs carried out by the supplier and/or the customer and/or the system management.

Internal defect procedure

Within a test team, there is an internal defect procedure containing agreements on the way in which testers should deal with defects. All defects detected during the preparation, specification and execution phases complete this procedure. The procedure involves the following:

- *Intake.* It is determined whether the deliverable is complete and testable, and whether it has been supplied in accordance with the schedule. If the deliverable is not (sufficiently) testable, this is signalled by means of a defect report, which is passed on to the external defect procedure.

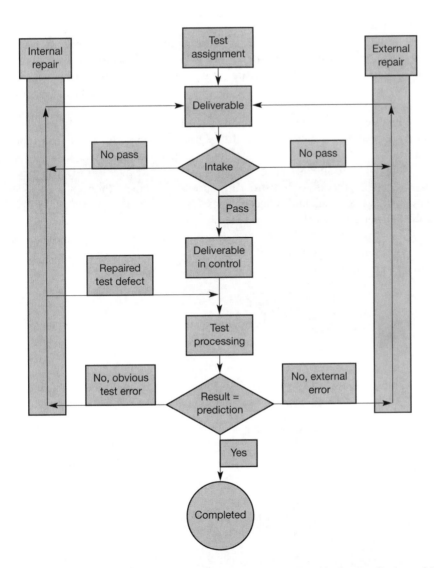

Figure 22.2
Deliverables and defects

- *Result ≠ prediction*. If the test result is not consistent with the prediction, this could point towards a defect in the test object. Firstly, it is determined whether the test has been prepared or executed properly. If necessary, test repair occurs. As a general rule, one may say that about 20 per cent of the defects require test repair. If there is no clarity about a defect, and it does not concern a test error, the defect is passed on by means of a defect report to the external defect procedure.

External defect procedure

The external defect procedure contains both the decision-making process and the repair process for defects. Such a procedure is available in most organizations or projects. It is important that any existing procedures are checked for usability before testing. Strict requirements apply to the possibility of influencing and tracing changes, and to the classification of defect reports. The procedure receives as input the change requests to the test basis and defect reports resulting from defects found in testing or in an audit. The defect reports resulting from defects derive from the internal defect procedure.

The procedure shown in Figure 22.3 is used for the decision-making process and the repair process. Two distinct functional units play a role in the processing of change requests and defect reports: the analysis forum and the decision forum. Depending on the size and form of the organization, the development and/or test phase, and the test type, these forums are implemented as actual meetings. Sometimes a 'paper' procedure will suffice, which requires occasional management decisions.

Figure 22.3
Making decisions on defect reports and change requests

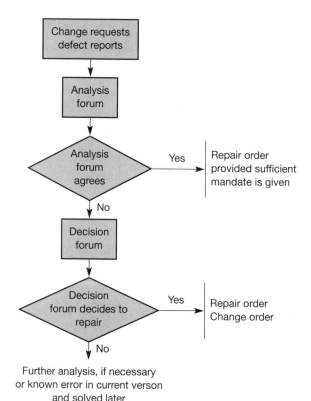

The analysis forum often appears in the form of, for example, the test meeting, the quality assurance meeting or the change control board. Apart from in the form of the change control board, the decision forum hardly ever occurs explicitly. Decisions are usually taken in the project management meeting or in the steering group.

The analysis forum can represent a group of employees at an operational level, such as:

- test
- quality management and quality assurance
- functional design
- technical design/construction
- system management
- application management and use.

The decision forum may represent a number of parties involved at a tactical/strategic level, such as:

- customer
- project management
- supplier (developer)
- test management (optional).

The procedure works as follows:

- All reported change requests and defect reports are dealt with initially by the analysis forum.
- In the case of a change request, the analysis forum decides whether the change is possible and, if so, what the consequences are in terms of work hours for the disciplines involved, e.g. test, technical design/construction and functional design.
- Subsequently, the change requests go to the decision forum, where it is decided whether the proposal will be converted into change assignment for this version, or it is passed on to a following version, or it is rejected.
- In the case of a defect report, the analysis forum investigates the defect. What is the cause of the defect? Where and how can it be solved? And what are the possible consequences in work hours for the disciplines involved? If the analysis forum is unanimous in its analysis, and the consequences of the repairs do not exceed the mandate, the analysis forum may decide to issue a repair assignment.
- If the analysis forum cannot agree, or if the consequences of the repairs exceed the mandate of the analysis forum, the defect report is submitted to the decision forum.
- The decision forum decides whether the defect should be solved or passed on to the following version (or even later), or whether further analysis is necessary.

- In addition to all change requests and defect reports, the decision forum also receives an overview of all defect reports that have been dealt with by the analysis forum.
- The analysis forum meets regularly (frequency depends on necessity), but can also meet on an ad hoc basis.
- In principle, the decision forum meets only periodically.

22.5.2 Defect reports

Defect reports should be supplied according to a standard. This standard depends on what the organization wants to achieve with a defect report:

- Defect reports may be designed solely as a means of communication.
- The retest may have to be performed on the basis of these defect reports.
- It may be necessary to make a reliable statement on the possible risks of going into production, e.g. the severity and cause categories, or the classification on the basis of quality characteristics.

In many organizations, there are resources or tools available for this purpose that make it easy to produce, register and consult defect reports. Sometimes reports and statistics are created automatically.

In order to ensure that the reports are reliable, a disciplined registration regime is important. There is no point (and it could even be counterproductive) in including certain characteristics if they are filled in incorrectly.

Time required for defects

Completing and updating the defects is a labour-intensive affair, and errors may be introduced if a suitable tool is not used. One should be prepared for about ten minutes per defect merely for registration and control of the defect. If we then include the time for defect consultation and handling in the analysis forum, we need an average of 45 minutes per defect.

Examples

To provide some insight into the possible types of defect report, we use examples of a simple defect report and a more extensive report. The simple defect report illustrated in Figure 22.4 constitutes a simple but effective means of recording and passing on defects. The fields are filled in as follows:

- *Project name.* The name of the (test) project or the system to be tested.
- *Number.* A unique (serial) number for the defect report for the benefit of controlling and tracing progress.
- *Tester.* The name of the tester who detected the defect.
- *Date.* The date when the defect was reported: dd/mm/ccyy.

<table>
<tr><td>Project name:</td><td></td></tr>
<tr><td>Number:
Tester:
Date:
Urgency:
Type:</td><td></td></tr>
<tr><td>Test object:
Version:
Test specification:
Description:

Appendices:
Remarks:</td><td></td></tr>
</table>

Figure 22.4
Simple defect report

- *Urgency.* A mix of the priority of the defect and the severity category. The standard (recorded in the test plan) is the degree of hindrance experienced by the tester when carrying out the test script, or the degree of hindrance experienced by production if this defect is not solved in this release. The following urgency classification is usually applied:
  - defect that blocks further execution of the test script, or immobilizes operations if the system were to go into production;
  - defect as a result of which the test script can be executed only to a limited degree, or that is too serious to allow the system to go into production;
  - minor defect or flaw that does not interfere with the completion of the test script or operation.
- *Type.* Indicates what the cause seems to be, e.g. TB (test basis: specification, requirements), PR (program software), DOC (documentation), TIS (technical infrastructure).
- *Test object.* The tested (part of the) test object must be indicated in this note, such as the name and number of a function. If possible, further details such as the name of the program or screen may be stated.
- *Version.* The version number or the version date of the system documentation or the software to which the defect report refers.
- *Test specification.* A reference to the test case to which the defect report refers, possibly with a link to the test basis.
- *Description.* The detected defect is described as fully as possible.
- *Appendices.* If further clarification is necessary, appendices are added, e.g. test scripts, hard copies of screens and prints, etc.
- *Remarks.* Additional space for further information, e.g. on corresponding defects or reproduction possibilities.

id	Project name		Number		STATUS

tst			**New**
	Tester ID		
	Test environment ID		
	Test basis ID		
	Test object ID		
	Test case ID		
	Provisional seriousness		
	Provisional priority		
	Provisional cause		
	Quality characteristic		

Description:

Note:

for			**Reported**
	Persons present		
	Final seriousness		
	Final priority		
	Final cause		
	Desired solving date		

Note:

Cancelled

sol	Deliverable before	Deliverable afer	By	Date	# hours	Being repaired

Solution:

ret			Re-test
	Re-tester ID		
	Test environment ID		
	Test basis ID		
	Test object ID		
	Test case ID		

No. follow-up		Follow-up no.

Note:

Solved

Figure 22.5 Extensive defect report

For many test processes, the extensive form shown in Figure 22.5 goes too far. Obviously, it is possible to use this form and leave a number of fields empty, or to use a form based on this, but geared more towards the situation at hand.

- The ID (identification) block is used to identify the defect report.
- The 'tst' (test execution) block is used to describe the definite defect.
- The 'for' (forum) block is used to display the decision of the analysis forum.
- The 'sol' (solution) block describes the solution to the defect.
- In the 'ret' (retest) block the result of the retest is noted down.
- The status of the defect is indicated in the right-hand column of the form.

The fields are completed as follows:
- *Project name*. The name of the (test) project or the system being tested.
- *Number*. A unique (serial) number of the defect report for the benefit of controlling and progress tracing.
- *Tester ID*. The name of the tester who detected the defect.
- *Test environment ID*. The test environment used, and the identification of the test data used, i.e. test environment, database identification, including the version of the data model and test data.
- *Test basis ID*. The test basis used, i.e. name of the test basis document, including the version number, possibly supplemented with a specific user requirement number.
- *Test object ID*. The object tested, i.e. the name of the (sub)system, including the version number.
- *Test case ID*. The unique test case to which the defect refers.
- *Provisional seriousness*. The severity category suggested by the tester. This severity category indicates the damage to operations, e.g.
  - blocking production: this immediately involves large sums of money because, for example, the defect immobilizes operations if the system goes into production;
  - serious: this concerns less money, because, for example, the user must manually repair or complete issues;
  - interfering: this concerns very little or no money, e.g. the truncation of alphanumerical data on the screen or issues regarding user-friendliness;
  - cosmetic: incorrect layout (position of fields) or colours.
- *Provisional priority*. The priority or urgency suggested by the tester for the execution of the test, e.g.
  - immediate repair necessary, e.g. to have a patch available within 48 hours to deal (provisionally) with the defect. The test process or present operation (if it concerns a defect report from production) is blocked in a serious manner;
  - repairs necessary within the present release: the present process could possibly continue with work-arounds, but production must not be saddled with this defect;

- repairs necessary in due course, but these need be only available in a subsequent release: the defect does not occur (at present) in production or the damage is slight.
- *Provisional cause.* The cause of the defect estimated by the tester. Possible causes are:

    TB   test basis is not right (functional design)
    TO   test object is not right (software)
    DM   data model version is not correct
    EN   environment: printer/network defects, memory problems
    LT   logical test specifications are not correct
    TS   test script is not correct
    TD   test data are not correct
    TE   error in test execution.

- *Quality characteristic.* The quality characteristic determined by the tester to which the defect refers.
- *Description.* The clearly formulated description of the defect detected.
- *Note.* Additional space to add further information, e.g. on corresponding defects or reproduction possibilities, or a description of a situation in the case of error guessing. The number of appendices can also be reported here.
- *New.* The date on which the defect was found.
- *Persons present.* The people involved in the analysis forum.
- *Final seriousness.* The final severity category as determined by the forum.
- *Final priority.* The final priority as determined by the forum.
- *Final cause.* The final cause as determined by the forum.
- *Desired solving date.* A date is set by when the defect must be solved. It is possible to also note a planned number of hours.
- *Note.* Additional space to add further information, e.g. on corresponding defects or reproduction possibilities. If the forum decides that a defect is not an error but a change is desired nevertheless, then the defect should be changed into a proposal for change. The identification of the proposal for change is recorded in the 'Note' field.
- *Reported.* The date on which the defect was dealt with by the forum.
- *Cancelled.* If it is decided to do nothing with the defect, then it can be set to 'Cancelled'. This means that even the testers do not need to change or retest anything. In this case, the reason for the cancellation should be written in the 'Note' field.
- *Deliverable before.* Identification of the deliverable that caused the defect.
- *Deliverable after.* Identification of the deliverable, including the version number for which the defect must be solved.
- *By.* The name of the person who adapted the deliverable concerned.
- *Date.* The date on which the deliverable was adapted.
- *# hours.* The number of hours spent on adapting the deliverable concerned.
- *Solution.* Space to indicate briefly and clearly what has been changed in order to solve the defect.

- *Being repaired.* The date on which the person who must solve the defect is informed that the defect must be solved.
- *Re-tester ID.* The name of the tester who executes the retest.
- *Test environment ID.* The test environment used for the retest and the identification of the test data used, i.e. test type (environment), database identification, including the version of the data model and the test data.
- *Test basis ID.* The test basis used for the retest, i.e. name of the test basis document, including the version number, possibly supplemented with a specific user requirement number.
- *Test object ID.* The object tested in the retest, i.e. the name of the (sub)system, including the version number.
- *Test case ID.* The full path of a test case number to be traced in a retest.
- *Re-test.* Date from when the retest can occur.
- *Follow-up no.* New defect number, number of the defect report listing the unsolved defect (with different IDs).
- *Followed up.* Date on which the defect was declared as being unsolved and to be followed up.
- *Solved.* Date on which the defect was declared as being solved.
- *Note.* Free field.

The fields on the right-hand side of the defect form ("New" to "Solved") constitute the status of the defect. The field with the most recent date is the present status.

22.6 Control and quality management

22.6.1 External and internal quality management

To control test processes, it is necessary to pay due attention to the quality management aspect. A test process is always part of a larger process, an organization or a project. This is the task of quality management in whatever form or on whatever level.

Although a test process may rely on external quality management, it is not its competence. The project or line manager is responsible for the quality of processes and deliverables, and hence also for quality management for the quality system. The test management may therefore expect that the conditions will be or have been created in order to produce high-quality work. This concerns not only measures and standards for methods, techniques and resources, and quality standards, but also support and training.

Test management may also rely on a regular process audit of the test process or a test deliverables review. Provided implementation is timely and professional, great advantages can be achieved by testing. Examples of processes and deliverables to be reviewed in this framework include the test plan, the test specifications, and the test execution process.

In larger projects and organizations, this external quality management is usually executed by a quality assurance (QA), quality management (QM) or methods and techniques (M&T) department/subproject. It is not advisable to include this external quality management in a test team.

What applies to quality management in general also applies to the internal quality management for testing. There is plenty of literature and experience available on quality management, so it is sufficient to mention here only the most important components of internal quality management for a test process. Using general knowledge of the quality management phenomenon, and applying TMap, an adequate quality system for testing can be created.

22.6.2 Internal quality management testing
Organization

Internal quality management of a test process comes under the responsibility of the test management. This should not be assigned to a single official, as the quality or quality management is achieved by each person involved in the test process. The test management is responsible for the facilities used to give shape to the quality management. The organization of internal quality management depends greatly on the size of the test object and the test process, as well as the degree to which external quality management is available. Special tasks of quality management, such as audits, reviews and risk analysis, are executed (on a part-time basis) by one or more employees, and sometimes by the test management itself. In larger projects, it is conceivable to organize a separate quality management role.

TMap: the ideal instrument for quality management

Internal quality management is effected by the application of TMap. Within the four cornerstones (lifecycle model, techniques, infrastructure and organization), all preventive and detective measures are described:

- management, planning, control (procedures) and organization;
- risk taxation and strategy development, and coordination with the customer;
- progress and quality monitoring (statistics);
- personnel aspects, such as training, support and motivation;
- methods, techniques for management, control and testing;
- facilities and special resources;
- reports.

Audit trail

Internal quality management of a test process must be organized in such a way that at least the following aspects are guaranteed:

- *Audit trail*. The audit trail is used to show the structural relationship between the test activities and the deliverables used and produced in the test project. An auditor or reviewer may, for example, trace the path from the test basis to the test result, and vice versa, on the basis of the available documentation. The audit trail links the test basis, test scripts, test files, test object, and test results deliverables. The audit trail also provides guarantees for the reproducibility and control of the tests in connection with possible retests and maintenance.

- *Degree of coverage*. Checks on the degree of coverage, as agreed in the test plan.
- *Time and budget*. The connection is made between the test planning, activities and deliverables on the one hand, and time and budget on the other.

Risk analysis on the test process

It is advisable to perform a risk analysis on the test process at set times. On the basis of this, (possible) measures can be taken in consultation with the customer. Times when a risk analysis is called for include:

- after fixing the test plan;
- at the beginning of the specification phase;
- at the beginning of the test execution;
- after the test object has been tested once.

The risks run during the test process can be grouped under the following items:

- cost and/or over-running the budget;
- exceeding the time;
- supplying incorrect or insufficient functionality;
- supplying incorrect or insufficient quality.

The cost and/or over-running the budget and exceeding the time are indicators for the efficiency of the test project implementation, while supplying the incorrect or insufficient functionality and/or quality is an indicator of the effectiveness of the (test) project implementation.

Various checklists included in Chapter 17 may offer support when carrying out the risk analyses.

Metrics **23**

23.1 Introduction

Test managers are often expected to answer awkward questions, such as:

- Why does testing take so long?
- Why has the test process not been completed yet?
- How many defects can I still expect during production?
- How many retests are still required?
- When can testing be stopped?
- When will the test team start the execution of the test?
- Tell me exactly what you are up to.
- What is the quality of the system that you have tested?
- When can I start production?
- Why was the previous test project much faster?
- What did you actually test?
- How many defects have been found, and what is their status?

Answering such questions with well-founded, fact-based answers is not easy. Most questions can be answered with reference to the periodic reports as described in section 22.2.5. These reports can be created only on the basis of correctly recorded relevant data. These data are converted into information, which is then used to answer the questions listed above.

Metrics on the quality of the test object and the progress of the test process are of great importance to the test process. They are used to control the test process, to substantiate test advice, and to compare systems or test processes with each other. Metrics are important for the improvement of the test process, to assess the consequences of certain improvement measures by comparing data before and after the measure has been taken.

In summary, this means that a test manager must record a number of items in order to be able to pass well-founded judgment on the quality of the object that is to be tested, as well as on the quality of the test process itself. We describe here a structured approach to arriving at a set of test metrics.

23.2   The goal–question–metric method in six steps

There are various ways of arriving at a certain set of metrics. The most common form is the goal–question–metric (GQM) method (Basili *et al.*, 1994; van Solingen and Berghout, 1999). This is a top-down method in which one or more goals are formulated, e.g. what information should I collect in order to answer those awkward questions posed in the introduction? These goals include questions that constitute the basis for the metrics.

The collected metrics must provide the answers to the questions. The answers will indicate, among other things, whether the goal has been achieved.

The GQM process is described below in six steps. This is a concise description that includes only those items relevant to the test manager. For a more detailed description, please see Basil *et al.* (1994) and van Solingen and Berghout (1999).

23.2.1 Step 1: defining the goals

Measuring purely to measure is of no use. Clear and realistic goals must be set beforehand. We distinguish two types of goals:

- *Knowledge goals* ('knowing where we are now') are expressed by terms such as 'evaluate', 'predict' or 'monitor'. One may think in terms of evaluating how many hours are actually spent on retesting or monitoring the test coverage. The goal here is to gain insight.
- *Improvement goals* ('where do we want to go?') are expressed by terms such as 'increase', 'decrease', 'improve' or 'achieve'. Setting such goals means that we must know that there are shortcomings in the present test process or the present environment, and that we wish to improve these.

An example of an improvement goal is to achieve a 20 per cent saving on the number of testing hours at a constant test coverage within a period of 18 months. In order to ascertain this, the following two knowledge goals must be included:

- insight into the total number of testing hours per project;
- insight into the achieved test coverage per project.

It is important to investigate whether the goals and the (test) maturity of the organization match. It is pointless to set a goal to achieve a certain test coverage if the necessary resources (knowledge, time, tools) are not available.

> Goal: provide insight into the quality of the test object

23.2.2 Step 2: asking questions for each goal

For each goal, several questions must be asked. The questions have to be formulated in such a way that they act as a specification of a metric. In addition, it is also possible to ask who is responsible for the test metrics supplied. From the above goal, various questions can be derived. We will limit the number of questions in this example to three:

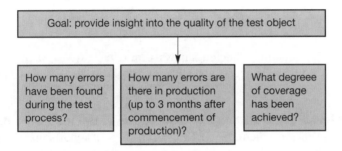

23.2.3 Step 3: from questions to metrics

From the questions we have to derive the metrics. The metrics are gathered during the test process. By asking the right questions, one arrives automatically at the correct set of metrics for a certain goal. It is important to define and specify each metric correctly. For example, what exactly is a defect?

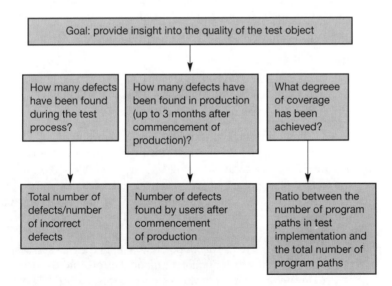

23.2.4 Step 4: data collection and analysis

During the test process a variety of data is collected. One way of keeping things simple is to use forms/templates (preferably electronic). The data must be complete and easy to interpret. In the design of these forms, attention should be paid to the following:

- Which metrics are collected on the same form?
- Validation: how easy is it to check whether the data are complete and correct?
- Traceability: forms including the date, project ID, configuration management data, data collector, etc. Take into consideration that it is sometimes necessary to preserve these data for a long time.
- Possibility of electronic processing.

As soon as the data are collected, analysis must be started. At this point it is still possible to make corrections. Waiting too long decreases the chance of restoring the data.

23.2.5 Step 5: presentation and distribution of the measured data
The collected measurements are used both in the test reports on the quality of the product to be tested and in those on the test process. Proper feedback is also of importance for the motivation of those involved and the validation of the measured data.

23.2.6 Step 6: relating the measured data to the questions and goals
This last step is used to investigate to what extent the indicators (answers to the questions) offer sufficient insight into the question of whether the goals have been achieved. This situation may be the starting point for a new GQM cycle. In this way, one is continually improving the test process.

23.3   Hints and tips

When metrics are being collected, the test manager must take the following issues into account:

- Start with a limited set of metrics and build them up slowly.
- Keep the metrics simple. The definition must appeal to the intuition of those involved, e.g. try to avoid using lots of formulas. The more complicated the formulas, the more difficult they are to interpret.
- Choose metrics that are relatively simple to collect and are easily accepted. The more difficult it is to collect data, the greater the chance that they will not be accepted.
- Collect data in as automated a way as possible. This is the quickest way of data collection, and avoids the introduction of manual errors into the data set.
- Keep an eye on the motivation of the testers to record accurately.
- Avoid complicated statistical techniques and models during presentations. Allow the type of presentation to depend on the data presented (tables, diagrams, pie charts, etc.).
- Provide feedback to the testers as quickly as possible. Show them what you do with the information.

23.4   Practical starting set of test metrics

Here we explain what test managers embarking on a metrics program should start with. The metrics set described is a starting set that can be used in practice with little cost and effort. Chapter 22 lists a number of more specific test statistics and progress reports.

- Record the number of hours spent using activity codes. Record the following for each tester: date, project, TMap phase, activity, number of hours. A 'comments' field is recommended, to check whether the data have been entered correctly. Recording the hours in this way enables you to obtain insight into the hours spent on each TMap phase (Figure 23.1). It also enables the customer to check the progress of the test process. It is advisable to compile this type of hour report on a weekly basis for projects that last for up to three or four months. For projects that last for more than six months, this can be done on a fortnightly basis. For projects that last for more than a year, it is best to report every month or so.

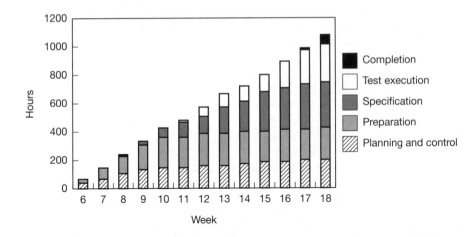

Figure 23.1
Example of time spent on test process in each phase

- Collect data about the test deliverables (test plans, test scripts, etc.), the test basis and test object. Record the following: document name, delivery date, TMap phase on delivery, version, and a characteristic that indicates the quantity. This may be the number of test cases for the test scripts, or the number of pages for the other documents. In the test basis, a function point analysis (FPA) or the number of user requirements can be included as a quantity characteristic.
- Report on the progress of the defects. Chapter 22 describes how a defect administration can be set up. An example of this type of reporting is shown in Figure 23.2.

Figure 23.2

Example of a progress
overview of defects

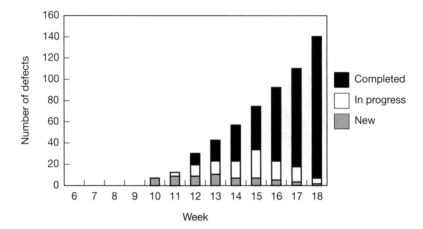

These elementary metrics (hours, documents and defects) can be used to assess the
productivity of the test process. Note that this productivity must be seen in relation to the required effort and size of the test project. For example, in the first ten
hours of testing one may find more defects per hour than in 400 hours of further
testing, simply because the first defects are found more quickly than the later ones.

The following metrics regarding productivity can be derived from this elementary set:

- number of defects per hour (and per hour of test execution);
- number of test cases carried out per hour;
- number of specified test scripts per hour (and per hour of test specification);
- number of defects per test script;
- division of hours spent over the TMap phases.

The following function points or number of kilolines of code (KLOC) of the
object to be tested can be found:

- number of test hours per function point (or KLOC);
- number of defects per function point (or KLOC);
- number of test cases per function point (or KLOC).

For the test basis, we can establish the following metrics:

- number of test hours per page of the test basis;
- number of defects per page of the test basis;
- number of test cases per page of the test basis;
- number of pages of the test basis per function point.

If it is also known how many defects occurred in the first three months of production, then the defect detection effectiveness of a test type can be
determined, i.e. the number of defects found in a test type divided by the total
number of defects present. The total number of defects present can be found by
adding the number of defects found to the number of defects occurring in production during the first three months after commencement of production.

By recording these metrics, completed with some specific issues, we arrive at the two checklists described in the following sections.

23.5   Checklist of test object metrics

The following metrics are possible indicators that can be used to assess the quality of the object to be tested. They can also be used in the report to the customer.

- *Number of defects found*. The ratio between the number of defects found and the size of the system per unit of testing time.
- *Defects as a result of modifications that are not tested*. Defects because of modifications that are not tested as a part of the total number of defects arising as a result of changes.
- *Defects after tested modifications*. Defects because of modifications that are tested as a part of the total number of defects arising as a result of changes.
- *Savings of the test*. Indicates how much has been saved by performing the test, i.e. what would the losses have amounted to if the test had not been performed?

23.6   Checklist of metrics for the benefit of the test process

The following metrics are possible indicators to measure the quality of the test process, and to compare it with the standard set by the organization. They can also be used in the report to the customer.

- *Executed instructions*. Ratio between the number of tested program instructions and the total number of program instructions. Tools are available that can produce such metrics.
- *Number of tests*. Ratio between the number of tests and the size of the system, e.g. expressed in function points. This indicates how many tests are necessary to test a part.
- *Number of tested paths*. Ratio between the tested and the total number of logical paths present.
- *Number of defects during production*. Gives an indication of the number of defects not found during the test process.
- *Number of defects found*. The total number of defects found during testing divided by the total number of defects – estimated partly on the basis of production data.
- *Test effectiveness in relation to the primary process*. Indicates how much testing has saved by enabling the primary process to continue normally, i.e. what would it have cost if the defect had been found in the production phase?
- *Test effectiveness in the definition study phase*. Ratio between the cost of testing and the number of defects found in the definition study phase.
- *Test effectiveness in the design phase*. Ratio between the cost of testing and the number of defects found in the design phase.

- *Test effectiveness in the programming phase.* Ratio between the cost of testing and the number of defects found in the programming phase.
- *Test effectiveness in the test phase.* Ratio between the cost of testing and the number of defects found in the test execution phase.
- *Test effectiveness in the implementation phase.* Ratio between the cost of testing and the number of defects found in the execution phase.
- *Test effectiveness in the maintenance phase.* Ratio between the cost of testing and the number of defects found in the maintenance phase.
- *Test costs.* Ratio between the test costs and the total development costs. A prior definition of the various costs is essential.
- *Cost per detected defect.* Total test cost divided by the number of defects found.
- *Budget utilization.* Ratio between the budget and the actual cost of testing.
- *Test efficiency.* The number of tests required versus the number of defects found.
- *Degree of automation of testing.* Ratio of the number of tests carried out manually to the number of tests carried out automatically.
- *Number of defects found (relative).* The ratio of the number of defects found to the size of the system (in function points or KLOC) per unit of testing time.
- *Defects as a result of modifications that are not tested.* Defects because of modifications that are not tested as a part of the total number of defects arising as a result of changes.
- *Defects after tested modifications.* Defects because of modifications that are tested as a part of the total number of defects arising as a result of changes.
- *Savings of the test.* Indicates how much has been saved by carrying out the test, i.e. what would the losses have amounted to if the test had not been carried out?

Structuring: the implementation of TMap

24

This chapter describes the way in which TMap is implemented in an organization, i.e. the structuring process. Then some aspects of such a process are highlighted, such as a lifecycle model, the organization, the required knowledge and skills, the expected resistance against changes, and the estimation of benefits and costs of an improved test process. The chapter ends with a number of factors for success and failure.

24.1   Introduction

If a universal approach to testing and a universal organization existed, issuing rules and training a few employees would be all that would be needed for introducing a structured approach to testing. However, this is only a utopian possibility.

TMap is a general model that must be adapted to the relevant test processes and the characterization of the organization. This was borne in mind throughout the development of TMap. The standard provides a wide range of components relating to aspects of testing as well as to the organization. TMap is therefore suitable for adapting to specific situations, since the required building blocks can be selected from the well-stocked standard set. TMap contains the planning and control phase and the strategy development technique for choosing the right components in terms of activities and techniques to suit an individual test project.

It becomes more difficult if TMap is to be implemented in an entire department or organization instead of in a single project because change in an organization always creates problems and resistance. This chapter examines this form of implementation. Emphasis is put on the process of change that an organization has to pass through in order to implement structured testing.

Such a process of change should be conducted gradually and in a controlled manner. This can be achieved by executing the process in phases. Moreover, in practice it is hard to decide which steps have to be taken in which sequence in order to structure testing. An attempt to implement the desired situation by (too) big steps usually ends in failure. Using smaller, more controllable steps gives a much bigger chance of success. Changing too much can generate a large number of problems and arouse so much resistance that this is counterproductive and the organization will soon fall back into old habits.

An important support for improving the test process is delivered by the test process improvement model (Koomen and Pol, 1999), which offers a frame of reference to improve the test process step by step. A summary of this model is included in Chapter 25.

24.2 The process of test structuring

The process of test structuring is, for most organizations, a change process because they are already testing in one way or another. Each process of change has the same general approach: based on certain aims, changes are carried out in order to move from the existing situation to the desired situation. Structuring a test process does not really differ from any other process of change. Figure 24.1 shows the lifecycle model of a process of change. Although the scheme may give the impression that there are single and subsequent phases, there is a certain overlap. Some phases, such as obtaining awareness, may even be regarded as a permanent process.

Figure 24.1
Process of change

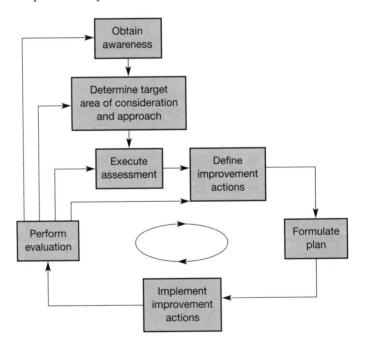

24.2.1 Obtaining awareness

A bad test process usually causes a lot of testing problems. The structuring of the test process is regarded as the solution. Important subjects in this initial phase imply that the various parties involved become aware of:

- the aim and the necessity to structure the test process;
- the fact that a process of change is the manner to do so.

This awareness also implies that the parties should mutually agree on outlines and give their commitment to the structuring process.

The choice of parties that should be involved from the beginning depends on the problems and the chosen scale of the structuring process. It is likely that it will involve the senior management, line managers, project managers, test managers and testers. If at a later stage the number of parties involved increases, those parties should still pass through the awareness phase. In fact, this awareness phase should be regarded not as a separate phase in the structuring process but as an essential precondition. If this commitment is insufficient, a structuring process should not be started because the chance of failure is quite high. If a structuring process fails once, there will be greater resistance to any further change.

Moreover, the commitment should not just be obtained at the beginning of the structuring process but should be retained during the entire process. This requires a continuous effort in the form of, for instance, information supply or discussion meetings.

It is also important that people see that higher management supports the structuring process, e.g. through brainstorming sessions. For this reason, the awareness process should start with the higher management, and involve lower management, test leaders and testers at a later stage. The long-term aims and the assets and liabilities are discussed with the higher management. With the testers, the discussion concerns shop-floor problems and short-term improvements. When one of the parties is left out, the structuring of the test process is likely to fail, especially if regular work and the process of change collapse on priorities at some stage.

24.2.2 Determining the target, area of consideration and approach

In this phase, the outlines of aim, scope and approach of the structuring process are determined.

Target

The ultimate target of structuring the test process is to optimize the required time, money and quality of testing in relation to the total information services for the organization. While this may be difficult, an attempt should be made to formulate the aims as concrete, feasible, mutually consistent and measurable as possible. A global indication of the milestones and costs are also given.

Conceivable aims are that testing should be x per cent cheaper, y per cent quicker after a certain time, or that there are z per cent fewer defects in production or the next test. The problem with such aims is:

- objective data about the present situation are seldom available in practice;
- it is difficult to determine to what extent structuring of the test process will lead to the desired aims, e.g. it is difficult to answer the question: 'Will the introduction of test specification techniques lead to 20 per cent fewer defects in production?';
- external factors, such as the quality of the development process, have a big impact on the quality and efficiency of the test process.

For these reasons, usually no guarantees can be given while determining these aims, and the risks and uncertainties should be stated clearly.

Other aims may be:

- increased insight and therefore better control of the test process;
- more insight into the quality of the test object by increased depth of testing;
- increased quality and timeliness of the test advises;
- shorter training period and better transferability by the utilization of uniform procedures;
- making the test process independent of particular people.

Area of consideration

The area of consideration of the structuring process has several variants:

- one test level in one project, e.g. the system test in project x;
- all test levels in one project;
- all tests of one test level in the entire organization, e.g. all acceptance tests;
- all test levels in the entire organization.

It is important to obtain clarity on the scope as soon as possible so that the right people and departments can be involved early in the structuring process.

Approach

Although in all cases the successive phases of the change process should be passed, the implementation depends very much on the chosen (long- or short-term) aims and scope. This has consequences for the approach of the structuring process. For a process with limited aims and scope, the changes can usually be implemented in a relatively short time. The costs are low and the number of involved people is small. The results of this phase should be recorded in a growth document, which should be enlarged or adapted with the results of the next phases.

24.2.3 Executing assessment

If you don't know where you are, a map won't help

(Humphrey, 1989)

In this phase, the state of the current test process is assessed. Based on the previously determined aims and the present situation, in the next phase the improvement actions are stated. Hereby the weak points are improved based on the strong points of the test process. The use of the test process improvement (TPI) model is an important aid to the assessment because it offers a frame of reference to inventory the strong and weak points of the investigated test process. An assessment consists of the following steps:

- preparation
- collecting information
- analysis
- reporting.

24.2.4 Defining improvement actions

Based on the improvement aims and the result of the assessment, the improvement actions are determined. These are stated in such a way that a gradual, step-by-step structuring is possible. In practice, it is impossible to implement the desired final situation in one step. The TPI model helps with the determination of these improvement actions.

The improvement actions should agree with, and lead to, the achievement of the aims of structuring the test process that have already been determined. This is one of the most difficult aspects of improvement. How can we prove that the implementation of some actions, such as the introduction of test-specification techniques, leads to the achievement of previously determined aims? For this reason, it is important that the formulated aims are measurable in some way. Periodically, an assessment should also be made of whether the improvement actions give the desired result and to what extent the aims are met.

For each improvement action the estimated costs, dependencies and priorities are recorded.

24.2.5 Formulating a plan

A plan is drawn up to implement (a part of) the improvement actions in the short term. In this plan, the aims are recorded and indications are given as to which improvements should be implemented in what time in order to achieve these aims. The plan should answer the following questions:

- Who is the customer?
- Who is the supplier and/or responsible for the implementation?
- What is (the scope of) the assignment?

- Which improvement actions have been chosen?
- How will these actions be implemented?
- What are the milestones at which the improvements should have been implemented?
- Who and what is needed when?
- How much does it cost?
- Which results should the action deliver (e.g. in the form of products)?
- How many and which (intermediate) measuring moments will be distinguished?
- What are the risks, and how they are made manageable?

The plan considers both the activities concerning content to structure the test process and the activities needed to steer the process of change in the right direction. The former may include:

- *Selecting and using pilot projects*. Pilot projects aim to try out the proposed improvement actions in practice. The experiences from this may lead to measures being adapted and may ease the further implementation. A pilot should be representative and have a limited size and impact.
- *Training*. Just delivering training is not sufficient. Training supplies a good foundation, but this should be built on with training on the job, supplying a mentor, coaching and periodical evaluations, etc.
- *Adaptation of procedures and manuals*. It is not sufficient to put a new manual on the shelf. The books and procedures should be used. Do not presume that the described procedures represent the reality.
- *Purchasing and using tools*. The word 'tool' often suggests increasing productivity many-fold. Such expectations should be corrected because this relates to a specific situation, not to the entire test process.
- *Involving test experts*. Test experts can support most test activities. However, using external test experts to train and coach external testers should be avoided – both parties leave at the end of project, and the organization has learned nothing.

Possible activities to steer the process of change in the right direction include:

- *Presentations*. All involved layers of the organization should be informed about the changes. Presentations are a suitable form of communication for this. If commitment has to be obtained, or many questions remain unanswered about the path to follow, discussion meetings are more appropriate;
- *Participation in consultative bodies*. Periodic participation in consultative bodies ensures that the change process remains in the picture. Too often, the structuring of the test process is introduced with great fanfare but is followed by a big silence. If the change team then shows up with products, the interest may have faded and nobody is likely to work with those products;

- *Publications.* It is often possible to approach a much wider public in an easier and cheaper way through publications, booklets, posters or reference cards than through presentations. This form of communication is suited not only for getting commitment, but also for retaining commitment, e.g. by writing periodical articles about the progress of the change process.

24.2.6 Implementing improvement actions

The plan is executed. Because it is in this phase that the consequences of the structuring process are felt most, much attention should be paid to communication, hence the need for such activities in the previous phase. People involved in the test process to be changed should be informed about what, why and how the actions are to be executed. It is helpful to create communication channels for this. The resistance that undoubtedly exists should be brought to the surface and be made open for discussion. Furthermore, a clearly visible and involved management is helpful.

The actions to be executed are measured as to what extent they have been initiated. Based on these results, an announcement can be made about the progress of the structuring process. An essential part of this phase is the embedding. The organization should maintain the changed procedures; communicating the results, training and a quality system could offer support here.

24.2.7 Performing evaluation

To what extent have the implemented actions delivered the desired result? In this phase, the degree to which actions were implemented successfully, and the degree to which the original objectives were achieved, is monitored. Based on these observations, the structuring process may proceed in different ways:
- The next improvement cycle is started.
- The improvement actions are adjusted.
- A new assessment is carried out, after which the structuring process continues by determining improvement actions, creating plans, etc.
- New aims or scopes are determined, after which the change process continues from that point.
- The structuring of the test process is stopped.

24.3   Organization of the change process

While setting up the organization of a change process, the scope in particular plays an important role. If the scope is relatively limited, one can opt for the installation of a single change team. This team performs the planning, preparation, execution and monitoring of all activities, from the raising of awareness up to the evaluation. The actual implementation of the measures is usually performed by those involved.

If the scope concerns a large organization with various departments or test levels, there may be more delegation, with a central change team but with similar teams at local level. The central team is concerned with raising the awareness, determining the objective, scope and approach, and assessing and formulating improvement actions. For the latter, the central group sets the frame and the guidelines. The local groups execute the activities in more detail, and are responsible for all activities from creating the plan to executing evaluation. The central group occupies itself more with supporting, coordinating and monitoring the various subactivities, maintaining commitment, and evaluating of the achieved results at a global level.

An important aspect of the organization of a change process is who will pay for it. A change process where each department or project is supposed to pay the costs of changes is likely to be unsuccessful. Which project leader is prepared to implement changes on the budget of the project when it is subsequent projects that will benefit? The same applies, to a lesser extent, for departments. Some departments will have to bear the costs for changes that are profitable for the entire organization but are charged to that department.

The solution is to address that level of management where the costs and benefits of the structuring of the test process come together. A change process does not usually give a return on investment at once, and always causes a shift of costs and benefits. One should take this into account from the beginning to reduce the chance that changes are obstructed from a cost point of view.

24.4   Required knowledge and skills

The change team should have a broad mix of knowledge and skills, including:
- social skills, such as:
  - consulting skills
  - handling conflicts
  - negotiating skills
  - enthusiasm and persuasiveness
  - honest and open attitude
  - immunity to panic, and capable of handling criticism
  - patience;
- profound knowledge of the organization;
- profound knowledge of the test process within the organization;
- profound knowledge of, and experience in, changing processes within organizations;
- profound test expertise.

This mix will rarely be found in one person. While composing the group, care should be taken that all the necessary knowledge and skills are present in the team. It is preferable for the leader of the change team to originate from the organization rather than be an external advisor who might withdraw and leave the organization to fall back into the original situation.

24.5   Resistance

Wherever there is change, some people will be against it. Often, such resistance is underestimated; however, resistance is predictable and influenceable. The change team should be able to handle resistance, and should work actively to reduce it. This requires insight into the relation between the phase the structuring process finds itself in, the behavior of the change team, and the amount of resistance.

At the start of the structuring process, only a few people are informed. The resistance will increase if the change plans and their influence are announced. After the announcement, adequate support should be available to reduce the resistance. During the application and the accompanying support, the test personnel bring proposals for improvement. These should be listened to carefully and eventually negotiated. A sensitive ear and acceptance of the proposals reduces the resistance considerably.

A steady continuation of support in this phase convinces the testers of the usefulness of changes. By timing the announcement of the change properly, the resistance curve may be influenced. By continuously predicting the resistance, helpful measures may be taken in advance. In this way, resistance is influenceable (Figure 24.2).

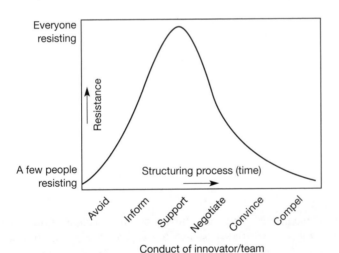

Figure 24.2
Resistance is predictable and can be influenced

An important message from this is that all these stages must be passed through. If the process is already in the phase in which improvement measures are implemented and no resistance can yet be noticed, the probable cause is that nothing has been implemented. For this reason, it is important to reveal the resistance and discuss it, instead of having agitation growing uncontrolled beneath the surface.

24.6   Benefits and costs

An important issue of the structuring process is to demonstrate the extent to which the set objectives have been achieved, and the extent to which the benefits of the structuring process are higher than the costs. Unfortunately this is one of the most difficult issues, because both the costs and benefits are difficult to quantify.

In Chapter 23, several metrics are mentioned that should be recorded. These deal with quality, costs and lifetime of the test process. Examples are the number of defects per hour, the percentage of code covered by testing, and the number of defects detected by testing in relation to the number of present defects. By the combined use of metrics, a good idea may be obtained of the benefits of structuring. Such metrics are much the best way of stating the benefits of the improved test process.

Common sense plays an important role in demonstrating the benefits. By means of evaluation meetings and interviews, for instance, the benefits of an improved test process may be revealed in a more subjective way. While stating the objectives, the limitations and uncertainties should be indicated clearly so that everybody is aware of this and accepts the procedure.

24.7   Critical factors

List in this section are some factors that are important to the success of the structuring process. These are divided into success and failure factors.

24.7.1 Success factors

- *Need for change*. When starting a structuring process, an important condition is the insight that the present situation is unacceptable. The various layers in the organization are firmly convinced that the test process should be improved.
- *Clarity of the desired situation*. The structuring process should have a well-defined objective so that it is clear to everybody what should be achieved. These objectives may differ per target group. For the higher management, the aim may be that the time to market for new products is shorter. For the testers, the aim may be that fewer (annoying) retests are needed. The various target groups should bear in mind the relevant objective for them.
- *Sponsor commitment*. Perhaps the most important factor of success (and failure) is the commitment of the management to the structuring process. The impatience of the management helps to obtain the commitment to change the organization, but may have a reverse effect if the expectations are not met soon enough. If it is not clear that the management supports the structuring process, that should be tackled first.

24.7.2 Failure factors

- *Exclusively top-down or bottom-up structuring*. Structuring cannot be implemented exclusively top down or bottom up. Top-down structuring by issuing directives – possibly by spreading a guideline – will not lead to success. On the other hand, bottom-up structuring without support from the management in the form of time and resources will not lead to the desired structural improvements. The structuring process should be supported actively by the management, as well as having sufficient support in the organization.
- *Unbalanced structuring*. The four cornerstones of a structured test approach (lifecycle, techniques, infrastructure and organization) should be balanced mutually. If, for instance, there is attention only on test techniques or the test organization, this will lead to disappointment.
- *Structuring only of high-level tests*. Structuring of the test process extends to all test levels and types. It is senseless to purchase a superb (high-level) safety net for the basic negligence of the developers. The structuring should also be directed to the low-level tests because that is where the most expensive defects are detected for the fewest costs.
- *Regarding test tools as the best option*. Test tools may support a test process. This means that when starting to use test tools, structuring testing should be present, and that tools only support, i.e. the test process cannot be overtaken completely by tools.
- *Unsuitable pilot project*. Choosing pilot projects should entail assessing whether they are suitable. A project under heavy time pressure is not so suitable because the improvement actions, which require an initial investment in time and money, will be the first to be cancelled if the pressure becomes too great. Do not choose a single project, because a setback may immediately delay the entire structuring process; also, do not choose too many projects because guidance becomes very labor intensive and adjusting is difficult. The organization and the infrastructure should be involved explicitly in the pilot.
- *Underestimation of the implementation*. The phases after improvement actions are often underestimated. The external experts finish their job and leave, and the internal steering group reduces the frequency of meetings because the organization now needs simply to implement the recommendations. These are, however, the toughest activities of the entire process, with the greatest resistance to be overcome.
- *No embedding in the organization*. Usually, structuring is carried out in a project context. After the completion of the project, no employees are available for the maintenance and improvement of the defined test approach. The creation of a lasting function in the line organization, e.g. a test coordinator, prevents this problem.

- *Too many promises*. Structuring the test process takes time and has its ups and downs. It is important not to build up expectations too much – in the short term, small successes may be achieved, but it is in the longer term that the advantages become clearer and more visible.

- *Going and growing concern*. During the structuring process, there are two more or less opposite interests: the structuring process, to be regarded as growing concern, and the regular activities, to be regarded as going concern. These two groups of activities are usually not separated sufficiently. For understandable reasons, the regular work soon becomes the main issue, while the minimal activities needed for the structuring are disturbed by ad hoc test activities, e.g. due to disturbances in the production.

- *Too little attention to measurements*. During the structuring process, time and money are available for the execution of test activities. It is important to measure during this phase in order to demonstrate the need for a structured test approach so that there is proof if resistance builds up against the introduction of structured testing again in the future.

The test process
improvement model

25

25.1 Introduction

Most organizations regard testing as a necessary precondition for successfully building and implementing information systems. Often, however, testing is experienced as a tedious process, the progress of which is impossible to control. Testing often takes longer and is much more expensive than originally planned, while there is little insight into the quality of the test process, and hence into the quality of the information system tested.

Many organizations realize that improving the test process may provide a solution. In practice, however, it often remains difficult to determine which steps should be taken, and in which order, to improve the process. We can make a comparison here with the improvement of the software process as a whole, where models such as the capability maturity model (Humphrey, 1989; SEI, 1995) offer support.

To facilitate the improvement of the test process, and to enable a more gradual progress, the test process improvement (TPI) model (Koomen and Pol, 1999) was set up based on the knowledge and experience of a large number of test professionals. The TPI model offers a reference framework to determine the strengths and weaknesses of an organization's current test process. It maps the maturity of the organization's test process. The model also offers support for the formulation of specific, feasible proposals for the improvement of this test process in terms of lead time, expenses and quality.

The basis of the model is TMap, complemented by various aspects from other models. The TPI model can also be applied in organizations that use methodologies other than TMap.

25.2 Description

Figure 25.1 shows an overview of the TPI model.

Figure 25.1

The TPI model

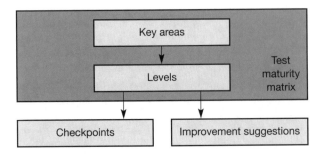

25.2.1 Key areas

For each test process, we can identify a number of key areas that require specific attention for the process to be set up successfully. These key areas also constitute a basis for the improvement and structuring of the test process. The TPI model distinguishes 20 key areas.

The scope of TPI usually includes high-level tests such as the system test and the acceptance test. Most key areas are adjusted to this. To give enough attention to the low-level tests such as the unit test and the integration test in improving more "mature" test processes, separate key areas are included for these.

Table 25.1 gives a brief description of the distinct key areas. The first column shows TMap cornerstone under which the key area is classified (L = life-cycle, O = organization, I = infrastructure and T = techniques).

Table 25.1

Key areas of TPI

Cornerstone	Key area	Description
L	Test strategy	The test strategy has to be focused on detecting the most important defects as early and as cheaply as possible. The test strategy defines which requirements and (quality) risks are covered by what tests. The better each test level defines its own strategy, and the more the different test level strategies are adjusted to each other, the higher the quality of the overall test strategy.
L	Lifecycle model	Within the test process, a number of phases can be defined, such as planning, preparation, specification, execution and completion. In each phase, several activities are performed. For each activity, the following aspects should be defined: purpose, input, process, output, dependencies, applicable techniques and tools, required facilities, documentation, etc. Using a lifecycle model implies an improved predictability and manageability of the test process because the different activities can be planned and monitored in mutual cohesion.

Table 25.1
continued

Cornerstone	Key area	Description
L	Moment of involvement	Although the actual execution of the test normally begins after the construction of the software, the test process must and can start much earlier. Earlier involvement of testing in the system development path helps to find defects as soon and as easily as possible, and perhaps even to prevent defects. A better adjustment between the different tests can be done, and the time that testing is on the critical path of the project can be kept as short as possible.
T	Estimating and planning	Test planning and estimating indicate which activities have to be carried out when, and what the necessary resources (people) are. Good estimating and planning are very important because this is the basis of, for example, allocating resources for a certain timeframe.
T	Test-specification techniques	A test-specification technique is a standardized way of deriving test cases from source information. Applying these techniques gives insight into the quality and depth of the tests, and increases the reusability of the test.
T	Static test techniques	Not everything can and should be tested dynamically, i.e. by running programs. Inspection of products without running programs, or the evaluation of measures that must lead to a certain quality level, are called static tests. Checklists are very useful for this.
T	Metrics	Metrics are quantified observations of the characteristics of a product or process. For the test process, metrics of the progress of the process and the quality of the tested system are very important. They are used to control the test process, to substantiate the test advices, and to make it possible to compare systems or processes. Why does one system have far fewer failures in operation than the other system? Or why is one testprocess faster and more thorough than the other? Specifically for improving the test process, metrics are important for evaluating consequences of certain improvement actions by comparing data before and after performing the action.

Table 25.1

continued

Cornerstone	Key area	Description
I	Test automation	Automation within the test process can take place in many ways, and has in general one or more of the following aims: • fewer hours needed • shorter lead time • more test depth • increased test flexibility • more and/or faster insight in test process status • better motivation of the testers.
I	Test environment	The test execution takes place in a test environment. This mainly comprises the following components: • hardware • software • communication means • facilities for building and using databases and files • procedures. The environment should be composed and set up in such a way that by means of the test results it can be determined optimally to what extent the test object meets the requirements. The environment has a large influence on the quality, lead time, and cost of the test process. Important aspects of the environment are responsibilities, management, on-time, sufficient availability, representativeness and flexibility.
I	Office environment	The test staff need rooms, desks, chairs, PCs, word-processing facilities, printers, telephones, etc. Good, timely organization of the office environment has a positive influence on the motivation of the test staff, on communication in and outside of the team, and on the efficiency of the work.
O	Commitment and motivation	The commitment and motivation of the people involved in testing are important conditions of a smooth-running test process. The people involved include not only the testers but also, for example, the project management and the line management. The latter are important mainly in the sense of creating good conditions. The test process thus receives enough time, money, and resources (quantitatively and qualitatively) to perform a good test, in which cooperation and good communication with the rest of the project results in a total process with optimum efficiency.

Table 25.1
continued

Cornerstone	Key area	Description
O	Test functions and training	In a test process, the right composition of a test team is very important. A mix is required of different disciplines, functions, knowledge and skills. Besides the specific test expertise, knowledge is required of the subject matter, the organization and IT in general. Social skills are also important. For acquiring this mix, training etc. is required.
O	Scope of methodology	For each test process in the organization, a certain methodology or working method is used, comprising activities, procedures, regulations, techniques, etc. When these methodologies are different each time, or when the methodology is so generic that many parts have to be drawn up every time, it has a negative effect on the test process efficiency. The aim is that the organization uses a methodology that is sufficiently generic to be applicable in every situation, but that contains enough detail so that it is not necessary to rethink the same items each time.
O	Communication	In a test process, communication with the people involved must take place in several ways within the test team as well as with parties such as the developer, the user, the customer, etc. These communication forms are important for a smooth-running test process, not only to create good conditions and to optimize the test strategy but also to communicate about the progress and the quality.
O	Reporting	Testing is not so much defect detection as giving insight into the quality level of the product. Reporting should be aimed at giving well-founded advice to the customer concerning the product and even the system development process.
O	Defect management	Although managing defects is, a project matter and not specifically for the testers, the testers are mainly involved in it. Good management should be able to track the lifecycle of a defect, and to support the analysis of quality trends in the detected defects. Such analysis is used, for example, to give well-founded quality advice.

Table 25.1
continued

Cornerstone	Key area	Description
O	Testware management	Products of testing should be maintainable and reusable, so they must be managed. As well as the products of the testing, such as test plans, specifications, databases and files, it is important that the products of previous processes as design and code are managed well because the test process can be disrupted if the wrong program versions, etc. are delivered. If testers make demands on version management of these products, a positive influence is exerted and the testability of the product is increased.
O	Test process management	For managing each process and activity, four steps are essential: plan, do, check and act. Process management is of vital importance for the implementation of an optimal test in an often turbulent test process.
All	Evaluation	Evaluation means inspecting intermediate products such as the requirements and the functional design. The importance of evaluation is that the defects are found in a much earlier stage in the development process than with testing. This makes the rework costs much lower. Evaluation can also be set up more easily because there is no need to run programs or to set up an environment.
All	Low-level testing	Low-level tests are carried out almost exclusively by the developers. Well-known low-level tests are the unit test and the integration test. Just as in evaluation, the tests find defects in an earlier stage of the system development path than the high-level tests. Low-level testing is efficient because it requires little communication, and often the finder is both the error producer and the one who solves the defect.

25.2.2 Levels in the TPI model

In the TPI model, the key areas are provided with a number of levels ascending in maturity. The lowest level of maturity is A, while the highest is D. The number of levels differs for each key area, but for the sake of applicability there are about three levels per key area. By using levels, we can determine the current situation of a test process and provide better targets for step-by-step improvement. To be classified at a level, the appropriate checkpoints must be met. The requirements (checkpoints) of a level also contain the requirements related to the lower levels. A test process classifying at the B level meets the requirements of both the A level and the B level. When a test process does not meet the requirements of the A level, then the process is at the starting level. There are no requirements for this lowest level. Table 25.2 shows the levels for the various key areas.

Table 25.2
Levels in the TPI model

Key area	Level A	B	C	D
Test strategy	Strategy for single high-level tests	Combined strategy for high-level tests	Combined strategy for high-level tests plus low-level tests or evaluation	Combined strategy for all test and evaluation levels
Lifecycle model	Planning, specification, execution	Planning, preparation, specification, execution and completion		
Moment of involvement	Completion of test basis	Start of test basis	Start of requirements definition	Project initiation
Estimating and planning	Substantiated estimating and planning	Statistically substantiated estimating and planning		
Test-specification techniques	Informal techniques	Formal techniques		
Static test techniques	Inspection of test basis	Checklists		
Metrics	Project metrics (product)	Project metrics (process)	System metrics	Organization metrics (≥ 1 system)
Test automation	Use of tools	Managed test automation	Optimal test automation	
Test environment	Managed and controlled test environment	Testing in the most suitable environment	Environment on call	
Office environment	Adequate and timely office environment			
Commitment and motivation	Assignment of budget and time	Testing integrated in project organization	Test engineering	

Table 25.2
continued

Key area	Level A	B	C	D
Test functions and training	Test manager and testers	(Formal) methodical, technical and functional support, management	Formal internal quality assurance	
Scope of methodology	Project specific	Organization generic	Organization optimizing, research and development activities	
Communication	Internal communication	Project communication (defects, change control)	Communication in organization about the quality of the test processes	
Reporting	Defects	Progress (status of tests and products), activities (cost and time, milestones), defects with priorities	Risks and recommendations, substantiated with metrics	Recommendations have a software process improvement character
Defect management	Internal defect management	Extensive defect management with flexible reporting facilities	Project defect management	
Testware management	Internal testware management	External management of test basis and test object	Reusable testware	Traceability system requirements to test cases
Test process management	Planning and execution	Planning, execution, monitoring and adjusting	Monitoring and adjusting in organization	
Evaluation	Evaluation techniques	Evaluation strategy		
Low-level testing	Low-level test lifecycle (planning, specification and execution)	White-box techniques	Low-level test strategy	

25.2.3 Test maturity matrix

Description

In analyzing a test process, the level of each key area is determined. On the basis of these levels, improvements can be suggested in the form of desired higher levels. The temptation can be, for example, to decide to bring all key areas to level B or to say something like 'The test process is on level A', but this is not the best way. There are several dependencies and priorities between the levels and the key areas, which we will illustrate with an example: Level A of key area 'metrics' states that metrics are kept per project. This means, for example, that for each unit of time, hours accounting data and defect data have to be recorded. Monitoring these data means that the test process for the key areas 'reporting' and 'defect management' are at least at level B and level A, respectively. This implies that 'metrics' level A is dependent of 'reporting' level B and 'defect management' level A. Such dependencies are present between many levels and key areas. In addition, various priorities can be distinguished. In a young test process, it is much more important to give attention to a good test strategy, use of a lifecycle model, and the use of test-specification techniques than to collecting metrics, using test tools, or describing the complete test methodology of the project.

On the basis of the dependencies and priorities, all levels and key areas are mutually related in a test maturity matrix (Table 25.3). In the matrix, the key areas are indicated vertically and the test maturity scales are indicated horizon-

Key area / Scale	0	1	2	3	4	5	6	7	8	9	10	11	12	13
Test strategy		A					B				C		D	
Lifecycle model		A		B										
Moment of involvement			A				B				C		D	
Estimating and planning				A							B			
Test-specification techniques		A	B											
Static test techniques					A		B							
Metrics						A			B			C		D
Test automation			A					B			C			
Test environment			A					B					C	
Office environment			A											
Commitment and motivation		A				B						C		
Test functions and training				A			B				C			
Scope of methodology				A							B			C
Communication			A	B								C		
Reporting		A		B			C					D		
Defect management		A			B			C						
Testware management			A		B					C				D
Test process management		A	B									C		
Evaluation						A			B					
Low-level testing			A				B	C						
			Controlled					Efficient					Optimizing	

Table 25.3 Test maturity matrix

tally. The levels have been entered in the boxes. This has led to a matrix with 13 scales of test maturity.

The open boxes between the levels indicate that reaching a higher degree of maturity for the given key area is related to the maturity of other key areas. There is no gradation applied in the model: if a test process has nearly (but not quite) reached level B for a certain key area, then the process is classified at level A. If the test process does not meet level A for a certain key area, then the process is set to the zero scale for this key area.

In general, the various scales of test maturity can be divided into three categories:

- controlled
- efficient
- optimizing.

Controlled

Scales 1–5 are aimed primarily at the control of the test process. The purpose of the levels is to provide a controlled test process that gives a sufficient degree of insight into the quality of the tested object. In concrete terms, this means that the test process is carried out in phases according to a strategy defined in advance. Informal test-specification techniques are used for testing, and defects are recorded and reported. The testware and test environment are controlled, well and the test staff are trained adequately.

Efficient

Scales 6–10 focus more on the efficiency of the test process. This efficiency is achieved by automating the test process, by a better integration between the different test levels and with the other parties within the system development, and by consolidating the working method of the test process in the organization.

Optimizing

A test process that is efficient today may not be so tomorrow. Changing circumstances, such as the introduction of new architectures and development techniques, each time require an adjustment of the test process. The levels in the last three scales are characterized by an increasing optimization of the test process. Their aim is that continuous improvement of the generic test process will be a part of the regular working method of the organization.

Using the matrix structure

A test maturity matrix is completed after the analysis of a test process. This gives everybody concerned a clear view of the level of each of the different key areas of the test process. The matrix can then also be used to make a better judgment about improvement actions. The intention here is to work from left to right, i.e. first to improve the key areas with a low test maturity. As a result of the interdependencies between the key areas, experience has taught that real peaks (a key area with a high scale of test maturity, whereas the other key areas have a low or average scale) are not very efficient. What is the use in keeping a very comprehensive defect administration if it is not used for analysis and reporting? Without acting contrary to the model's principles, we can deviate from it – but only if there is a good reason.

In Table 25.4, the test process does not meet the lowest level (level ≤ A) of the key area 'test strategy'. It uses a lifecycle model (level A), and is involved in the test process during system development around the time of completion of the test basis (level A).

Key area	Scale	0	1	2	3	4	5	6	7	8	9	10	11	12	13
Test strategy			A						B				C		D	
Lifecycle model			A				B									
Moment of involvement				A					B				C		D	

Table 25.4 Test maturity matrix for a test process that does not meet the lowest level for key area 'test strategy'

This matrix can be used to discuss any improvements. In this example, the choice was made to coordinate the strategy between high-level tests (=≥ level B) and a full lifecycle model (=≥ level B). Earlier involvement is (currently) not considered relevant. The desired situation is shown in Table 25.4.

Key area	Scale	0	1	2	3	4	5	6	7	8	9	10	11	12	13
Test strategy			A	–					B				C		D	
Lifecycle model			A	–		B										
Moment of involvement				A					B				C		D	

Table 25.5 Test maturity matrix showing improvements (see text for details)

25.2.4 Checkpoints

To determine objectively the level of a key area a test process is at, the model provides a measuring instrument called checkpoints. Each level has a number of checkpoints. A test process must meet these points in order to be classified at that level. These checkpoints are cumulative, which means that for level B the checkpoints for that level must be met, as well as the checkpoints for the preceding level A.

For example, for a Level A strategy for a single high-level test:

● a motivated consideration of risks takes place, for which knowledge of the system, its use and its operational management has been contributed;
● there is a differentiation in test depth, depending on the risks and, if present, the acceptance criteria; not all subsystems are tested equally thoroughly, and not every quality characteristic is tested (equally thoroughly).

25.2.5 Improvement suggestions

The checkpoints of a certain level are an aid for process improvement. Other aids are the improvement suggestions per level. It is emphasized that these suggestions are meant as hints and tips, and not as mandatory steps to achieve that level. Each level has a number of these improvement suggestions in order to achieve the level concerned.

For example, for a Level A strategy for a single high-level test:

- involve the various interested parties, such as end users, systems manager, and project manager in determining the test strategy;
- deal with the various subsystems/quality characteristics, and try to determine the relative importance of each subsystem/quality characteristic.

In fact, the various stages, techniques, checklists and procedures of TMap constitute a large collection of improvement suggestions.

25.2.6 Characteristics

For the higher scales of the TPI model, we can mention the following characteristics:

- *Development from project to organization.* The lower scales of the model focus on achieving a properly set-up test process within a project. As projects are, by definition, temporary, the aim of the higher scales of the model is that the organization provides structural support for a good set-up of test processes. This prevents the situation in which each project reinvents the wheel (test process), possibly in its own way.
  Key areas: metrics, scope of methodology, communication, test process management.
- *Earlier start.* Starting to test at an earlier stage of system development means not only that defects can be detected earlier but also that coordination between the various tests and evaluations and between testing and design/building is easier.
  Key areas: test strategy, moment of involvement, evaluation, low-level testing.
- *Greater involvement in previous stages.* Involving testing in earlier stages such as design and building has the advantage of improved communication, and also helps to increase the testability of the system. This enables the test process to work more efficiently, and any defects can be detected at an earlier stage, or even prevented.
  Key areas: moment of involvement, commitment and motivation, communication, reporting.
- *Increasing automation of the test process.* Automation of the test process makes it possible to achieve advantages such as shorter lead times, lower costs, and higher quality of the test process. As for all automation, this must be seen as a means and not an objective in itself.
  Key areas: test automation.

- *Professionalization of testing*
  Testing must be given the attention that it deserves. It is expected that the test process is improved, that the testers give expert advice, etc. This means that the people involved must be capable enough. Test training courses, job descriptions and organizational support may help here.
  Key areas: test functions and training, commitment and motivation.

Infrastructure   PART V

Test environments 26

The infrastructure for testing includes all facilities and resources required for adequate testing. We distinguish between facilities needed for the execution of tests (test environment, see Chapter 26), facilities needed to support the tests (test tools, see Chapter 27), and facilities needed for the office environment (see Chapter 28).

26.1 Introduction

26.1.1 Test environment

The execution of the dynamic tests, i.e. by running the programs, requires a suitable test environment. This environment comprises the following key components:

- hardware
- software
- means of communication
- facilities for the construction and use of files
- procedures.

The checklist "test facilities" included in Chapter 17 offers a detailed overview of the possible components of which a test environment can consist.

The environment should be composed and set up in such a way that the test results can be used to determine optimally to what extent the test object meets the requirements. The unit test usually requires a completely different set-up from a production acceptance test. Sometimes, such an environment is very limited in size (e.g. a single PC when testing a word processor), while at other times it contains a large collection of devices, software and procedures, set up in various locations (e.g. for testing the booking system of an airline company). Apart from the test level and type, other aspects also play an important role, such as the operational standards, the type of application, the organization structure and, not least, the budgets available. Even if we ignore the large variety of hardware and software offered, it is impossible to describe the ideal test environment. This chapter will therefore remain general, aiming to provide some support when choices must be made.

26.1.2 General requirements of the test environment

In order to guarantee a reliable execution of tests, the test environment must meet a number of requirements:

- The test environment should be as representative as possible for the intended test, e.g. identical to the ultimate production environment.
- To ensure that the test object functions constantly under the same circumstances, the test environment must be stable. The test environment should be manageable in combination with the test object. Changes in any components of the environment (hardware and software, test object, procedures, etc.) should be carried out only after permission has been given by the test management.
- It must be possible for the set-up of the test environment to be adapted quickly (within the standards of manageability).
- In some situations, it is necessary to have several (physical) test environments. This is important in particular to ensure that tests that are carried out simultaneously do not influence each other.
- It is sometimes necessary to execute tests on a different date than the system date. To be able to do so, it must be possible to manipulate the system date. In practice, this is often not possible because several applications run on the same computer simultaneously. This requires separate facilities (e.g. an individual date facility).
- There should be a back-up/restore possibility for the test environment.
- In cases where continuity is very important for testing, alternatives for the test environment must be arranged.

26.1.3 Relation to TMap lifecycle

The infrastructure for testing grows with the application of the TMap lifecycle, as does the test environment, along with the other test activities. A TMap user is more or less forced to give due consideration to the test environment on time. The following activities are distinguished within the TMap lifecycle:

- *Planning and control phase*: defining the infrastructure.
- *Preparation phase*: specifying the infrastructure.
- *Specification phase*: specifying the review of the test object and infrastructure; setting up the infrastructure.
- *Execution phase*: review of test object and infrastructure.

26.2   Types of test environment

26.2.1 Common approach

In the common approach, there are three types of environment available for testing purposes. These environments are related directly to the test level.

Deviating from this relation is not customary and often not even possible. For the low-level tests, there is a laboratory or development environment; for the system tests, there is the system test environment; and the acceptance tests are carried out in the simulated production environment (Figure 26.1).

Test types

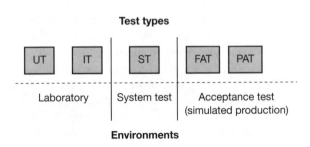

Figure 26.1
Traditional test
environments

FAT, functional acceptance test; IT, integration test;
PAT, production acceptance test; UT, unit test; ST, system test

Laboratory environment

The unit test and integration test (low-level tests) are executed in the same environment as the one in which the software and other system components are developed. The set-up of the environment and the test activities are organized as part of the development process. The test environment is usually organized by the programmers themselves, but sometimes by a colleague or the team leader. The development environment often provides standard facilities for testing, including files, test tools and procedures for matters such as version control, release, defects and rework. Such facilities offer testers enough possibilities for managing the test process properly. If no special demands are made on low-level tests, and the above standard facilities are available, then the tests can be executed successfully.

An important aspect that low-level testers have to deal with is the manageability of the test environment. In practice, programmers are often working on five or more versions of a program. Preserving the relationship between the test cases, the test results and the test object requires a great deal of attention.

System test environment

The system test environment is meant for testing both the technical and the functional aspects of (parts of) the system. The system test should be executed in a controllable environment separate from the laboratory. The term 'controllable' implies that there are means available for releasing and managing items such as the software, documentation, test databases and testware. The system tester must be able to check the transfer of new or modified software. Tests should be as reproducible as possible. It should also be possible for the individual tests of one (sub)system to be executed separately from the tests of other (sub)systems. In particular, the concurrent use of test databases causes a lot of problems in this area. The nature of the environment (controllable laboratory) gives the tester an opportunity to use a wide range of tools in order to determine the test object's functional quality. The use of this kind of tool is not normally allowed in a simulated production environment.

Experience has shown that many organizations suffer from uncontrollability and proliferation of the system test environment. To obtain greater certainty about the quality of the test object, many developers strive towards simulated production facilities in the system test environment. Without adequate facilities and procedures, this results in an enormous amount of program duplication and large files, which are saved for an unnecessarily long period. This redundancy demands a considerable storage capacity at similar costs.

Acceptance test environment

The acceptance test environment enables future users and systems managers to test the test object in an environment that reflects the production environment as much as possible. An acceptance test is usually divided into a functional acceptance test (FAT) and a production acceptance test (PAT). During FAT, the test object is tested to find out whether it provides the required functionality and quality in association with simulated production facilities and procedures. During PAT, the system is tested to find out whether it meets control and production standards both in respect of procedures and in aspects such as volume processing and performance. FAT and PAT activities are sometimes carried out in the same environment, sequentially or otherwise. In other instances, two separate environments may be available.

Bottlenecks

Many system development processes face the problem of bottlenecks in the PAT environment. During the final stages of the development process, the system is often tested on real production aspects for the first time. The effects of correcting a detected defect are then often drastic and time-consuming, at a stage when time is usually lacking. Conflicts are not difficult to find at that moment. In order to prevent this, the simulated production environment must be available at a much earlier stage in the process.

Rigidity of system management

In this framework, testers also encounter the phenomenon of rigidity of system management. Testers feel that they often have to deal with inflexibility and bureaucracy, as a result of which they can influence the progress of the tests to only a limited extent. In fact, they are experiencing simulated production. The rigid attitude of system management, often justifiable, is still the insurance premium for manageability of the information services. Being confronted with this phenomenon is an indispensable part of the test, because in production at least the same rules will apply. This requires timely consultation and respect for each other's interests and points of view. With respect to the test team, it is recommended to have the position of technical support filled by an employee of system management. This will certainly have a positive effect. In addition, every self-respecting system management department always strives for higher service levels.

Order and planning times
To have the required test facilities at the right time, we must take into account the considerable order and installation periods. This means that the test environment must often be ordered at a time when there is still too little knowledge about its composition and the schedule. In general, the required degree of detail cannot (yet) be defined reliably. Incomplete orders and incorrect planning can result in serious stagnation of the test process. It is very important to make timely agreements with suppliers of the test facilities about the order and planning dates and the possibility of changing the agreements. Again, having the technical support provided by an employee of the system management can have a positive effect. TMap initiates this in the planning and control phase, during the activity of defining the infrastructure.

26.2.2 Variations
Combination of the system test and functional acceptance test environment (integrated environment)
During the system test, the developer checks the functional quality of the system; the acceptance tester does the same during the FAT. The difference is in the representativeness of the environment and the origin of the test cases. System testers have laboratory facilities at their disposal and test functional and technical aspects. The acceptance tester tests in a simulated production environment, and will include in the tests only functional aspects as well as subject matter and use aspects. Applying these two filters is important and must be guaranteed as much as possible. By allowing the acceptance test cases to be executed first in the system test environment, one may achieve a major optimization. Sometimes it is decided to set up a special integrated test environment for this purpose (Figure 26.2). By using this approach, defects are detected sooner, and sophisticated test tools can be used for the acceptance test cases. It is also usually possible to execute several tests simultaneously.

When the system is found to be functionally clean, the actual acceptance test is carried out in the simulated production environment. This test will produce, at the most, a few defects with regard to control and use.

Note

- As indicated above, full integration of the functional test cases of the system and acceptance tests is strongly discouraged, as the filter effect of the respective tests would be seriously reduced.
- The (timely) recording of agreements concerning tasks and responsibilities is an important precondition for the successful application of an integrated test environment.

Figure 26.2

Integrated test
environment

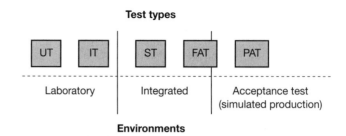

Test types

Laboratory　　　Integrated　　　Acceptance test
(simulated production)

Environments

Set-up according to test type

The consistent linking of a test level to one environment has great disadvantages. Because of the sequential nature of the test processes in the environments, major defects are discovered too late. It is more efficient to relate the set-up and provision of the test environment to the test type, i.e. directly to the quality characteristics. This implies that the delivery of the parts of the test object to be tested must also be related to the test type (and the accompanying environment).

In this construction, the situation may arise that the user is carrying out some tests in the low-level test environment, while a programmer tests some aspects in the simulated production environment. The realization of this is a challenge for the test management and others involved. It requires great organizational and persuasive powers, in particular in the field of responsibilities and separation of functions. Whereas everything is usually centered around the owner of the environment, the focus is now on the test. The test environment is purely a facilitating factor for whatever type of test is being run. The time that can be saved by parallel execution of tests and the reduction of re-work by early detection of defects is well worth the effort.

It is therefore very important to suit the test environment to the test type. In general, this is possible within the traditional test environments of laboratory, system test and simulated production.

26.3　Choices and considerations

26.3.1 Quality characteristics, test type and test environment

Table 26.1 shows a number of test types and their accompanying quality characteristics, which are related to the most obvious environments: laboratory (lab), system test environment (st) and simulated production (sp). After the test strategy has been determined, this table must be drawn up and effected (i.e. defining the infrastructure in the planning and control phase) when the (master) test plan is being set up.

Table 26.1
Test types and test
environments

Test type	Quality characteristic	Environment
Checks	Correctness, data controllability	sp
Functionality	Functionality	lab, st, sp
Interfaces	Connectivity	lab, st, sp
Load and stress	Continuity, performance	sp
Manual support	Suitability	st, sp
Regression	All	lab, st, sp
Security	Security	sp
Standards	Security, user-friendliness	st, sp
Use of resources	Efficiency	sp

26.3.2 Organizational factors

The organization of the test environment is different for each test process. Any number of factors play a role in this process, including:

- *Test level.* Unit, integration, system or acceptance test or possibly an integrated test;
- *Test type.* Which quality characteristics/test types are relevant (Table 26.1)?
- *Requirements of the environment.* Does the environment need to comply with explicit requirements e.g. reproducibility, security, simulated production, parallel execution, date manipulation?
- *Available test environments.* Are there test environments available within the organization or the project? Are these usable? How can individual demands be effectuated?
- *Standards.* Are there (system management) standards for setting up the test environment?
- *Platform (hardware and software architecture).* Which development or production platform is being used? What possibilities are offered, and what restrictions may there be as a result?
- *Organization of system development.* The methods, techniques and lifecycle model used for system development have an impact on the test environment when it comes to procedures;
- *Type of application.* The test environment is related strongly to the corresponding test object, e.g. batch, online, mainframe, PC application, tailor-made or software package;
- *Data communication, decentralized processing.* To what extent does data communication play a role? In which form? Is the network or the network software part of the test object? Are decentralized test locations being used?
- *Boundaries of the test.* Is it necessary to also test manual processes and, for example, input and output processing? If so, then several things need to be arranged with respect to the test environments;

- *Budget.* Is there a budget for setting up the test environments, and what possibilities are offered?
- *Geographical location.* The test environments of the developer and the acceptance tester should not be too far apart. Although telephone, fax and email can cover part of the communication needs, frequent meetings must still occur between the various parties involved. A suitable choice of location can save much time and money;
- *Use of test tools.* The use of test tools often makes demands on the test environment in terms of security, data storage and communication facilities;
- *Availability of testware.* To what extent is testware available with the test object? Using existing testware makes demands on the environment and especially the storage of data.

26.4   Facilities for the construction and use of test files

Test files are of crucial importance for the ability to test or retest. To avoid working with incorrect test files during the execution of the test, thought must be given at an early stage to the method of creating files and the usage strategy to be applied. In the TMap lifecycle, this is dealt with during the planning and control phase (in the organizing control activity) and the specification phase (in the defining initial test databases activity). The actual filling of the files occurs during the execution phase (in the setting up initial test databases activity).

26.4.1 Construction of files
For the construction of files, one can choose from three alternatives:
- constructing with regular system functions;
- constructing with separate loading software;
- converting production data.

Constructing with regular system functions has the disadvantage that the functions themselves have not been tested exhaustively, and that the data entered must therefore be checked thoroughly. The advantage is that during the construction of the databases, the regular functions are tested simultaneously (implicitly).

Constructing with separate loading software has the disadvantage that many 'impossible situations' are suddenly possible because there is no check on the input. This means that technical support is necessary during the construction, and (tested) loading software must be available. The advantage is that the files can be constructed relatively quickly.

Converting production data has the disadvantage that although testing is carried out with a large amount of data, these data differ very little from each other. With production data, the 'good path' is usually tested, but hardly any of the 'wrong path' is tested. In addition, it is not always known which test situations are covered by the data. Also, the disk space taken up is often much more than that which is necessary. Another disadvantage is that it is not always allowed (because of privacy regulations, susceptibility to fraud) to work with production data. This creates the need to encrypt private data. The advantage is that files can be constructed quickly, and that any conversion software is tested implicitly.

Apart from the problems relating to planning and budgets, the first option is preferred. If the test team has permission to retrieve test files from production, it is also possible to combine the three options. Select a set of production data in such a way that a certain coverage is available for each type of data (client, order, invoice, etc.). This subset is loaded in the test environment (maintaining the consistency between the different data), then regular system functions are used to make changes in these data in order to create the desired initial situation.

26.4.2 Using files

The use of the various test files requires an individual strategy. This mainly concerns the choice between:

- the cumulative construction of files;
- the freeze/unfreeze principle;
- the use of several parallel versions.

In addition, agreements will have to be made concerning the simultaneous use of data and change control.

In the case of cumulative construction, the files grow in parallel with test progress. New test data are created, modified, etc., as needed. On the one hand, this gives testers a great deal of freedom and flexibility. On the other hand the data will quickly become polluted and the demand for storage capacity will increase rapidly. To reduce these disadvantages, adequate control instruments are necessary.

A second strategy is a periodic reset of a basic data set, e.g. once a day or once a week. Each test is then based on this data set. In order to test removal functionality, the creating of data is recorded first, and so on. A special control procedure can provide the structural addition of data to the basic set. A great advantage is the manageability of the data, but disadvantages are the dependability on the time of refreshing and the extra work needed to arrive at the relevant test situation. The latter, however, can be promoted with the aid of a recording and playback tool (see Chapter 27).

A third option is the use of several parallel versions of the data. Each tester has his or her own test files. Sometimes it suffices to have a partially 'private' availability, while other data can be shared. The advantage of this approach is the parallel execution of the tests. The amount of time gained is substantial. Although the independence of the tests prevents conflicts between testers, the isolation of the tests means that the integral test aspects are dealt with only later.

For all aspects relating to the ordering, organizing, installing and use of the test environments, it is advisable to involve personnel from the organization that has to deliver the test environments (usually the system management). If possible, they should be – usually on a part-time basis – part of the test team. One cannot do without the specific knowledge of the infrastructure and the procedures. Lack of these costs a great deal of time and money.

Test tools   **27**

The description of test tools in this chapter is merely a snapshot. It describes the present state of affairs in a constantly changing market. The reader should be aware of this and read the chapter from this perspective.

27.1   Introduction

At a time when information services are becoming more and more widespread, the deciding factor between competitors, timeliness and the quality of the information system are of strategic importance for many organizations. Applying the latest development methods and tools has shortened the time it takes to develop new systems. This means that in relation to development, testing is on the critical path even more clearly and is threatening to become a hindering factor for decisive information services and business operations. All this while testing of information systems was already regarded as a time-consuming and costly activity. This development is being aggravated by the fact that more and stricter quality demands are made on the systems, and the negative impact of insufficient quality is becoming greater. In order to gain sufficient insight into this quality, the importance of a good test is increasing.

In order to break free from this negative spiral, faster and better testing has become an important aim for many test organizations. Test tools are regarded as almost indispensable instruments for achieving this aim. To be able to discuss test tools, it is important to define what a test tool is: *a test tool is an automated resource that offers support to one or more test activities, such as planning and control, specification, constructing initial test files, execution of tests, and analysis.* The emphasis is on support. The use of the test tool must make it possible to achieve higher productivity levels and/or greater effectiveness. This means that a test tool is a useful resource only if using it yields a result; it should not be an aim in itself to use a tool.

The critical success factor for the automation of the test process by means of tools is the presence of a structured test approach and a test organization. On the basis of the structured test approach and the corresponding techniques, the implementation of one or more test tools should be given shape. In a properly controlled process, tools can certainly provide a major added value, but their effect is counterproductive in an insufficiently controlled test process. Automation requires a certain level of repeatability and standardization of the activities to be supported. An unstructured process cannot comply with these conditions. Because automation imposes a certain standard procedure, it may contribute to the implementation of a structured approach. However, structuring and automation must at least go hand in hand. In other words: *structure and tool*.

While in the development process, methods and techniques preceded the arrival of supporting tools, in testing it appears to be the opposite. It is remarkable that the interest in test tools is often greater than the interest in test methods and techniques.

27.2   A closer look at test tools

Within some testing areas, activities take place that are relatively standard but nevertheless must be carried out with great accuracy. Examples are the comparison of extensive reports to find out whether both reports are identical with each other, or executing the same test over and over again when no differences are expected. These types of routine activities are often very suitable for automation, and therefore require the support of a test tool.

Within software development, a similar evolution occurred some time ago. Programmers are no longer needed to write the object code. They have been replaced by compilers, 4GL resources or code generators. A programmer does not need to retype the entire program to make a change. Nevertheless, this is what often happens when information systems are being tested: the test input is not saved, which means that the tester must execute the whole test again. Even the logical and physical test cases and their results are produced and assessed manually.

The use of test tools to support a structured test approach is clearly the next step towards high-quality testing and software. Judging by the present status of test tools, testing may receive support in particular during the execution of tests and to a lesser degree in test design and test planning. Usable test tools that support test specification techniques (as described in Chapter 15) are available only to a limited degree, and then only for specific situations. The test tools available focus mainly on the execution phase. A distinction should be made between tools for high-level testing and those for low-level testing; at present, there are more tools – especially more usable test tools – for low-level testing than for high-level testing.

Being able to use test tools can be assumed to be a basic skill for a tester these days. The wider concept of automation of the test process, on the other hand, requires specialist and in-depth knowledge of (the possibilities of) automation and tools. This knowledge is certainly not present in all testers. This has created a new type of specialism: the test automation specialist. Chapter 19 describes the roles of architect and engineer, which come under this specialism.

27.3 Advantages

Automation of the test process may lead to less effort being required for the execution of routine test activities. As a result, employees with (often scarce) test and subject matter knowledge are able to concentrate on the complex test activities and on providing a higher test quality. Provided that test tools are used in combination with a structured test approach, there will be advantages in using them. These advantages may be quite considerable, as the area of application of most test tools – the execution of the test – often claims about 40 percent of the total test effort for new construction (even more in maintenance tests).

Automation of the test process offers the following advantages:

- A large number of tests can be carried out unattended and automatically, e.g. at night.
- Automation of routine and often boring test activities leads to greater reliability of the activities carried out manually, and to a higher degree of work satisfaction in the test team. This results in higher productivity in test team.
- Retesting can, to a large extent, be done automatically. Automating the process of retesting makes it possible to perform a full regression test, so that it can be determined whether the unchanged software still functions according to the specifications.
- Test tools ensure that the test data are the same for consecutive tests so that there is certainty about the reliability of the initial situation with respect to the data.
- Tools can trace defects that are difficult to detect manually. Using the tool, it is in principle possible to find all incidences of these types of defects.
- Generating large amounts of test data can be done automatically with the aid of a test tool. Entering initial data sets need be done only once instead of every time a test is run.

In summary, it can be concluded that the use of test tools makes it possible to carry out more test activities in less time, and increases both the quality and the productivity of the test process.

27.4 Considerations

27.4.1 Is test automation the only solution?

Automation of the test process may contribute to the improvement of the quality of the software and the test process, and to higher productivity, but it is not the solution to all problems. In many areas of IT, an overwhelming enthusiasm has emerged with regard to various new technological solutions. The use of 4GL and CASE tools was supposed to lead to error-free software. More recently, generators and the object-oriented development were designed to solve all problems. At the moment, the ultimate solution is component-based development.

The best solution is a combination of several good solutions, not necessarily the latest innovation. Test process automation is no exception to this rule. Clear aims must be formulated at the start, and only if a tool can be proven to create improvements it should be included in the test process.

27.4.2 Management commitment

Although testing is mature enough for the application of tools, it is not always certain that the desired advantages will be achieved. One of the most important success factors for automation of the test process is the management's commitment. Management should be made aware of the fact that use of a tool is an investment in both money and time, which can often be earned back only over a longer period of time in terms of faster and/or better testing. If such awareness is insufficient, there is a risk that use of the tool will be discontinued at the first disappointment. Even more when the tool is used for the first time in a time-critical project: if the project is under severe time pressure, then chances are that further use will be stopped.

Another aspect of management commitment is the degree to which support is given to the structured test approach. Some test tools contribute to more effective testing, while others lead to higher productivity. Neither of these types of tools will yield the desired improvements if testing is unstructured. In particular, when the test activity is to be executed under great time pressure, the principles of structured testing should be maintained. At times like these, it will become clear to what extent the management actually supports the structured test approach and the idea of quality.

27.4.3 Interpretation of tool results

Test automation often leads to an increase in the number of tests executed. In addition, tools often provide a quantification regarding certain quality aspects and the test process. The explicitness and high level of detail of such quantifications often inspire unjustifiable conclusions. For example, if a test tool indicates that 100 percent statement coverage has been achieved, it does not follow that the system has been 100 percent tested. It is therefore very important to analyze carefully the meaning of the results, and to ensure that misinterpretations do not occur.

27.5   Overview of test tools

Test tools may offer support to the test activities with respect to all phases of TMap. Figure 27.1 shows various test tools that are available in relation to the various TMap phases. The test tools are explained in more detail below. This overview is not meant to be exhaustive, and highly specific types of test tools in particular have not been included. Word processors and spreadsheets can also be extremely useful test resources.

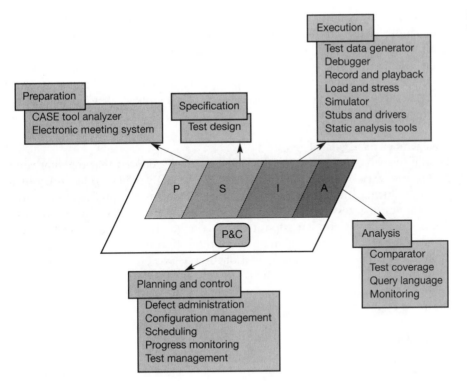

Figure 27.1
Test tools and TMap

We include only test tool types and do not give brand names of test tools. Readers who want more information are referred to the various suppliers, test conferences and the Internet. There are also reports that give inventories of the available test tools (Ovum, 1999).

27.5.1 Planning and control phase
Various test tools are available for the planning and control phase. Most of the tools mentioned below are in fact project management tools and have not been developed specifically for testing:
- defect administration
- configuration management
- scheduling
- progress monitoring
- test management.

Defect administration
During the test process, defects are found. During the preparation and specification phases, most of the defects concern the test basis, while during the execution phase they concern the test object. The number of defects depends

on the size and quality of the test object, and may reach hundreds or even thousands. Defect management (described in section 22.5) is therefore a complex and often sizeable activity. To support this activity, there are tools for registering defects and tracing and monitoring their lifecycle (defect tracking). Some tools also provide the possibility of producing reports and statistics. This functionality is highly desirable and can be used to write reports on the quality of the test object.

Configuration management

During the test process, a variety of deliverables is produced that together constitute the testware. It is very important for the deliverables to be controlled properly during the test process. After their creation and quality checks, the deliverables (e.g. test cases and test documentation) should be frozen. At this point, they become configuration items. A configuration management tool can support the (logical) management of configuration items and their changes. Such a tool supports the management of the versions of objects (i.e. also of the testware) that have emerged in the course of time and of the possible relations between the objects. Product control (described in Chapter 22) is supported by means of configuration management tools.

Scheduling

To support the scheduling process in large-scale test processes, a tool is indispensable. Before a schedule can be entrusted to a progress monitoring package, it is essential to calculate fully, its start date (and possibly end date) and the resources allocated to it. Many planning packages offer 'what if?' analyses, and are capable of generating both strip and network schedules. An important aspect in the selection of planning packages is the possibility of creating management information, e.g. reports of resources and costs. The functionalities of a planning package are often integrated with the functionalities of a progress-monitoring package.

Progress monitoring

A tool is almost indispensable for progress monitoring in large-scale processes. Progress monitoring packages should provide the functionality that is necessary to:
- gain knowledge on the progress made in relation to the budget, time and deliverables, as well as to be able to report on this;
- accurately predict the time and resources necessary to complete the test process.

A progress-monitoring package is a tool for measuring and controlling project progress. To be able to do so, the activities to be carried out are divided into independent tasks. Hours planned, hours worked, and hours still to be spent are registered for each task, after which reports can be drawn up on the basis of these data. The functionalities of a progress-monitoring package are often integrated with the functionalities of a planning package.

Test management

This tool offers an integrated set of functions in the fields of planning, progress control, defect management and configuration management. The functionality for each area is usually not as extensive as would be the case with a specific tool, the power of a test-management tool lying in the integration of the various areas. Often, the tools are also integrated with other tools, such as record and playback or load and stress tools. The use of the tool guides the test process from making a test plan to reporting on the results.

27.5.2 Preparation phase

CASE tool analyzer

If the test basis is recorded in a CASE tool, this tool can usually perform various checks on the completeness and consistency of the test basis. Examples include checks as to whether obsolete attribute names are still being used somewhere.

Electronic meeting system

Testing (not only of the test basis but also of other intermediate deliverables) involves various people, expertise and departments. In practice, communication between all these parties is often laborious. Electronic meeting systems (EMSs) help to structure the communication between all parties, e.g. by supporting the creation and registration of defect reports. The use of EMS also facilitates distributed evaluation of a document.

27.5.3 Specification phase

Test design

The interest in tools that support the specification of test cases using test-specification techniques is increasing. If the test basis has been described in formal notation, then in principle a tool can use this to generate test cases. However, the use of such tools is not simple. Often, the tester must provide an additional description of the system in the language of the tool. The required description may have a graphic form (e.g. a data flow diagram) or a formal language form (e.g. pseudo-code). The test tool can then generate test cases on the basis of this description that guarantee a certain degree of coverage. Usually, these test cases must be edited further, e.g. by giving the test cases a physical content.

27.5.4 Execution phase

There are many types of test tools available for the execution phase. They can be divided into execution and analysis tools. Tools that support the execution of tests include:

- test data generator
- debugger
- record and playback
- load and stress

- simulator
- stubs and drivers
- static analysis tool.

Tools that support the assessment of test results include:
- comparator
- test coverage tool
- query language
- monitoring tool.

Test data generator

This tool helps with the construction of physical test sets. Test data generators can be used to provide a random content on the basis of file and/or database specifications. This makes it possible to create a large test set relatively quickly, e.g. for a real-life test. To some extent, these tools also belong to the specification phase because a great deal of work can already be carried out there: the rules for generating test data must be specified in advance in the tool. This includes defining restricted sets from which a selection can be made, and the relationship between the data (consistency rules).

Debugger

Strictly speaking a debugger is not a test tool. A debugger can be used to detect specific defects that are difficult to find and subsequently to solve them. Depending on the tool, debugger tools make it possible to view and/or manipulate program logic and data at source and/or object level.

Record and playback

A record and playback tool records the test input (data and actions) in a script. The tool may play this script again later so that the test can be repeated easily (the term 'script' in this context should not be confused with the manual test scripts that are part of the test specifications). Usually, this type of tool offers the possibility of changing stored input data, and provides support for the creation of test input. In general, record and playback tools are combined with comparators to enable analysis of the test results. The combination of tool, test cases, scripts and recorded results is referred to as a test suite.

The main advantage of record and playback tools is that a test can be repeated automatically at a later stage. This advantage can be undone if the test object is changed to such an extent that the automated script crashes when it is run. For efficient use of the tool, it is therefore necessary not to only use the record functionality, but also to apply software development techniques (see section 27.6). In addition, a certain degree of stability of the test object is desired. This stability is usually present in regression tests, making the tool very suitable for this type of test.

A record and playback tool can contain the following functionalities:

- automatic creation of test scripts, and the possibility of manual mainte-nance of the test scripts if the situation changes;
- logging of a specific terminal or terminals for performance tests;
- multiplying the test scripts for volume tests;
- the possibility of automatic and interactive comparison of recorded and current output;
- the possibility of stopping the test and restarting it later from the point where it was stopped;
- a test control language that can be used to combine various test scripts to create a test scenario.

Load and stress

These tools can place a load on the information system by simulating (large num-bers of) users to test whether the system will continue to function correctly under the expected workload during production. To measure the results, the tools often have a monitoring function (see *Monitoring tools* below).

Simulator

A simulator imitates the operation of the environment of (part of) the system to be tested. A simulator is used to test software for which it is too costly, dan-gerous or even impossible to execute tests in the actual environment, such as the control software of an aeroplane or a nuclear reactor, or chemical process monitoring software. The simulator provides input for the test objects, which the test object treats as if it were the real input. The output of the test object is intercepted by the simulator before the indicated actions are carried out.

Stubs and drivers

A system is usually tested in parts. Parts can be a program, module or compo-nent. For reasons of simplicity, we will refer only to the term 'program' here. The initial desire is often to test a program that is related to programs that have not yet been created. In this case, stubs and drivers are made that replace the missing programs and simulate the interface between the programs in a simple manner. A stub is called from the program to be tested; a driver calls a program to be tested (Figure 27.2).

A stub or driver is also used if testing with the real programs would demand too great an effort, e.g. is testing a reporting function that prints the salaries per employee. Within this function, the (previously tested) salary calcu-lation program is called. This particular test is only meant to check that all employees are selected, and that each employee's

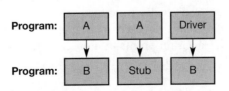

Figure 27.2
Stubs and drivers

salary is printed. Preparing the test database with all the data required for the various salary calculations may involve a great amount of work. A stub that returns a certain salary value (e.g. based on the employee number entered) can decrease the test effort considerably. Of course, the interface between the programs must always be tested at some stage.

Static analysis tools

There are packages that take the program code as input and use this to carry out a variety of static analyses and checks. The aim is not so much to trace hard defects, as to detect unsafe programming and error-prone code. Besides detecting defects, this provides the tester with information on, for example, the maintainability of the system. This information is also used to identify system components that carry larger risks. These components can then be given a relatively greater test effort. The problem with this type of tool is that they are often dependent on the environment (hardware, software, etc.) in which development takes place.

We are dealing here with a static test, as opposed to a dynamic test in which the software actually runs. This means that no input data and no output predictions are necessary, and that the software does not generate output. The functionalities on which static analysis tools focus can be divided into four groups:

- *Program structure analyses*. Has the program been set up in a structured way? The tool may try to generate a Nassi–Shneiderman diagram. If this fails, a structure defect is signalled. Structure analyses are used to assess the program architecture.
- *Lines of code*. Has programming taken place according to the standards? Do all fields in a program receive a value before they are used? Are infinite loops being avoided? Are the different types of variables not being mixed up? Compilers often provide functionalities for answering these questions. For example, they may, by default, build both syntax checks and certain run-time checks, and detect non-initialized variables, unused code, and infinite loops. Most compilers also create a report of variables and their use (cross-reference reports).
- *Style guide*. Does the software comply with the style guide used (e.g. are there sufficient comment lines, and is indenting correct)?
- *Software metrics*. This functionality can be used to generate metrics on the software, e.g. in terms of size, complexity or comment frequency. An example of a complexity metric is McCabe's formula (McCabe, 1976), in which a statement is made about the degree of complexity of the programs. Complexity is defined as the number of paths that can be taken in a program, the basis of the theory being that an increase in the number of decision points in a program increases the complexity of the program and hence the chance of defects.

Static analysis tools can be purchased, but they are often created in-house. An example of such a tool is one that checks the program code for adherence to some or all of the standards.

Comparator

The comparator compares data and reports to detect the differences. These differences must then be analyzed to determine whether each difference is according to expectations. A comparator may be used to compare:
- the test output with the test output of the previous test;
- a data set before and after one or more test actions;
- the results of the simulated operation with the results of production.

The tools are often an integral part of record and playback tools, but very simple file comparison utilities or even the revision function of a word processor can also be used.

Test coverage tool

This tool provides information on the degree to which the structure of the software has been covered by the tests that have been carried out, and as such offers useful support for measuring the effect of the use of test-specification techniques. The measurements can be made at program or subsystem level. This makes it possible, for example, to determine that during testing each program statement is carried out at least once. However, 100 percent test coverage of the program statements (statement coverage) by no means guarantees that defects cannot occur anymore. For more information on the types of coverage, see Chapter 15.

Query language

A tester can use a query language to retrieve information on the contents of files by means of short, concise commands. A query language is an excellent tool for investigating a defect in greater detail. Some query languages also offer the possibility of manipulating data, which means that they can be used to maintain the initial data set.

Monitoring tool

In order to gain insight into aspects such as memory usage, central processing unit use, network load and performance, monitoring tools can be used during the test process. A variety of data on utilization of resources can be measured and stored. The measured data are then made available to the test team in the form of a report.

Making sure monitoring tools are present is often a complex matter. On the other hand, system management often has monitoring tools available to monitor the operational production environment that may also be usable in the test environment. In the case of load and stress tools, the monitoring functionality is often an integral part.

27.6 Automation of the execution of tests

With the term 'test automation', people often refer strictly to the automation of the execution of the test, and when they speak of 'test tools' they refer only to record and playback tools. Although incorrect, this confusion is understandable because this type of test automation promises the most benefits. Automation not only shortens the lead time but also yields a higher quality execution of the test. There are no longer any doubts as to whether the tester forgot to execute test cases or made an error when entering data. This section deals with this type of automation in greater detail.

27.6.1 Record and playback

At the beginning of the 1990s, there was a strong increase in the supply of record and playback (R&Pb) tools because the expected advantages for the automation of the execution of tests were very attractive:

- It is possible to record a very large number of tests in a short space of time.
- Little or no knowledge of the tool is necessary, so the learning time is short.

In practice, it was found that there were also major disadvantages:

- Each new test case must first be recorded in a (tool) script before it can be run automatically. This recording costs more time than entering the test case manually. Initially, there is always loss of time in relation to manual testing.
- Adapting a recorded test because of a change in the test object is very costly. For example, adding a field to a certain screen in a new release of the system to be tested means that every test case in which this screen is used must be adapted.
- The automated testware is insufficiently maintainable because the relation between the automated test cases and the test object and the test basis is not known. Usually, this is caused by the fact that no test-specification techniques have been used.

For these reasons, it often costs so much time to execute a previously recorded test in full that the advantages of the test suite compared with manual testing disappeared. In many cases, this led to the tools no longer being used after a short period of time; they gathered dust as they sat on the bookshelf, which gave rise to the terms 'dustware' and 'shelfware'.

27.6.2 Testing, automation, knowledge, tools

The problems mentioned above can be traced back to insufficient quality of the test suite (the combination of tool, test cases, scripts, and recorded results). A test suite must pay for itself in terms of faster and better testing when new releases are retested. The effort needed to adapt a test suite to a new release must therefore be minimal. The main quality demands that the test suite should meet are maintainability, flexibility, robustness and reusability.

To develop test suites that meet these demands, the test automation approach, testing, automation, knowledge, tools (TAKT[1]) is used (Figure 27.3). Like TMap, this practical approach also uses the cornerstones of techniques, infrastructure, organization and lifecycle. TAKT distinguishes clearly between the development phase, in which development takes place, and the operation phase, in which use and maintenance of automated tests occurs.

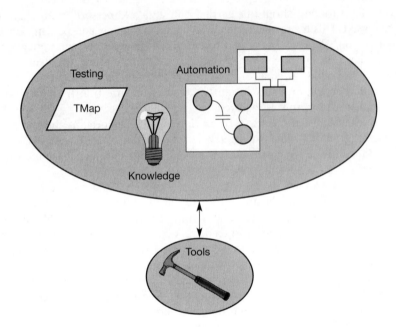

Figure 27.3
Testing, automation, knowledge, tools.

Although it uses the same cornerstones as TMap, TAKT can be applied independently of the test methods and brands of test tools used. A necessary precondition for a successful application of TAKT, however, is that testing is done in a structured way. Test automation within a test process that does not use a lifecycle model or test-specification techniques, or that has not organized control properly, is almost never cost-effective.

Technique: data-driven approach

A suitable technique for making it easier to adapt a recorded test when the test object is changed is the data-driven approach (Figure 27.4). In this approach, the test cases are not hard-coded in the tool scripts but are stored separately in a

---

[1] TAKT is based not only on TMap but also on Andersen Consulting (1995), Fewster and Graham (1999), Kaner (1997) and Hayes (1995).

Figure 27.4

Data-driven approach

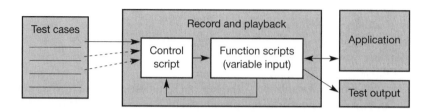

table. Each line in the table represents one test case. For each test case, it is indicated which function should be carried out (e.g. 'add person') and which data must be used. This means that there may be lines such as 'add person; Johnson; P.; 07-06-1963; 12, The Green; Newtown'. In the programming language of the R&Pb tool, scripts are programmed that can be used to read and execute the test cases from the tables. Such a control script reads the table line by line, interprets the function script, and subsequently executes it, entering the data from the table whenever test input is required.

The selection of the tests to be carried out, the reports on the test results, and the logging of events during the test execution can be dealt with by the standard facilities of the test tool. If the facilities of the test tool are inadequate, special scripts can be programmed.

The great advantage of the data-driven approach is that only a few changes need to be made to the control and/or function scripts when the test object is changed. Maintenance of the table containing the test cases is carried out outside the tool. The table may be produced by a spreadsheet or database program. Adding extra test cases is easy and (very) quick, and adapting previously recorded tests to changes in the test object is much simpler. It is also very important for maintainability that test cases can be related to the test basis and the test object. The use of test-specification techniques is therefore an important precondition.

Below is an example of the difference between 'normal' R&Pb scripts and data-driven scripts for 30 test cases that are used to test the 'add person' function.

'Normal' R&Pb:
1   Add person 1 script.
2   Add person 2 script.
3   Add person – script.
4   Add person 30 script.

When something changes in the function, e.g. 'close' using F10 instead of F12, then all 30 scripts will have to be adapted.

Data-driven approach:
1   Function script 'add person' (variable input).
2   Table (created outside the R&Pb tool using, for example, a spreadsheet or a simple database program) with:

- – 'Add person', test data 1.
- – 'Add person', test data –.
- – 'Add person', test data 30.
3   Control script that reads the table calls the function script 'add person' and provides the test data.

When something changes in the function, e.g. 'close' with F10 instead of F12, only the function script 'add person' needs to be adapted. When an extra attribute is added to the entity 'person', then not only must the function script be extended with a attribute but also the table containing the test data. In both cases, this costs much less effort than in 'normal' R&Pb. Another advantage is that the (subject matter expert) testers can maintain the table with test cases, while tool specialists can maintain the scripts. The (often scarce) subject matter expert testers can concentrate on specifying the test cases using selected test-specification techniques without the need to first learn how to use the tool.

Infrastructure: framework architecture
Each script is a small program. Use of the basic principles of modular program-ming increases the maintainability of the scripts: each group of successive actions that must be carried out repeatedly (e.g. moving to a certain screen in the application) is best stored as a separate module. If something changes in the group of activities (e.g. because of a different menu set-up), then only one module will need to be adapted. Modules exist at different levels of abstraction, varying from activating or checking a specific object of the system to be tested, to carrying out a business process.

A framework architecture is a library of reusable modules. Having such an architecture makes it possible for new test suites (for new systems) to be created in a short period of time, because many of the necessary building blocks (mod-ules) are already present in the library.

To construct a test suite in such a modular fashion, expertise in the fields of testing and software development is required.

Organization
Successful automation of testing requires knowledge in the fields of testing, automation and the tool to be used. A test team or test organization that wants to introduce automated testing, must introduce new test roles:
- the test automation architect, whose task is to design the test suite;
- the test automation engineer, a tool specialist who creates the test suite in accordance with the design.

These roles are described in detail in Chapter 19.

To find qualified personnel, the manager of the test organization has the following options:

- training interested testers in software development;
- training interested programmers in testing and tools;
- hiring expertise in the field of test automation.

People with test experience who have specialized in software development are preferred.

Lifecycle

The aim to test faster and better is not achieved merely by purchasing a standard test tool or a ready-made test suite. Like automation of book-keeping, the automation of testing is a step that must be approached in a structured and well-planned way (Figure 27.5). The test tool can be regarded as a development environment for building the automated test suite.

Figure 27.5
Lifecycle of test automation

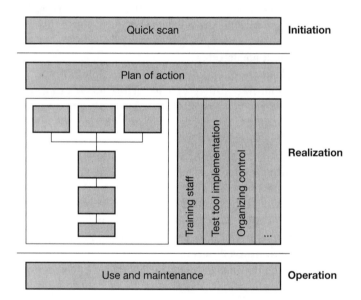

Initiation
When applying TAKT, an inventory is first made of the current test organization and approach, the applications that are to be tested, and the specific test automation aims and their feasibility. This provides answers to questions such as:
- Should we automate only one application for the time being, or introduce automated testing throughout the company?
- Should we automate only the functionality tests, or also the performance tests?
- Who is going to construct the test suite? Who is going to maintain it, and who is going to control it?

A pilot project is selected in which the chances of success and the gains to be made are high. The desired schedules are determined: at what moment will which parts of the test suite be used in an operational test project? When should the internal test organization be capable of taking over all maintenance of the test suite? This inventory is the basis for a go/no-go decision. After a 'go', one proceeds to the following phase.

Construction
In consultation with the customer, the architect decides which approach to use. Accordingly, a plan of action is set up. This plan should provide answers to questions such as 'Who is going to do what when?' Topics dealt with in the plan include:
● aims (time, money, quality)
● scope (which tests to automate)
● personnel and organization
● technical infrastructure
● activities

and optionally:
● selection and implementation of the test tool
● training employees
● organizing control.

The test suite is constructed according to plan, and the following activities are carried out (Figure 27.6). The architect translates the general aims into test automation aims, analyzes the system (test object) to be tested, and analyzes the present test approach (including the test environment, tools and available testware). The architect then designs the test suite on the basis of the analysis results in such a manner that the test automation aims can be completed in full.

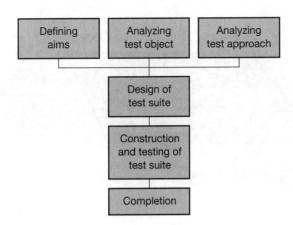

Figure 27.6
Activities during the construction phase

The engineer then constructs the design of the test suite with the aid of the test tool chosen in the phase development and testing of test suite. Because maintainability of the test suite is a primary requirement, concepts such as the data-driven approach and framework architecture are applied. The constructed modules are tested separately for correct functioning, and subsequently integrated with other modules and the data-driven tables, and tested again. Finally, during the completion phase, the test suite is delivered clean and documented.

Operation

This is the phase in which the automated tests are used and maintained. Usually, this concerns testing new releases in the maintenance phase of the system. However, it also applies to newly constructed systems in the iterative route of testing–repairs–retesting–etc. (Figure 27.7). This is the phase in which the original aims and the degree to which they have been achieved are evaluated. New aims can be formulated and the process can be repeated, partly or in full.

The operation phase of automated testing is part of the test process as a whole. For this reason, the activities to be carried out in this phase are included in the lifecycle used in the overall test process.

Changes in the application usually mean that test cases need to be adapted or new test cases must be made. This is the regular route of structured testing, in which such items as test strategy and test-specification techniques play an important role. For the automated part of the test process, this means that the necessary adjustments must be made to the test suite in the preparation and specification phases: the scripts and the framework are adapted, and the new or changed test cases are entered into the tables with the test cases. The necessary effort is minimized by the high degree of maintainability of the test suite. Once the system to be tested is supplied to the test team, the automated tests can be executed immediately.

Figure 27.7
Operation lifecycle

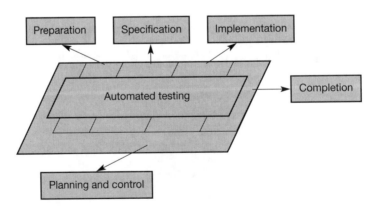

Office environment 28

An aspect that is often forgotten in testing is the availability of an effective and efficient office environment for the test teams. This concerns the office environment in the widest sense because the testers must also be able to carry out their work under favourable circumstances.

28.1 Office space

Testing is usually carried out as a project, which means that, in addition to the office space available for regular (line) activities, extra office space is needed. It is advisable to assign the test team to one location or room – this constitutes the basis for successful cooperation and coordination within the team. If it is not possible to make one room available, then the distribution of the team members across the various rooms must match the distribution of the testers across the various system parts, the test techniques to be applied, etc.

Testing is characterized by a great deal of consultation, both internally within the test team and externally with the various parties involved. It is therefore necessary to reserve a number of conference rooms where such meetings can take place. The advantage of a structured approach is the fact that these meetings will often occur at set times, meaning that the locations can be reserved in advance.

It is advisable to place the test team in a location that is close to the development team, the designers, the change control team, etc. Experience has shown that if the physical distance between those involved is too great, this leads to less cooperation and coordination.

28.2 Workspaces

A tester's workspace often differs from a regular workspace. To set up and maintain the test documentation, use is made of PCs, whereas test execution could be done on a terminal connected to a mainframe. The development of test documentation is often done with the standard packages available on PCs within the organization. This may be word processors, spreadsheet programs, drawing programs, etc.

This means that the correct PC configurations, networks and printers must be made available on time. Another aspect concerns the availability of storage capacity for digital versions of the test documentation, e.g. in the form of a server, and the hard copy documentation, e.g. in the form of sufficient cabinet space.

The test teams also need a number of standard office facilities, including telephone extensions, fax and photocopy machines, and a supply of office materials, such as writing pads, pens, staplers, etc.

28.3 Access control

Many companies have access regulations for their employees. This requires the provision of access passes for employees. It may also be important to make the test team aware of any procedures that are used by the department or the organization. These include registering holidays, reporting sickness, account of hours, registering presence, etc.

28.4 Catering

Despite the use of a structured approach, testing is often characterized by working under a great deal of pressure, in particular during the execution phase. Overtime is a regular occurrence, which means that catering facilities are no superfluous luxury. A hungry tester will want to go home as soon as possible!

Variations

PART VI

Variations on the theme   **29**

29.1   Introduction

TMap is a generic model. Its approach, originally designed for high-level testing in development projects, has developed into a practical basis for almost every type of test and test activity relating to software. The TMap cornerstones – lifecycle, techniques, infrastructure and organization – are used as standards for purposes such as:

- low-level (unit and integration) tests and high-level (system and acceptance) tests;
- testing applications and systems software, hardware, documentation, etc.
- testing new information systems and testing in maintenance situations;
- tests ranging from mega-projects ($\geq$ £30 million/$50 million) to very small projects;
- tests for tailor-made software and packages;
- tests for conventional and modern infrastructures;
- tests for conventional and modern development methods.

This makes considerable demands on the developers of the TMap standards as well as on its users. It is assumed that the TMap developers will have constructed the standard in modular form, and will support the user in selecting the required components. Users are expected to find the right solution between a dogmatic selection of TMap standard components and a more pragmatic one. It is vitally important to arrive at a reliable test process that is neither inadequate nor excessive. As far as lifecycle, techniques and organization are concerned, TMap is constructed in such a way that it is nearly always possible to do less.

The instrument for arriving at a suitable selection is provided by TMap itself in the form of the test strategy development technique. A test process sometimes requires extras in the form of special techniques or a different organizational structure, which as a rule are derived easily from the standard. Because of the great diversity of applications, it is clearly impossible to specify just one standard test infrastructure: TMap provides a generic framework on which to base an appropriate infrastructure.

29.2   Variations

Any standard approach will give rise to variations that, to some extent, develop as specific subsets of the standard. Variations of this kind are sometimes temporary, but a substantial expansion of the standard also occurs. Several areas where this happens are described in the following sections:

- testing in maintenance situations
- integrated testing
- client/server testing
- graphical user interfaces
- object-oriented development
- rapid application development and evolutionary system development
- testing of packages
- testing e-business.

29.3   Testing in maintenance situations

TMap can be used for new information systems as well as for the maintenance of existing information systems. It is simply a matter of approaching from a different angle, which gives rise to a number of changes in emphasis. Here, too, the test strategy development technique provides for differentiation in the way the standard is applied. There are several areas where most differences occur, e.g. regarding the test basis. A catching-up operation is frequently required when systems are maintained. Functional specifications are often missing, and a set of testware related to the functional specifications simply does not exist. It may well be possible to carry out this catching-up operation along with testing a new maintenance release, which may reduce the cost.

If it is impossible to compile any functional specifications, an alternative test basis should be sought by way of compromise. A search should be made for documentation that is closest to the functional specifications and that can be managed by developers as well as testers. In such cases, it is advisable to draw the customer's attention to the lower test quality that is likely to be achieved. Anything, however, is to be preferred to the notorious daily production, because in that case nobody knows what is being tested. Reproducibility should always be of paramount importance.

One aspect that in many cases differs somewhat from the development situation is the type of test organization. New developments and their appropriate test activities are usually carried out as parts of a project, whereas maintenance tests are normally executed as an activity in the line organization. As a result, there will usually be some lack of resources and flexibility, and the test process will experience more competition from other line activities.

In general, however, it may be argued that testing for maintenance purposes may be dealt with in the same way as it is for new development.

29.3.1 Development and test process

The development and test process applicable to new developments does not change fundamentally for maintenance purposes. It is a matter of a low-level unit and integration test, and a high-level system and acceptance test (Figure 29.1). A maintenance test process usually begins with the receipt of an application for a change or a release plan. The high-level test manager drafts a test plan by order of (and in cooperation with) the customer. On receipt of the new or changed functional specifications, corresponding test cases are specified or adapted. On receipt of the test object the tests and possible retests are executed. On completion of the tests, the testware is preserved (once again).

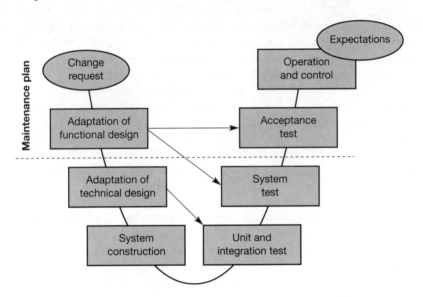

Figure 29.1

System maintenance in the V-model

29.3.2 Types of maintenance

From the point of view of testing, there are two types of maintenance. There is maintenance for which testing may be planned, and there is ad hoc corrective maintenance, which cannot be planned at all. Ad hoc corrective maintenance takes place when the search for solutions to defects cannot be delayed. Special test procedures are required at that time.

Planned maintenance

The category of planned maintenance includes:

- perfecting maintenance (adapting software to the user's wishes, e.g. by supplying new functions or enhancing performance);
- adaptive maintenance (adapting software to environmental changes, such as new hardware, new system software or new legislation);

●   corrective planned maintenance (deferrable correction of defects and shortcomings).

The standard TMap approach is fully applicable to planned maintenance. On
average, planned maintenance represents more than 90 percent of all maintenance work on information systems.

Ad hoc corrective maintenance

Ad hoc corrective maintenance is concerned with defects requiring an immediate solution. Imagine a production run which dumps late at night, a network
goes down with a few hundred users online, or a mailing has incorrect
addresses. There are different rules and different procedures for solving problems of this kind. It will be impossible to take the steps required for a structured
approach to testing. If, however, a number of activities are carried out before a
potential malfunction, it may be possible to achieve a situation in which reliable tests can be executed in spite of panic stations all round.

A risk analysis of the operational information systems should be performed
in order to establish which functions or programs constitute the greatest risk to
the information services in the event of disaster. It is then established – in
respect of the functions at risk – which (test) actions should be performed if a
particular malfunction occurs. Several types of malfunctions may be identified,
and there will be various ways of responding to them for each function at risk.
A possible reaction might be that a relevant function at risk should always be
tested, or that under particular circumstances testing might be carried out in ret-
rospect (the next day, for instance). If it is decided that a particular function at
risk should always be tested whenever relevant, a number of standard tests,
which could be executed almost immediately, should be prepared for this purpose. The standard tests would obviously be prepared and maintained in
accordance with the TMap approach.

Even in the event of ad hoc maintenance, it is therefore possible to bring
about an improvement in quality by adopting a specific test approach. It is
important to make a thorough risk analysis of the information system, and to
specify a set of standard tests accordingly.

29.4   Integrated testing

In many organizations, system testing and acceptance testing are combined
either completely or in part. This phenomenon is called integrated testing. It
usually concerns the functional acceptance test, the aspect that may be tested
largely in an environment unrepresentative of production and that is also the
most important aim of the system test. However, it is hard to imagine many reasons why integrated tests should be limited to functionality, since there are
several quality characteristics that are eminently suitable for this procedure.

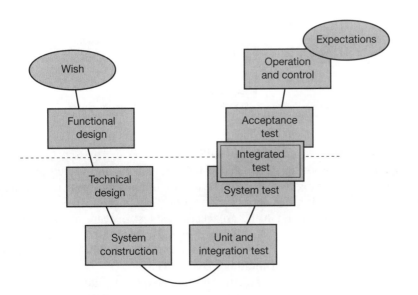

Figure 29.2
The integrated test in the
V-model

In the event of an integrated test, the parties (development and user representatives) agree in advance which aspects will be covered in which specific test, and to what level they will be tested. The usual procedure is to allocate quality characteristics and, depending on them, the test types and the techniques that are to be employed, and the degree of coverage that is to be achieved. Developers and users both specify their own test cases, independently of one another as much as possible and parallel to the technical design phase and the system realization (Figure 29.2)

An integrated test is preceded by a (reduced) system test. The developers subject the agreed aspects to a system test up to the agreed level. The users do not play any part in this. After the system test has been executed, developers and users join forces in confronting the system with the test cases agreed on for the integrated test.

This test is executed in a properly controllable laboratory environment, e.g. the system test environment, in which optimum use can be made of test tools and (rapid) recovery procedures. With expertise on both sides, and the opportunities presented by the test environment and the test tools, the tests may proceed quite quickly. After the execution of an integrated test in the system test environment, the functional test cases are ideally used or executed again in the simulated production environment. The developers do not play any part in this. As for functionality, this test will merely produce defects about interfaces to other systems and manual procedures. If the system and acceptance test are carried out by means of an integrated test, the production acceptance test will remain unchanged, focusing on other quality characteristics.

It should be noticed that the developer will remain fully responsible for the product that is to be presented for acceptance. The user's participation in the integrated test should be regarded merely as support for the development process. The user accepts the system by executing an acceptance test (Figure 29.3)

Figure 29.3
Responsibilities during
integrated testing

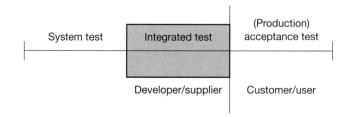

29.4.1 Why use the integrated test?

The reasons for choosing an integrated test are varied – and sometimes wrong. An example of a wrong reason would be an attempt at a late stage to eliminate a backlog caught during the development process by more or less skipping the system test and simply retaining an acceptance test instead, or by leaving the specification and execution of the functional test cases to the users only. Each set of tests has its own background, has its own filtering process, and produces its own defects; such filters should not be removed.

Legitimate reasons for organizing an integrated test include:

- the opportunity presented to the users of first testing functionality thoroughly in a more suitable environment subjected to less stringent procedures;
- the test environment's suitability for first (artificially) testing aspects such as stress and authorization;
- identifying and, above all, correcting relatively important defects in an early stage by using test cases belonging to the acceptance test;
- an early exchange of information about the system by the developer and about the subject matter by the user;
- the joint use of the test environment and its control procedures;
- the use of test tools by users, including the technical support. This is, for security reasons, not normally allowed in a simulated production environment;
- timely conveying information about testing and especially the use of test tools to users and possibly to (future) system and application managers;
- early involvement in testing will encourage users to take an active part in thinking about testing and implementation, which will increase the degree of acceptance;
- as a result of an integrated test, the best possible use will be made of resources. Staff and test facilities will be employed from a single point, and priority conflicts will be averted timely;
- the execution of an integrated test will also increase mutual understanding and thus improve communication between parties.

29.4.2 Risks, measures and considerations

The integrated test can be applied only after clear agreements have been made on a large number of aspects, including:

- responsibilities for progress, quality and reporting;
- division of quality characteristics, degree of coverage, test strategy and, if appropriate, the test techniques to be employed;
- staff and facilities to be employed by each party, but also simple matters such as working hours, travelling time, and holiday arrangements;
- management, recovery and escalation procedures;
- ownership of testware and other test deliverables.

The reduced independence of those concerned is one of the major risks of an integrated test. Although it is possible to make formally sound agreements, conflicts may arise about all kind of matters, including:

- the employment and the amount of effort required on the part of staffing of either party;
- the release of common test environments and data;
- quality of release for the integrated or acceptance test;
- test coverage agreed and achieved;
- defects, their urgency and recovery cycles;
- different understanding of test approach and terminology.

One of the risks of an integrated test is the late discovery that one of the parties has not prepared the test satisfactorily. At this stage, it is often impossible to repair the damage.

Calling in a third party with the authority to check is one way of avoiding conflicts or the late discovery of inadequate preparations for testing. This task may be performed by a quality assurance employee, who checks periodically whether the agreements are adhered to, and whose recommendations are regarded as binding.

It should be noted that a system-development process in which one or more parties operate on the basis of a fixed price, and possibly a fixed date, is less appropriate for an integrated test. For an integrated test, a considerable number of agreements will have to be made throughout the frequently extensive contractual negotiations relating to the fixed commission. These agreements will require a lot of discussion during their preparation and application, not only between the parties themselves, but also with their respective accountants and perhaps lawyers. Consequently, the cost of an integrated test may well exceed the expected benefits.

29.5 Client/server testing

29.5.1 Introduction

More and more information systems are operated in areas other than classic mainframe infrastructures. The limitations of mainframe environments inhibit an organization's ability to respond quickly to changing market requirements. It must be possible for services and products to be developed with competitive speed. The slogan these days is 'time to market'. To operate effectively in this context, the user will want reliable information to be available quickly, and will therefore require a flexible information infrastructure. In order to achieve this objective, the user will wish to employ all available applications and data directly from his or her workstation. The integration of hardware and applications, tools and (local) networks, open systems and so on will be required for this purpose. Client/server technology may involve all these facilities.

A wide range of technologies and development methods is usually linked to the client/server technology, including:

- graphical user interfaces (GUIs, see section 29.6);
- object-oriented (OO) development (see section 29.7);
- rapid application development (RAD) and evolutionary system development (see section 29.8).

The almost unlimited distribution of applications and data, the multiplicity of (different) components, and the related technologies and development methods make the client/server technology particularly interesting for testing. In the following sections, the technologies associated with client/server systems (GUIs, OO and RAD) are discussed. It is not our intention to explain the various technologies in detail or to value them. The vast differences between products and the unpredictability of technological developments impose restraints to the authors in this respect. Testers will have to make themselves thoroughly familiar with the relevant circumstances – as they do for any test process – and subsequently use the TMap standard as the basis for the organization and execution of their test processes.

29.5.2 Definition and properties

The client/server technology consists of a large number of elements for development as well as for operational purposes. It is pointless to seek clear-cut limits to the composition of these elements, since the phenomenon changes daily and no one can predict what the outcome will be. For the time being, the phenomenon client/server may be described as a technology by which information systems are subdivided into independent processes, initiated by clients and executed by servers, using a standard communication protocol.

For testing purposes, it is important to be clear about the logical design of the client/server applications. Client/server systems are generally divided into three logical parts (Figure 29.4):

- presentation (screens and reports)
- application (software)
- data (including integrity rules).

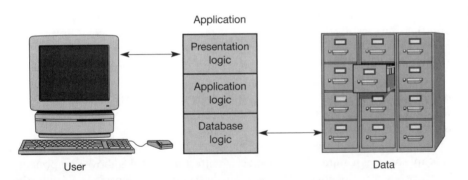

Application

Figure 29.4
Logical application
architecture

User

Data

This logical distinction plays a major role in the physical distribution of components of an application over several hardware platforms linked by means of a network. In this context, Gartner Group (1995) identified five client/server architectures within which the logical application components are distributed among client and server (Figure 29.5):

● distributed presentation
● remote presentation
● distributed functionality
● remote data access
● distributed data management.

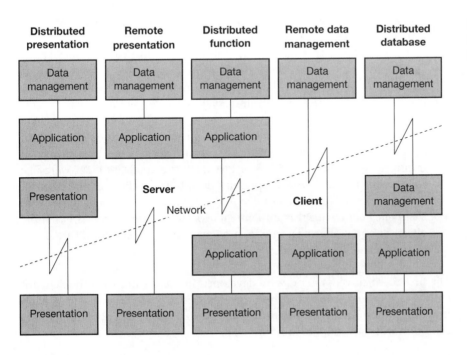

Figure 29.5
Client/server
architecture

This distribution has a major effect on testing, particularly on the test strategy and the test-specification techniques that are to be applied. Depending on the organization of the client/server architecture, there is decentralization of functionality and data, much more than in traditional environments, e.g.

- on both sides of the network;
- in several places on the client as well as the server side (redundancy);
- on various machines of various makes, and usually from various suppliers;
- in the use of various techniques, procedures and protocols.

It is an essential feature of client/server architecture that the above components or processes are implemented autonomously and independently. As a result, the data part, for example, consists not only of the tables in which the data are stored, but also the software with which the integrity rules are implemented. This prevents the inconsistencies that may occur if each of the various applications carries out its own validations and amends the data directly. This problem is avoided by accommodating data maintenance in a single autonomous process that all applications are obliged to use.

Technically, the translation from a logical subdivision to a physical distribution may be effected in many different ways. The options are linked closely to the development tools used. In practice, the following technical forms of implementation occur:

- *Structured query language (SQL).* In this form, the client comprises presentation and application software, and the server comprises the data, while SQL is used for communication purposes (remote data access).
- *Stored procedures.* In this variant, the application programs are kept as stored procedures in the database management system (DBMS). Here, the server therefore comprises both application and data. Presentation on the client side communicates with the server by way of remote procedures calls (remote presentation).
- *Transactions.* Here, the application programs are accommodated in a transaction processing monitor. This is software specialized in dealing with transactions, for instance CICS or ENCINA. The application software plays the role of the server for the presentation, but is a client of the data software (distributed functionality).
- *Distributed objects.* In this implementation form, the system is based on a object-oriented approach in which client and server communicate by way of an object request broker.

The first client/server systems were developed in accordance with the SQL principle. Since then, favor has shifted towards stored procedures and transaction processing monitoring. It is expected that the distributed object implementation form will predominate in future.

The current client/server systems were often implemented in conjunction with Windows™, GUIs, PC networks and relational database management systems (RDBMSs). In the foreseeable future, developments will continue in the direction of wide area networks (WANs), workflow management (WFM), groupware, etc. This development will result in increasingly complex client/server systems, which will demand a sound and in-depth approach to testing.

29.5.3 Test strategy

Testing a client/server system should be organized in the same way as any other test process. Its specific features, however, give rise to a number of specific points that need to be considered when test strategy is discussed. In this section, special attention is devoted to the specific aspects of testing and quality characteristics that are of importance here.

Functionality

Client/server systems have a modular structure, since they are divided into independent autonomous processes. This is an advantage in functionality testing. The principle of incremental testing is very suitable here. Incremental testing means that the elementary building blocks are tested first, then the components that make use of these elementary building blocks, and so on. The integration test is executed after the various components have been tested separately. The following approach to incremental testing is generally applicable to client/server systems:

- *Data*. First the components that create data storage are tested. Here, too, an incremental approach may be adopted. The integrity rules of individual attributes should be tested first (limit values, defaults, etc.). Then the integrity rules concerned with the relations between attributes within a single entity are tested and consequently between entities. Finally, the functions by which the data can be accessed are tested.
- *Application*. In testing, the application the components and/or the functions are tested with which the processing has been implemented. Once it has been established that data processing functions correctly, all this test needs to do is focus on processing algorithms. They are tested one by one, and subsequently their inter-relationship is tested.
- *Presentation*. Finally, the user interface is tested. By this stage, there is no further need to focus on the correct operation of functions, which are called by the user interface. However, it must be checked whether the correct function is called. The user interface of a client/server application is often a GUI. The special approach required for testing GUIs is described in general terms in section 29.6.

In some client/server systems, components are reused. If greater use is made of components of this kind, which have been tested thoroughly already, the main emphasis will be on the integration tests. It should be noted that the incremental approach to testing described here works only when the client/server concept has been applied in accordance with the definition. If the data, application and presentation have not been set up with sufficient autonomy and independence, then the test process will become considerably more complex.

Operational reliability (integrity of the database)

In a client/server architecture, there may be several DBMSs, which may be in different physical locations. Even linked entities may be distributed over several locations. There may be clients who approach the data via the server in a protected manner, but there may also be some clients who approach the data directly. In practice, the increase in the architecture's complexity may, if testing is inadequate, lead to inconsistencies in the database and hence poor performance. To preserve the integrity of the data in the database, the following aspects should be considered during testing:

- *Autonomy of the (database) server*. This is relevant if the databases can be called (and updated) in various ways, e.g. by way of a low-level interface, intermediate server layers that have to guarantee the consistency, or an end-user tool. A detailed analysis should prove whether the direct approach to the data may upset the required consistency and integrity. In this case, test cases should be created for verifying all integrity rules that should apply to the database in respect to the various approaches.
- *Multiple access*. During testing, the inter-related data are read and updated simultaneously by several clients. This may lead to problems with inconsistency and performance due to locking problems.
- *Message overload*. A message overload is tested by means of a stress test. As many actions as possible for approaching the database are generated. In this way, the database server is tested for sensitivity to stress. Possible consequences of stress sensitivity include omission of updates and perhaps also performance problems.
- *Roll-back, back-up/restore*. If there are several linked DBMSs, an extensive test should be executed in respect of the roll-back mechanism and back-up and restore procedures.

Robustness

Even client/server systems that have been tested thoroughly may, in practice, have many problems of robustness. The application may loop, the system may crash, or the performance may be greatly reduced for no apparent reason. This kind of problem is not usually detected during testing if a structured test focusing on functionality is the only one executed. Supplementary tests are needed that simulate the extent and, as much as possible, the unpredictable nature of its practical use, and also allow for the diversity of the environments. The following tests may be executed when the robustness of a client/server application is tested:

- *Randomizing events*. The largest possible number of predictable situations that may occur in practice are created during this test. Many different combinations of actions (events) are generated in order to simulate the largest possible number of practical situation in which an application might be placed.
- *Transaction marathon*. This test checks whether a deterioration in the performance level occurs during the long-term use of an application. Contrary to the purpose of randomizing events, the objective here is not to try to crash the application as a result of a specific combination of events but to attempt to achieve this situation on the basis of quantity and duration. In the course of this test, defects relating to the incorrect use of system resources are most likely to be detected.

The execution of this kind of real-life test needs to be supported adequately by test tools.

Portability

Because users often do not have exactly the same configuration at their disposal, tests should be executed in order to establish whether applications continue to function correctly in different configurations. This applies to both client and server. Especially in decentralized organizations, the same system is often implemented in several locations and therefore configurations. If testware is available from former tests, e.g. of the functionality test, it may be reused, perhaps with the aid of a tool, to verify whether the system continues to function correctly in a (somewhat) different environment. It is important to test whether the exchange of data between the various parts of the client/server system continues to function properly. Tests should also be executed to find out whether existing systems continue to function correctly if the new application is added to the environment.

It is, of course, possible to execute this test only if the various configurations are available to the test team. There are two possibilities:
- The test environment contains all required configurations: this is the ideal situation, but it is also costly and therefore often unrealistic.
- The test is executed in the production environment outside office hours: a number of additional measures are required for reasons of security and privacy.

In the ideal situation, all tests are executed on all configurations. In practice, however, it will nearly always be necessary to make a representative selection of the tests that are to be executed and the configurations, based on a risk analysis.

Security

The security and authorization requirements for a client/server system are basically the same as for any other kind of system. The implementation of the accompanying measures, however, is more complex as a result of the distribution of the data, the application and the presentation logic. The security measures should therefore be applied to a large number of client and server components. This creates the risk of elements being forgotten, measures counteracting one another, or being inconsistent, etc. Testing security in a client/server system consequently acquires an extra dimension.

The following approach to testing security may be adopted:

- Making a checklist of essential security measures based on current requirements.
- Making an inventory for each set of measures showing in which client/server component(s) the measures should have been implemented. This will provide a matrix of security measures versus client/server components.
- Testing whether the individual measures have been implemented correctly, e.g. by using the semantic test technique.
- Establishing whether the various are coordinated properly, and together cover the security requirements adequately.

Maintainability

There are generally two main aspects that need to be managed: the data and the software and/or the application. In client/server systems, an extra dimension is added, since both data and software may be distributed and interactions are possible between the various operational applications. This increases the complexity and therefore the risks associated with management, and makes maintainability something that needs to be considered when client/server systems are tested. Extra attention should be paid to:

- back-up and restore facilities, especially in respect of tables distributed over various locations;
- the way in which data and software are distributed;
- version and configuration management, particularly because of the great diversity of components and the fact that components are used by several applications.

29.5.4 Other points to be considered

As explained above, the tester in a client/server environment is faced with new or anomalous situations in many areas. This section lists a number of other points that require consideration. They may be used as a checklist when the test strategy is developed, and also during the execution of a test in a client/server environment:

- Study the way in which the client/server application has been created, and make good use of this knowledge when deciding on the approach to be adopted.
- It is advisable to begin actual testing at the earliest possible stage. The tester may sometimes even take the initiative to start incremental system development. This provides learning points early on, not only for the tester but also for the developer. Experience has shown that this kind of approach will benefit the quality of the system.

- For large client/server systems, draw up a master test plan that indicates clearly who is to test which part of the system and in what depth. This prevents duplication and/or the lack of specific tests.
- When testing, pay special attention to the integration of applications. Also take into account word processors or spreadsheets that form an integral part of the system.
- When testing, take into account the (sometimes considerable) complexity and above all the diversity of hardware and systems software, including the accompanying networks. This may give rise to application defects resulting from the underlying technical infrastructure.
- Pay attention to the installability of the application in various environments.
- Testing client/server applications requires special tools that are compatible with the technical aspects of the client/server application. They should, for example, be able to deal with GUIs, be able to test the various components by way of interfaces, and be capable of generating load on the servers and the network. A number of tools geared specifically to client/server systems are available.
- The organization and the lifecycle model of testing must be geared to each other. By definition, there is not just one test team that executes the tests after the test object has been supplied. Testing the whole system may be spread over various test teams of various compositions, which carry out activities (in time) independently of one another. The master test plan referred to earlier in this book is clearly essential in situations of this kind.

29.6   Graphical user interfaces

The transformation from character-oriented to graphics-oriented software for user interfaces also requires a transformation in test methods and, for the time being, a greater test effort. GUIs are distinguishable from traditional interfaces by a large number of user-friendly features, including:
- control and feedback at a glance on a single screen;
- easy exchanges between applications;
- the use of illustrations alongside the text;
- reduced typing by using clicking and dragging instead;
- movable windows in variable sizes.

A number of levels may be identified for testing purposes:
- individual windows;
- interaction between windows;
- individual applications;
- interfaces between applications.

The various screen attributes, such as buttons and boxes, also need to be considered in the above context. Aspects such as screen filling, use of fonts, use of keyboard and mouse, dealing with errors, consistency of screen layout, releasing memory space, etc. also require attention. Despite the fact that user-friendliness is one of the prime reasons for the development of GUIs, a specific test focusing on this aspect should not be overlooked. GUIs are not, by definition, user friendly.

It is important to organize the GUI tests at the indicated levels. The tests are set up in overlapping order, with the operation of an attribute or component being approved after each test, up to and including the integral operation of the total interface.

Perhaps even more than in other tests, the number of test situations in GUI tests is unlimited. It is advisable always to analyze carefully where things can go wrong. Part of the test is about analyzing the development process and the tools used for it. In this respect, note that specific knowledge of the way the development tool works is of importance. Putting a lot of energy into testing the development tool should be avoided, however necessary it may sometimes be.

It is highly recommended to use test tools when testing GUIs. Record and playback tools, which may (re)test the many screen interactions accurately and quickly, are very useful – or even compulsory.

29.7   Object-oriented development

29.7.1 Introduction

Object orientation (OO) is increasingly popular, especially among developers. Customers switch over to OO because developers indicate that by doing so they can build systems quicker and adapt in a simpler and cheaper way. In addition, customers like to use state-of-the-art technology.

OO contains both the methodology and the technology to build systems. In the OO development methodology, the system to be built is modeled in terms of objects. An object represents the data and the behavior of one appearance from the real world (e.g. the person 'John Johnson'). While analyzing the system, an inventory is made of objects that play a role and which interactions exist between objects. By using the case modeling technique, the behavior of the system and the way it is used may be described in terms of 'actors' and 'use cases' (Jacobson *et al.*, 1992). An actor is a representation of a user, and a use case is a logical connected series of actions executed by this user with the system. For instance, the placing of an order by a client might be a use case.

By OO programming, the object-oriented models are realized and classes are programmed, from which objects are created during execution of the programs. The classes are the blueprint of the objects that are created and manipulated by the system, for instance the class 'Person'.

Important concepts in developing and programming object-oriented systems are inheritance, polymorphism, and information hiding and encapsulation:

- At inheritance, there is a matter of a hierarchy where lower classes automatically take (inherit) the properties of higher classes in the hierarchy. This technique is used to isolate the common properties of different classes, and to describe them solely in a higher class. For instance, the common properties of the classes 'Male' and 'Female' may be described in a single class 'Person'. The classes 'Male' and 'Female' are 'specializations' of the class 'Person'.
- Polymorphism means that whoever starts an object should not know what the (specialized) class of that object is. This implies that existing software should change less or not at all if new (specializations of) classes are built.
- In OO, the concept of information hiding is applied strictly. The internal structure of objects of the data and the functionality is screened completely from the outside world. This phenomenon is called encapsulation. Data in the object may not be updated or consulted directly. An object may be manipulated only by the activation of its methods.

Inheritance, polymorphism and information hiding/encapsulation are regarded as important elements that improve the reusability and the maintainability of systems.

For the sake of readability, the term 'object' is used when programming 'classes' is meant.

In order to achieve a specific test approach for object-oriented systems, we must discuss the most important disciplines involved, and the influence the application of OO has on them.

29.7.2 Specific risks for object orientation

In general, most acceptance testers (and/or users) are used to test incrementally, i.e. from function level via subsystem level to system level. If they have to test object-oriented systems, they will tend to do the same, i.e. start by testing the single objects. Testers soon find out that they lack the technical expertise to fathom the behavior of objects. Moreover, it turns out that testing of a subsystem level is not a matter of grouping a number of objects that are already tested. Objects do not belong to a subsystem. This is the notorious pitfall of testing object-oriented systems. One should realize that testing details of objects is not the same as testing a detailed business functionality.

In reality, the developers and the users represent two completely different worlds. Because testing is about reducing risks, and because developers and users have their own views on the risks involved, this will lead to two test strategies.

The developer's point of view

One of the main reasons for developers to apply OO is the realization of flexibility and maintainability while using reusable building blocks. This is a long-term aim that normally will require an extra investment to develop and build such building blocks. Under time pressure, developers will be tempted to choose a pragmatic, short-term solution for a particular problem, which will ultimately damage the flexibility and maintainability. Moreover, they deal with the technical characteristics of OO that ease the building but often complicate the testing. This leads to problems and risks from the point of view of the developer, including:

- *Will the design decision hurt the long-term aims?* An example of such a problem is the realization of a variant of an existing business product. This may be achieved by the creation of a new subclass. Wrong choices in this aspect may lead to an obscure tree of classes and hence a badly maintainable system.

- *Which code will actually be executed while carrying out a particular test?* Thanks to the powerful mechanisms of inheritance and polymorphism, the system decides at run time which code is applicable at that moment and has to be executed. Moreover, objects may start an event in other objects at their turn in a kind of a chain reaction. This makes it very difficult to master completely the situations to be tested, and to predict and analyze the results.

- *What is happening inside during the execution of a particular test?* Data in the object may be consulted only by especially programmed functions (methods) of that object. Data that are used solely within the object are fully invisible and unapproachable even for the users of these objects. This far-reaching form of data encapsulation reduces the chance of inconsistent data, but also makes the way of processing within the object invisible. This makes it more difficult to check the intermediate results of the test, and more difficult to 'debug'.

The user's point of view

The user wants an information system that supports their business processes. In this aspect, they do not care whether the system is built by a classical development method or by OO – the user deals with the same risks and has the same need to test. The main noticeable difference for the user in the application of OO is at the level of the kind of product they receive. Instead of receiving specific programs for each single business application, the user gets a set of objects which interact in such a way that the desired business functionality is realized. Moreover, the objects are not made specifically for particular business applications but may be a part of many different applications. This leads to the following problems and risks from the user's point of view:

- *Does the set of objects realize exactly the desired business functionality?* It is inherent to reusability that the programmed classes can be used in several applications. This means that the classes are programmed by preference in such a way that they are generally applicable, independent of specific applications that make use of these objects. This implies that objects are often capable of doing more things than needed by a specific application. Together with the high degree of interaction between objects, this makes the system behavior unpredictable to some extent.

- *What is the impact of installing new versions of objects?* In order to build a new (version of an) application, it may be necessary to adapt several objects. These objects, however, may well be used by other applications. These applications may then function unintentionally in a different way or even crash. The risk is more threatening by the fact that the customer often does not know exactly which applications use which objects.
- *Do the objects function properly in a large-scale production environment?* OO is a new technology of which there has been relatively little experience and where defects by bad programming have not yet been banned. In fact, there are studies that even show a deterioration in terms of continuity and maintainability (Hatton, 1998). Some defects manifest themselves simply in large-scale situations – performance problems and memory leakages are notorious problems of OO systems in production.

A test approach integrating both points of view

The test approach of OO consists of two elements:

1 The demarcation of two test types, that are separately implemented and executed.
2 The coordination of these test types by a master test plan.

The first element in the test approach is the distinction of two fundamentally different strategies. These are based on the two different worlds of developer and user with their different expertise, their points of view to OO, and the related risks:

- *Testing 'in the small'*. This is about low-level tests in a development environment. The emphasis is on the technical OO characteristics and the detailed behavior of the objects. This is the test type that most people think about when testing of OO is mentioned.
- *Testing 'in the large'*. These are high-level tests in the production lookalike environment. It is not about the correctness of the objects but the extent to which they are appropriate to reach the business aims.

The second element in the test approach is to determine to what extent there is interaction between the worlds of user and developer. If necessary, special coordination between the two test types must be organized. If the involvement of the customer does not go beyond the purchasing of the ready-to-use final product, they will execute their own acceptance test only in the large. If the customer orders the delivery of a tailor-made solution, generally during the development process there will be close cooperation between the developer and the customer. In this case, it makes sense to tune the test activities in the small and in the large, and to coordinate with a master test plan. A tailor-made solution involves a growth scenario and requires a well-organized configuration management. As soon as new or changed objects come through the testing in the small successfully, they may be passed (possibly by group) to a stable test environment to be tested in the large. Damage to existing applications by these new objects is prevented by the continuous execution of regression tests, preferably automated, thus enabling the OO system to grow in a safe and controlled way.

29.7.3 Testing in the small

In testing in the small, the emphasis is on specific OO characteristics and the technical details. Detailed knowledge and experience of OO technology is needed. That is why testing in the small is typically the domain of developers and OO programmers. In order to reduce the risks from the developer's point of view, the test strategy should contain special measures regarding the cornerstones lifecycle and infrastructure.

For the lifecycle:

- *Evaluation.* For the long-term aims (reusability, flexibility and maintainability), it is crucial that the OO system is well designed and that the programmers build according to this design. For instance, it is vital that the hierarchical class structure should not be too deep or too wide. Evaluation and the use of an OO-specific checklist are powerful measures to prevent problems of this kind. Tools that state complexity or analyze interdependencies between classes may have a supporting role here.
- *Low-level module tests of class libraries.* These do not really differ from traditional unit tests. For OO in particular, it is important to strive for at least 100 percent statement coverage due to the generally applicable character of objects.
- *Integration tests.* An integration test should be carried out to ensure that the interaction between various objects leads to the desired business functionality. The test basis for the design of such test cases consists of the interaction diagrams from the use case modeling technique (Jacobson *et al.*, 1992). The interaction diagrams describe at a detailed level which objects are involved while executing a use case, and how they interact. Use cases are a useful reference for logical test cases, and the detailing to object level helps the low-level tester to track and analyze intermediate results (debug trail).

For the infrastructure:

- *Extra code for testability.* To obtain detailed information about the behavior of an object, it may be necessary to add code. For instance, extra functions may have to be programmed to consult internal data or to initialize particular desired values. Such extra code for testing is sometimes called 'hooks' because it gives the tester a hold to penetrate to the core of objects. In organizations with a mature development process, and that feel strongly about 'design for testability', this is common procedure.

- *Test driver to manipulate objects*. Objects usually cannot be manipulated by the standard user interface. A special interface layer should be built to activate the objects with the desired parameters, and to collect the resulting output from the objects to compare the results with the predicted ones. This usually leads to a special test system (also called test engine or test harness) that is built with the same OO technology as the objects to be tested. This is complex software that preferably is designed in such a way that it supports automated testing. Modern test-automation techniques, such as data-driven testing, (see Chapter 27) are particularly applicable here.

29.7.4 Testing in the large

In testing in the large, the emphasis is on business functionality and the suitability for use in production. This is typically the domain of business experts and acceptance testers. The test approach is largely the same as for traditionally developed systems. The impact of OO at system level from the user's point of view leads to some test types that deserve extra attention in the test strategy:

- *Business functionality tests and regression tests*. It is here that control is exerted over whether the combined action of the set of objects leads to the desired business functionality and does not touch other applications. The main test basis for the development of test cases consists of the use case model (which describes the use of the system) and the administrative organization procedures (which describe the business processes that should be supported by the system). The emphasis should be on the correct course of total business transactions and not so much on input validations. The latter is realized perhaps completely within a particular object, and would have been covered while testing in the small. This is an example of how a master test plan may have an additional value.
- *User-friendliness tests*. Due to the inheritance mechanism, objects automatically inherit a particular behavior that may be undesirable. If a particular object is changed on request, the user may find that other objects do not function smoothly any more. One cannot presume that a new release does not affect the user-friendliness, and this should be taken into account when deciding whether a proposal for changes should be honored or whether stated defects should be resolved.
- *Security tests*. Security rules may be realized within an object by implementing rules in the class concerned. This means that the software that is enforcing the security is scattered through the information system. This makes the total view on security obscure and increases the chance of holes, inconsistency and redundancy.
- *Installation and configuration tests*. Installing new OO applications usually entails installing many objects in various locations and directories. It is important to check whether the set of objects is complete and has the right version. The actual composition may, however, differ with each user's con-

figuration and platform. Moreover, the possibility that identical objects with another (usually older) version have been installed is dealt with correctly. Obviously, a good configuration management is essential.
- *Performance and load and stress tests.* It should be tested explicitly whether the system continues in large-scale environments under realistic load – the notorious problem areas of performance and memory leakages should be paid explicit attention.

29.7.5 The future

OO is an important step to more flexible and maintainable software. The next step in this evolution seems to be component-based development (CBD). Here, reusable building blocks of a higher level (e.g. the complete billing process) are built, usually applying OO technology. This development shows a sharpening of the demarcation between the two different worlds of developer and user. The testing of objects and components will increasingly be the exclusive responsibility of the developers and will not matter to the customer.

29.8 Rapid application development and evolutionary system development

29.8.1 Introduction

Several kinds of novel development methods are being used to find solutions quickly and to reduce the limitations of the waterfall method as much as possible. Firm definitions of the various methods do not exist (yet). In broad outline, the emphasis in rapid application development (RAD) is on specifying, prototyping and creating system components in small teams of users and developers, whilst making use of the most advanced tools. The evolutionary approach may basically suggest RAD, but it places more emphasis on the step-by-step development or adaptation of small system components in order to reach the ultimately desired total solution. There are other methods, such as iterative application development (IAD) and the dynamic systems development method (DSDM). Whatever the differences, in this kind of situation it is important for the tester to concentrate on what system development is doing and how it is being done, i.e. what products will be supplied, and when are they to be expected? In this section, the term RAD will be used for all types of evolutionary development methods.

Testing in development processes of this kind is easier if the agreed method is applied consistently. The subdevelopments may be regarded as roof tiles, each of which undergoes its own test process. Both the test basis (the specifications) and the test object are established like overlapping tiles and may, as such, serve as input for the specification and execution of white-box and black-box tests. There are corresponding test cycles depending on the development approach and internal release sequence. The major difference between RAD and the traditional waterfall method is the way in which the various (intermediate) products are created. The number of different versions is a multiple of the number applicable to system development by means of the waterfall method; the specifications are adapted continuously, as is the corresponding software. Basically, each new version should be tested fully. The use of adequate test tools can help to limit the ever-threatening shortage of time in this kind of process.

The relationship between test cases and specifications is a very important aspect of testing during system development processes of this type in which a large number of temporary versions of the ultimate information system are completed. Functionalities are added, changed or removed in each new version. A new functionality results in one or more test cases being added. If an existing functionality is removed, then the corresponding test cases should also be removed. The situation, however, is often more complex in reality since several functionalities, rather than just one, are often tested with a single test case. In practice, the relationship between functionality and test cases is not one to one but usually one to n, or even n to m. This complex relationship between functionality and test cases makes the maintenance of test cases for the purpose of testing new versions more difficult. Which test cases should be changed or even removed? It is therefore essential for the relationship between functionality, consisting of the test object and corresponding specifications, and the test cases (an extensive two-dimensional matrix) to be established clearly at the outset, and then to be maintained meticulously in order to ensure an adequate and controlled test process. All this will result in an approach that may be regarded as a configuration management approach. A change is analyzed, after which the relevant identified configuration items (specifications, programs and test cases) can be adapted. The availability of (configuration management) tools is obviously an essential condition for applying this approach. The approach basically combines internal and external product control (as described in section 5.4) to form a single type of product control: high-level configuration management for the benefit of both developer and tester.

It is important to note that the purpose of RAD is to deliver an adequate system in a short period of time. It will not be the perfect solution, but it will be an adequate one for the business needs, and it will be acceptable for the users.

29.8.2 Problems with testing rapid application development

Most RAD methods concentrate on system development and pay little or no attention to the impact on testing. If anything is said about it at all, it is usually an effort to squeeze traditional test approaches into the RAD cycles. In practice, this often leads to compromises, resulting in lower quality or delays in system delivery.

Some special problems in testing RAD are:

- For preparing test cases, testers require detailed specifications and sufficient time. In RAD cycles, specifications are not ready until the very end.

- Even if all component parts of the system have been tested in each RAD cycle, this provides no confidence that the system as a whole will work as intended. A separate system test in a controlled environment is still needed. This may have a negative effect on the rapidness of the project.
- Some aspects of the system cannot be tested effectively in the informal RAD environment. Examples are performance issues and integration with other applications.
- The customer may insist on an additional, independent acceptance test in spite of the users' responsibilities and authorizations in the project.

There seems to be a choice between two bad situations:
- A tester may forget about structured testing, and just test whatever is possible at any given time in the RAD cycles. The project will retain its rapidness, but confidence in quality will be low.
- A tester may stick to structured testing, prepare tests on the basis of the final specifications, and carry them out in a controlled environment. Quality will be high, but the project will no longer be rapid.

The next sections describe a solution to this dilemma: the concept of negotiability. It offers testers a view of the cause of their testing problems and provides them with a workable solution. Often, the cause of the problem lies in the way in which RAD is (incorrectly) implemented in the organization.

29.8.3 The negotiability concept
The problems concerned with testing in RAD situations should not result in disqualifying RAD itself. There are many examples of successful RAD projects, including:
- small projects
- simple functionality
- users decide on functionality and presentation.

It is a characteristic of RAD that developers and users work together to negotiate a suitable solution. In fact, whenever users and developers can truly negotiate about how the system should work, RAD works fine. In situations in which there is no room for negotiation, RAD will tend to create confusion. This is the essence of the negotiability concept. Some examples of negotiable issues are listed below. The system under development will work adequately independently of what is finally decided about these issues: there are no wrong choices, that directly cause business loss.
- Which functionality will be presented in which screen or window?
- Which information will be presented, and in what layout?
- What is the best query for retrieving the required information?

- What options must be given with a function?
- What are default values, error messages and input validations?

Examples of non-negotiable issues include:
- When is authorization required, and by whom?
- Which VAT percentage is applicable?
- What discounts are permitted, and for which products?

Decisions on these non-negotiable issues cannot be made by users and developers alone. The customer will want to check the results and formally agree to them. Non-negotiable items in a RAD project are often the source of problems. Because the item is not negotiable, certain rules exist. Developers must know these rules in order to build the item correctly, and testers must know them in order to test it. Each non-negotiable item needs to be planned and managed separately; this is actually achieved more easily with traditional development methods.

29.8.4 A test approach to rapid application development

In order to avoid the RAD testing problems, it must be understood that some elements are suitable for development under RAD and some are not, even within one IT project. This section describes a test approach that uses the negotiability concept as the key to decide which situation applies. The steps are summarized here:
- Identify the non-negotiable items in the project.
- Test the non-negotiable items in a classical structured way in a controlled test environment.
- Test the negotiable items in the RAD environment in a way that corresponds to the nature of RAD.
- Coordinate the two in a master test plan.

Testing the negotiable items

The third step of the test approach mentioned above is described in more detail here. Typical RAD issues in the test approach are connected to the negotiable items to be tested. Here, the role of the tester is fundamentally different from the traditional one. Traditionally, the role of the tester is to reduce risks by checking where the product shows wrong behavior with regards to those risks. Classically, the major risk is that the product does not work as intended by the user. Therefore, the role of the tester is to check whether the product works in conformity with the requirements. When using RAD, however, the user decides how the negotiable item is built. The product that is delivered at the end of a RAD cycle is, consequently, according to the user's needs. In fact, the acceptance of the product is already performed by the user in the RAD cycle. Because the classical risk (product does not work as intended) does not exist with negotiable items in RAD, there is no need for testers to engage in the classical role of testing against the specifications. Test teams that stick to this role in a RAD project usually come out of it frustrated.

Testers should concentrate on the specific risks that apply to RAD, and engage in activities that reduce them. When items are developed and accepted in iterative RAD cycles, the major risks are:

- Does the user know exactly what he or she has accepted? In one of the evaluation meetings, the developer should have showed the product's new version and asked the user if it was according to their needs. When the user said 'yes', what exactly was it that they accepted? Did they only agree to the screen layout and the input fields? Or did they also check that correct default values were shown, that input fields were validated correctly, and that certain options became disabled under specific circumstances? The user may have evaluated the product only on a limited number of aspects, while the developer may assume that they have agreed on everything.

- Does the product still conform to former agreements after having gone through several evaluation meetings? Usually, the product needs some iterations in order to become accepted. There is a risk that changes accepted in earlier cycles are over-ruled in the next cycles, unnoticed.

Testers have new tasks in these situations related to the RAD risks mentioned above. Their value may lie in supporting the evaluation process. Testers can help users in making the correct decisions when evaluating the developers' new product version, and at the same time keep track of decisions made and changes proposed. A checklist of aspects to be evaluated may come in useful here. Testers may use their experience and expertise to point out weak spots and risky areas for further attention. It is the user's role to decide whether the product is according to their needs, it is the tester's role to identify weaknesses that appear to have been overlooked.

It is important to capture the results of an evaluation in test cases. When agreements have been reached during evaluation sessions, the tester must assure that they can be reproduced for future cycles. This is done by insisting on explicit examples of the required system behavior, the examples subsequently being treated as test cases. Record and playback tools can obviously be of help here: in later evaluation meetings, the recorded test cases are replayed, in this way checking whether the agreements of previous evaluations still apply to the new version of the product. This can be seen as a form of regression testing. In building such an automated regression test, the tester should aim for a high level of portability. The organization can benefit greatly from this regression test during the later phases of the project, when the automated test suite can also be executed for integration and production test purposes.

29.9　General impact

In general, the impact of the conglomerate client/server and related technologies and development methods is, for the time being, concentrated largely on the following aspects.

29.9.1 Applicability of TMap

TMap provides sufficient building blocks for the set-up and execution of test processes. The lifecycle model is eminently suitable, perhaps in more iterations. Most test-specification techniques are very well applicable. For testing GUIs, the semantic and syntactic test-specification techniques should be extended. The technique for developing the test strategy is suitable for establishing the test effort and the TMap building bricks to be used. The descriptions of test functions, staffing, organization and consultation structures and management provide sufficient support for the slightly more difficult setting-up of the organization and test administration. Several tasks relating to the test environment and the test tools may well require more attention.

Heavy demands will also be made on the methodological support when this kind of new development method is first introduced. The aspect of function separation will need extra attention as cooperation between developers and users increases. The set-up of the test environment and test tools is, of course, highly specific. The set-up of the TMap lifecycle model will provide a useful guide in this respect.

29.9.2 Greater focus on the development process and the employed tools

The focus will move from the test object to the development process, and particularly to the consistent application of the tools used for the purpose. Testers should study this so that they can assess the likelihood of defects. It is pointless searching for defects that cannot be made.

29.9.3 Starting from the consistent application of development standards

Tests will be tuned to the strict application of standards for matters such as modularity, OO and the use of tools. The guarantees provided by such methods and tools are used in the development of the test strategy. On the basis of the properties of the development process and tools, it may be possible to omit integration and validation tests (e.g. in the case of proper use of data dictionary systems). Such a strategy introduces the risk that deviations from the standards are not noted until a very late stage, and it may be necessary to organize extra tests for which there is usually no time available. Checks should be carried out throughout the entire development process to ensure that the standards are actually being applied. There will be a shift from dynamic to static testing, from testing to evaluation, and from validation to verification.

29.9.4 New test types and levels

New or divergent types and levels of testing will be needed for some aspects. New test techniques will be developed for testing synchronization of processes, the use of data, network components and modularity of the applications. Tests relating to performance and resource utilization will acquire a different character as a result of more widely distributed processing.

29.9.5 Technology push

Testers are faced constantly with unremitting technology push. The stability of the infrastructure, development methods and products has come under increasing pressure. The degree of innovation is extremely high, and testers will need a lot of time and empathy to keep up to date.

29.9.6 Technology immaturity

The multitude, complexity and innovative character of the applied technological tools are in themselves sources of defects, and may obstruct the proper working of the information system, even if the functional design is implemented correctly.

29.9.7 Relationship between development and testing effort

Experience has shown that technological developments are aimed first at the technical infrastructure, then at development and management aspects, and then at providing appropriate test instruments. As a result, the balance between test effort and development effort is threatened. This is aggravated further by the pattern of expectations aroused during the transformation brought about by new technologies: the test effort may be reduced considerably as it is no longer possible to make errors. As a result of the application of evolutionary and rapid development methods, the tester is, in this context, also faced with the later availability of the test basis (the specifying documentation). The test cases must therefore be developed in relatively less time without the required advanced test tools being available. The usual pressure of time during testing will therefore increase for the time being.

Testers should anticipate this when deciding on test strategy. It will therefore be necessary to seek an even better balance between:

- duration and quality of the test process;
- testing and evaluation (more evaluation than previously);
- low-level and high-level testing (more integration).

29.10 Testing packages

29.10.1 Introduction

In order to form an opinion of testing packages, it is important to be aware of the background of the phenomenon. Why do people opt for packages? What are the advantages and disadvantages? What kinds of packages are there, and to what extent are the envisaged objectives usually achieved? How does the implementation proceed, and what specific risks are there for packages? Is testing really necessary?

In this section, we attempt to provide answers to these questions, after which the special aspects of testing packages are considered. In most instances, thorough testing will be required.

Packages

Purchasing a package instead of developing software oneself occurs with increasing frequency. Instead of having tailor-made software developed, many organizations prefer to choose from the wide range of available packages. A package may best be described as a set of software and procedures for automating a part of business processes. The set should be applicable in several organizations. A package is therefore not just software, but includes documentation as well. More extensive packages also provide other products and services, such as an installation manual, help-desk, training, (control) procedures, and often testware.

Advantages

The most common reason to buy a package is to reduce costs and to reduce the time to market. Costs are saved on the resources required for system development, maintenance and therefore also testing. Throughput time reduction is achieved because the required applications can be made available almost immediately. The available training and supplier's support are other major advantages.

Consequences

Several consequences, however, put a damper on the good news. The functionality offered by a package rarely coincides with the functionality required by the organization. A certain amount of cutting and pasting is required, i.e. the package has to be customized. The same applies to the organization and the corresponding administrative procedures, and in many cases to the infrastructure as well. All this leads to a need for development, control and test capacity, including the required standards and infrastructure. One of the major risks is that people usually underestimate these consequences and realize far too late, for example, that they really require a sound test organization.

Types of package

Several types of package are available. In this book, the concept of packages is approached in the same broad terms as that of tailor-made products. The application and attendant risks determine the test strategy. In the case of packages, the test effort is linked directly to the extent to which functionality and/or flexibility may be affected. Packages in which the user has hardly any influence on functionality, e.g. word processors, need little or no test effort. Packages that can be customized as required usually call for the same amount of test effort as any other tailor-made product.

What is the appropriate package?

Supplying information is an ancillary process of primary business management. A package must fit in with such management (business process and administrative organization), and with the architecture of the information services (policy, standards, technical infrastructure and already existing applications). Experience has shown that it is hardly ever possible to find a package that fits completely. Apart from the integration with the existing information services architecture, the package usually offers insufficient functionality in some areas but too much in other areas. Obviously, the art lies in choosing the package that is most appropriate (Figure 29.6).

Figure 29.6
The appropriate
package?

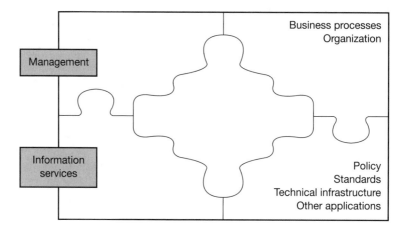

Customizing a package usually entails setting parameters for the various options and sometimes adding new functionality. In the case of more extensive packages, their own development environment is sometimes offered as well. This, in turn, must also fit, and so on. There is consequently a powerful connection between the extent to which a package needs adapting and the test effort that will be required (Figure 29.7).

29.10.2 Lifecycle

As with tailor-made software, it is highly recommended for packages to start test activities as soon as possible. Testing here may have also a major preventive effect on quality. Considering test aspects at the time of selecting a package may also prevent the occurrence of frequently expensive disappointments later on. Testability after setting and/or adding extensions is a major precondition for buying or rejecting a package. There are various selection and implementation models available for packages. Larger packages often have their own lifecycle model for this purpose (Figure 29.8)

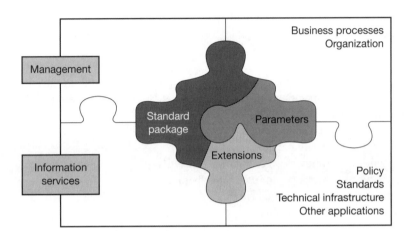

Figure 29.7
The appropriate package

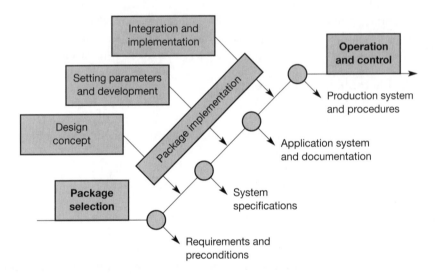

Figure 29.8
Package lifecycle

Introduction of a package

The introduction path for a package consists of three main phases: selection, implementation, and operation and control.

1 The requirements and preconditions for the package to be implemented must be established by the end of the selection phase.
2 The implementation phase consists of the activities specification and design, setting parameters and development, and integration and implementation. Specification and design provides the system specifications on the basis of which parameters are set or the package is extended if required. The system that becomes available, plus the corresponding documentation, must be integrated with the existing systems and infrastructure.

3   After an assessment of the quality – or rather the risks – the package may be used, i.e. put into operation and control.

Releases

In the event of a subsequent release, all activities of the implementation phase are repeated from specification to integration. Releases are initiated for all sorts of reasons, including:

- amendment of the package by the supplier;
- amendment of the parameter settings;
- amendment following a customized extension;
- putting new package modules into operation;
- amendments to the infrastructure;
- a combination of the above.

Testing and the package lifecycle

Testing forms an integral part of the activities during the introduction of the package, as well as in the event of subsequent releases. Whenever tests are to be executed, TMap will provide the required support, just as it does for tailor-made processes.

29.10.3 Is testing really necessary?

Depending on the type of package, testing is likely to be required in most instances. The following questions basically require a positive answer. If that proves impossible, organizing a test is at least worth considering, depending on the risks. Relevant questions are

- Does the package comply with the supplier's specifications?
- Does the package meet the user's functional requirements?
- Have the parameters been set properly?
- Are components that are not suited for use well screened off for users?
- Do the customized extensions comply with the specifications?
- Are customized extensions compatible with the package?
- Is the package compatible with existing systems, control procedures, technical infrastructure, administrative organization, etc.?
- Are the authorizations defined and implemented properly?
- Are the manuals sufficiently clear to the users?
- Have the performance requirements been met?
- Does the resource utilization remain within the set limits?
- Is training available and appropriate?
- Are the converted data correct and applicable?
- Do possible service level agreements (SLAs) also cover the package's control (and maintenance)?

What is different?

The TMap standard is suitable for testing packages, and no amendments to life-cycle, infrastructure, techniques or organization will be required. The sole differences relate to the test basis (requirements and criteria) and the test levels. That reveals itself in the determination of the test strategy.

The principal difference is in the approach. Testers will concentrate far more on not testing than they do when testing tailor-made products. Anything that is standard and applied frequently by many users (in other organizations) – and therefore well tried – does not require further testing in its unaltered form. The question people should ask when testing packages should be 'What cannot go wrong?' Things that cannot go wrong do not need testing.

29.10.4 Requirements and criteria

A number of criteria that are not relevant to tailor-made products will apply to packages. The importance of some quality characteristics is different. The requirements and criteria (the test basis) for testing packages fall into three groups:

- properties of packages;
- preconditions for package use;
- functional and non-functional quality characteristics.

Properties of packages

Packages have a number of properties that are particularly relevant during the selection and first implementation. While developing the test strategy, it is necessary to decide whether these properties should be considered during testing, and to what extent. These properties include:

- the amount of capacity required, and the operating costs related to managerial staff and technical infrastructure;
- supplied facilities for maintenance and control;
- the presence, accessibility and quality of a service and help-desk;
- the quality of supplied training, including frequency and facilities;
- the extent to which a development environment and support for tailor-made work are provided;
- the degree of quality assurance (also in respect of testing);
- the level of reliability, service and supplier's warranties;
- the organization and support in the event of releases and possible checks on alterations that have been introduced.

Preconditions for package use

Packages have some special preconditions for their use. These are basic principles that should be added to the existing policy on information services, which usually focuses on tailor-made work. Important questions in this context include:

- Are packages installed as they are delivered by the supplier? In other words, is it permitted to change or extend the package except for parameter setting?
- Will the organization and the corresponding processes (administrative organization) be adapted?
- Will the existing technical infrastructure take the lead?
- How will control be organized? Who is allowed to do what? What is the supplier allowed to do?
- Will the package's or the supplier's standards be adopted?

Functional and non-functional quality characteristics

Besides functionality, the same set of quality characteristics will apply as for tailor-made products. In the case of packages, however, some quality characteristics require either more or less test effort. The requirements relating to, for example, suitability, flexibility, portability and perhaps performance are more stringent. They will therefore require more attention on the part of the testers, whereas maintainability and continuity, for instance, need fewer tests because of the large number of existing users. The functionality of the package itself will not require much effort until people start tinkering with it.

29.10.5 Test strategy

In the case of packages, deciding on the test strategy is the best way of communicating about risks, and is the basis for making strategic choices relating to the test process. Again, the obvious purpose is to find major defects as soon as possible and at the lowest possible cost. The package's properties and its preconditions form an extra dimension when compared with the development of the test strategy in the case of tailor-made software. They will need to be translated into relevant quality characteristics, which will result particularly in test activities during package selection. Figure 29.9 shows a survey of relevant test aspects. These aspects should get the appropriate attention in the test strategy.

For testing packages, four test levels are distinguished. Because these test levels differ from the conventional TMap, this treatment concentrates on that. The four test levels are:
- tests during selection;
- standard functionality tests;
- customization tests;
- integration tests.

Tests during selection

A large number of requirements and criteria should be considered during the process of package selection. There should be no doubt about the package's characteristics, preconditions and functionality before implementation commences. This also implies largely to quality characteristics crucial to packages, including suitability and flexibility. These requirements and criteria can usually

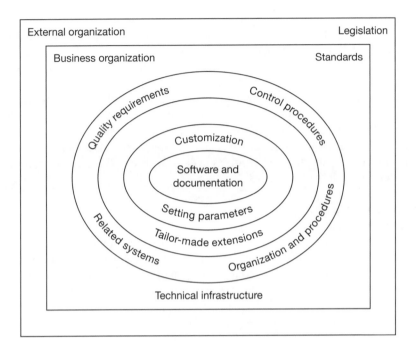

Figure 29.9
Aspects of testing

be assessed during selection in the form of both static and dynamic tests. It is obviously important for them to be executed on time.

Standard functionality tests

A process for testing a package focuses primarily on the package's standard functionality, the software and the corresponding documentation. In the event of its being unchanged, little or no testing will be required. The execution of a supplier's test may well be all that is needed. Most packages are currently provided with a standard test set, which may be used for executing a first test. During the execution of this test, it is important to assess whether the results comply with the (supplier's) predicted results. The test may be used to establish whether the package functions properly in the organization's infrastructure.

Customization tests

Adequate tests should be executed if the package needs customizing, either in the form of setting parameters or by adding tailor-made software. Both the operation of the parameter setting and the functionality of the customized software must be tested carefully. The unchanged functionality, validations, calculations and most non-functional quality characteristics are included implicitly in these tests. Any required data conversion will be tested for functionality. The most suitable test techniques in this instance are the data flow test and the process cycle test – or best of all a mixture of the two. The error guessing technique is also suitable for this purpose.

Integration tests
During the integration test, functionality is tested integrally, combined with the non-functional quality characteristics, control procedures, administrative procedures, interfaces with related systems and the functioning in the existing technical infrastructure. Quality characteristics explicitly dealt with here include performance, resource utilization, security and portability. Functionality and user-friendliness, for instance, are tested implicitly. Any requested conversions are tested with regard to throughput time and required resources. Business standards and other relevant relationships are included automatically in the tests. In addition to the data flow and process cycle test, the real-life test technique is used during the integration tests.

29.10.6 Test planning
Generic and specific test plan components
It is possible when testing packages to develop largely generic test plans first, e.g. during the introduction. For subsequent releases, the preparation of test plans may be limited to a few variable components or to specific elements. Table 29.1 provides an indication of the generic and specific components.

Table 29.1
Generic and specific test plan components

Planning activities	Generic	Specific (per release)
General review and study	X	X
Establishing test basis		X
Developing test strategy	X	X
Setting up organization	X	
Specifying infrastructure	X	
Organizing management and control	X	
Estimation and planning		X

Estimation and planning test activities
Test point analysis (TPA) is unsuitable for testing packages. Testers will therefore be obliged to rely on their own and other people's experience. It is, however, important to build up statistics so that subsequent releases may be planned with greater precision. The planning schedule for testing packages does not differ from that for testing tailor-made products. In package testing, it is extremely important for the test activities to be prepared and executed in parallel as much as possible. Improving time to market is, after all, one of the principal aims of buying packages. Just as in the case of tailor-made products, it is essential to have flexible planning that anticipates setbacks.

29.11 Testing e-business

The Internet can be described as a collection of computers that communicate with each other over a telecommunications network. This network covers the whole world. During the last few years, there has been an uncontrolled explosion of Internet use, and it seems that this current growth rate is likely to increase in the coming years. However, there has been a visible change in the way the Internet is used. Organizations no longer only publish information about their business on the Web; they also develop more complex applications that make use of the possibilities that the Internet offers. This new generation of applications offers new possibilities, but at the same time more risks, for business development. This explains the increasing demand for testing because *no risk = no test*.

This chapter looks at the testing of Internet applications. The emphasis is on applications that offer the most risk and therefore applications where testing is of most importance: e-business.

29.11.1 The Internet

First we will look at some important aspects of Internet applications. Note that our aim is not to explain all aspects of the Internet.

Application types

The Internet fulfills a versatile role in a growing number of situations. Internet applications are used for information delivery, marketing, entertainment, distribution, image building, public relations, relationship development, customer service, sales, interaction/feedback with customers, internal communications, and many other things.

The type of application is important when testing an Internet application as this determines the level of risk.

A company does not run much risk when it only publishes a homepage with its name and address details. However, if customers can buy (and pay for) articles from the company on the Internet site, then the risks are much higher. Such applications are called e-commerce. E-commerce means the buying and selling of goods and services or the transfer of money over the Internet, especially the World Wide Web.

An extension of e-commerce is e-business, which as well as sales transactions includes servicing customers and collaborating with business partners. We will use the term 'e-business'.

E-business applications can be split into two types:

- *Business-to-consumer (B-to-C, B2C)* is used by individual consumers. Examples are the sale of books, CDs or PCs. It is not usually known beforehand who the consumers are.

- *Business-to-business (B-to-B, B2B)* is used for doing business with other companies. According to Forrester (1999), the turnover generated from B-to-B applications will grow explosively in the coming years (much faster than that from B-to-C applications).

Furthermore, there are two special forms of internet applications: intranet and extranet. An intranet is a network running within an organization. Only users of the organization network can use the intranet. An extranet is an organization network available via the Internet, but only to users whose identity is verified. Extranet users consist of staff and/or business partners of the organization. Both cases are simplified versions of the 'normal' Internet because the type and number of users is known beforehand.

Architecture

The (technical) architecture of an Internet application is a form of client/server architecture. Figure 29.10 shows the components of this architecture. The user controls the application via a browser on a PC, mobile telephone, TV or other device (the client). A mobile telephone communicates first via the wireless application protocol (WAP) with the server that is connected via a fixed line to the Internet. The exchange between the client and server takes place via a network connection (with TCP/IP protocol) allowing communication with the Web server. Often, external connection is protected via a firewall located on the Web server. The Web server delivers the received information request to the application server (e.g. via the Common Gateway Interface (CGI) protocol), which in turn communicates with the database server in order to query and manipulate the relevant data. These components are not always present. For example, a site that only delivers information may require only a Web server.

Figure 29.10
Internet architecture

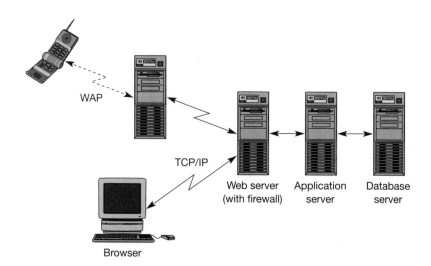

WAP

TCP/IP

Web server (with firewall)   Application server   Database server

Browser

This architecture is characterized by the fact that it comprises a large number of relatively independent components. Many of these components are standard, and are supplied by a third party. It has been estimated that 80–90 percent of the code for an average Internet application comes from third-party software. Additionally, this architecture is not fixed, and it is very difficult to keep pace with the changes in functionality. Browsers from different manufacturers are available (Microsoft Internet Explorer™, Netscape Navigator™), with different versions (IE3, IE4, IE5; NN3, NN4, etc.). In general, the application must at least be suitable for the latest browser versions, otherwise large groups of customers will not be able to use it.

Internet application components include:

- Hypertext Markup Language (HTML) pages
- Applications that that can run on a web page:
  - applets
  - Java scripts
  - plug-in applications
  - cookies
- Applications that run on the server side:
  - CGI scripts
  - database interfaces
  - logging applications
  - dynamic page generators
  - messaging agents
- Security:
  - firewalls
  - encryption
  - passwords
- The (possible) situation on the client side:
  - browsers: Netscape, Internet Explorer, etc.
  - operating systems: Windows 3.1/95/98/2000, Macintosh, UNIX, etc.
  - types of connection: modem, ISDN, local area network (LAN), etc.
  - varying connection speed.

E-business architecture can also be seen at a higher level of abstraction that shows its relationship with other information systems in the organization, i.e. back-office systems. These information systems are meant solely for internal use and have no direct contact with the customers.

E-business systems and voice-response systems facilitate new communication channels that have direct contact with the customers. These applications are therefore referred to as front-office applications. However, these applications still make use of the traditional back-office information systems. This makes another type of architecture necessary: multi-channel architecture (Figure 29.11). Back-office applications often have to be updated to a degree so that

Figure 29.11
Multi-channel
architecture

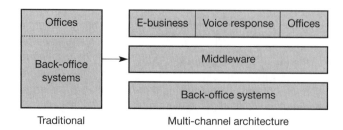

they can also be used with the new applications. Usually, a middle layer (middleware) is used to make the communication between the front-office and the back-office systems as efficient and flexible as possible.

System development

As a first step, an organization usually develops a site for the distribution of company information. The client is not an IT department but, more likely, the marketing department. The most important requirement is that the site must visually look good. As a consequence, these first developers are often not professional developers. They are more likely to be people with a more creative background, e.g. advertising staff or graphical artists. The fact that these people concentrate more on the appearance of the application than on whether it functions properly is not really a problem for these relatively simple sites.

However, the increasing professionalism of Internet sites in the form of e-business means that a site that is visually appealing is not enough. The user of such a site expects that it functions and performs well, and that financial and private (sensitive) transactions are secure. The high frequency with which updates are released means that the application should be easy to maintain and adapt. Therefore, the demand for professional software engineers to develop technically complex e-business applications is increasing.

The high update frequency combined with short time to market means that it is important that the development period is as short as possible. Usually, a project with a short development period is set up in order to get a first release with limited functionality quickly into production. The functionality is extended with the following releases. Due to this kind of system development and maintenance, the use of the traditional waterfall method is not required. Instead, some sort of RAD approach is used. In practice, it seems that all these approaches have two things in common: there is minimal documentation, and many ad hoc decisions are taken. This, of course, generates a conflict of interest with the importance of a well-designed and maintainable application.

29.11.2 More, less or another way of testing?

The degree to which the testing approach is different for an e-business application can be split into two parts:

- How does an e-business application differ from a traditional application?
- What effects do these differences have on using TMap?

What is different?

The most important generic differences between an e-business and a traditional custom-made application are:

- Time-to-market is even more important for e-business applications. The necessary time needed to get an application into production is no longer measured in years or months, but in weeks or even days.
- For the majority of organizations, e-business applications are new, therefore it is also a new communications channel for customer and supplier contact. The introduction has a far-reaching effect on the existing procedures of an organization.
- Often, the department that has led the development of an e-business application is not the IT department, e.g. it can be led from marketing or sales. Usually, there is little IT knowledge in these departments.
- Higher demands are made of aspects such as security, user-friendliness and performance. Specific knowledge is needed to reach this higher level of quality.
- The system documentation is often of a lower quality and quantity.
- During the development of an application, a large number of standard components are used. Development involves much more integration than programing.
- The users of e-business applications, unlike the IT systems of the internal organization, are outside of the direct influence of the organization. Also, little is known about the users.
- As e-business applications are aimed at customers and the suppliers of an organization, and thus the primary business processes, the damage due to insufficient quality is much higher than when an application is used internally. With this in mind, it is often said that a competitor is 'only one click away'.
- Maintenance requires a continuous effort and investment because the application is never finished and the functionality is constantly being extended.
- The Internet changes rapidly. A large degree of change is due to the environment. New components are introduced hastily and are often unstable.

These differences affect the test process in many ways, from the test-specification techniques used, to the choice of test tools. Risk analysis plays an important role here. A risk is the estimated chance of failure in relation to the expected damage. Most of the differences described above can, in one way or another, be translated into risks. These risks have consequences for the quality attributes to be tested. These risks have consequences for what to test, and how thoroughly to test. For instance, testing the security or performance aspects is much more important than for traditional applications.

With regard to the elements of TMap, we will discuss the following:

- quality attributes
- test levels
- test basis
- lifecycle model
- techniques
- infrastructure
- organization.

Quality attributes

The overview in Table 29.2 lists the quality attributes that demand more attention when testing an e-business application than when testing a traditional application. This is a generic overview, and is not meant to replace the test strategy: whether or not to test a quality attribute, and how thoroughly to test, is always a decision to be made for each particular situation.

Table 29.2
The most important quality attributes when testing an e-business application

Continuity
Effectivity
Maintainability
Manageability
Performance
Portability/(suitability of) infrastructure
Security
Suitability
User-friendliness

As an example, it should be realized that the importance applied to the quality attributes during testing of intranet or extranet applications is normally very much different to that when testing an open Internet application. Intranet applications are not generally used for financial transactions, therefore the potential damage in case of failure is much less. The number and type of user for intranet and extranet applications is known beforehand, therefore:

- application overload can be prevented more easily (refer to the quality attribute continuity);
- the users can be trained beforehand (refer to user-friendliness);
- security is easier to organize and the risks of insufficient security are less.

Continuity

Continuity is considered to be a very important quality attribute for e-business applications. Increasing numbers of users have often overloaded applications, rendering the application no longer available. The risks are relatively high, as it is difficult to estimate the number of users beforehand, the application must be available night and day, and failure of the application means a loss of earnings. It is often quoted that due to failure, 20 percent of the transactions are lost and the remaining 80 percent are completed later.

In the USA, Forrester (1999) studied the loss of revenue when a site is down for one hour: for Amazon this is estimated at $22 500 at daily revenues of $2.7 million, and for Intel $274 980 at daily revenues of $33 million. An important element of the required continuity is the scalability: the ability to change the number of servers being used depending on the load. A term related to this is 'webfarm'. A webfarm is a group of servers that are located together in one location. The number of active servers depends on the load. Failure of a server can be recovered by activating one of the other servers.

Effectivity
Related in some ways to user-friendliness, effectivity is the way the application helps the user. Does the application have added value for the user? For example, does it simplify the sales process? An example is the possibility of searching for the required item in different ways. Another is if you find a book or CD interesting, then the site recommends other books or CDs that you might also be interested in. A further step is that the application stores information about the customer. The application can then supply the information that best suits this customer profile. The effectivity aspect is crucial for a Web site's success.

Maintainability
A feature of e-business applications is that they must be changed quickly and often. Precautions to make the application as maintenance-friendly as possible include good documentation (including test documentation), and the use of HTML pages generated dynamically from a database instead of static pages.

Manageability
A number of aspects make operating the application for system managers more complex than normal, including the large number of components, and the fact that the supplied (system administration) documentation is often insufficient.

Performance
This quality attribute is linked strongly with continuity. Will the performance of the application be acceptable? A general rule of thumb is that a user gets impatient after waiting for more than eight seconds for a web page to appear. It should be noted that overall performance depends on a number of external elements that the organization cannot control: the user's computer and modem, the telephone network and the infrastructure of the provider. The performance of an application can also be compared with that of competitor sites.

Portability/(suitability of) infrastructure

The large diversity of components that comprise an e-business application means that these quality attributes are more important than normal. Does the application work with an old browser version? Does it work with a new version? If the user does not accept cookies, then can they still use the application? If not, should the user be informed? A confusing factor for the portability quality attribute is that although standards are defined (e.g. for HTML), usually they are not adhered to. For example, the browsers from Microsoft and Netscape contain all sorts of additional functionality not included in the HMTL standard.

Suitability

At the moment, e-business applications represent a new way of working for most organizations. This means that the organization must set up staff and procedures to work with the application. It is unsatisfactory when handling incoming requests takes days. One of the most difficult aspects is keeping the information shown on the site up to date and accurate.

Security

Security is often one of the first causes for concern. Connection with the Internet means that the organization is vulnerable to undesired intrusion from outside. Furthermore, information that is exchanged is vulnerable to interception or manipulation. How sure is the customer that their credit card payment is not intercepted and misused? Generally, the following kinds of intrusion can be distinguished:

- *Unqualified entry*. The system (program, data, network traffic, etc.) is entered by people who do not have the right to do this. No changes are made, but information can be stolen. This type of intrusion can come from an internal (own staff) or external (hacker) source, and targets the infrastructure of the organization or the user, or the communication between the two.
- *Changing information/pages*. A more severe form of intrusion is when intruders actually change information, programs or Web pages.
- *Affecting availability (denial of service)*. The performance of a system can be influenced so that it is effectively no longer available. An example of this is the email bomb: a bulky message that is used to overload the handling capacity of the recipient's post box.
- *Viruses*. Programs or text (via macros) can contain viruses. Normally, a virus spreads itself first and then becomes visible. As well as infecting all of the programs on the PC of the recipient, the virus can also spread itself via the network or via email (by automatically sending itself to all of the addresses in the address list, a chain reaction occurs). When a virus exposes itself it can unexpectedly change text or even delete data from the PC.

Precautions against such forms of intrusion are the use of firewalls, virus-detection software, logging and secured transactions (secure socket layer (SSL) and secure electronic transaction (SET)) and mail (pretty good privacy (PGP)). It must be noted that security is a continuous technological struggle between intruders and system administrators. A system that is optimally secured today can become a security worry tomorrow. The security risk posed by intranet applications is less because there is no connection with the outside world. Also, this sort of application is used to disperse information rather than facilitate financial transactions where the potential damage is highest.

User-friendliness

The fact that an unknown Internet user should be able to use the application without training demands more user-friendliness than a traditional application, especially when the user can just as easily do business with a competitor. Aspects that play a part in user-friendliness are learnability, operability, comprehensibility and clarity. The following aspects are also important:

- *Attractiveness*. Is the application designed well – does it look attractive and logical?
- *Accessibility*. Can a user find the application easily? If the Internet address is not known, is it simple to find it via a search engine?

Functionality (does it do what it is supposed to do?), probably the most important attribute for testing, is not classed as one of the quality attributes requiring more attention than usual. However, testing the functionality is still very important and still demands a large part of the test effort.

Functionality

When an average e-business application does not function correctly, it usually causes more damage than a traditional application. However, the risk is also defined by the chance of failure. Currently, the functionality of e-business applications is not regarded as extensive or complex. There is also less chance of failure (although it is still present), as many standard components are used during development. The higher degree of damage is therefore compensated by the lower chance of failure, so that the testing of functionality does not demand any more attention than normal.

As so many standard components are used, testing should take care not to test these components extensively. Just as when testing an ERP package, one should ask 'What doesn't need to be tested?' For instance, user acceptance testing of the Netscape browser is a bit of a waste of time. Knowledge of the test object is indispensable. As the number of components and combinations of components is numerous, the integration of (standard) components should be an important test objective. Attention should be paid to the fact that standard components contain a certain degree of instability. During testing, this results in large number of non-repeatable defects. As it is not repeatable, the cause of the defect cannot be analyzed and therefore cannot be fixed. A well-known example of a non-repeatable defect is the locking of a browser while working with an application. It is much easier to find the cause of non-repeatable defects during low-level testing (especially the integration testing done by developers) when only a few components are tested together than during high-level testing when the complete application is tested.

Test levels
When testing e-business applications, we can use the traditional test level classification:

- unit test
- integration test
- system test
- acceptance test

along with a new test level:

- production test.

During production the application is tested to check that it still functions correctly and that the performance has not decreased. The reason for this level of test is that there are all sorts of elements (number of users, browser, provider, bandwidth, external links) that the organization has no control over. If it is not tested, a poor response from a provider or a link that does not work any longer will remain unnoticed. Another cause of performance degradation can be due to the increased use of the application. This is very difficult to predict beforehand.

Along with testing, evaluation activities such as reviews and inspections are important elements of quality control for an e-business application. All the different test aspects should be covered by one or more of the test or evaluation levels.

The coordination of the different test levels plus evaluation is very important when trying to develop an optimal test strategy: to find the most important defects as early and as cheaply as possible. To achieve this, prepare (and monitor) a master test plan (also called a validation and verification plan). The advantage of a master test plan is that it makes a coordinated overview of the test process possible, and makes it possible to share scarce knowledge and resources optimally over the different test levels.

Test basis
Testing is basically comparing. Based on defined input, the actual output of the software is compared with the expected output; the differences found are called defects. In order to determine the expected output, a point of reference, e.g. documentation, is needed. This is called the test basis. All references from which the requirements of an information system can be inferred form the test basis. From this, test cases are derived.

A RAD type of approach is normally used during systems development for e-business applications. The functionality of the application is determined in workshops by the developers and users. The quantity and quality of the system documentation is often minimal.

Possible forms of test basis are:

- *Requirements documentation*. In these documents, the objectives and requirements to be fulfilled by the application are defined. This documentation is essential as there is not a lot of attention paid to the functional and technical specifications. Business scenarios and use cases are often part of this documentation.
- *Functional and technical specifications*. This form of test basis is usually less extensive for Internet applications than for traditional applications.
- *Norms and standards*. As well as norms and standards defined for the project, existing norms and standards of the organization or even external norms and standards can be used. An example of the latter is the eight-second performance rule.
- *External references*. A competitor site is a very useful test basis.

If the documentation for a test basis is incomplete, then the testers can usually gather complementary information through interviews, attendance of workshops, (jointly) defining business scenarios, etc. (as such, the knowledge of individuals forms the test basis). A sufficient amount of test cases can therefore be defined to provide confidence in the quality of the test. Involving the test team at an early stage in the development process can facilitate the collection of information for a test basis. The test team should advise clearly on the risks involved with an insufficient test basis.

While defining the strategy, it can be agreed not to test but to measure some aspects due to a lack of requirements. The result of such a measurement could be that a maximum of 100 users can work with the application at the same time before the performance begins to degrade exponentially. Testing is more than measuring because it also expresses whether measured results are satisfactory. For instance, the resulting 100 users measured is less than the required 500 users, therefore the application will not perform as required.

Lifecycle model

The TMap lifecycle model offers five phases: planning, preparation, specification, execution and completion. This remains valid for e-business testing. The only point of attention is that acquiring a usable test basis for e-business applications demands more time than usual.

Techniques

The quality attributes to test, and the type of test basis, have a large influence on the choice of test-specification techniques. In practice, this results in the choice of informal test-specification techniques, such as error guessing.

The reuse of existing testware is an important option when developing test cases. An e-business application often contains the same functionality as the existing traditional office application, so testware of this application can perhaps be reused.

Many checklists, derived from practical experiences, are used. Below, we give some specific hints and directions for testing certain quality attributes:

- *User-friendliness and effectivity.* For the testing of this quality attribute, techniques such as eye-catching are available. These tests are usually performed in a usability lab because of the specific infrastructure required. Checklists such as software usability measurement inventory (SUMI) or Web analysis and measurement inventory (WAMMI) are also used.
- *Security.* If actual testing takes place, this is called penetration testing. In this form, ethical hackers attempt to break into the application. They have the tools and the knowledge to test the security thoroughly. Security audits are also widely used.
- *Continuity and performance.* Load and stress testing is the common term for testing the attributes of continuity and performance. The system is tested to see whether it remains sufficiently available (and the effect on performance) when subjected to normal and maximum expected load, and to find the bottlenecks. The situations to be tested are:
  - simulation of one user;
  - simulation of the average number of users expected;
  - simulation of the maximum number of users that the system should be able to handle;
  - a heavier load than the maximum expected, in order to determine the level of load at which the availability degrades markedly.

  These test situations are based on the presumption that the availability degrades slowly up until a certain level of loading, but thereafter degrades at a quicker rate (Figure 29.12). At which point(s) is the degradation to be measured? An e-business application comprises a large number of components. A first variant is to measure the response over the complete application. How long does it take before information from the database is displayed to the user? Another variant is to measure phases, e.g. between user and Web server, between Web server and application server, and between application server and database server. The choice of variant depends on the risks and how difficult it is to analyze the bottlenecks. For this form of testing the use of test tools (load/stress) is required. Employing a large number of real users to attain system loading can be done once with a lot of effort, but often not for a second time. In reality, these tests should be repeated periodically as changes are often made to the hardware and software.
- *Portability.* During the testing of different browsers, the standard settings (colors, fonts, use of Java) are often changed. Constructions that are incorrect, such as the hard coding of settings in the programing, are thus detected quickly.

Infrastructure

Test tools

A large number of test tools specific for the Internet are available. Suppliers put a lot of effort into marketing, so at conferences the testing of Internet applications seems to be synonymous with the use of test tools. A reason for the

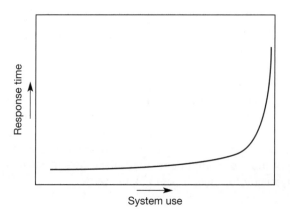

Figure 29.12
Degradation curve

popularity of test tools for testing Internet applications is that it is relatively simple to automate many of the operations. The number of test tools, some of which are free, is extensive. Operations where test tools are widely used include:

- spell-checkers
- image analysis (size, bandwidth, time to load an image, etc.)
- structure controls (dead links, loose ends, old parts, etc.)
- portability controls (differing browsers)
- monitor width controls (does the application fit smaller monitors/settings?)
- external link controls
- HTML validators
- Web page syntax and style controls.

As well as the test tools specific to Internet applications, traditional test tools can be used, e.g.

- defect administration tools;
- record and playback: as e-business applications have to be updated often and quickly, a good regression test is important. The automation of this test is recommended, especially when we consider the later tests (during maintenance) when regression tests become even more important. See also Chapter 27 for a structured approach (TAKT) used to set up these tests properly;
- load and stress: these tools generate load by simulating a large number of users in order to test whether the system still functions properly and quickly enough under the expected production load. These tools often have monitoring functionality to measure the results. For the measurement of continuity and performance, these tools are virtually a necessity;
- monitoring tools: in order to get an indication of aspects such as memory requirements, CPU use, network strain and performance, monitoring tools can be used. Data about resource use are measured and recorded. Tools specific for the Internet are available that periodically measure the availability and performance of a live production application.

Test environment

During the development of the first generation of Internet applications, there was often only one environment: the production environment. The user was often informed that the site was under construction. This is not acceptable for e-business applications, and there is usually a separate development environment. However, a separate environment for testing is not usual. It is expected that this will change in the near future due to the increasing importance of e-business applications and the testing of them. Continuity and performance testing are the main factors that make a separate environment necessary.

The large number of components used makes the installation and management of the (test) environment a complex matter.

Organization

Knowledge

The most important organizational difference between e-business and traditional applications is the knowledge required in the testing team. Knowledge can be split into the following:

- *System.* As a large number of standard components are used, it is important during testing to check that this standard functionality is not tested. This demands knowledge of the internal structure and functionality of the test object. A developer is more likely than a tester to have this knowledge. Insufficient knowledge of the architecture of the Internet application leads to time lost on tests that are not needed.
- *Testing.* As well as generic test knowledge (such as TMap), additional specialist knowledge (depending on the quality attributes to be tested) is needed. Examples of this are the testing of security, effectivity and user-friendliness.
- *Test tools.* To use a test tool, knowledge of the tool is required. The array of test tools available for Internet applications means that the test team must acquire knowledge of many of them.
- *Subject matter and organization.* As the system documentation is often insufficient, knowledge of what the application is supposed to do is an alternative form of test basis.

Different (often specialist) kinds of knowledge are required. The test manager needs good organizational skills in order to bring together multi-talented test teams with the right composition of knowledge at the right time.

Organizational forms

The different test levels need to be adjusted to correspond with the complete system-development process. The most important question to ask is whether the test level is organized as an independent process or as part of another process. The organization always depends on the situation. However, Table 29.3 shows the preferences.

Test level	Organizational form
Unit test	Part of the development process.
Integration test	Part of the development process.
System test	Part of the development process. A test leader should be appointed who leads and/or performs test activities (not development activities). This is done to prevent the test from being snowed under by the rest of the development process.
Acceptance test	Independent: can be split into a user acceptance test and a production acceptance test. It is possible to contract out some of the activities, e.g. testing the user-friendliness or the security.
Master test plan	The above test levels are best coordinated centrally by a test manager or test coordinator.
Production test	Part of the system management process; can be contracted out.

Table 29.3
Preferred organizational forms for different test levels.

Parties involved

E-business applications are often initiated by non-IT departments, such as purchasing, sales, marketing or support. Often, the application has an impact on other departments. It is important to involve these departments for their knowledge of the subject and the organization; this improves the quality of the application and therefore the degree of acceptance. It should be understood that people from these departments often have little knowledge of IT, and many make comments such as 'Testing isn't necessary, as the developer has enough knowledge of the subject.' Some test awareness activities are often necessary to make clear the importance of testing and what it (globally) involves.

Operation and maintenance

At a certain point, the application has been developed and is in production. For traditional applications, a reasonably stable situation is attained: most changes to the system and infrastructure are manageable and can be planned easily, and the use is predictable. This is not the case with e-business applications: many changes cannot be managed, and the application is much less predictable. Links to other sites suddenly do not seem valid, the search engines no longer work effectively, newer versions of browsers and system software are released, and use of the system multiplies from one day to the next. This means that more maintenance (testing) takes place more often, and it is therefore necessary to perform a regression test in order to ascertain whether the complete system still works satisfactorily. This test validates not only the functionality of the application, but also the portability and performance. A consideration is to perform this test periodically, regardless of whether a change has been made, as part of the production test. The high frequency with which this test is performed justifies its automation. This test automation is best started during the initial development phase, as most knowledge is available at this point and the automation can be used for a longer period.

29.11.3 The future of e-business testing

As with e-business in general, a number of trends can be witnessed in the testing of e-business applications that are a result of the increase of e-business and the growing competition (Figure 29.13):

- The development of e-business applications is performed increasingly in a professional way. This results in an increased awareness of the importance of testing. This, in part, means that testing in the future will be performed in a more traditional way.
- The growing importance of e-business also means that there is a switch of the effort from development to testing. This in turn demands increased technical knowledge for testing.

Generally, three types of organization (shown from left to right in Figure 29.13) can be defined:

- Group I represents the newcomers to the e-business market. These companies often have a product or service that clearly differentiates them from competitors. To take advantage of this temporary lead, time to market is extremely important. The quality of the e-business application is therefore less important. The organization relies on the differentiating power of the product or service.
- Group II organizations have gained some experience developing e-business applications. Usually they do not have much experience with IT for support of the primary business processes. Although time to market is still very important, the quality of the e-business application is also important. However, the role that testing plays is still unclear. Organizations that

Figure 29.13
Classification of
e-organizations

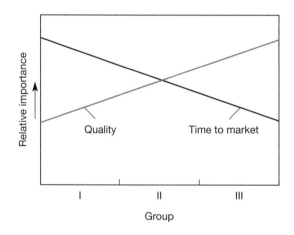

belong to this group operate in industry, the trading world, publishing and governmental services. Companies for which e-business is the primary business ('dot.com' companies) also often belong in this group.

- Group III companies have used IT to support the primary business processes for a longer time. Time to market remains important, but, the (direct and indirect) potential damage that can result from insufficient quality of the application in production is very high, therefore the quality aspect is very important. There is a belief that structured testing is important in order to determine the level of quality of the application. Organizations from the world of banking, insurance, telecommunications, some governmental services and some dot.com companies are examples of this group.

Appendix **A**
Model of a test plan

Introduction

This appendix contains a detailed example of a test plan. The example concerns the acceptance test of the information system for Watching Officially Obliged Fees (WOOF) intended for the tax office of the community of Grayhound. This information system is developed for the department that is dealing with tax regulations concerning pets. The department also keeps the tax accounts, including collection of tax regulations concerning pets. Until now, dog fees have been dealt with manually using mainly temporary employees. Several contracts will expire by the end of the year. The automated dog fee system (WOOF) should be introduced on 1 October.

Formulation of assignment

Customer
The customer of the acceptance test is the head of the local tax office of the community of Grayhound. Every week, the progress of the test project and the quality of the WOOF system will be reported to the customer.

Contractor
The test team WOOF will execute the acceptance test of the WOOF system. The activities will be referred to as the test project.

Scope
The scope of the acceptance test covers:

- release 1 of the WOOF system;
- the automated interfaces;
- the administrative organization.

The infrastructure does not belong to the scope of the acceptance test. The supplier of the infrastructure is responsible for the availability and the quality.

Aim

The aim of the acceptance test is two-fold:

- Regarding the test project, the aim is to determine the extent to which the new WOOF, which should be introduced according to planning on 1 October, meets the functional requirements of the local tax office, and the extent to which it fits in with the administrative organization. Indicate which parts of the system do not function properly so that they may be repaired. Advise on release of the WOOF system based on the test experiences and the risks.
- Regarding the testware, to compile the testware in such a manner that it can be reused during maintenance of WOOF.

Preconditions

The preconditions imposed externally to the test project are:

- the functional detailed design will be delivered to the test team by 14 August;
- the supplier of the test object, i.e. the WOOF application, delivers usable and testable units. The complete delivery takes place on 11 September;
- the test environment and test tools will be available on 1 September;
- the execution phase of the test project should be completed by 30 September;
- the users of the local tax office will be involved in the execution phase of the test project.

Starting points

The conditions imposed by the test project on third parties are:

- changes in the delivery planning of the WOOF system have to be tuned with the test management at least one week before effectuation in order to prevent a delay of the test project;
- before delivering the WOOF system, the unit and (sub)system test of the functional units concerned must have been executed;
- changes in the delivery planning of the test environment and the test tools have to be tuned with the test management at least one week before effectuation in order to prevent a delay of the test project;
- during the test project, immediate support must be available to correct defects in the test environment and/or the test tools that delay or obstruct the progress of the test project;
- the test management must be informed immediately about implemented changes in the test basis;

- during the test project, support must be available from the pet department to correct defects in the test basis that delay or obstruct the progress of the test project;
- the test project will execute a planned test twice at most (a first test and a retest);
- the effort and presence of employees of the local tax office is, according to the planning, set down in this test plan.

Test basis

The test basis is formed by:
- *Product descriptions*:
  1 general functional design, version 1.1;
  2 detailed functional design, which will be delivered according to plan on 14 August;
  3 administrative organization, which will be delivered according to plan on 14 August.
- *Standards:*
  4 standards for test products, version 2.0;
  5 the book *Software Testing: a guide to the TMap approach.*
- *User guides*:
  6 the user manual for the utilization of the test environment, which will be delivered according to plan on 1 September.
  7 the user manual for the test tools, which will be delivered according to plan on 1 September.
- *Interfaces*:
  8 all documents regarding relations and connections to neighboring systems, as far as they have not been described in the documents mentioned above, will be used for testing the functioning of WOOF as an entity. At this moment it is not known which documents are concerned here.

For creating this test plan, the following documents have been consulted:
- *Plan of approach*:
  9 project plan WOOF, version 1.0.
- *Planning*:
  10 planning development team WOOF, version 1.0;
  11 planning supplier test environment and test tools, version 1.1.
- *Other documentation*:
  12 Function point analysis (FPA) WOOF, version 1.1.

Test strategy

This test strategy is based on the assumption that the unit tests and the (sub)system tests have already been executed by the development team. Therefore, the acceptance test team will focus on testing the user point of view, i.e. black-box testing.

Well-founded choices have been made regarding the depth of the tests to be executed. Some system parts deserve more attention than others. Some properties (quality characteristics) are regarded as more important than others. The basis for this are the business risks involved.

The test strategy is the link between the significance attached to various aspects (subsystems and quality characteristics) and the tests to be executed.

Quality characteristics

In cooperation with the customer, the quality characteristics have been selected that are to be tested by the acceptance test of WOOF. The relative importance of the selected quality characteristics has been determined by weighing the risks per quality characteristic (Table A.1).

Table A.1
Relative importance of the quality characteristics to be tested by the WOOF acceptance test

Quality characteristic	Relative importance
Security	10
Functionality	50
User-friendliness	10
Performance	5
Data controllability	5
Suitability	20
Total	**100%**

Subsystems

Based on the general functional design (1) and the test assignment, the following subsystems have been distinguished:

- Principal data, consisting of the processes:
    - register factor data
    - modify factor data
    - look up factor data
    - approve/delete factor data
    - report factor data
    - register age group/tariff
    - modify age group/tariff
    - report age group/tariff
    - approve/delete age group/tariff.

- Tax assessment data, consisting of the processes:
  - register Grayhound citizen's data
  - modify Grayhound citizen's data
  - look up Grayhound citizen's data
  - approve/delete Grayhound citizen's data
  - create/print tax assessment
  - calculate tax amount
  - report tax assessment data
  - delete tax assessment register.

Based on the test assignment and the selected quality characteristics of the principal data and tax assessment data, the entire system is distinguished (Table A.2). This serves the purpose of indicating that some quality characteristics can be evaluated effectively only with the help of an integral test that tests the coherence of the various subsystems.

	Relative importance
Principal data	30
Tax assessment data	50
Entire system	20
Total	**100%**

Table A.2
Distinguishing the entire system

Strategy matrix
In cooperation with the customer, the relative importance within the information system is determined for each subsystem. A plus indicates whether a particular quality characteristic is applicable for a particular subsystem; two pluses indicates that relatively more attention is given to the combination quality characteristic/subsystem. Table A.3 is the strategy matrix for the acceptance test of WOOF.

Quality characteristic	Subsystem	Principal data	Assessment data	Entire system	Relative importance (%)
Functionality		+	++		50
Performance			+	++	5
Security		++	+		10
Suitability				++	20
User-friendliness		+	++	+	10
Data controllability			**++**		**5**
Relative importance (%)		30	50	20	100

Table A.3
Strategy matrix for the acceptance test of WOOF

Test techniques per subsystem

Based on the strategy matrix, the characteristics of the various available test techniques and the characteristics of the distinguished subsystems, test techniques have been assigned to the subsystems, as shown in Table A.4.

Subsystem	Test techniques
Principal data	Semantic test
	Data combination test
	Checklist user-friendliness
Tax assessment data	Semantic test
	Elementary comparison test
	Checklist data controllability
	Checklist user-friendliness
	Statistics on performance
Entire system	Process cycle test
	Real-life test
	Checklist user-friendliness

Effort estimation

Based on the FPA (12) and several investigated documents, an effort estimation for the test process has been drawn up using test point analysis (TPA) (Table A.5). In the effort estimation, the required effort for functional and technical support has not been included.

Activity	Test team	Users	Total effort
Writing test plan	32		32
Planning and control phase	140		140
Test management	*56*		*56*
Control	*28*		*28*
Methodological support	*56*		*56*
Preparation phase	96		96
Specification phase	408		408
Execution phase	336	112	448
Completion phase	64		64
Total hours	**1076**	**112**	**1188**

Because the creation of a test plan is not part of TPA, this is included as a separate activity. Also, the effort for the users that is required for their participation in the execution phase is not part of the TPA. Methodical support and control are also not included in the TPA calculation.

A detailed description of the TPA calculation is given later.

Test organization

The test process will be part of the test management's responsibility. They will report on a weekly and, if requested, ad hoc basis to the customer.

Test functions
Within the test project, the following test functions will be distinguished:
- testers
- test management
- methodological support
- technical support
- subject matter support
- control.

Testers
The test function contains the basic test tasks. The following tasks will be carried out:
- review of the test basis;
- specification of logical and physical test cases and initial data set;
- setting up the initial files and data;
- executing test cases (dynamic testing);
- executing checks and investigations (static testing);
- registering defects;
- preserving testware.

Test management
The test management is responsible for the planning, coordination, monitoring, controlling and execution of the test process. Test management report to the customer on the progress of the test process and the quality of the test object. The following tasks will be carried out:
- drafting, obtaining approval and maintaining the test plan;
- executing the test plan within the planning and the budget:
  - everyday control of the test activities;
  - conducting internal meetings;
  - participating in project meetings, etc.;
  - maintaining external contacts;
  - internal quality management;
  - recognizing, anticipating and reporting project risks.

- reporting on the progress of the test process and the quality of the test object:
  - creating periodical and ad hoc reports;
  - creating advise on release;
  - creating evaluation report.

Methodological support

This function supports the test process in the field of methodology. The following tasks will be carried out:

- establishing test techniques;
- creating test regulations;
- advising and supporting the application of all kinds of test techniques.

Technical support

This function supports the test process in the technical field. The control and manageability of the test environment, test tools and office environment should be guaranteed. The following tasks will be carried out:

- establishing control and maintenance of the test environment and the test tools;
- physical configuration management;
- solving problems regarding the test environment and test tools.

Subject matter support

This function supports the test process in the functional field. Subject matter support cares about the knowledge of the information system and its intended use as well as about how this has been specified functionally. They will support and advise on the functionality of the test object at:

- testability review (the specifications);
- specification of test cases and initial data set;
- executing test cases (dynamic testing);
- executing checks and investigations (static testing);
- analyzing test results and defects.

Control

Control is an administrative and logistic function. The function has the responsibility for registration of, storage of and making available all control objects of the test process. The following tasks will be carried out:

- progress control;
- supervision of test documentation;
- administration of defects and collecting statistics;
- logical control of testware, including files.

Organizational structure

Figure A.1 shows the relations and reporting lines within and outside the test team.

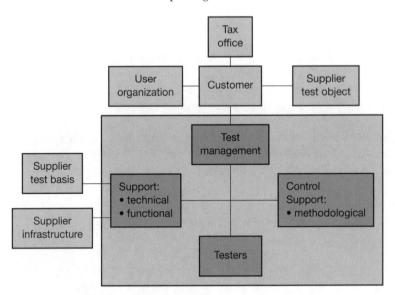

Figure A.1
Organization of
acceptance test team

The following reporting lines are implemented:

- Every week and, if requested, ad hoc, the test management reports to the customer on the progress of the test process and the quality of the test object.
- The content of these reports corresponds with the concept content of progress report as described in the chapter 'Test control' of the book *Software Testing: a guide to the TMap approach* (5).
- The communication between the test team and the local tax office, and the communication between the test team and the various suppliers (test basis, test object, test environment and test tools), about changes will pass the customer.
- Control cares about the communication between the test team and the supplier of the test object over the delivery and transfer of the test process and the defects.
- technical and subject matter support are part of the test team. They take care of the communication between the test team and the suppliers of the test basis and infrastructure about the defects relating to the test basis or to the infrastructure.
- All members of the test team report on a weekly basis on the progress of the assigned tasks and the hours spent.

Training

The appointed user will follow the course *Testing according to TMap* preceding the beginning of the execution phase. The other members of the test team are sufficiently familiar with the test phenomenon in general, and TMap in particular.

Structure of meetings

Test team meetings will be held every week in order to tune and coordinate the test process:

- *Aim*: tuning and progress control.
- *Frequency*: weekly.
- *Permanent participants*: test management, control, methodology support, testers.
- *Optional participants*: subject matter support, technical support.
- *Agenda*: among others, planning, progress control, activities, monitoring spend hours, quality, defects, changes and reports.

This meeting forms the basis of the progress and quality reports. The decision-making process regarding the defects (analysis and decision panel) occurs at project level and has been described in the project plan (9).

Test staff

Table A.6 shows the test staff required.

Table A.6
Test staff functions and full-time equivalents

Function	Name	Full-time equivalents
Test management	Leo Leader	0.20
Control	Conny Control	0.10
Methodological support	Harry Helper	0.20
Testers	Chris Check	1.00
	Tony Testman	1.00
User local tax office		1.00 (in execution phase)
Subject matter support		0.10–0.20
Technical support		0.10–0.20

Test deliverables

The results of the test project will be recorded in several ways. There is a distinction between testware and project documentation.

Project documentation

The project documentation of the test project will consist of:

- *Test plan*: this document and possible previous/new versions.
- *Defects*: the procedural settlement and layout of defect reports has been described in this test plan (see Chapter 22).
- *Weekly reports*: the progress and quality reports that are drawn up by the test management for the customer.

- *Ad hoc report*: the ad hoc report drawn up by the test management at the request of the customer.
- *Evaluation report*: after completion of the test project, there will be an evaluation report based on the defects to outline the quality of the test object and the productivity of the test process.

Testware
The test project will deliver test documentation, which will be used after the project for maintenance purposes. The test documentation itself should be transferable and maintainable.

- *Test specifications*: contains the logical description of the tests executed during the acceptance test.
- *Test scripts*: contains the physical description of the tests executed during the acceptance test.
- *Test scenario*: describes the sequence in which the test scripts have been executed by the test team.
- *Initial data set*: (a description of) the files containing the physical data needed to start the test and a program to fill the database with these data. The format of the files is based on the technical specification of the system.
- *Test documents*: in addition to the test specification, the test script and the initial data set, these documents contain hard copies of screens, lists, etc. If available, the descriptions of the aids used are included in these documents.

Storage
At the central server, a separate directory structure has been set up for the test team in order to store the test products digitally. This structure is:

```
ATWOOF
    PDATWOOF            Project documentation
        TPATWOOF        Test plan
        WRATWOOF        Weekly reports
        AHATWOOF        Ad hoc reports
        ERATWOOF        Evaluation report
    WDATWOOF            Work directory testware
        SPATWOOF        Test specifications
        SCATWOOF        Test scripts
        SOATWOOF        Test scenario
        IDATWOOF        Initial data set
    TWATWOOF            Final version testware
        SPATWOOF        Test specifications
        SCATWOOF        Test scripts
        SOATWOOF        Test scenario
        IDATWOOF        Initial data set
    DDATWOOF            Defects
    ODATWOOF            All other documentation
```

Naming conventions

The following naming conventions will be applied for the various test products:

$$\leq SRT \geq \leq CODE \geq \leq VRS \geq .DOC$$

where ≤SRT≥ can be TP (test plan), WR (weekly report), AH (ad hoc report), ER (evaluation report), SP (test specification), SC (test script), SO (test scenario), ID (initial data set) or OD (other documentation); ≤CODE≥ can be ATW (documentation on project and system) or XXX (three-letter code (XXX) assigned to user functions of WOOF; and ≤VRS≥ is 9_9 (the version number of the document concerned assigned by control to documents delivered by the test team).

In addition to the automated storage mentioned above, a paper version of each test product is available at the test team's office. The test documents are not stored automatically. After execution of the test, the tester will store the latest version of the test document concerned in the central system. The physical set of initial data will be stored in a directory to be decided on by the technical support. In addition to this, a print-out of these files and a date will be added to the accompanying test documentation.

Infrastructure

The infrastructure consists of the facilities and the resources needed to test properly. The facilities for the test execution (test environment), to support testing (test tools) and the office environment are distinguished.

Test environment

In order to execute the acceptance test properly, the test team should have at least the following at their disposal:
- *Hardware*:
  - five PCs type x.x.x.x.;
  - one PC type x.x.x.x., equipped as server;
  - one printer to print lists and similar, type x.x.x.x.;
  - one printer to make screen prints, type x.x.x.x.;
- *Software*:
  - graphical operating sytstem, version x.;
  - visual advanced dialog, version x.x.x;
  - date manipulation (still to be determined);
  - one logical test environment (still to be determined);
  - back-up and recovery (still to be determined).
- *Facilities to build and use files*:
  - storage devices such as tapes, cassettes, disks and diskettes (still to be determined).

During the preparation phase, a specification of the test environment will occur if necessary.

Test tools
The following test tools will be used during the test project:
- Function Point Analysis Tool (FPAT), for FPA and TPA.
- Planner, for creating a planning and recording of the progress.
- Change Management, for the control of the test products.
- Defect Management, for the management of the defects.

At this point, an investigation is carried out within the local tax office with the available record and playback tools. The results of this investigation may lead to the use of the selected tool during the test project.

Office environment
For a proper execution of the test activities the following office environment is required for the test project:
- *Test room: HB01.14*. This room will contain five desks for the test team. In addition, there are three telephone connections, and space for five PCs and several printers. There is also sufficient cupboard space.
- *Meeting room: HB00.01*. This room may be used for the test team meetings and other meetings. Reservations should be registered at the project secretariat WOOF, phone 212.

Control

Test process control
Test process control aims to control the test process and the quality of the test object. Control is responsible for the test process control.

Progress and spending of budget and time
In the test planning, the activities and deliverables are related to hours, resources, lead time and dependencies. The test team reports on a weekly basis on the extent of completion of the activities and test deliverables.

Every week, per activity and test deliverable, the following are stated:
- status of progress (not started, in process, suspended, percentage of completeness, completed);
- hours and resources (planned, spend, still to go, over/underspending).

Based on this information it is possible to obtain insight into the status of the test project as a whole, as well as into the progress in detail.

Defects

For the registration and settlement of the test defects, the test team uses the procedure defects control.

Metrics

The following metrics are recorded:

- Number of outstanding defects per category of severity, i.e. the number of outstanding defects.
- Number of solved defects in a period per category of severity, i.e. the number of solved defects in the period concerned.
- Number of reported defects in a period per category of severity, i.e. the number of reported defects in the period concerned per category of severity.
- Number of retests, i.e. the number of retests with the spend hours per test unit.

Control of infrastructure

The control of the infrastructure is the responsibility of the technical support.

Changes to infrastructure

During the process, the infrastructure is subject to changes by all sorts of internal and external causes.

Changes in the infrastructure may be implemented only with the consent of the test management. The changes are recorded using the procedure control of infrastructure. Depending on the type and size of the change, these will generally be announced to the test team.

The testers should report disturbances in the infrastructure to the technical support, who will analyze the disturbance and repair it immediately, depending on the severity. For those disturbances that cannot be remedied directly, the tester will write a defect report.

The technical support submits periodically, and on request, data for reports on the availability of the test infrastructure, and the course and duration of any disturbances.

Control of test deliverables

It is important to distinguish the various test products, and to control them in an unequivocal manner. The following deliverables will be distinguished for the test project:

- *External deliverables*:
  - test basis
  - test object.
- *Internal deliverables*:
  - testware
  - test documents.

External deliverables
The control of the external deliverables is an external responsibility by the WOOF project. The necessary procedures have been laid down in the project plan WOOF (9).

Internal deliverables
The procedure control of test deliverables is used for the control of the internal products.

Planning

Table A.7 shows the planning of the test project. The start and end dates of the various activities are given, including the hours spent by the test team.

Activity	Start	End	Test management	Methodolgy support	Subject matter support	Technical support	Control	Testers	Users (= local tax office)
Creating test plan	14–08	18–08	32						
Planning and control	24–08	03–10							
Test management			48						
Control							24		
Methodology support				48					
Preparation	24–08	25–08						32	
Specification	28–08	08–09						136	
First execution round	11–09	19–09						112	56
Repair of defects	13–09	22–09							
Final execution round	25–09	27–09						48	24
Contingency	28–09	29–09						?	
Completion	02–10	03–10						16	

Table A.7 Planning of the test project

Figure A.2 shows the sequence and dependencies of the phases. In addition, the agreed delivering dates of the various suppliers are given. The planning and control phase is not shown.

In this example, only a global planning of the test project is included. The detailed planning of the phases preparation, specification, execution and completion still has to be determined, and so is lacking.

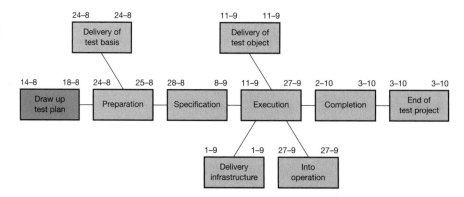

Threats, risks and measures

Based on the global review and study, some possible threats have been identified that may harm the test process:

- *Critical planning of the development process.* The development team indicated that the planning of the development process is critical. In the test plan a possible phased delivery of the WOOF-system has been taken in account.
- *The users' contribution (timely and quality).* The availability of users of the local tax office is hard to implement because the daily activities should not be delayed. The available users are not skilled in testing. After consultation with the customer, it has been decided to appoint one user as soon as possible to follow the course *Testing according to Tmap* and to be involved full-time during the execution phase.
- *Global FPA.* The FPA calculation (12) of the acceptance test is a global calculation based on the general functional design (1). The function point calculation will be done again at the delivery moment of the detailed functional design (2). Consequences for the budget estimation of the test project will be communicated with the customer.
- *Critical planning administrative organization (3).* The planning of the administrative organization is critical in view of the limited availability of the users. At this point, the test process has taken no measures. The test management will be extra alert to this point.

Test point analysis in detail

Calculation of the D_f factor
Table A.8 shows the calculation of the D_f factor.

User functions	D$_f$ factor	Ue	Uy	I	C	U	D$_f$
Register Grayhound citizen's data		12	2	4	3	1	1.05
Modify Grayhound citizen's data		6	2	4	3	1	0.75
Look up Grayhound citizen's data		3	2	2	3	1	0.50
Approve/delete Grayhound citizen's data		12	2	4	3	1	1.05
Create/print tax assessment		12	2	2	12	1	1.40
Calculate tax amount		12	4	4	12	1	1.60
Register factor data		12	2	4	3	1	1.05
Modify factor data		6	2	4	3	1	0.75
Look up factor data		3	2	2	3	1	0.50
Approve/delete factor data		12	2	4	3	1	1.05
Report factor data		3	2	2	3	1	0.50
Register age group/tariff		12	2	8	3	1	1.25
Modify age group/tariff		6	2	8	3	1	0.95
Report age group/tariff		3	2	2	3	1	0.50
Approve/delete age group/tariff		12	2	4	3	1	1.05
Report tax assessment data		6	2	2	6	1	0.80
Delete tax assessment register		6	2	8	3	1	0.95
Error messages		6	4	4	3	1	0.85
Help screens		6	2	4	3	1	0.75
Application menu		6	4	4	3	1	0.85

Table A.8 Calculating the D$_f$ factor

Calculation of the Q$_d$ factor

Table A.9 shows the calculation of the Q$_d$ factor.

Quality characteristics	Value
Dynamic explicit measurable quality characteristics	
Functionality	5
Security	3
Suitability	4
Performance	3
Q dynamic explicit	1.15
Dynamic implicit measurable quality characteristics	
User-friendliness	Y
Efficiency	N
Performance	N
Maintainability	N
Q dynamic implicit	0.02
Q dynamic	1.17

Table A.9
Calculating the Q$_d$ factor

Calculation of the direct test points

Table A.10 shows the calculation of the direct test points.

User functions	FP	D_f	Q_d	TP_f
Register Grayhound citizen's data	10	1.05	1.17	12.29
Modify Grayhound citizen's data	3	0.75	1.17	2.63
Look up Grayhound citizen's data	3	0.50	1.17	1.76
Approve/delete Grayhound citizen's data	3	1.05	1.17	3.69
Create/print tax assessment	4	1.40	1.17	6.55
Calculate tax amount	11	1.60	1.17	20.59
Register factor data	7	1.05	1.17	8.60
Modify factor data	3	0.75	1.17	2.63
Look up factor data	3	0.50	1.17	1.76
Approve/delete factor data	3	1.05	1.17	3.69
Report factor data	4	0.50	1.17	2.34
Register age group/tariff	12	1.25	1.17	17.55
Modify age group/tariff	4	0.95	1.17	4.45
Report age group/tariff	4	0.50	1.17	2.34
Approve/delete age group/tariff	3	1.05	1.17	3.69
Report tax assessment data	5	0.80	1.17	4.68
Delete tax assessment register	3	0.95	1.17	3.33
Error messages	4	0.85	1.17	3.98
Help screens	4	0.75	1.17	3.51
Application menu	4	0.85	1.17	3.98
TP_f = total dynamic test points				114.04

Calculation of Q_s

Table A.11 shows the calculation of Q_s.

Statically measurable quality characteristics		
	Flexibility	N
	Testability	N
	Security	Y
	Continuity	Y
	Manageability	N
Q static		32

Calculation of the total number of test points

Table A.12 shows the calculations for the total number of test points.

TP_f		114.04
$(FP \times Q_s) / 500$	+	32
		———
TP = total number of test points		146.04

Table A.12
Calculating the total
number of test points

Calculation of the environment factor

Table A.13 shows the calculation of the environment factor.

Environment factor	Value
Test tools	2
Development testing	8
Test basis	3
Development environment	8
Test environment	1
Testware	4
O-factor (= environment factor/21)	1.24

Table A.13
Calculating the
environment factor

Calculation of the primary test effort

Table A.14 shows the calculation of the primary test effort.

TP = test points		146.04
S = skill factor	×	2.0
E = environment factor	×	1.24
		———
PT = primary test effort		362.18
Team size		3
Management tools	+	4
		———
Management addition		7
Primary test effort		362.18
Management addition	×	1.07
		———
Total test effort		383.53 = 384

Table A.14
Calculating the primary
test effort

Appendix: ISO/IEC 9126-1 quality characteristics

B

Definitions

Functionality
The capability of the software product to provide functions that meet stated or implied needs when the software is in use under specified conditions.

- *Suitability*
The capability of the software product to provide an appropriate set of functions for specified tasks and user objectives.

- *Accuracy*
The capability of the software product to provide the right or agreed results or effects with the needed degree of precision.

- *Interoperability*
The capability of the software product to interact with one or more specified systems.

- *Security*
The capability of the software product to protect information and data so that unauthorized persons or systems cannot read or modify them, and authorized persons or systems are not denied access to them.

- *Functionality compliance*
The capability of the software product to adhere to standards, conventions or regulations in laws and similar prescriptions relating to functionality.

Reliability
The capability of the software product to maintain a specified level of performance when used under specified conditions.

- *Maturity*
The capability of the software product to avoid failure as a result of faults in the software.

- *Fault tolerance*
The capability of the software product to maintain a specified level of performance in cases of software faults or of infringement of its specified interface.

- *Recoverability* — The capability of the software product to re-establish a specified level of performance and recover the data directly affected in the case of a failure.

- *Reliability compliance* — The capability of the software product to adhere to standards, conventions or regulations relating to reliability.

Usability — The capability of the software product to be understood, learned, used and attractive to the user under specified conditions.

- *Understandability* — The capability of the software product to enable the user to understand whether the software is suitable, and how it can be used for particular tasks and conditions of use.

- *Learnability* — The capability of the software product to enable the user to learn its application.

- *Operability* — The capability of the software product to enable the user to operate and control it.

- *Attractiveness* — The capability of the software product to be attractive to the user.

- *Usability compliance* — The capability of the software product to adhere to standards, conventions, style guides or regulations relating to usability.

Efficiency — The capability of the software product to provide appropriate performance, relative to the amount of resources used, under stated conditions.

- *Time behavior* — The capability of the software product to provide appropriate response and processing times and throughput rates when performing its function under stated conditions.

- *Resource behavior* — The capability of the software product to use appropriate amounts and types of resources when the software performs its function under stated conditions.

- *Efficiency compliance* — The capability of the software product to adhere to standards or conventions relating to efficiency.

Maintainability — The capability of the software product to be modified. Modifications may include corrections, improvements or adaptation of the software to changes in environment, and in requirements and functional specifications.

- *Analyzability*   The capability of the software product to be diagnosed for deficiencies or causes of failures in the software, or for the parts to be modified to be identified.

- *Changeability*   The capability of the software product to enable a specified modification to be implemented.

- *Stability*   The capability of the software product to avoid unexpected effects from modifications of the software.

- *Testability*   The capability of the software product to enable modified software to be validated.

- *Maintainability compliance*   The capability of the software product to adhere to standards or conventions relating to maintainability.

Portability   The capability of the software product to be transferred from one environment to another.

- *Adaptability*   The capability of the software product to be adapted for different specified environments without applying actions or means other than those provided for this purpose for the software considered.

- *Installability*   The capability of the software product to be installed in a specified environment.

- *Co-existence*   The capability of the software product to co-exist with other independent software in a common environment sharing common resources.

- *Replaceability*   The capability of the software product to be used in place of another specified software product for the same purpose in the same environment.

- *Portability compliance*   The capability of the software product to adhere to standards or conventions relating to portability.

Translation from ISO 9126 quality characteristics to TMap

Table B.1 shows how ISO 9126 quality characteristics translate to TMap.
The TMap quality characteristics (suitability of) infrastructure and reusability have no equivalence within ISO 9126.

Translation from TMap quality characteristics to ISO 9126

Table B.2 shows how TMap quality characteristics translate to ISO 9126.
    The ISO 9126 quality characteristics stability, co-existence, replaceability and compliance have no equivalence within TMap.

ISO 9126	TMap
Functionality	
Suitability	Suitability
	Effectivity
	Data controllability (specific functions)
	Flexibility (specific functions)
Accuracy	Functionality
Interoperability	Connectivity
Security	Security
Functionality compliance	–
Reliability	*Continuity*
Maturity	Operational reliability
Fault tolerance	Robustness
Recoverability	Recoverability
	Degradation possibilities
	Possibility of diversion
Reliability compliance	–
Usability	
Understandability	User-friendliness
	Effectivity
Learnability	User-friendliness
	Effectivity
Operability	User-friendliness (end user)
	Manageability (operator user)
	User-friendliness
Attractiveness	User-friendliness
Usability compliance	–
Efficiency	
Time behavior	Performance
Resource utilization	Efficiency
Efficiency compliance	–
Maintainability	
Analyzabilty	Maintainability
Changeability	Maintainability
Stability	–
Testability	Testability
Maintainability compliance	–
Portability	
Adaptability	Portability
Installability	Portability
Co-existence	–
Replaceability	–
Portability compliance	–

TMap	ISO 9126
Connectivity	Interoperability
Continuity	Reliability
Degradation possibilities	Fault tolerance
Possibility of diversion	Recoverability
operational reliability	Maturity
Recoverability	Recoverability
Robustness	Fault tolerance
Data controllability	Suitability
Effectivity	Learnability
	Operability
	Suitability
	Understandability
Efficiency	Resource utilization
Flexibility	Suitability
Functionality	Accuracy
(Suitability of) infrastructure	–
Maintainability	Analyzabilty
	Changeability
Manageability	Operability
Performance	Time behavior
Portability	Adaptability
	Installability
Reusability	–
Security	Security
Suitability	Suitability
Testability	Testability
User-friendliness	Attractiveness
	Learnability
	Operability
	Understandability

Table B.2
Translation of TMap quality characteristics to ISO 9126

Glossary

Acceptance test	A test executed by the user(s) and system manager(s) in an environment simulating the operational environment to the greatest possible extent, which should demonstrate that the developed system meets the functional and quality requirements.
Audit trail	Determining a track by which the original input data may be traced back from the results of data processing. This facilitates result checking.
Black-box test technique	Test-specification technique that derives test cases from the externally visible properties of an object without having knowledge of the internal structure of this object.
Boundary value analysis	Test principle based on the fact that a test around a boundary has a greater chance to detect a defect.
Clone	A function point analysis (FPA) function that has been specified already or constructed within another or the same user function within the project.
Completeness	The certainty that all inputs and changes are processed by the system.
Connectivity	The ease with which a link with a different information system or within the information system can be made and modified.
Continuity	The certainty that the information system will continue uninterruptedly, which means that it can be resumed within a reasonable time even after serious interruptions.
Correctness	The degree to which the system processes the input and changes entered correctly, in accordance with the specifications, to produce consistent data sets.

Coverage	The relation between what is tested by the test set and what may be tested. The concept is applied frequently in relation to the program code ('by the available test cases, *x*% statement or condition coverage is achieved'), but the application is also conceivable regarding functional specifications (paths, conditions, interfaces).
Data controllability	The ease with which the correctness and completeness of the information (in the course of time) can be checked.
Defect (fault)	The result of an error residing in the code or document.
Degradation possibilities	The ease with which the core of the information system can continue after a part has failed.
Driver	A simulation program that replaces a program that should take care of the control and/or the calling of the test object.
Dummy	A function point analysis (FPA) function, of which the functionality should not be specified or constructed but is available because that has been undertaken outside of the project.
Dynamic testing	Testing by execution of the test object and/or the running of programs.
Effectivity	The degree to which the information system meets the demands of the organization and the profile of the end users for whom it is intended, as well as the degree to which the information system contributes to the achievement of business objectives.
Efficiency	The relationship between the performance level of the system (expressed in the transaction volume and overall speed) and the amount of resources (central processing unit cycles, disk access time, memory and network capacity, etc.) that are used.
Equivalence class	Set of possible input values that will lead to an identical processing (a known principle to derive test cases).
Error	A mistake (done by a human).
Evaluation	The reviewing and inspecting of the various intermediate products and/or processes in the system development cycle. Within the scope of this book, only the evaluation of the intermediate products is described.

Failure	The result or manifestation of one or more faults.
Fault (defect)	The result of an error residing in the code or document.
Flexibility	The degree to which the user may introduce extensions or modifications to the information system without changing the program itself. Or the degree to which the system can be modified by the controlling organization without being dependent on the IT department for maintenance.
Function point	Unit used to measure the functionality and/or the size of application software.
Function point analysis (FPA)	Method aiming to measure the size of the functionality of an automated system. The measurement is independent of the technology. This measurement may be used as a base for the measurement of productivity, the estimation of the needed resources, and project control.
Function point analysis (FPA) functions	Subdivision of user functions in FPA functions: logical set of data, links, input functions, output functions, reading functions. These FPA functions are the elementary building blocks to determine the functionality of a system.
Functionality	The certainty that data processing is correct and complete in accordance with the description in the functional specifications.
High-level tests	These involve testing whole, complete products. As their focus is often the externally visible properties of an object, high-level tests commonly use black-box techniques. Well-known high-level tests are the system and acceptance test.
Infrastructure (suitability of)	The suitability of hardware, network, systems software and database management system for the application concerned and the degree to which the elements of this infrastructure interrelate.
Initial data set	The set of data (files or database) that should be loaded at the start of a test execution. The initial data set contains physically all the necessary data. The initial data set is composed once and will be loaded for every test.
Integrated test	Test approach by which the system test and the functional acceptance test are combined into a single test level.

Integration test	A test executed by the developer in a laboratory environment that should demonstrate that a logical set of programs meets the requirements set in the design specifications.
Known errors	Defects that have been found but have not been solved (yet).
Logical test case	A series of situations to be tested, running the test object concerned (e.g. a function) from start to finish. Logical test cases are used when the individual test situations cannot be approached directly during the testing, or when it is not possible to check the result of a certain test situation immediately.
Low-level tests	These involve testing the separate components, e.g. programs, of a system, individually or in a combination. As the low-level tests require good knowledge of the internal structure of the software, mainly white-box testing techniques are applicable. The tests are executed almost exclusively by developers. Well-known low-level tests are the unit and integration test.
Maintainability	The ease with which the information system can be adapted to new demands from the user, to changing external environments, or in order to correct defects.
Manageability	The effort needed to get and keep the information system in its operational state.
Master test plan	Test plan by which the various test levels are geared to one another.
Online	Function mode of an information system in which the information system immediately processes the commands and directly shows the answer (output) on the screen (or otherwise).
Operational reliability	The degree to which the information system remains free from interruptions.
Performance	The speed with which the information system processes interactive and batch transactions.
Physical test case	Detailed description of a test situation or logical test case containing a starting situation, actions to be taken, and the result checks to be performed. The level of detail is such that when the test is executed at a later stage, this is done as efficiently as possible.

Portability	The diversity of the hardware and software platforms on which the information system can run, and how easy it is to transfer the system from one environment to another.
Possibility of diversion	The ease with which (part of) the information system can continue elsewhere.
Pretest	Testing the delivered product in such a way that it is determined whether the product is of sufficient quality to execute a complete test of this product.
Quality	According to ISO (1994), the totality of features and characteristics of a product or service that bear on its ability to satisfy stated or implied needs.
Quality assurance	According to ISO (1994), all the planned and systematic activities implemented within the quality system, and demonstrated as needed, to provide adequate confidence that an entity will fulfill requirements for quality.
Quality characteristic	Property of an information system.
Recoverability	The ease and speed with which the information system can be restored after an interruption.
Regression test	A phenomenon that the quality of a system as a whole declines due to individual modifications. Regression testing aims to check that all parts of the system still function correctly after the implementation of a modification.
Reusability	The degree to which parts of the information system or the design can be reused for the development of different applications.
Risk reporting	A description of the extent to which the system meets the specified quality requirements and the risks associated with bringing a particular version into production, including any available alternatives.
Robustness	The degree to which the information system proceeds as usual even after an interruption.
Security	The certainty that data can be viewed and changed only by those who are authorized to do so.
Static testing	Testing by examining products (such as manuals or source code) without any programs being executed.
Stub	A simulation program.
Suitability	The degree to which manual procedures match the automated information system, and the fitness for use of these manual procedures for the organization.

System management	Responsible for technical operation of the software in its intended infrastructure in production
System test	A test executed by the developer in a (properly controlled) laboratory environment that should demonstrate that the developed system or subsystems meet the requirements set in the functional and quality specifications.
Test action	An action in a previously defined start situation that produces a result. A test action is part of a test case.
Test basis	All documents from which the requirements of an information system can be inferred The documentation on which the test is based. If a document can be amended only by way of formal amendment procedure, then the test basis is called a frozen test basis.
Test case	A description of a test to be executed, focused on a specific test aim.
Test infrastructure	The environment in which the test is performed, consisting of hardware, system software, test tools, procedures, etc.
Test level	A group of test activities that are organized and managed together. A division can be made into high- and low-level tests.
Test measure	Indicates to which extent the dependencies between successive decision points are tested. At test measure n, all dependencies of actions before a decision point and after $n-1$ decision points are verified by putting all possible combinations of n actions in test paths.
Test object	The information system (or part of it) to be tested.
Test organization	The whole of the test functions, facilities, procedures and activities, including their relationships.
Test plan	In a test plan, the general structure and the strategic choices with respect to the test to be executed are formulated. The test plan forms the scope of reference during the execution of the test and also serves as an instrument to communicate with the customer of the test. The test plan is a description of the test project, including a description of the activities and the planning, therefore it is not a description of the tests themselves.

Test point	Unit of measurement for the size of the high-level test to be executed.
Test point analysis (TPA®)	A method with the possibility to perform a technology-independent measurement of the test size of an information system on the basis of a function point analysis, and to use this measurement as a basis for a productivity measurement, an estimate of the required resources, and project management.
Test process	The collection of tools, techniques and working methods used to perform a test.
Test scenario	A scheme for the execution of test scripts. The test scripts are included in the test scenario in their context and in the order in which they are to be executed.
Test script	A sequence of related actions and checks, related to test cases, of which the sequence of execution is indicated. A description of how the testing is done.
Test set	A collection of test cases specifically aimed at one or multiple quality characteristics and one or more test units.
Test-specification technique	A standardized method of deriving test cases from reference information, e.g. the test basis.
Test strategy	The distribution of the test effort and coverage over the parts to be tested, or aspects of the test object aimed at finding the most important defects as early and as cheaply as possible.
Test team	A group of people who, led by a test manager, undertake test activities.
Test technique	A set of actions aimed at creating a test deliverable by a universal method.
Test tool	An automated aid that supports one or more test activities, such as planning and control, specification, building initial files and data, test execution and test analysis.
Test type	A group of test activities aimed at checking the information system on a number of interrelated quality characteristics.
Test unit	A set of processes, transactions and/or functions that are tested collectively.
Testability	The ease with which the functionality and performance level of the system can be tested (after each modification), and the speed at which this can be done.

Testability review	The detailed check of the test basis on testability.
Testing	A process of planning, preparing, executing and analyzing aimed at establishing the characteristics of an information system, and demonstrating the difference between the actual status and the required status. According to ISO/IEC (1991), a technical operation that consists of the determination of one or more characteristics of a given product, process or service according to a specified procedure.
Testware	All the test documentation, such as test specifications, test scripts, a description of the test infrastructure, etc., that is produced during the test process. This test documentation can be reused for maintenance purposes, therefore it should be transferable and maintainable.
Unit test	Test is executed by the developer in a laboratory environment that should demonstrate that a program meets the requirements set in the design specifications.
User function	Property recognized by the user that the delivered product should meet. Generally speaking, the user functions are best described as objects and processes.
User-friendliness	The ease with which end users use the system. This general definition is often divided into how easy it is for end users to learn to work with the information system, and how easy it is for trained users to work with.
White-box test techniques	Test-specification techniques that derive test cases from the internal properties of an object, with knowledge of the internal set-up of the object.

Bibliography

The publications mentioned below are an interesting selection from the extensive range of test literature:

General testing

Beizer, B. (1984) *Software System Testing and Quality Assurance*, John Wiley & Sons, New York.

Beizer, B. (1990) *Software Testing Techniques*, International Thomson Computer Press, Boston.

Beizer, B. (1995) *Black-Box Testing: techniques for functional testing of software and systems*, John Wiley & Sons, New York.

Black, R. (1999) *Managing the Testing Process*, Microsoft Press, Redmond.

Deutsch, M.S., *Software Verification and Validation*, Prentice-Hall, Englewood Cliffs, NJ.

Hetzel, W.C. (1988) *The Complete Guide to Software Testing*, 2nd edn, John Wiley & Sons, New York.

IEEE (1998) *829 – Standard for Software Test Documentation*, Secretary Institute of Electrical and Electronic Engineers Standards Board, New York.

IEEE (1998) *1012 – Standard for Software Verification and Validation*, Secretary Institute of Electrical and Electronic Engineers Standards Board, New York.

IEEE (1993) *1008 – Standard for Software Unit Testing*, Secretary Institute of Electrical and Electronic Engineers Standards Board, New York.

Kaner, C., Falk, J. and Nguyen, H.Q. (1999) *Testing Computer Software*, 2nd edn, John Wiley & Sons, New York.

Kirakowski, J. and Corbett, M. (1993) 'SUMI: the software usability measurement inventory', *British Journal of Educational Technology*, **24** (3).

Kit, E. (1995) *Software Testing in the Real World*, Addison-Wesley, London.

Lindgaard, G. (1993) *Usability Testing and System Evaluation*, Chapman & Hall, London.

Mosley, D.J. (1993) *The Handbook of MIS Application Software Testing*, Yourdon.

Myers, G.J. (1979) *The Art of Software Testing*, Wiley-Interscience Publications, New York.

Nielsen, J. (1993) *Usability Engineering*, Addison-Wesley, London.

Perry, W.E., *A Structured Approach to Systems Testing*, QED Information Sciences, Wellesley.

Perry, W.E. (1995) *Effective Methods for Software Testing*, John Wiley & Sons, New York.

Perry, W.E. and Rice, R.W. (1997) *Surviving the Challenges of Software Testing*, Dorset House Publishing, New York.

Roper, M. (1994) *Software Testing*, McGraw-Hill, New York.

Rubin, J. (1994) *Handbook of Usability Testing*, John Wiley & Sons, New York.

Schmitz, B. and Van Megen, *Software-Qualitätssicherung-Testen im Software-Lebenszyklus*, Vieweg & Sohn, Braunschweig/Wiesbaden.

SIGIST (Specialist Interest Group in Software Testing) (1998) *Working Draft: Glossary of terms used in software testing, version 6.2*, British Computer Society, London.

Van Veenendaal, E. and Trienekens, J. (1995) 'Testing software based on user's quality needs', presented at Proceedings EuroSTAR Conference 1995, London.

Test metrics

Basili, V.R., Galdiera, G. and Rombach, H.D. (1994) *The Goal Question Metric Approach*, John Wiley & Sons, New York.

Boehm, B.W. (1981) *Software Engineering Economics*, Prentice-Hall, Englewood Cliffs, NJ.

De Panfilis, S., Kitchenham, B. and Morfuni, N. (1997) *Experiences Introducing a Measurement Program*, Information and Software Technology.

Fenton, N.E. and Pfleeger, S.L. (1996) *Software Metrics, a Rigorous and Practical Approach*, International Thomson Publishers.

Grady, R. (1992) *Practical Software Metrics for Project Management and Process Improvement*, Prentice-Hall PTR, NJ.

Grady, R. and Caswell, D.L. (1987) *Software Metrics: establishing a company-wide program*, Prentice-Hall, Englewood Cliffs, NJ.

Hetzel, W.C. (1993) *Making Software Measurement Work*, John Wiley & Sons, New York.

Hetzel, W.C. (1993) *Making Software Metrics Work*, QED Publishing Group, New York.

Pulford, K., Kuntzmann-Combelles, A. and Shirlaw, S. (1995) *A Quantitative Approach to Software Management: the AMI handbook*, Addison-Wesley, London.

Van Solingen, R. and Berghout, E. (1999) *The Goal/Question/Metric method: a practical handguide*, McGraw-Hill, New York.

Auditing, reviews and inspections

Aerts, H., van Genuchten, M. and Rooijmans, J. (1996) 'Software quality in consumer electronic products', *IEEE Software*, January.

Fagan, M.E. (1976) 'Design and code inspection to reduce defects in program development', *IBM Systems Journal*, **15** (3).

Fagan, M.E. (1986) 'Advances in software inspections', *IEEE Transactions on Software Engineering*, July.

Freedman, D.P. and Weinberg, G.M. (1990) *Handbook of Walkthroughs, Inspections and Technical Reviews*, Dorset House Publishing, New York.

Gilb, T. and Graham, D.R. (1993) *Software Inspection*, Addison-Wesley, London.

Jenkins, B., Perry, R. and Cooke, P. (1986) *An Audit Approach to Computers*, Coopers & Lybrand Deloitte, UK.

Paulk, M.C. (1999) 'Using the software CMM with good judgement', *Software Quality Professional*, June.

Van Veenendaal, E.P.W.M. (1999) 'Practical quality assurance for embedded software', *Software Quality Professional*, June.

Weber, R. (1988) *EDP Auditing, Conceptual Foundations and Practice*, McGraw-Hill, Singapore.

Organization

Bainbridge, C. (1996) *Designing for Change: a practical guide to business transformation*, John Wiley & Sons, New York.

Burns, T. and Stalker, G.M. (1995) *The Management of Innovation*, Oxford University Press, Oxford.

Burnstein, I., Suwannasart, T. and Carlson, C.R. (1996) *Developing a Testing Maturity Model: Part I and II*, Illinois Institute of Technology.

Deming, W. E. (1992) *Out of the Crisis*, Cambridge University Press, Cambridge.

Drucker, P.F. (1999) *Management Challenges for the 21st Century*, HarperBusiness, New York.

El Emam, K. and Drouin, J. (eds) (1998) *Spice: the theory and practice of software process improvement and capability determination*, IEEE Computer Society.

Ericson, T., Subotic, A. and Ursing, S. (1996) 'Towards a test improvement model', presented at EuroSTAR Conference 1996, Amsterdam.

Gates, B. (1995) *The Road Ahead*, Penguin Books, London.

Gelperin, D. (1996) 'A testability maturity model', presented at STAR Conference 1996.

Koomen, T. and Pol, M. (1999) *Test Process Improvement: a practical step-by-step guide to structured testing*, Addison-Wesley, London.

Kuvaja, P. *et al.* (1994) *Software Process Assessment and Improvement: the Bootstrap approach*, Blackwell.

McFeeley, B. (1996) *IDEALsm: a user's guide for software process improvement*, Software Engineering Institute.

Robbins, S.P. (1986) *Organizational Behavior, Concepts, Controversies, and Applications*, 3rd edn, Prentice Hall, NJ.

Software Engineering Institute, Carnegie Mellon University (1994) *The Capability Maturity Model: guidelines for improving the software process*, Addison-Wesley, London.

Software Engineering Institute, Carnegie Mellon University (1995) *The Capability Maturity Model*, Addison-Wesley, London.

Zahran, S. (1998) *Software Process Improvement: Practical guidelines for business success*, Addison-Wesley, London.

Infrastructure and tools

Andersen Consulting (1995) *Technology Discussion on Testing Tools: establishing 'parameterized testing' environment (data-driven testing)*, Andersen Consulting.

Dustin, E. (1999) *Automated Software Testing: introduction, management and performance*, Addison-Wesley, London.

Fewster, M. and Graham, D. (1999) *Software Test Automation*, Addison-Wesley, London.

Gilad, Z. (1993) 'How automation can help in client/server testing', presented at EuroSTAR Conference 1993, London.

Graham, D. Herzlich, P. and Morelli, C. (1996) *Computer Aided Software Testing, The CAST-report*, Cambridge Market Intelligence Limited.

Hatton, L. (1998) 'Does OO sync with how we think?', *IEEE Software*, May/June.

Hayes, L.G. (1995) *The Automated Testing Handbook, Software Testing Institute*, Richardson, TX.

Kaner, C. (1997) 'Improving the maintainability of automated test suites', *Software QA*, **4** (4).

Von Mayrhauser, A. (1991) 'Testing and evolutionary development', *Software Engineering Notes*, **16** (4).

Ovum (1997) *Ovum Evaluates: software testing tools*, Ovum Ltd, London.

Ovum *Ovum Evaluates: CASE products*, http://www.ovum.co.uk (evaluations of leading CASE products and methods; continuously updated).

Quality management

Crosby, P.B. (1980) *Quality is Free: the art of making quality certain*, McGraw-Hill, New York.

Hall, T.J. (1995) *The Quality Systems Manual: the definitive guide to the ISO 9000 family and tickit*, John Wiley & Sons, New York.

Horch, J.W. (1996) *Practical Guide to Software Quality Management*, Artech House Publishers.

Humphrey, W.S. (1989) *Managing the Software Process*, Addison-Wesley, London.

Imai, M. (1990) *Kaizen: the key to Japan's competitive success*, Kluwer Bedrijfswetenschappen, Deventer.

ISO (1994) *ISO 8402: quality management and quality assurance – vocabulary*, International Organization of Standardization.

Trienekens, J. and van Veenendaal, E. (1997) *Software Quality from a Business Perspective*, Kluwer BedrijfsInformatie, Deventer.

Product quality

Crandall, V., and Jarvis, A. (1997) *Inroads to Software Quality*, Prentice Hall PTR, New Jersey.

Gilb, T. (1988) *Principles of Software Engineering Management*, Addison-Wesley, London.

Humphrey, W.S. (1997) *Introduction to the Personal Software Process*, Addison Wesley, London.

ISO (1991) *ISO/IEC Guide 2: general terms and definitions concerning standardization and related activities*, International Organization of Standardization.

ISO (1998) *ISO/IEC WD 9126-2: software quality characteristics and metrics – part 2: external metrics*, International Organization of Standardization

ISO (1999) *ISO/IEC 9126 part 1: information technology – software product quality – part 1: quality model*, International Organization of Standardization.

ISO (1999) *ISO/IEC WD 9126 part 3: information technology – software product quality – Part 3: internal metrics*, International Organization of Standardization.

Jarvis, A., and Crandell, V. (1997) *Inroads to Software Quality*, Prentice-Hall Englewood Cliffs, NJ.

Juran, J.M. (1988) *Juran's Quality Control Handbook*, McGraw-Hill, New York.

McCall, J.A., Richards, P.K. and Walters, G.F. (1977) *Factors in Software Quality*, RADC-TR-77-363 Rome Air Development Center, Griffis Air Force, Rome (New York, USA).

Musa, J.D. (1998) *Software Reliability Engineering: more reliable software, faster development and testing*, McGraw-Hill, New York.

Van Veenendaal, E. and McMullan, J. (eds) (1997) *Achieving Software Product Quality*, Tutein Nolthenius, 's-Hertogenbosch.

Other

Bazzana, G. and Fagnoni, E. (1999) *Testing Web-based Applications*, SQE Europe, http://net.onion.it/.

Berson, A. (1992) *Client/Server Architecture*, McGraw-Hill, New York.

De Marco, T. and Lister, T. (1999) *Peopleware*, Dorset House Publishing, New York.

IEEE (1992) *610 – Standard Computer Dictionary*, Secretary Institute of Electrical and Electronic Engineers Standards Board, New York.

IFPUG (1994) *Function Point Counting Practices, release 4.0*, International Function Point User Group, USA.

Jacobson, I., Christerson, M., Johnsson P. and Overgaard, G. (1992) *Object-oriented software engineering: a use case driven approach*, Addison-Wesley, London.

Leebaert, D. (1995) *The Future of Software*, MIT Press.

Macfarlane, I.J. and Warden, R. (1996) *Testing an IT Service for Operational Use*, HMSO London.

Mosley, D.J. (1993) *The Handbook of MIS Application Software Testing*, Prentice Hall, New Jersey.

Neumann, P.G. (1995) *Computer Related Risks*, ACM Press, New York.

Ottevanger, I.B. (1998) 'Test factory (TSite): a next step in structured testing', presented at EuroSTAR Conference 1998, Munich.

Pressman, R.S., *Software Engineering*, McGraw-Hill, New York.

Reynolds, M.T. (1996) *Test and Evaluation of complex Systems*, John Wiley & Sons, New York.

Robbins, H. and Finley, M. (1996) *Why Change Doesn't Work*, Peterson's, Princeton, NJ.

Samaroo, A., Allot, S. and Hambling, B. (1999) *E-ffective Testing for E-business*, Imago^{QA}.

Schaefer, H. (1996) 'Surviving under time and budget pressure', presented at EuroSTAR Conference 1996, Amsterdam.

Weinberg, G.M. (1971) *The Psychology of Computer Programming*, Van Nostrand Reinhold, New York.

TMap-related publications

English-language publications

Pol, M. and van Veenendaal, E. (1999) *Structured Testing of Information Systems: an introduction to TMap*, tenHagenStam uitgevers, The Hague.

Koomen, T. and Pol, M. (1999) *Test Process Improvement: a practical step-by-step guide to structured testing*, Addison-Wesley, London.

German-language publications

Pol, M., Koomen, T. and Spillner, A. (2000) *Managument und Optimierung des Testprozesses: ein Leitfaden für erfolgreiches Testen von Software mit TPI und TMap*, dpunkt-verlag, Heidelberg.

Dutch-language publications

Broekman, B., Hoos, C. and Paap, M. (2001) *Automatisering van de testuitvoering, een praktische handleiding*, tenHagenStam uitgevers, The Hague.

Koomen, T. and Pol M. (1998) *Test Process Improvement®, leidraad voor stapsgewijs beter testen*, tenHagenStam uitgevers, The Hague.

Pol, M., Teunissen, R. and van Veenendaal, E. (1996) *Gestructureerd testen: een introductie tot TMap®*, Tutein Nolthenius, 's-Hertogenbosch.

Pol, M., Teunissen, R. and van Veenendaal, E. (1999) *Testen volgens TMap®*, Tutein Nolthenius, 's-Hertogenbosch.

References

Andersen Consulting (1995) *Technology Discussion on Testing Tools: establish 'parameterized testing' environment (data-driven testing)*, Andersen Consulting, London.

Basili, V.R., Galdiera, G. and Rombach, H.D. (1994) *The Goal–Question–Metric Approach*, John Wiley & Sons, New York.

Beizer, B. (1990) *Software Testing Techniques*, International Thomson Computer Press, Boston.

Boehm, B.W. (1981) *Software Engineering Economics*, Prentice-Hall Inc., Englewood Cliffs, NJ.

British Standards Institute (1998a) *BS7925-1, Software Testing Vocabulary*, British Standards Institute, London.

British Standards Institute (1998b) *BS7925-2, Software Component Testing*, British Standards Institute, London.

Fagan, M.E. (1986) 'Advances in software inspections', *IEEE Transactions on Software Engineering*, July.

Fewster, M. and Graham, D. (1999) *Software Test Automation*, Addison-Wesley, London.

Forrester (1999) www.forrester.com.

Gartner Group (1995) *Client/server Architectures*, http://www.gartner.com.

Gilb, T. and Graham, D.R. (1993) *Software Inspection*, Addison-Wesley, London.

Hatton, L. (1998) 'Does OO sync with how we think?', *IEEE Software*, May/June.

Hayes, L.G. (1995) *The Automated Testing Handbook*, Software Testing Institute, Richardson, TX.

Hetzel, W.C. (1993) *Making Software Measurement Work*, John Wiley & Sons, New York.

Humphrey, W.S. (1989) *Managing the Software Process*, Addison-Wesley, London.

IEEE (1990) *610.12 – IEEE Standard Glossary of Software Engineering Terminology*, Secretary Institute of Electrical and Electronic Engineers Standards Board, New York.

IEEE (1993) *1008 – Standard for Software Unit Testing*, Secretary Institute of Electrical and Electronic Engineers Standards Board, New York.

IEEE (1994) *IEEE Software Engineering Standards Collection*, Institute of Electrical and Electronic Engineers, New York.

IEEE (1998) *829 – Standard for Software Test Documentation*, Secretary Institute of Electrical and Electronic Engineers Standards Board, New York.

IEEE (1998) *1012 – Standard for Software Verification and Validation*, Secretary Institute of Electrical and Electronic Engineers Standards Board, New York.

IFPUG (1994) *Function Point Counting Practices, release 4.0*, International Function Point User Group, USA.

ISO (1991) *ISO/IEC Guide 2: general terms and definitions concerning standardization and related activities*, International Organization of Standardization.

ISO (1994) *ISO 8402: Quality management and quality assurance – vocabulary*, International Organization of Standardization.

ISO (2001) *ISO/IEC 9126 part 1: information technology – software product quality – part 1: quality model*, International Organization of Standardization.

Jacobson, I., Christerson, M., Johnsson, P. and Overgaard, G. (1992) *Object Oriented Software Engineering: a use case driven approach*, Addison-Wesley, London.

Kaner, C. (1997) 'Improving the Maintainability of Automated Test Suites', *Software QA*, **4** (4).

Kirakowski, J. and Corbett, M. (1993) 'SUMI: the software usability measurement inventory', *British Journal of Educational Technology*, **24** (3).

Kit, E. (1995) *Software Testing in the Real World*, Addison-Wesley, London.

Koomen, T. and Pol, M. (1999) *Test Process Improvement: a practical step-by-step guide to structured testing*, Addison-Wesley, London.

McCabe, T.J. (1976) 'A complexity metric', *IEEE Transactions on Software Engineering*, **2**.

McCall, J.A., Richards, P.K. and Walters, G.F. (1977) 'Factors in software quality', RADC-TR-77-363 Rome Air Development Center, Griffis Air Force, Rome (New York, USA).

Myers, G.J. (1979) *The Art of Software Testing*, Wiley-Interscience, New York.

Nielsen, J. (1993) *Usability Engineering*, Addison-Wesley, London.

Ovum (1999) *Ovum Evaluates: software testing tools*, Ovum Ltd, London.

Paulk, M.C. (1999) 'Using the software CMM with good judgement', *Software Quality Professional*, June.

Perry, W. (1995) *Effective Methods for Software Testing*, John Wiley & Sons, New York.

Pol, M. and van Veenendaal, E. (1998) *Structured Testing of Information Systems: an Introduction to TMap*, Kluwer Bedrijfsinformatie, Deventer.

Schaefer, H. (1996) 'Surviving under time and budget pressure', presented at EuroSTAR Conference 1996, Amsterdam.

Software Engineering Institute, Carnegie Mellon University (1995) *The Capability Maturity Model*, Addison-Wesley, London.

SIGIST (Specialist Interest Group in Software Testing) (1998) *Working Draft: glossary of terms used in software testing, version 6.2*, British Computer Society, London.

Van Solingen, R. and Berghout, E. (1999) *The Goal–Question–Metric method: a practical handguide*, McGraw-Hill, New York.

Van Veenendaal, E.P.W.M. (1999) 'Practical quality assurance for embedded software,' *Software Quality Professional*, June.

Software Control

Software Control is a client-oriented organization that offers services such as the implementation of structured testing, test management, quality control, process improvement, auditing and information security. With more than 450 staff and a structured approach to research and development, Software Control is a trend setter and market leader.

The internationally recognized market standards developed by Software Control are openly available in book form:

- TMap®, the approach for a structured testing;
- TPI®, the approach for test process improvement.

There are additional approaches based on the above:

- effective automated testing;
- structured performance testing;
- setting up and exploiting testing in an organisation;
- testing embedded software.

Software Control has a generic model for process improvement. This model is distinguished by the joint consideration of 'hard' and 'soft' aspects of process improvement, and can be applied in combination with the market standards. The approach 'Quality Tailor Made' is used for setting up quality control in projects.

Software Control employees chose quality control and testing as their profession. Structured career paths are used for staff development. Knowledge management ensures that the portfolio of services is matched with the needs of the client.

Established since 1986, Software Control is a part of IQUIP Informatica B.V. and is ISO-9002 certified. IQUIP Deutschland GmbH, founded in 1999, is the German representative of Software Control. It offers testing and quality assurance services.

IQUIP Informatica B.V.   IQUIP Deutschland GmbH
Software Control   Schiessstrasse 72
Postbus 263   40549 Dusseldorf
1110 AG Diemen   Germany
The Netherlands

Internet: www.iquip.nl/tmap   *Internet*: www.iquip.de
Email: info@iquip.nl   *Email*: info@iquip.nl

Gitek nv

Gitek nv was founded in 1986, and is specialized in software testing, in addition to the design and development of software. Gitek employs more than 130 people, with 50 professional software test engineers. Its customers include companies in the pharmaceutical, financial, telecoms and insurance industries.

Gitek is an enthusiastic team of professionals specialized in customized IT solutions and structured testing. A personal approach forms the basis of our success. This ensures services that are better adapted to the customer's specific requirements, and a committed and motivated team ensuring optimal efficiency. Gitek is the exclusive distributor of TMap®, TPI® and TAKT© in Belgium.

Gitek provides services that offer a complete solution for testing:

- Participation in the operational test process:
  – test planning and test management
  – test design and test execution.
- Complete test projects and fixed price projects.
- Test advice and support.
- Defining and implementing a structured test process.
- Selection and implementation of test tools.
- Improving the test process.
- Training and coaching in testing.

Gitek nv
St Pietersvliet 3
B-2000 Antwerp
Belgium
Internet: http://www.gitek.be
Email: gitek@gitek.be

Index

acceptance criteria 20–21, 454–7
acceptance tests 17
  definition 531
  environment *421*, 422–3
  example test strategy 151–2
  integrated testing 21, *21*, 454–7, *455*
  lifecycle 71
  model test plan 505–23
  test point analysis 157–77
  test team organization 348
ad hoc corrective maintenance 155, 454
administrative organization 247–55
algorithm test 181, 204, 206, 207–12, *209*
analysis forum 373–4
application integrator 333–4
architecture
  client/server systems 459, *459*
  framework architecture 443
  Internet 488–90, *488*, *490*
  see also functional system architecture; technical system architecture
assembly tests 17
audit trails 380–1, 531
automation
  architect role 334–5
  e-business testing 501
  engineer role 335–6
  object-oriented testing 471
  process cycle test 247–55

test process improvement model 406, 409
  test tools 429–32, 440–6, *444*

black-box test techniques
boundary value analysis 202–3, 531
British Computer Society 340
browsers 494, 501
budgets 77–8, 119, *136*, 356–8
business functionality tests 471

career structure, test staff 341–3, *341*, *342*, *343*
CASE tool analyzer 435
causal analysis meeting 191, 195
chance of failure 135, 136–8, 155
change processes 392–8, *392*, 399, 400
checklists
  information system global investigation 300
  infrastructure 67
  packages 482, 483, 484
  quality characteristics 277–96
  structuring 303–6
  test facilities 306–8
  test plans, preconditions and assumptions 301–2
  test project evaluation 298–9
  test project risks 302–3
  testability review of test basis 180, 181–9